WHERE THERE IS NO DOCTOR

a village health care
handbook

FOUNDATION FOR TEACHING AIDS AT LOW COST

INSTITUTE OF CHILD HEALTH
30 Guilford Street London WCIN IEH

Telephone: Admin.Sec. St Albans (0727) 53869

A non-profitmaking Trust providing low cost teaching aids and books
to raise the standard of health care in developing countries

The Foundation for Teaching Aids at Low Cost - TALC - is a registered Charity which provides books and teaching aids to raise the standards of child health world-wide. While the material has been developed primarily for use in developing countries, much is appropriate for use in Europe and the U.S.A.

The organisation in St. Albans, U.K., distributes about one third of a million slides a year. Each set of slides comprises 24 transparencies (2 x 2 inch, 50 x 50 mm) and are sent with a detailed script describing each slide.

The following titles are examples from the fifty sets available:-

BREAST FEEDING, CHARTING GROWTH, SEVERE MEASLES, MENTAL RETARDATION (48 slides), ONCHOCERCIASIS, PRIMARY CHILD CARE (240 slides), MALNUTRITION IN AN URBAN ENVIRONMENT etc.

The Tropical Child Health Unit of the Institute of Child Health has for many years encouraged the use of simple growth charts for primary health care. TALC has charts available in five languages. A number of teaching aids are also available for use with them.

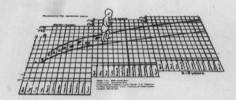

Health workers need and love books

Health for all by the year 2000 will require distribution of books on health care throughout the villages of the world in the local language. TALC provides appropriate low cost books mainly in English and a few other major languages.

Examples of popular books available are:-

WHERE THERE IS NO DOCTOR — D. Werner
PRIMARY CHILD CARE — M. King
SEE HOW THEY GROW — D. Morley
BREAST FEEDING - THE BIOLOGICAL OPTION — G.J. Ebrahim

Some low cost books and pamphlets which are not available through bookshops are also in stock. Write for further details including lists of slides, books and accessories to:-

Barbara Harvey
T.A.L.C.
P.O. Box 49
St. Albans
Herts AL1 4AX England

Where There Is No Doctor

a village health care handbook

by
David Werner

with drawings by the author

M
MACMILLAN PUBLISHERS

© The Hesperian Foundation, Box 1692, Palo Alto, California 94302, USA

First English edition 1977, revised from the Spanish *Donde No Hay Doctor.* Second
slightly revised printing March 1978. Third, slightly revised printing September 1978.

This edition published 1979; reprinted with slight revision 1980 (twice)
Reprinted 1981 (three times), 1982 (twice), 1983 (twice), 1984 (twice), 1985 (three
times), 1987 (twice), 1988, 1989, 1990

Published by *Macmillan Publishers Ltd*
London and Basingstoke
Associated companies and representatives in Accra,
Auckland, Delhi, Dublin, Gaborone, Hamburg, Harare,
Hong Kong, Kuala Lumpur, Lagos, Manzini, Melbourne,
Mexico City, Nairobi, New York, Singapore, Tokyo

British Library Cataloguing in Publication Data

Werner, David
　Where there is no doctor. – (Macmillan tropical
　community health manuals).
　1. Underdeveloped areas – Medical care
　I. Title
　610'.9172'4　　　RA394

　ISBN 0-333-26257-3
　ISBN 0-333-26258-1 Pbk

Any parts of this book, including the illustrations, may be copied, reproduced, or adapted
to meet local needs, without permission from the author or publisher, provided the parts
reproduced are distributed free or at cost - not for profit. For any reproduction with
commercial ends, permission must first be obtained from the publisher, the author or the
Hesperian Foundation. The publisher and author would appreciate being sent a copy of
any materials in which text or illustrations have been used.

> **THIS BOOK CAN BE IMPROVED WITH YOUR HELP.**
> If you are a village health worker, doctor, mother, or
> anyone with ideas or suggestions for ways this book
> could be changed to better meet the needs of your people,
> please write to the author at the Hesperian Foundation
> address. Thank you for your help.

If you are unable to obtain copies of this book locally, you can send for copies to:

The Hesperian Foundation   English
P O Box 1692   Spanish
Palo Alto, California 94302   Portuguese
USA

or

TALC (Teaching Aids at Low Cost)   English
Institute of Child Health   Spanish
30 Guilford Street   Portuguese
London WC1N 1EH
England

or

Rural Communications   English
17 James Street
South Petherton
Somerset TA13 5BS
England

or

Editorial Pax-Mexico   Spanish
Rep. Argentina 9
Mexico 1, D. F.
Mexico

or

Edições Paulinas   Portuguese
Caixa Postal 8107
01000 São Paulo, SP
Brazil

This book may be sold at a lower price to those living in poor countries than to those in
rich countries. Lower prices are also available for those working with health projects or
programmes in poor countries (or poor communities within rich countries). For information contact the Hesperian Foundation or one of the other addresses.

Where There is No Doctor — A new edition for Africa

**A special English language edition is now available for use in Africa. It
has been edited to take into account medical conditions which are more
prevalent in Africa, as well as social and cultural factors. The illustrations
have been placed in the African context.
It is available from Macmillan Publishers and from TALC.**

ISBN 0-333-44410-8

THANKS

I would like to thank the following persons for their important contributions to the preparation and review of the original Spanish edition of this book:

Val Price, pediatrician
Al Hotti, internist
Rodney Kendall, dermatologist
Max Capestany, obstetrician and gynaecologist
Rudolf Bock, opthalmologist
Kent Benedict, pediatrician
Alfonzo Darricades, general practitioner
Carlos Felipe Soto Miller, general practitioner and surgeon
Paul Qintana, pediatrician

For this English edition I would especially like to thank Dr. David Morley, pediatrician, Dr. Val Price, pediatrician, Bill Bower, medical educator, and Allison Orozco, physician's assistant, for their careful review and valuable suggestions; also Susan and Greg Troll, practical midwives, for their help in the revision of the chapter for mothers and midwives.

I would also like to thank the medical and health personnel in parts of Africa, Asia, and Indonesia for their suggestions of what to include; and to thank Dr. Jack Lange of Lange Medical Publications for helping make contact with many of these persons.

I thank McGraw-Hill Book Company for permission to use drawings appearing on pages 85 and 104 taken from *Emergency Medical Guide* by John Henderson, illustrated by Neil Hardy. My thanks to Dale Crosby for drawings on pages 29, 32, 35, 100, 181, and 300. And to my father, Carl Werner, for drawings on pages 5-8, 121, 187, 229, 231, 235-238, 240, 245, 256, 276, and 281.

For assistance in translation from the Spanish, I would like to thank Roger Bunch, Lynne Coen, George Kent, Jack May, Greg and Susan Troll, Dr. Rudolf Bock, Oliver Bock, Bill Gonda, and Ray Bleicher; and for help in graphics, Jesús Manjarrez and Bill Bower.

My appreciation to Hal Lockwood for his patience, hard work, and care in the typesetting. For the long hard job of getting the manuscript into useful shape and ready for printing I warmly thank the team that helped put it together: Carol Westberg, Bill Bower, Lynn Gordon, Myra Polinger, and Trude Bock.

Trude Bock deserves very special thanks, for not only helping on the book in many ways, but for generously providing her home, meals, and understanding to those who put this book together.

This book can be made available at low cost because most of the work was done on a volunteer basis and because Oxfam and Misereor helped cover part of the costs of this edition. My heart-felt thanks to all those who, by giving of their time, money, and concern, made this possible.

CONTENTS

A list of what is discussed in each chapter

Chapter 10

FIRST AID 75

Chapter 11

NUTRITION: WHAT TO EAT TO BE HEALTHY 107

Chapter 12

PREVENTION: HOW TO AVOID MANY SICKNESSES 131

Chapter 13

SOME VERY COMMON SICKNESSES 151

Chapter 14

SERIOUS ILLNESSES THAT NEED SPECIAL MEDICAL ATTENTION 179

Chapter 15

SKIN PROBLEMS. 193

Chapter 20

FAMILY PLANNING—
HAVING THE NUMBER OF CHILDREN YOU WANT 283

Chapter 21

HEALTH AND SICKNESSES OF CHILDREN 295

Chapter 22

HEALTH AND SICKNESSES OF OLDER PEOPLE..................323

Chapter 23

THE MEDICINE KIT...331

TEAR OUT SHEETS

Making Medical Reports
Dosage Instructions for Persons Who Cannot Read

INTRODUCTION TO THE ENGLISH EDITION

This handbook has been written primarily for those who live far from medical centers, in places where there is no doctor. But even where there are doctors, people can and should take the lead in their own health care. So this book is for everyone who cares. It has been written in the belief that:

1. **Health care is not only everyone's right, but everyone's responsibility.**

2. <u>Informed self-care</u> **should be the main goal of any health program or activity.**

3. **Ordinary people provided with clear, simple information can prevent and treat most common health problems in their own homes—earlier, cheaper, and often better than can doctors.**

4. **Medical knowledge should not be the guarded secret of a select few, but should be freely shared by everyone.**

5. **People with little formal education can be trusted as much as those with a lot. And they are just as smart.**

6. **Basic health care should not be delivered, but encouraged.**

Clearly, a part of informed self-care is knowing one's own limits. Therefore guidelines are included not only for **what to do,** but for **when to seek help.** The book points out those cases when it is important to see or get advice from a health worker or doctor. But because doctors or health workers are not always nearby, the book also suggests **what to do in the meantime**—even for very serious problems.

This book has been written in fairly basic English, so that persons without much formal education (or whose first language is not English) can understand it. The language used is simple but, I hope, not childish. A few more difficult words have been used where they are *appropriate* or fit well. Usually they are used in ways that their meanings can be easily guessed. This way, those who read this book have a chance to increase their language skills as well as their medical skills.

Important words the reader may not understand are explained in a word list or *vocabulary* at the end of the book. The first time a word listed in the vocabulary is mentioned in a chapter it is usually written in *italics*.

Where There Is No Doctor was first written in Spanish for farm people in the mountains of Mexico where, for the past 13 years, the author has helped form a health care network now run by the villagers themselves. *Donde No Hay Doctor* is now being used throughout Latin America.

This experimental English edition has been prepared as a result of many requests to adapt it for use in Africa and Asia. In spite of help and suggestions from persons with experience in these parts of the world, I am still not completely satisfied with this edition. It has lost much of the flavor and usefulness of the original Spanish edition, which was written for a specific area, and for people who have for years been my neighbors and friends. In rewriting the book to serve people in many parts of the world, it has in some ways become too general.

To be fully useful, this book should be adapted by persons familiar with the health needs, customs, special ways of healing, and local language of specific areas.

———•———

Persons or programs who wish to use this book, or portions of it, in preparing their own manuals for villagers or health workers are encouraged to do so. Permission from the author or publisher is not needed — **provided the parts reproduced are distributed free or at cost — not for profit.** It would be appreciated if you would (1) include a note of credit and (2) send a copy of your production to The Hesperian Foundation, Box 1692, Palo Alto, California 94302, U.S.A. and to The Macmillan Press, Houndmills, Basingstoke, Hants, U.K.

For local or regional health programs that do not have the resources for revising this book or preparing their own manuals, it is strongly suggested that if the present edition is used, leaflets or inserts be supplied with the book to provide additional information as needed.

In the Green Pages (the Uses, Dosage, and Precautions for Medicines) blank spaces have been left to write in common brand names and prices of medicines. Once again, local programs or organizations distributing the book would do well to make up a list of generic or low-cost brand names and prices, to be included with each copy of the book.

———•———

This book was written for anyone who wants to do something about his own and other people's health. However, it has been widely used as a training and work manual for community health workers. For this reason, an introductory section has been added for the health worker, making clear that **the health worker's first job is to share his knowledge and help educate his people.**

Today in over-developed as well as under-developed countries, existing health care systems are in a state of crisis. Often, human needs are not being well met. There is too little fairness. Too much is in the hands of too few.

Let us hope that through a more generous sharing of knowledge, and through learning to use what is best in both traditional and modern ways of healing, people everywhere will develop a kinder, more sensible approach to caring—for their own health, and for each other.

—D. W.

WORDS TO THE VILLAGE HEALTH WORKER

Who is the village health worker?

A village health worker is a person who helps lead family and neighbors toward better health. Often he or she has been selected by the other villagers as someone who is especially able and kind.

Some village health workers receive training and help from an organized program, perhaps the Ministry of Health. Others have no official position, but are simply members of the community whom people respect as healers or leaders in matters of health. Often they learn by watching, helping, and studying on their own.

In the larger sense, **a village health worker is anyone who takes part in making his village a healthier place to live.**

This means almost everyone can and should be a health worker:

- Mothers and fathers can show their children how to keep clean;
- Farm people can work together to help their land produce more food;
- Teachers can teach schoolchildren how to prevent and treat many common sicknesses and injuries;
- Schoolchildren can share what they learn with their parents;
- Shopkeepers can find out about the correct use of medicines they sell and give sensible advice and warning to buyers (see p. 338);
- Midwives can counsel parents about the importance of eating well during pregnancy, breast feeding, and family planning.

This book was written for the health worker in the larger sense. It is for anyone who wants to know and do more for his own, his family's or his people's well-being.

If you are a community health worker, an auxiliary nurse, or even a doctor, remember: this book is not just for you. It is for **all the people.** Share it!

Use this book to help explain what you know to others. Perhaps you can get small groups together to read a chapter at a time and discuss it.

THE VILLAGE HEALTH WORKER LIVES AND WORKS AT THE LEVEL OF HIS PEOPLE. HIS FIRST JOB IS TO SHARE HIS KNOWLEDGE.

Dear Village Health Worker,

This book is mostly about people's **health needs.** But to help your village be a healthy place to live, you must also be in touch with their **human needs.** Your understanding and concern for people are just as important as your knowledge of medicine and sanitation.

Here are some suggestions that may help you serve your people's human needs as well as health needs:

1. BE KIND. A friendly word, a smile, a hand on the shoulder, or some other sign of caring often means more than anything else you can do. **Treat others as your equals.** Even when you are hurried or worried, try to remember the feelings and needs of others. Often it helps to ask yourself, "What would I do if this were a member of my own family?"

HAVE COMPASSION.
Kindness often helps more than medicine. Never be afraid to show you care.

Treat the sick as people. Be especially kind to those who are very sick or dying. And be kind to their families. Let them see that you care.

2. SHARE YOUR KNOWLEDGE. As a health worker, your first job is to teach. This means helping people learn more about how to keep from getting sick. It also means helping people learn how to recognize and manage their illnesses—including the sensible use of home remedies and common medicines.

There is nothing you have learned that, if carefully explained, should be of danger to anyone. Some doctors talk about **self care** as if it were dangerous, perhaps because they like people to depend on their costly services. But in truth, **most common health problems could be handled earlier and better by people in their own homes.**

LOOK FOR WAYS TO SHARE YOUR KNOWLEDGE.

3. RESPECT YOUR PEOPLE'S TRADITIONS AND IDEAS.

Because you learn something about modern medicine does not mean you should no longer appreciate the customs and ways of healing of your people. Too often the human touch in the art of healing is lost when medical science moves in. This is too bad, because . . .

> **If you can use what is best in modern medicine, together with what is best in traditional healing, the combination may be better than either one alone.**

In this way, you will be adding to your people's culture, not taking away.

Of course, if you see that some of the home cures or customs are harmful (for example, putting excrement on the freshly cut cord of a newborn baby), you will want to do something to change this. But do so carefully, with respect for those who believe in such things. Never just tell people they are wrong. Try to help them understand WHY they should do something differently.

People are slow to change their attitudes and traditions, and with good reason. They are true to what they feel is right. And this we must respect.

Modern medicine does not have all the answers either. It has helped solve some problems, yet has led to other, sometimes even bigger ones. People quickly come to depend too much on modern medicine and its experts, to overuse medicines, and to forget how to care for themselves and each other.

So go slow—and always keep a deep respect for your people, their traditions, and their human dignity. Help them build on the knowledge and skills they already have.

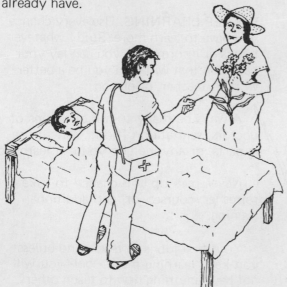

WORK WITH TRADITIONAL HEALERS AND MIDWIVES— NOT AGAINST THEM.

Learn from them and encourage them to learn from you.

4. KNOW YOUR OWN LIMITS.

No matter how great or small your knowledge and skills, you can do a good job as long as you know and work within your limits. This means: **Do what you know how to do.** Do not try things you have not learned about or have not had enough experience doing, if they might harm or endanger someone.

But use your judgment.

Often, what you decide to do or not do will depend on how far you have to go to get more expert help.

For example, a mother has just given birth and is bleeding more than you think is normal. If you are only half an hour away from a medical center, it may be wise to take her there right away. But if the mother is bleeding very heavily and you are a long way from the health center, you may decide to massage her womb (see p. 265) or inject an oxytocic (see p. 266) even if you were not taught this.

I KNOW IT'S A LONG WAY TO THE HEALTH CENTER, BUT HERE WE CANNOT GIVE HIM THE TREATMENT HE NEEDS. I'LL GO WITH YOU.

KNOW YOUR LIMITS.

Do not take unnecessary chances. But when the danger is clearly greater if you do nothing, do not be afraid to try something you feel reasonably sure will help.

Know your limits—but also use your head. Always do your best to protect the sick person rather than yourself.

KEEP LEARNING—Do not let anyone tell you there are things you should not learn or know.

5. KEEP LEARNING. Use every chance you have to learn more. Study whatever books or information you can lay your hands on that will help you be a better worker, teacher, or person.

Always be ready to ask questions of doctors, sanitation officers, agriculture experts, or anyone else you can learn from.

Never pass up the chance to take refresher courses or get additional training.

Your first job is to teach, and unless you keep learning more, soon you will not have anything new to teach others.

6. PRACTICE WHAT YOU TEACH.

People are more likely to pay attention to what you do than what you say. As a health worker, you want to take special care in your personal life and habits, so as to set a good example for your neighbors.

Before you ask people to make latrines, be sure your own family has one.

Also, if you help organize a work group—for example, to dig a common garbage hole—be sure you work and sweat as hard as everyone else.

> **A good leader does not tell people what to do. He sets the example.**

PRACTICE WHAT YOU TEACH
(or who will listen to you?)

7. WORK FOR THE JOY OF IT.

If you want other people to take part in improving their village and caring for their health, you must enjoy such activity yourself. If not, who will want to follow your example?

Try to make community work projects fun. For example, fencing off the public water hole to keep animals away from where people take water can be hard work. But if the whole village helps do it as a 'work festival'—perhaps with refreshments and music—the job will be done quickly and can be fun.

Children will work hard and enjoy it, if they can turn work into play.

You may or may not be paid for your work. But never refuse to care, or care less, for someone who is poor or cannot pay.

This way you will win your people's love and respect. These are worth far more than money.

WORK FIRST FOR THE PEOPLE—NOT THE MONEY.
(People are worth more.)

8. LOOK AHEAD—AND HELP OTHERS TO LOOK AHEAD.

A responsible health worker does not wait for people to get sick. He tries to stop sickness before it starts. He encourages people to take action **now** to protect their health and well-being in the future.

Many sicknesses can be prevented. Your job, then, is to help your people understand the causes of their health problems and do something about them.

Most health problems have many causes, one leading to another. To correct the problem in a lasting way, you must look for and deal with the **underlying causes.** You must get to the root of the problem.

For example, in many villages diarrhea is the most common cause of death in small children. The spread of diarrhea is caused in part by lack of cleanliness (poor *sanitation* and *hygiene*). You can do something to correct this by digging latrines and teaching basic guidelines of cleanliness (p. 133).

But the children who suffer and die most often from diarrhea are those who are poorly nourished. Their bodies do not have strength to fight the infections. So to prevent death from diarrhea we must also prevent poor nutrition.

And why do so many children suffer from poor nutrition?

- Is it because mothers do not realize what foods are most important (for example, breast milk)?

- Is it because the family does not have enough money or land to produce the food it needs?

- Is it because a few rich persons control most of the land and the wealth?

- Is it because the poor do not make the best use of land they have?

- Is it because parents have more children than they or their land can provide for, and keep having more?

- Is it because fathers lose hope and spend the little money they have on drink?

- Is it because people do not look or plan ahead? Because they do not realize that by working together and sharing they can change the conditions under which they live and die?

HELP OTHERS TO LOOK AHEAD.

You may find that many, if not all, of these things lie behind infant deaths in your area. You will, no doubt, find other causes as well. As a health worker it is your job to help people understand and do something about as many of these causes as you can.

But remember: to prevent death from diarrhea will take far more than latrines, pure water, and nutrition centers. You may find that family planning, better land use, and fairer distribution of wealth, land, and power are more important in the long run.

The causes that lie behind much sickness and human suffering are short-sightedness and greed. If your interest is your people's well-being, you must help them learn to share, to work together, and to look ahead.

MANY THINGS RELATE TO HEALTH CARE

We have looked at some of the causes that underlie diarrhea and poor nutrition. Likewise, you will find that such things as **food production, land distribution, education,** and **the way people treat or mistreat each other** lie behind many different health problems.

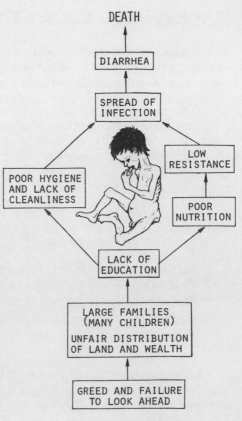

The chain of causes leading to death from diarrhea.

If you are interested in the long-term welfare of your whole community, you must help your people look for answers to these larger questions.

Health is more than not being sick. It is well-being: in body, mind, and community. People live best in healthy surroundings, in a place where they can trust each other, work together to meet daily needs, share in times of difficulty and plenty, and help each other learn and grow and live, each as fully as he can.

Do your best to solve day-to-day problems. But remember that your greatest job is to help your community become a more healthy and more human place to live.

You as a health worker have a big responsibility.

Where should you begin?

TAKE A GOOD LOOK AT YOUR COMMUNITY

Because you have grown up in your community and know your people well, you are already familiar with many of their health problems. You have an inside view. But in order to see the whole picture, you will need to look carefully at your community from many points of view.

As a village health worker, your concern is for the well-being of **all the people** —not just those you know well or who come to you. Go to your people. Visit their homes, fields, gathering places, and schools. Understand their joys and concerns. Examine with them their habits, the things in their daily lives that bring about good health, and those that may lead to sickness or injury.

Before you and your community attempt any project or activity, carefully think about what it will require and how likely it is to work. To do this, you must consider **all** the following:

1. **Felt needs**—what people feel are their biggest problems.
2. **Real needs**—steps people can take to meet these problems in a lasting way.
3. **Willingness**—or readiness of people to plan and take the needed steps.
4. **Resources**—the persons, skills, materials, and/or money needed to carry out the activities decided upon.

As a simple example of how each of these things can be important, let us suppose that a man who smokes a lot comes to you complaining of a cough that has steadily been getting worse.

1. His **felt need** is to get rid of his cough.

2. His **real need** (to correct the problem) is to give up smoking.

3. To get rid of his cough will require his **willingness** to give up smoking. For this he must understand how much it really matters.

4. One **resource** that may help him give up smoking is information about the harm it can do him and his family (see p. 149). Another is the support and encouragement of his family, his friends, and you.

Finding Out the Needs

As a health worker, you will first want to find out your people's most important health problems and their biggest concerns. To gather the information necessary to decide what the greatest needs and concerns really are, it may help to make up a list of questions.

On the next 2 pages are samples of the kind of things you may want to ask. But think of questions that are important **in your area.** Ask questions that not only help you get information, but that get others asking important questions themselves.

Do not make your list of questions too long or complicated—especially a list you take from house to house. Remember, **people are not numbers** and do not like to be looked at as numbers. As you gather information, be sure your first interest is always in what individuals want and feel. It may be better not even to carry a list of questions. But in considering the needs of your community, you should keep certain basic questions in mind.

Sample Lists of Questions

To Help Determine Community Health Needs
And at the Same Time Get People Thinking

FELT NEEDS

What things in your people's daily lives (living conditions, ways of doing things, beliefs, etc.) do they feel help them to be healthy?

What do people feel to be their major problems, concerns, and needs—not only those related to health, but in general?

 ## HOUSING AND SANITATION

What are different houses made of? Walls? Floors? Are the houses kept clean? Is cooking done on the floor or where? How does smoke get out? On what do people sleep?

Are flies, fleas, bedbugs, rats, or other pests a problem? In what way? What do people do to control them? What else could be done?

Is food protected? How could it be better protected?

What animals (dogs, chickens, pigs, etc.), if any, are allowed in the house? What problems do they cause?

What are the common diseases of animals? How do they affect people's health? What is being done about these diseases?

Where do families get their water? Is it safe to drink? What precautions are taken?

How many families have latrines? How many use them properly?

Is the village clean? Where do people put garbage? Why?

 ## POPULATION

How many people live in the community? How many are under 15 years old?

How many can read and write? What good is schooling? Does it teach children what they need to know? How else do children learn?

How many babies were born this year? How many people died? Of what? At what ages? Could their deaths have been prevented? How?

Is the population (number of people) getting larger or smaller? Does this cause any problems?

How often were different persons sick in the past year? How many days was each sick? What sicknesses or injuries did each have? Why?

How many people have chronic (long-term) illnesses? What are they?

How many children do most parents have? How many children died? Of what? At what ages? What were some of the **underlying** causes?

How many parents are interested in not having any more children or in not having them so often? For what reasons? (See Family Planning, p. 283.)

NUTRITION

How many mothers breast feed their babies? For how long? Are these babies healthier than those who are not breast fed? Why?

What are the main foods people eat? Where do they come from?

Do people make good use of all foods available?

How many children are underweight (see p. 113) or show signs of poor nutrition? How much do parents and schoolchildren know about nutritional needs?

How many people smoke a lot? How many drink alcoholic or soft drinks very often? What effect does this have on their own and their families' health? (See p. 148 to 150.)

LAND AND FOOD

Does the land provide enough food for each family? How long will it continue to produce enough food if families keep growing?

How is farm land distributed? How many people own their land?

What efforts are being made to help the land produce more?

How are crops and food stored? Is there much damage or loss? Why?

HEALING, HEALTH

What role do local midwives and healers play in health care?

What traditional ways of healing and medicines are used? Which are of greatest value? Are any harmful or dangerous?

What health services are nearby? How good are they? What do they cost? How much are they used?

How many children have been vaccinated? Against what sicknesses?

What other preventive measures are being taken? What others might be taken? How important are they?

SELF-HELP

What are the most important things that affect your people's health and well-being—now and in the future?

How many of their common health problems can people care for themselves? How much must they rely on outside help and medication?

Are people interested in finding ways of making self-care safer, more effective, and more complete? Why? How can they learn more? What stands in the way?

What are the rights of rich people? Of poor people? Of men? Of women? Of children? How is each of these groups treated? Why? Is this fair? What needs to be changed? By whom? How?

Do people work together to meet common needs? Do they share or help each other when needs are great?

What can be done to make your village a better, healthier place to live? Where might you and your people begin?

USING LOCAL RESOURCES TO MEET NEEDS

How you deal with a problem will depend upon what resources are available.

Some activities require outside resources (materials, money, or people from somewhere else). For example, a vaccination program is possible only if vaccines are brought in—often from another country.

Other activities can be carried out completely with local resources. A family or a group of neighbors can fence off a water hole or build simple latrines using materials close at hand.

Some outside resources, such as vaccines and a few important medicines, can make a big difference in people's health. You should do your best to get them. But as a general rule, it is in the best interest of your people to

> ## Use local resources whenever possible.

The more you and your people can do for yourselves, and the less you have to depend on outside assistance and supplies, the healthier and stronger your community will become.

Not only can you count on local resources to be on hand when you need them, but often they do the best job at the lowest cost. For example, if you can encourage mothers to breast feed rather than bottle feed their babies, this will build self-reliance through a top quality local resource— breast milk! It will also prevent needless sickness and death of many babies.

In your health work always remember:

Encourage people to make the most of local resources.

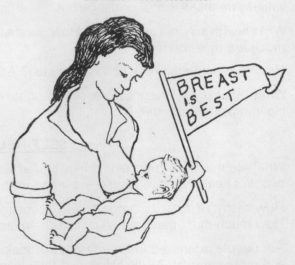

BREAST MILK—A TOP QUALITY LOCAL RESOURCE—BETTER THAN ANYTHING MONEY CAN BUY!

> ## The most valuable resource for the health of the people is the people themselves.

DECIDING WHAT TO DO AND WHERE TO BEGIN

After taking a careful look at needs and resources, you and your people must decide which things are more important and which to do first. You can do many different things to help people be healthy. Some are important immediately. Others will help determine the future well-being of individuals or the whole community.

In a lot of villages, poor nutrition plays a part in other health problems. **People cannot be healthy unless there is enough to eat.** Whatever other problems you decide to work with, if people are hungry or children are poorly nourished, better nutrition must be your first concern.

There are many different ways to approach the problem of poor nutrition, for many different things join to cause it. You and your community must consider the possible actions you might take and decide which are most likely to work.

Here are a few examples of ways some people have helped meet their needs for better nutrition. Some actions bring quick results. Others work over a longer time. You and your people must decide what is most likely to work in your area.

POSSIBLE WAYS TO WORK TOWARD BETTER NUTRITION

FAMILY GARDENS

CONTOUR DITCHES
to prevent soil from washing away

ROTATION OF CROPS
Every other planting season plant a crop that returns strength to the soil—like beans, peas, lentils, alfalfa, peanuts or some other plant with seed in pods (legumes).

This year maize

Next year beans

MORE WAYS TO WORK TOWARD BETTER NUTRITION

IRRIGATION OF LAND

FISH BREEDING

BEEKEEPING

NATURAL FERTILIZERS

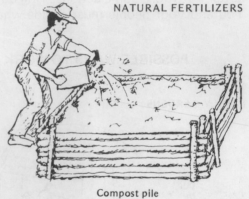

Compost pile

BETTER FOOD STORAGE

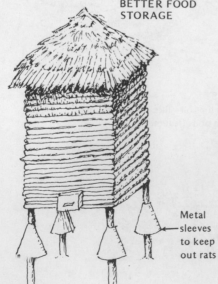

Metal sleeves to keep out rats

SMALLER FAMILIES

THROUGH FAMILY PLANNING
(p. 283)

TRYING A NEW IDEA

START SMALL

Not all the suggestions on the last pages are likely to work in your area. Perhaps some will work if changed for your particular situation and resources at hand. Often you can only know whether something will work or not by trying it. That is, by experiment.

When you try out a new idea, **always start small.** If you start small and the experiment fails, or something has to be done differently, you will not lose much. If it works, people will see that it works and can begin to apply it in a bigger way.

Do not be discouraged if an experiment does not work. Perhaps you can try again with certain changes. You can learn as much from your failures as your successes. But start small.

Here is an example of experimenting with a new idea.

You learn that a certain kind of bean, such as soya, is an excellent body-building food. But will it grow in your area? And if it grows, will people eat it?

Start by planting a small patch—or 2 or 3 small patches in different conditions of soil or water. If the beans do well, try preparing them in different ways, and see if people will eat them. If so, try planting more beans in the conditions where you found they grew best. But try out still other conditions in more small patches to see if you can get an even better crop.

There may be several conditions you want to try changing. For example, type of soil, addition of fertilizer, amount of water, or different varieties of seed. To best understand what helps and what does not, be sure to change only **one** condition at a time and keep all the rest the same.

For example, to find out if animal fertilizer (manure) helps the beans grow, and how much to use, plant several small bean patches side by side, under the same conditions of water and sunlight, and using the same seed. But before you plant, mix each patch with a different amount of manure, something like this:

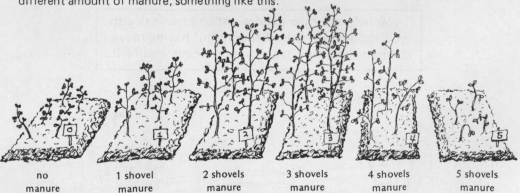

| no manure | 1 shovel manure | 2 shovels manure | 3 shovels manure | 4 shovels manure | 5 shovels manure |

This experiment shows that a certain amount of manure helps, but that too much can harm the plants. This is only an example. Your experiments may give different results. Try for yourself!

WORKING TOWARD A BALANCE BETWEEN PEOPLE AND LAND

As a health worker you should do all you can to protect the lives and health of children. If, through your efforts, fewer children die, you must also consider how this affects the future well-being of your community and the children to come. Fewer deaths means more people. And in time this can mean hunger, for the land can only feed a certain number.

The growing number of people in your village may be able to hold off hunger for a while by better use of land, so that it produces more food. But if parents continue to have big families, and their children in turn have big families, the time will come when there is not enough land or food for all the people.

It would be very sad if preventing children's deaths now means more must starve in the future. Yet this may happen if parents continue to have large families. It is already happening in many parts of the world.

One of your most important jobs may be to help people realize how important it is to limit the size of their families. This is especially true if many of your people already do not have enough land to feed their families properly.

Chapter 20 gives information on different methods of family planning. Find out which methods are possible in your area, and which your people prefer. Help inform and supply parents and local midwives.

People will often come to you with health problems that relate to having large families. When you see a mother who has had one child after another, and who is very tired, anemic, or fails to produce milk for her baby, or when you see a child who is badly nourished or bears the marks of crowding and poverty, talk to the parents about family planning. Often a mother will not want another child, but will not mention this until you ask.

Family planning may be one of the most important preventive measures you can help with. Unless people learn to distribute their land and wealth more fairly and to have smaller families, all other preventive measures may only mean that in time more people starve.

> **If you help your people prevent children's deaths, you should also help them prevent having more children than they can clothe, educate, and feed.**

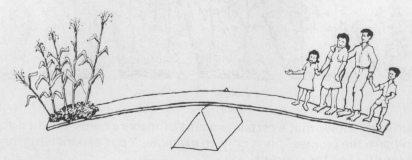

A LIMITED AMOUNT OF LAND CAN ONLY SUPPORT A LIMITED NUMBER OF PEOPLE.

WORKING TOWARD A BALANCE BETWEEN

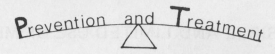
Prevention and Treatment

A balance between treatment and prevention often comes down to a balance between immediate needs and long-term needs.

As a health worker you must go to your people, work with them on their terms, and help them find answers to the needs they feel most. People's first concern is often to find relief for the sick and suffering. Therefore, **one of your first concerns must be to help with healing.**

But also look ahead. While caring for people's immediate felt needs, also help them look to the future. Help them realize that much sickness and suffering can be prevented and that they themselves can take preventive actions.

But be careful! Sometimes health planners and workers go too far. In their eagerness to prevent future ills, they may show too little concern for the sickness and suffering that already exist. By failing to respond to people's present needs, they may fail to gain their cooperation. And so they fail in much of their preventive work as well.

Treatment and prevention go hand in hand. Early treatment often prevents mild illness from becoming serious. If you help people to recognize many of their common health problems and to treat them early, in their own homes, much needless suffering can be prevented.

> **Early treatment is a form of preventive medicine.**

If you want their cooperation, **start where your people are.** Work toward a balance between prevention and treatment that is acceptable to them. Such a balance will be largely determined by people's present attitudes toward sickness, healing, and health. As you help them look farther ahead, as their attitudes change, and as more diseases are controlled, you may find that the balance shifts naturally in favor of prevention.

You cannot tell the mother whose child is ill that prevention is more important than cure. Not if you want her to listen. But you can tell her, while you help her care for her child, that prevention is equally important.

> **Work toward prevention— do not force it.**

Use treatment as a doorway to prevention. One of the best times to talk to people about prevention is when they come for treatment. For example, if a mother brings a child with worms, carefully explain to her how to treat him. But also take time to explain to both the mother and child how the worms are spread and the different things they can do to prevent this from happening (see Chapter 12). Visit their home from time to time, not to find fault, but to help the family toward more effective self-care.

> **Use treatment as a chance to teach prevention.**

SENSIBLE AND LIMITED USE OF MEDICINES

One of the most difficult and important parts of preventive care is to educate your people in the sensible and limited use of medicines. A few modern medicines are very important and can save lives. But **no medicine is needed for most sicknesses.** The body itself can usually fight off sickness with rest, good food, and perhaps some simple home remedies.

People may come to you asking for medicine when they do not need any. You may be tempted to give them some medicine just to please. But if you do, when they get well, they will think that you and the medicine cured them. Really their bodies cured themselves.

Instead of teaching people to depend on medicines they do not need, take time to explain **why** they should not be used. Also tell the person **what he can do himself** to get over his sickness.

This way you are helping the person to rely on a local resource (himself), rather than on an outside resource (medicine). Also, you are protecting the person, for **there is no medicine that does not have some risk in its use.**

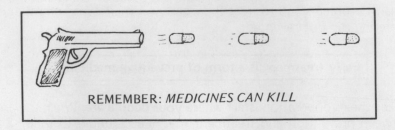

REMEMBER: *MEDICINES CAN KILL*

Three common health problems for which people too often request medicines they do not need are (1) the common cold, (2) minor cough, and (3) diarrhea.

The common cold is best treated by resting, drinking lots of liquids, and at the most taking aspirin. Penicillin, tetracycline, and other antibiotics do not help at all (see p. 163).

For minor coughs, or even more severe coughs with thick mucus or *phlegm,* drinking a lot of water will loosen mucus and ease the cough faster and better than cough syrup. Breathing warm water vapor brings even greater relief (see p. 168). Do not make people dependent on cough syrup or other medicines they do not need.

For most diarrhea of children use of medicines does not make them get well. Many of those commonly used (neomycin, streptomycin, kaolin-pectin, *Lomotil, Entero-Vioform,* chloramphenicol) may even be harmful. What is most important is that the child get lots of liquids and enough food (see p. 155 to 156). **The key to the child's recovery is the mother, not the medicine.** If you can help mothers understand this and learn what to do, many children's lives can be saved.

Medicines are often used too much, both by doctors and by ordinary people. This is unfortunate for many reasons:

- It is wasteful.
- It makes people depend on something they do not need (and often cannot afford).
- Every medicine has some risk in its use. There is always a chance that an unneeded medicine may actually do the person harm.
- What is more, when some medicines are used too often for minor problems, they lose their power to fight dangerous sicknesses.

An example of a medicine losing its power is chloramphenicol. The extreme overuse of this important but risky antibiotic for minor infections has meant that in some parts of the world chloramphenicol no longer works against typhoid fever, a very dangerous infection. Frequent overuse of chloramphenicol has allowed typhoid to become *resistant* to it (see p. 58).

For all the above reasons the use of medicines should be limited.

But how? Neither rigid rules and restrictions nor permitting only highly trained persons to decide about the use of medicines has prevented overuse. Only when the people themselves are better informed will the limited and careful use of medicines be common.

To educate people about sensible and limited use of medicines is one of the important jobs of the health worker.

This is especially true in areas where modern medicines are already in great use.

WHEN MEDICINES ARE NOT NEEDED, TAKE TIME TO EXPLAIN WHY.

For more information about the use and misuse of medicines, see Chapter 6, page 49. For the use and misuse of injections, see Chapter 9, page 65. For sensible use of home remedies, see Chapter 1.

FINDING OUT WHAT PROGRESS HAS BEEN MADE (EVALUATION)

From time to time in your health work, it helps to take a careful look at **what** and **how much** you and your people have succeeded in doing. What changes, if any, have been made to improve health and well-being in your community?

You may want to record each month or year the health activities that can be measured. For example:

- How many families have put in latrines?
- How many farmers take part in activities to improve their land and crops?
- How many mothers and children take part in an *Under-Fives Program* (regular check-ups and learning)?

This kind of question will help you measure **action taken.** But to find out the result or **impact** of these activities on health, you will need to answer other questions such as:

- How many children had diarrhea or signs of worms in the past month or year— as compared to before there were latrines?
- How much was harvested this season (corn, beans, or other crops)—as compared to before improved methods were used?
- How many children show normal weight and weight-gain on their Road to Health Charts (see p. 297)—as compared to when the Under-Fives Program was started?

To be able to judge the success of any activity you need to collect certain information both before and after. For example, if you want to teach mothers how important it is to breast feed their babies, first take a count of how many mothers are doing so. Then begin the teaching program and each year take another count. This way you can get a good idea as to how much effect your teaching has had.

You may want to set goals. For example, you and the health committee may hope that 80% of the families have latrines by the end of one year. Every month you take a count. If, by the end of six months, only one-third of the families have latrines, you know you will have to work harder to meet the goal you set for yourselves.

> **Setting goals often helps people work harder and get more done.**

To evaluate the results of your health activities it helps to count and measure certain things **before, during,** and **after.**

But remember: **The most important part of your health work cannot be measured.** It has to do with the way you and other people relate to each other; with people learning and working together; with the growth of kindness, responsibility, sharing, and hope. You cannot measure these things. But weigh them well when you consider what changes have been made.

TEACHING AND LEARNING TOGETHER—
THE HEALTH WORKER AS AN EDUCATOR

As you come to realize how many things affect health, you may think the health worker has an impossibly large job . And true, you will never get much done if you try to deliver health care by yourself.

> **Only when the people themselves become actively responsible for their own and their community's health, can important changes take place.**

Your community's well-being depends on the involvement not of one person, but of nearly everyone. For this to happen, responsibility and knowledge must be shared.

This is why **your first job as a health worker is to teach**—to teach children, parents, farmers, schoolteachers, other health workers—everyone you can.

The art of teaching is the most important skill a person can learn. To teach is to help others grow, and to grow with them. **A good teacher is not someone who puts ideas into other people's heads; he is someone who helps others build on their own ideas, to make new discoveries for themselves.**

Teaching and learning should not be limited to the schoolhouse or health post. They should take place in the home and in the fields and on the road. As a health worker one of your best chances to teach will probably be when you treat the sick. But you should look for every opportunity to exchange ideas, to share, to show, and to help your people think and work together.

On the next few pages are some ideas that may help you do this. They are only suggestions. You will have many other ideas yourself.

TWO APPROACHES TO HEALTH CARE

TAKING CARE OF OTHERS ENCOURAGES DEPENDENCY AND LOSS OF FREEDOM.

HELPING OTHERS LEARN TO CARE FOR THEMSELVES ENCOURAGES SELF-RELIANCE AND EQUALITY.

Tools for Teaching

Flannel-graphs are good for talking with groups because you can keep making new pictures. Cover a square board or piece of cardboard with a flannel cloth. You can place different cutout drawings or photos on it. Strips of sandpaper or flannel glued to the backs of cutouts help them stick to the flannelboard.

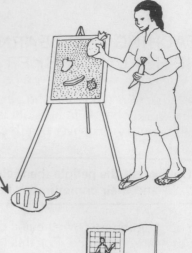

Posters and displays. "A picture is worth a thousand words." Simple drawings, with or without a few words of information, can be hung in the health post or anywhere that people will look at them. You can copy some of the pictures from this book.

If you have trouble getting sizes and shapes right, draw light even squares in pencil over the picture you want to copy.

Now draw the same number of squares lightly, but larger, on the poster paper or cardboard. Then copy the drawing, square for square.

If possible, ask village artists to draw or paint posters. Or have children make posters on different subjects.

Models and demonstrations help get ideas across. For example, if you want to talk with mothers and midwives about care in cutting the cord of a newborn child, you can make a doll for the baby. Pin a cloth cord to its belly. Experienced midwives can demonstrate to others.

Color slides and filmstrips are available on different health subjects for many parts of the world. Some come in sets that tell a story. Simple viewers and battery-operated projectors are also available.

A list of addresses where you can send for teaching materials to use for health education in your village can be found on pages 389 and 390.

Other Ways to Get Ideas Across

Story telling. When you have a hard time explaining something, a story, especially a true one, will help make your point.

For example, if I tell you that sometimes a village worker can make a better diagnosis than a doctor, you may not believe me. But if I tell you about a village health worker called Irene, who runs a small nutrition center in Central America, you may understand.

One day a small sickly child arrived at the nutrition center. He had been sent by the doctor at a nearby health center because he was badly malnourished. The child also had a cough, and the doctor had prescribed a cough medicine. Irene was worried about the child. She knew he came from a very poor family and that an older brother had died a few weeks before. She went to visit the family and learned that the older brother had been very sick for a long time and had coughed blood. Irene went to the health center and told the doctor she was afraid the child had tuberculosis. Tests were made, and it turned out that Irene was right. . . . So you see, the health worker spotted the real problem before the doctor—because she knew her people and visited their homes.

Stories also make learning more interesting. It helps if health workers are good story tellers.

Play acting. Stories that make important points can reach people with even more force if they are acted out. Perhaps you, the schoolteacher, or someone on the health committee can plan short plays or 'skits' with the schoolchildren.

For example, to make the point that food should be protected from flies to prevent the spread of disease, several small children could dress up as flies and buzz around food. The flies dirty the food that has not been covered. Then children eat this food and get sick. But the flies cannot get at food in a box with a wire screen front. So the children who eat this food stay well.

> **The more ways you can find to share ideas,**
> **the more people will understand and remember.**

Working and Learning Together for the Common Good

There are many ways to interest and involve people in working together to meet their common needs. Here are a few ideas:

1. **A village health committee.** A group of able, interested persons can be chosen by the village to help plan and lead activities relating to the well-being of the community—for example, digging garbage pits or latrines. The health worker can and should share much of his responsibility with other persons.

2. **Group discussions.** Mothers, fathers, schoolchildren, young people, folk healers, or other groups can discuss needs and problems that affect health. Their chief purpose can be to help people share ideas and build on what they already know.

3. **Work festivals.** Community projects such as putting in a water system or cleaning up the village go quickly and can be fun if everybody helps. Games, races, refreshments, and simple prizes help turn work into play. Use imagination.

4. **Cooperatives.** People can help keep prices down by sharing tools, storage, and perhaps land. Group cooperation can have a big influence on people's well-being.

CHILDREN CAN DO AN AMAZING AMOUNT OF WORK WHEN IT IS TURNED INTO A GAME!

5. **Classroom visits.** Work with the village schoolteacher to encourage health-related activities, through demonstrations and play acting. Also invite small groups of students to come to the health center. Children not only learn quickly, but they can help out in many ways. If you give children a chance, they gladly become a valuable resource.

6. **Mother and child health meetings.** It is especially important that pregnant women and mothers of small children (under five) be well informed about their own and their babies' health needs. Regular visits to the health post are opportunities for both check-ups and learning. Have mothers keep their children's health records and bring them each month to have their children's age and weight recorded (see the Road to Health Chart, p. 297). Mothers who understand the chart often take pride in making sure their children are eating and growing well. They can learn to understand them even if they cannot read. Perhaps you can help train interested mothers to organize and lead these activities.

7. **Home visits.** Make friendly visits to people's homes, especially homes of families who have special problems, who do not come often to the health post, or who do not take part in group activities. But respect people's privacy. If your visit cannot be friendly, do not make it—unless children or defenseless persons are in danger.

Ways to Share and Exchange Ideas in a Group

As a health worker you will find that the success you have in improving your people's health will depend far more on your skills as a teacher than on your medical or technical knowledge. For only when the whole community is involved and works together can big problems be overcome.

People do not learn much from what they are told. They learn from what they think, feel, discuss, see, and do together.

So the good teacher does not sit behind a desk and talk **at** people. He talks and works **with** them. He helps his people to think clearly about their needs and to find suitable ways to meet them. He looks for every opportunity to share ideas in an open and friendly way.

TALK WITH PEOPLE . . . . NOT AT THEM

Perhaps the most important thing you can do as a health worker is to awaken your people to their own possibilities . . . to help them gain confidence in themselves. Sometimes villagers do not change things they do not like because they do not try. Too often they may think of themselves as ignorant and powerless. But they are not. Most villagers, including those who cannot read or write, have remarkable knowledge and skills. They already make great changes in their surroundings with the tools they use, the land they farm, and the things they build. They can do many important things that people with a lot of schooling cannot.

If you can help people realize how much they already know and have done to change their surroundings, they may also realize that they can learn and do even more. By working together it is within their power to bring about even bigger changes for their health and well-being.

Then how do you tell people these things? Often you cannot!

But you can help them find out some of these things for themselves—by bringing them together for discussions. Say little yourself, but start the discussion by asking certain questions. Simple pictures like the drawing on the next page of a farm family in Central America may help. You will want to draw your own picture, with buildings, people, animals, and crops that look as much as possible like those in your area.

Show a group of people a picture similar to this and ask them to discuss it. Ask questions that get people talking about what they know and can do. Here are some sample questions:

- Who are the people in the picture and how do they live?

- What was this land like before the people came?

- In what ways have they changed their surroundings?

- How do these changes affect their health and well-being?

- What other changes could these people make? What else could they learn to do? What is stopping them? How could they learn more?

- How did they learn to farm? Who taught them?

- If a doctor or a lawyer moved onto this land with no more money or tools than these people, could he farm as well? Why or why not?

- In what ways are these people like ourselves?

This kind of group discussion helps build people's confidence in themselves and in their ability to change things. It can also make them feel more involved in their community.

At first you may find that people are slow to speak out and say what they think. But after a while they will usually begin to talk more freely and ask important questions themselves. Encourage everyone to say what he feels and to speak up without fear. Ask those who talk most to give a chance to those who are slower to speak up.

You can think of many other drawings and questions to start discussions that can help people look more clearly at problems, their causes, and possible solutions.

━━━━━━━━●━━━━━━━

What questions can you ask to get people thinking about the different things that lead to the condition of the child in the following picture?

Try to think of questions that lead to others and get people asking for themselves. How many of the causes underlying death from diarrhea (see p. w7) will your people think of when they discuss a picture like this?

MAKING THE BEST USE OF THIS BOOK

Anyone who knows how to read can use this book in his own home. Even those who do not read can learn from the pictures. But to make the fullest and best use of the book, people often need some instruction. This can be done in several ways.

A health worker or anyone who gives out the book should make sure that people understand how to use the list of Contents, the Index, the Green Pages and the Vocabulary. Take special care to give examples of **how to look things up.** Urge each person to carefully read the sections of the book that will help him understand **what may be helpful to do, what could be harmful or dangerous,** and **when it is important to get help** (see especially Chapters 1, 2, 6, and 9, and also the SIGNS OF DANGEROUS ILLNESS, p. 42). Point out how important it is to **prevent sickness** before it starts. Encourage people to pay special attention to Chapters 11 and 12, which deal with **eating right** (nutrition) and **keeping clean** (hygiene and sanitation).

Many of these things can be explained briefly. But the more time you spend with people **discussing** how to use the book or **reading and using it together,** the more everyone will get out of it.

You as a health worker might encourage people to get together in small groups to read through the book, discussing one chapter at a time. Look at the biggest problems in your area—what to do about health problems that already exist and how to prevent similar problems in the future. Try to get people looking ahead.

Perhaps interested persons can get together for a short class using this book (or others) as a text. Members of the group could discuss how to recognize, treat, and prevent different problems. They could take turns teaching and explaining things to each other.

To help learning be fun in these classes you can act out situations. For example, someone can act as if he has a particular sickness and can explain what he feels. Others then ask questions and examine him (Chapter 3). Use the book to try to find out what his problem is and what can be done about it. The group should remember to involve the 'sick' person in learning more about his own sickness— and should end up by discussing with him ways of preventing the sickness in the future. All this can be acted out in class.

As a health worker, one of the best ways you can help people use this book correctly is this: When persons come to you for treatment, have them look up their own or their child's problem in the book and find out how to treat it. This takes more time, but helps much more than doing it for them. Only when someone makes a mistake or misses something important do you need to step in and help him learn how to do it better. In this way, **even sickness gives a chance to help people learn.**

Dear village health worker—whoever and wherever you are, whether you have a title or official position, or are simply someone, like myself, with an interest in the well-being of others—make good use of this book. It is for you and for everyone.

But remember, the most important part of health care you will not find in this book or any other. The key to good health lies within you and your people, in the care, the concern, and the appreciation you have for each other. If you want to see your community be healthy, build on these.

> **Caring and sharing are the key to health.**

Yours truly,

David

David Werner

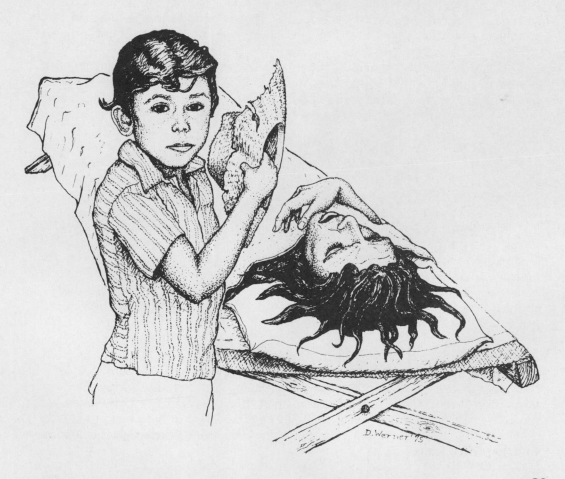

NOTICE

This book is to help people meet most of their common health needs for and by themselves. But it does not have all the answers. In case of serious illness or if you are uncertain about how to handle a health problem, get advice from a health worker or doctor whenever possible.

CHAPTER

1

HOME CURES
AND POPULAR BELIEFS

Everywhere on earth people use home remedies. In some places, the older or *traditional* ways of healing have been passed down from parents to children for hundreds of years.

Many home remedies have great value. Others have less. And some may be risky or harmful. Home remedies, like modern medicines, must be used with caution.

> **Try to *do no harm.*
> Only use home remedies if you are sure they are safe
> and know exactly how to use them.**

HOME CURES THAT HELP

For many sicknesses, time-tested home remedies work as well as modern medicines —or even **better.** They are often **cheaper.** And in some cases they are **safer.**

For example, many of the herbal teas people use for home treatment of coughs and colds do more good and cause fewer problems than cough syrups and strong medicines some doctors prescribe.

Also, teas or sweetened drinks many mothers give to babies with diarrhea are often safer and do more good than any modern medicine. What matters most is that a baby with diarrhea get plenty of liquids (see p. 151).

FOR COUGHS, COLDS, AND COMMON DIARRHEA, HERBAL TEAS ARE OFTEN *BETTER, CHEAPER, AND SAFER* THAN MODERN MEDICINES.

The Limitations of Home Remedies

Some diseases are helped by home remedies. Others can be treated better with modern medicine. This is true for most serious infections. Sicknesses like pneumonia, tetanus, typhoid, tuberculosis, appendicitis, diseases caused by sexual contact, and fever after childbirth should be treated with modern medicines as soon as possible. For these diseases, do not lose time trying to treat them first with home remedies only.

It is sometimes hard to be sure which home remedies work well and which do not. More careful studies are needed. For this reason:

> **It is often safer to treat very serious illnesses with modern medicines—following the advice of a health worker if possible.**

Old Ways and New

Some modern ways of meeting health needs work better than old ones. But at times the older, traditional ways are best. For example, traditional ways of caring for children or old people are often kinder and work better than some newer, less personal ways.

Not many years ago everyone thought that mother's milk was the best food for a young baby. They were right! Then the big companies that make canned and artificial milk began to tell mothers that bottle feeding was better. This is not true, but many mothers believed them and started to bottle feed their babies. As a result, thousands of babies have suffered and died needlessly from infection or hunger. For the reasons **breast is best,** see p. 271.

> **Respect your people's traditions and build on them.**

BELIEFS THAT CAN MAKE PEOPLE WELL

Some home remedies have a direct effect on the body. Others seem to work only because people believe in them. **The healing power of belief can be very strong.**

For example, I once saw a man who suffered from a very bad headache. To cure him, a woman gave him a small piece of yam, or sweet potato. She told him it was a strong painkiller. He believed her—and the pain went away quickly.

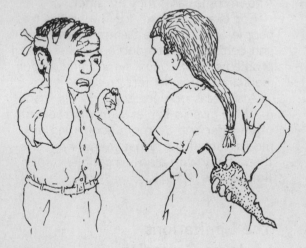

Clearly, it was his faith in her treatment, and not the yam itself, that made him feel better.

Many home remedies work in this way. They help largely because people have faith in them. For this reason, they are **especially useful to cure illnesses that are partly in people's minds, or those caused in part by a person's beliefs, worry, or fears.**

Included in this group of sicknesses are: bewitchment or hexing, unreasonable or hysterical fear, uncertain 'aches and pains' (especially those of teenage girls or older women), anxiety or nervous worry, and some cases of asthma, hiccups, indigestion, stomach ulcers, migraine headaches, and even warts.

For all of these problems, **the manner or 'touch' of the healer can be very important.** What it often comes down to is showing you care, helping the sick person believe he will get well, or simply helping him relax.

Sometimes a person's belief in a remedy can help with problems that have completely physical causes.

For example, Mexican villagers have the following home cures for poisonous snakebite:

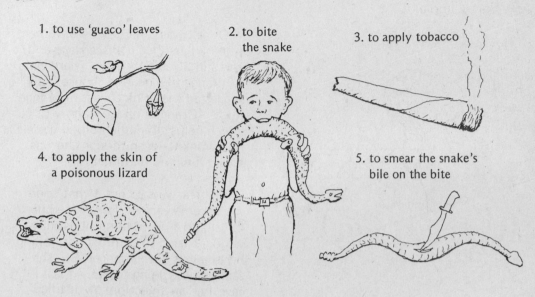

1. to use 'guaco' leaves

2. to bite the snake

3. to apply tobacco

4. to apply the skin of a poisonous lizard

5. to smear the snake's bile on the bite

In other lands people have their own snakebite remedies—often many different ones. As far as we know, **none of these home remedies has any direct effect against snake poison.** The person who says that a home remedy kept a snake's poison from harming him at all was probably bitten by a non-poisonous snake!

Yet any of these home remedies may do some good if a person believes in it. If it makes him less afraid, his pulse will slow down, he will move and tremble less, and as a result, the poison will spread through his body more slowly. So there is less danger!

But the benefit of these home remedies is limited. In spite of their common use, many people still become very ill or die from snakebite. As far as we know:

> **No home cure for poisonous bites**
> **(whether from snakes, scorpions, spiders, or other poisonous animals)**
> **has much effect beyond that of the healing power of belief.**

For snakebite it is usually better to use modern treatment. Be prepared: obtain *'antivenins'* or 'serums' for poisonous bites **before** you need them (see p. 105). Do not wait until it is too late.

BELIEFS THAT CAN MAKE PEOPLE SICK

The power of belief can help heal people. But it can also harm them. If a person believes strongly enough that something will hurt him, his own fear can make him sick. For example:

Once I was called to see a woman who had just had a *miscarriage* and was still bleeding a little. There was an orange tree near her house. So I suggested she drink a glass of orange juice. (Oranges have vitamin C, which helps strengthen blood vessels.) She drank it—even though she was afraid it would harm her.

Her fear was so great that soon she became very ill. I examined her, but could find nothing physically wrong. I tried to comfort her, telling her she was not in danger. But she said she was going to die. At last I gave her an injection of distilled (completely pure) water. Distilled water has no medical effect. But since she had great faith in injections, she quickly got better.

Actually, the juice did not harm her. What harmed her was her **belief that it would make her sick.** And what made her well was her faith in injections!

In this same way, many persons go on believing false ideas about witchcraft, injections, diet, and many other things. Much needless suffering is the result.

Perhaps, in a way, I had helped this woman. But the more I thought about it, the more I realized I had also wronged her; I had led her to believe things that were not true.

I wanted to set this right. So a few days later, when she was completely well, I went to her home and apologized for what I had done. I tried to help her understand that not the orange juice, but her **fear** had made her so sick. And that not the injection of water, but her **freedom from fear** had helped her get well.

By understanding the truth about the orange, the injection, and the tricks of her own mind, perhaps this woman and her family will become freer from fear and better able to care for their health in the future. For **health** is closely related to **understanding** and **freedom from fear.**

> **Many things do harm only because
> people believe they are harmful.**

WITCHCRAFT—BLACK MAGIC—AND THE EVIL EYE

If a person believes strongly enough that someone has the power to harm him, he may actually become ill. Anyone who believes he is bewitched or has been given the *evil eye* is really the victim of his own fears (see Susto, p. 24).

A 'witch' has no power over other people, except for her ability to make them believe that she has. For this reason:

> **It is impossible to bewitch
> a person who does not believe
> in witchcraft.**

Some people think that they are 'bewitched' when they have strange or frightening illnesses (such as *tumors* of the *genitals* or *cirrhosis* of the liver, see p. 328). Such sicknesses have nothing to do with witchcraft or black magic. Their causes are natural.

Do not waste your money at 'magic centers' that claim to cure witchcraft. And do not seek revenge against a witch, because it will not solve anything. If you are seriously ill, go for medical help.

If you have a strange sickness:	do not blame a witch,	do not go to a magic center,	but ask for medical advice.

QUESTIONS AND ANSWERS ON SOME FOLK BELIEFS AND HOME REMEDIES

These examples are from the mountains of Mexico, the area that I know best. Perhaps some of the beliefs of your people are similar. Think about ways to learn which beliefs in your area lead to better health and which do not.

When people think someone is bewitched, is it true that he will get well if his relatives harm or kill the witch?

FALSE! No one is ever helped by harming someone else.

Is it true that when the 'soft spot' on top of a baby's head sinks inward this means the baby will die of diarrhea unless he gets special treatment?

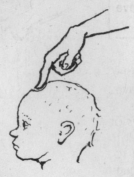

This is often true. The 'soft spot' sinks because the baby has lost too much liquid (see p. 151). Unless he gets more liquid soon, he may die (see p. 152).

Is it true that if the light of the eclipsing moon falls on a pregnant mother, her child will be born deformed or retarded?

This is not true! But children may be born retarded, deaf, or deformed if the mother does not use iodized salt, or for other reasons (see p. 318).

Is it true that mothers should give birth in a darkened room?

It is true that soft light is easier on the eyes of both the mother and the newborn child. But there should be enough light for the midwife to see what she is doing.

Is it true that a newborn baby should not be bathed until the cord falls off?

True! The stump of the cord should be kept dry until it falls off. But the baby can be gently cleaned with a clean, soft, damp cloth.

How many days after giving birth should a mother wait before she bathes?

A mother should wash with warm water the **day after giving birth.** The custom of not bathing for weeks following childbirth can lead to infections.

Is it true that traditional breast feeding is better than 'modern' bottle feeding?

TRUE! Breast milk is better food and also helps protect the baby against infection.

What foods should women avoid in the first few weeks after childbirth?

In the weeks following childbirth, women should not avoid any nutritious foods. Instead, they should eat plenty of fruit, vegetables, meat, milk, eggs, whole grains, and beans (see p. 276).

Is it a good idea to bathe a sick person, or will it do him harm?

It is a good idea. Sick people should be bathed in warm water every day.

Is it true that oranges, guavas, and other fruits are harmful when one has a cold or a fever?

NO! All fruits and juices are helpful when one has a cold or a fever. They do not cause congestion or harm of any kind.

Is it true that when a person has a high fever, he should be wrapped up so that the air will not harm him?

NO! When a person has a high fever, take off all covers and clothing. Let the air reach his body. This will help the fever go down (see p. 76).

Is it true that tea made from willow bark will help bring fever down and stop pain?

True. It helps. Willow bark has a natural medicine in it very much like aspirin.

SUNKEN FONTANEL OR SOFT SPOT

The *fontanel* is the soft spot on the top of a newborn baby's head. It is where the bones of his skull have still not formed completely. Normally it takes a year to a year and a half for the soft spot to close completely.

Mothers in different lands realize that when the soft spot sinks inward, their babies are in danger. They have many beliefs to explain this. In Latin America mothers think the baby's brains have slipped downward. They try to correct this by sucking on the soft spot, by pushing up on the roof of the mouth, or by holding the baby upside down and slapping his feet. This does not help because . . . **A sunken soft spot is really caused by dehydration** (see p. 151).

This means the child is losing more liquid than he is drinking. He is too dry—usually because he has diarrhea, or diarrhea with vomiting.

Treatment:

1. Give the child plenty of liquid: Rehydration Drink (see p. 152), breast milk, or boiled water.

2. If necessary, treat the causes of the diarrhea and vomiting (see p. 152 and 161). No medicine is usually needed.

TO CURE A SUNKEN SOFT SPOT . . .

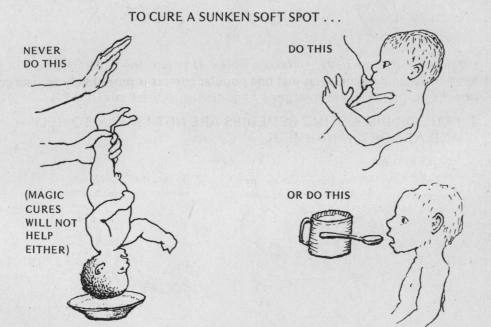

NEVER DO THIS

(MAGIC CURES WILL NOT HELP EITHER)

DO THIS

OR DO THIS

Note: If the soft spot is swollen or bulges **upward,** this may be a sign of meningitis. Begin treatment at once (see p. 185), and get medical help.

WAYS TO TELL WHETHER A HOME REMEDY WORKS OR NOT

Because a lot of people use a home cure does not necessarily mean it works well or is safe. It is often hard to know which remedies are helpful and which may be harmful. Careful study is needed to be sure. Here are four rules to help tell which remedies are least likely to work, or are dangerous. (Examples are from Mexican villages.)

1. THE MORE REMEDIES THERE ARE FOR ANY ONE ILLNESS, THE LESS LIKELY IT IS THAT ANY OF THEM WORKS.

For example: In rural Mexico there are **many** home remedies for goiter, **none** of which does any real good. Here are some of them:

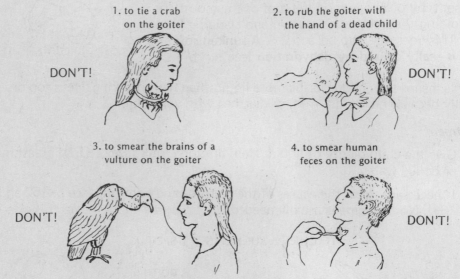

Not one of these many remedies works. If it did, the others would not be needed. **When a sickness has just one popular cure, it is more likely to be a good one.** For prevention and treatment of goiter use iodized salt (p. 130).

2. FOUL OR DISGUSTING REMEDIES ARE NOT LIKELY TO HELP— AND ARE OFTEN HARMFUL.

For example:

These two remedies do not help at all. The first one can cause dangerous infections. Belief in remedies like these sometimes causes delay in getting proper medical care.

3. REMEDIES THAT USE ANIMAL OR HUMAN WASTE DO NO GOOD AND CAN CAUSE DANGEROUS INFECTIONS. NEVER USE THEM.

Examples:

1. Putting human feces around the eye does not cure blurred vision and can cause infections.

2. Smearing cow dung on the head to fight ringworm can cause tetanus and other dangerous infections.

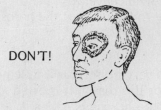

DON'T!

DON'T!

Also, the droppings of rabbits or other animals do not help heal burns. To use them is very dangerous. Cow dung, held in the hand, cannot help control fits. Teas made from human, pig, or any other animal feces do not cure anything. They can make people sicker. **Never** put feces on the navel of a newborn baby. This can cause tetanus.

4. THE MORE A REMEDY RESEMBLES THE SICKNESS IT IS SAID TO CURE, THE MORE LIKELY ITS BENEFITS COME ONLY FROM THE POWER OF BELIEF.

The association between each of the following illnesses and its remedy is clear in these examples from Mexico:

1. for a nosebleed, using *yesca* (a bright red mushroom)

2. for deafness, putting powdered rattlesnake's rattle in the ear

3. for dog bite, drinking tea made from the dog's tail

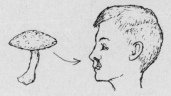 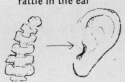 

4. for scorpion sting, tying a scorpion against the stung finger

5. to prevent diarrhea when a child is teething, putting a necklace of snake's fangs around the baby's neck

6. to 'bring out' the rash of measles, making a tea from kapok bark

 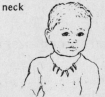 

These remedies, and many other similar ones, have no curative value in themselves. They may be of some benefit if people believe in them. But for serious problems, be sure their use does not delay more effective treatment.

MEDICINAL PLANTS

Many plants have curative powers. Some of the best modern medicines are made from wild herbs.

Nevertheless, not all 'curative herbs' people use have medical value . . . and those that have are sometimes used the wrong way. Try to learn about the herbs in your area and find out which ones are worthwhile.

 CAUTION! Some medicinal herbs are very poisonous if taken in more than the recommended dose. For this reason it is often safer to use modern medicine, since the dosage is easier to control.

Here are a few examples of plants that can be useful if used correctly:

ANGEL'S TRUMPET *(Datura arborea)*

The leaves of this and certain other members of the nightshade family contain a drug that helps to calm intestinal cramps, stomach-aches, and even gallbladder pain.

Grind up 1 or 2 leaves of Angel's Trumpet and soak them for a day in 7 tablespoons (100 ml.) of water.

Dosage: Between 10 and 15 drops every 4 hours (adults only).

 WARNING: Angel's Trumpet is very poisonous if you take more than the recommended dose. It is safer to use standard antispasmodic pills when possible (see p. 367).

CORN SILK (the tassels or 'silk' from an ear of maize)

Sometimes a tea made from corn silk can help reduce swelling of the feet—especially in pregnant women (see p. 176 and 248).

Boil a large handful of corn silk in water and drink 1 or 2 glasses. It is not dangerous.

CARDON CACTUS *(Pachycerius pectin-aboriginum)*

Cactus juice can be used to clean wounds when there is no boiled water and no way to get any.

Cardon cactus also helps stop a wound from bleeding, because the juice makes the cut blood vessels squeeze shut.

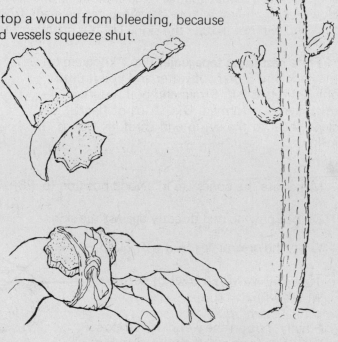

Cut a piece of the cactus with a clean knife and press it firmly against the wound.

When the bleeding is under control, tie a piece of the cactus to the wound with a strip of cloth.

After 2 or 3 hours, take off the cactus and clean the wound with boiled water and soap. There are more instructions on how to care for wounds and control bleeding on pages 82 to 87.

PAPAYA

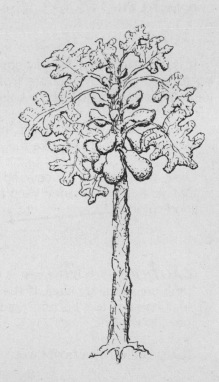

Ripe papayas are rich in vitamins and also aid digestion. Eating them is especially helpful for weak or old people who complain of upset stomach when they eat meat, chicken, or eggs. Papaya makes these foods easier to digest.

Papaya can also help get rid of intestinal worms, although modern medicines often work better.

Collect 3 or 4 teaspoons (15-20 ml.) of the 'milk' that comes out when the green fruit or trunk of the tree is cut. Mix this with an equal amount of honey and stir it into a cup of hot water. If possible, drink along with a laxative.

HOMEMADE CASTS—
FOR KEEPING BROKEN BONES IN PLACE

In Mexico several different plants such as *tepeguaje* (a tree of the bean family) and *solda con solda* (a huge, tree-climbing arum lily) are used to make casts. However, any plant will do if a syrup can be made from it that will dry hard and firm and will not irritate the skin. Try out different plants in your area.

For a cast using tepeguaje: Put 1 kilogram of the bark into 5 liters of water and boil it until only 2 liters is left. Strain and boil it until a thick syrup is formed. Dip strips of flannel or clean sheet in the syrup and carefully use as follows.

Make sure the bones are in a good position (p. 98).

Do **not** put the cast directly against the skin.

Wrap the arm or leg in a soft cloth.

Then follow with a layer of cotton or wild kapok.

Finally, put on the wet cloth strips so that they form a cast that is firm but not too tight.

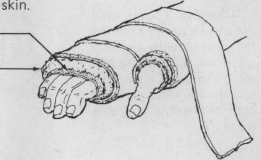

It is important that the cast cover enough of the arm or leg to keep the broken bones from moving—usually the joint above and the joint below the break.

For a broken wrist, the cast should cover almost the whole arm, like this:

Leave the finger tips uncovered so that you can see if they keep a good color.

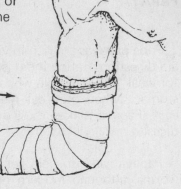

CAUTION: Even if the cast is not very tight when you put it on, the broken limb may swell up later. If the person complains that the cast is too tight, or if his fingers or toes become cold, white, or blue, take the cast off and put on a new, looser one.

Never put on a cast over a cut or a wound.

ENEMAS, LAXATIVES, AND PURGES: WHEN TO USE THEM AND WHEN NOT TO

Many people give enemas and take laxatives far too often. The 'urge to purge' is world wide.

Enemas and purges are very popular home cures. And they are often very harmful. Many people believe fever and diarrhea can be 'washed out' by giving an **enema** (running water into the gut through the anus) or by using a *purge,* or strong laxative. Unfortunately, such efforts to clean or purge the sick body often cause more injury to the already damaged gut.

> **Rarely do enemas or laxatives do any good at all.**
> **Often they are dangerous—especially strong laxatives.**

CASES IN WHICH IT IS DANGEROUS TO USE ENEMAS OR LAXATIVES:

Never use an enema or laxative if a person has a severe stomach-ache or any other sign of appendicitis or 'acute abdomen' (see p. 93), even if he passes days without a bowel movement.

Never give an enema or laxative to a person with a bullet wound or other injury to the gut.

Never give a strong laxative to a weak or sick person. It will weaken him more.

Never give a laxative or purge to a child with high fever, vomiting, diarrhea, or signs of dehydration (see p. 151).

Do not make a habit of using laxatives often (see Constipation, p. 129).

THE CORRECT USES OF ENEMAS

1. Simple enemas can help relieve constipation (dry, hard, difficult stools). Use warm water only, or water with a little soap in it.

2. When a person with vomiting is dehydrated, you can try giving an enema of Rehydration Drink **very slowly** (see p. 152).

PURGES AND LAXATIVES THAT ARE OFTEN USED:

CASTOR OIL SENNA LEAF CASCARA (cascara sagrada)	These are irritating purges that often do more harm than good. It is better not to use them.
MAGNESIUM CARBONATE MILK OF MAGNESIA EPSOM SALTS (magnesium sulfate) (see p. 368)	These are salt purges. Use them only in low doses, as laxatives for constipation. Do not use them often and **never when there is pain in the belly.**
MINERAL OIL (see p. 368)	This is sometimes used for constipation in persons with piles . . . but it is like passing greased rocks. Not recommended.

CORRECT USES OF LAXATIVES AND PURGES:

Laxatives are like purges but weaker. All the products listed above are laxatives when taken in small doses and purges when taken in large doses. Laxatives soften and hurry the bowel movement; purges cause diarrhea.

Purges: The only time a person should use a strong dose of a purge is when he has taken a poison and must clean it out quickly (see p. 103). At any other time a purge is harmful.

Laxatives: One can use milk of magnesia or other magnesium salts in small doses, as laxatives, in some cases of constipation. People with *hemorrhoids* (piles) who have constipation can take mineral oil but this only makes their stools slippery, not soft. The dose for mineral oil is 3 to 6 teaspoons at bedtime (never with a meal because the oil will rob the body of important vitamins in the food). This is not the best way.

A BETTER WAY:

Foods with fiber. The healthiest and most gentle way to have softer, more frequent stools is to eat more foods with lots of natural fiber, or 'roughage' like *cassava,* or *bran* and other whole grain cereals (see p. 129). Drinking lots of water and eating plenty of fruits and vegetables also helps.

People whose tradition it is to eat lots of food with natural fiber suffer much less from piles, constipation, and cancer of the gut than do people who eat a lot of refined 'modern' foods. For better bowel habits, avoid refined foods and eat foods prepared from unpolished or unrefined grains.

2

SICKNESSES THAT ARE OFTEN CONFUSED

WHAT CAUSES SICKNESS?

Persons from different countries or backgrounds have different ways to explain what causes sickness.

A baby gets diarrhea. But why?

People in small villages may say it is because the parents did something wrong, or perhaps because they made a god or spirit angry.

A doctor may say it is because the child has an infection.

A public health officer may say it is because the villagers do not have a good water system or use latrines.

A social reformer may say the unhealthy conditions that lead to frequent childhood diarrhea are caused by an unfair distribution of land and wealth.

A teacher may place the blame on lack of education.

People see the cause of sickness in terms of their own experience and point of view. Who then is right about the cause? Possibly everyone is right, or partly right. This is because . . .

Sickness usually results from a combination of causes.

"Why my child?"

Each of the causes suggested above may be a part of the reason why a baby gets diarrhea.

To prevent and treat sickness successfully, it helps to have as full an understanding as possible about the common sicknesses in your area and the combination of things that causes them.

In this book, different sicknesses are discussed mostly according to the systems and terms of modern or scientific medicine.

To make good use of this book, and safe use of the medicines it recommends , you will need some understanding of sicknesses and their causes according to medical science. Reading this chapter may help.

DIFFERENT KINDS OF SICKNESSES AND THEIR CAUSES

When considering how to prevent or treat different sicknesses, it helps to think of them in two groups: infectious and non-infectious.

Infectious diseases are those that spread from one person to another. Healthy persons must be protected from people with these sicknesses.

Non-infectious diseases do not spread from person to person. They have other causes. Therefore, it is important to know which sicknesses are infectious and which are not.

Non-infectious Diseases

Non-infectious diseases have many different causes. But they are never caused by germs, bacteria, or other living organisms that attack the body. They never spread from one person to another. It is important to realize that *antibiotics,* or medicines that fight germs (see p. 55), do not help cure non-infectious diseases.

> *Remember:* **Antibiotics are of no use for non-infectious diseases.**

EXAMPLES OF NON-INFECTIOUS DISEASES

Problems caused by something that wears out or goes wrong within the body:	Problems caused by something from outside that harms or troubles the body:	Problems caused by a lack of something the body needs:
rheumatism heart attack epileptic fits stroke migraines cataract cancer	allergies asthma poisons snakebite cough from smoking stomach ulcer alcoholism	malnutrition pellagra anemia goiter cirrhosis of the liver (part of the cause)

Problems people are born with:		Problems that begin in the mind (mental 'illnesses'):
harelip crossed or wall-eyes other deformities	epilepsy (some kinds) retarded (backward) children birthmarks	fear that something is harmful when it is not (paranoia) nervous worry (anxiety) belief in hexes (witchcraft) uncontrolled fear

Infectious Diseases

Infectious diseases are caused by bacteria and other *organisms* (living things) that harm the body. They are spread in many ways. Here are some of the most important kinds of organisms that cause infections and examples of sicknesses they cause:

EXAMPLES OF INFECTIOUS DISEASES

Organism that causes the sickness	Name of the sickness	How it is spread or enters the body	Principal medicine
bacteria (microbes or germs)	tuberculosis	through the air (coughing)	antibiotics
	tetanus	dirty wounds	
	some diarrhea	dirty fingers, water, flies	
	pneumonia (some kinds)	through the air (coughing)	
	gonorrhea and syphilis	sexual contact	
	earache	with a cold	
	infected wounds	contact with dirty things	
	sores with pus	direct contact (by touch)	
virus (germs smaller than bacteria)	colds, flu, measles, mumps, chickenpox, infantile paralysis, virus diarrhea	from someone who is sick, through the air, by coughing, flies, etc.	aspirin and other painkillers (There are no medicines that fight viruses effectively. Antibiotics do not help.) Vaccinations help prevent some virus infections.
	rabies	animal bites	
	warts	touch	
fungus	ringworm	by touch or from clothing	sulfur and vinegar ointments: undecylenic, benzoic, salicylic acid griseofulvin
	athlete's foot jock itch		
internal parasites (harmful animals living in the body)	In the gut: worms amebas (dysentery)	feces-to-mouth lack of cleanliness	different specific medicines
	In the blood: malaria	mosquito bite	chloroquine
external parasites (harmful animals living on the body)	lice fleas bedbugs scabies	by contact with infected people or their clothes	insecticides, lindane

Bacteria, like many of the organisms that cause infections, are so small you cannot see them without a microscope—an instrument that makes tiny things look bigger. Viruses are even smaller than bacteria.

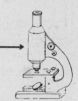

Antibiotics (penicillin, tetracycline, etc.) are medicines that help cure certain illnesses caused by bacteria. **Antibiotics have no effect on illnesses caused by viruses,** such as colds, flu, mumps, chickenpox, etc. **Do not treat virus infections with antibiotics.** They will not help and may be harmful (see **Antibiotics**, p. 57).

SICKNESSES THAT ARE HARD TO TELL APART

Sometimes diseases that have different causes and require different treatment result in problems that look very much alike. For example:

1. **A child who slowly becomes thin and wasted, while his belly gets more and more swollen, could have any (or several) of the following problems:**

   - malnutrition (see p. 112)

   - a 'heavy' roundworm infection, p. 140, (usually together with malnutrition)

   - advanced tuberculosis (p. 179)

   - a long-term severe urinary infection (p. 234)

   - any of several problems of the liver or spleen

   - leukemia (cancer of the blood)

2. **An older person with a big, open, slowly growing sore on the ankle could have:**

   - bad circulation that results from varicose veins or other causes (p. 213)

   - diabetes (p. 127)

   - infection of the bone (osteomyelitis)

   - leprosy (p. 191)

   - tuberculosis of the skin (p. 212)

   - advanced syphilis (p. 237)

The medical treatment for each of these diseases is different, so to treat them correctly it is important to tell them apart.

Many illnesses at first seem very similar. But if you ask the right questions and know what to look for, you can often learn information and see certain signs that will help tell you what illness a person has.

This book describes the typical history and signs for many illnesses. But be careful! Diseases do not always show the signs described for them—or the signs may be confusing. **For difficult cases, the help of a skilled health worker or doctor is often needed.** Sometimes special tests or analyses are necessary.

Work within your limits!
In using this book, remember it is easy to make mistakes.
Never pretend you know something you do not.
If you are not fairly sure what an illness is and how to
treat it, or if the illness is very serious—get medical help.

SICKNESSES THAT ARE OFTEN CONFUSED
OR GIVEN THE SAME NAME

Many of the common names people use for their sicknesses were first used long before anyone knew about germs or bacteria or the medicines that fight them. Different diseases that caused more or less similar problems—such as 'high fever' or 'pain in the side'—were often given a single name. In many parts of the world, these common names are still used. City-trained doctors often neither know nor use these names. For this reason, people sometimes think they apply to 'sicknesses doctors do not treat'. So they treat these **home sicknesses** with herbs or home remedies.

Actually, most of these home sicknesses or 'folk diseases' are the same ones known to medical science. Only the names are different.

For many sicknesses, home remedies work well. But for some sicknesses, treatment with modern medicine works much better and may be life-saving. This is especially true for dangerous infections like pneumonia, typhoid, tuberculosis, or infections after giving birth.

To know which sicknesses definitely require modern medicines and to decide what medicine to use, it is important that you try to **find out what the disease is in the terms used by trained health workers and in this book.**

If you cannot find the sickness you are looking for in this book, look for it under a different name or in the chapter that covers the same sort of problem. Use the list of CONTENTS and the INDEX.

If you are unsure what the sickness is—especially if it seems serious—try to get medical help.

The rest of this chapter gives examples of common or *traditional* names people use for various sicknesses. Often a single name is given to diseases that are different according to medical science.

Examples cannot be given for each country or area where this book may be used. Therefore, I have kept those from the Spanish edition, with names used by villagers in western Mexico. They will not be the same names you use. However, people in many parts of the world see and speak of their illnesses in a similar way. So the examples may help you think about how people name diseases in your area.

Can you think of a name your people use for any of the following 'folk diseases'? If you can, write it in after the Spanish name, where it says,

Name in your area:_____

EXAMPLES OF LOCAL NAMES FOR SICKNESSES

Spanish Name: *EMPACHO* (STOPPED-UP GUT) Name in Your Area: _____

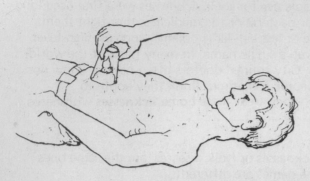

In medical terms *empacho* (impaction) means that the gut is stopped up or **obstructed** (see p. 94). But in Mexican villages any illness causing stomach-ache or diarrhea may be called *empacho.* It is said that a ball of hair or something else blocks a part of the gut. People put the blame on witches or evil spirits, and treat with magic cures and *cupping* (see picture). Sometimes folk healers pretend to take a ball of hair and thorns out of the gut by sucking on the belly.

Different illnesses that cause stomach pain or discomfort and are sometimes called *empacho* are:

- diarrhea or dysentery with cramps (p. 153)

- worms (p. 140)

- swollen stomach due to malnutrition (p. 112)

- indigestion or stomach ulcer (p. 128)

- and rarely, true gut obstruction (p. 94)

Most of these problems are not helped much by magic cures or cupping. To treat *empacho,* try to identify and treat the sickness that causes it.

Spanish Name: *DOLOR DE IJAR* (SIDE PAINS) Name in Your Area: _____

This name is used for any pain women get in one side of their belly. Often the pain goes around to the mid or lower back. Possible causes of this kind of pain include:

- an infection of the urinary system (the kidneys, the bladder, or the tubes that join them, see p. 234)

- an infection, cyst, or tumor in the womb or ovaries (see p. 243)

- cramps or gas pains (see diarrhea, p. 153)

- appendicitis (p. 94)

Spanish Name: *LA CONGESTIÓN* (CONGESTION) Name in Your Area:_____

Any sudden upset or illness that causes great distress is called *la congestión* by Mexican villagers. People speak of *congestión* of:

the head,   the chest,   the stomach,   or the whole body.

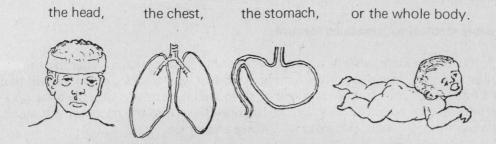

It is said that *la congestión* strikes persons who break 'the diet' (see p. 124), by eating foods that are forbidden or *taboo* after childbirth, while taking a medicine, or when they have a cold or cough. Although **these foods usually cause no harm** and are sometimes just what their bodies need, many people will not touch them because they are so afraid of getting *la congestión.*

Different illnesses that are sometimes called *la congestión* are:

- Food poisoning, from eating spoiled food: causes sudden vomiting followed by diarrhea, cramps, and weakness (see p. 135).

- A severe allergic reaction, in allergic persons after they eat certain foods (shellfish, chocolate, etc.), take certain medicines, or are injected with penicillin. May cause vomiting, diarrhea, cold sweat, breathing trouble, itchy rash, and severe distress (see p. 166).

- Any sudden upset of the stomach or gut: see diarrhea (p. 153), vomiting (p. 161), and acute abdomen (p. 93).

- Sudden or severe difficulty breathing: caused by asthma (p. 167), pneumonia (p. 171), or something stuck in the throat (p. 79).

- Illnesses that cause fits or paralysis: see fits (p. 178), tetanus (p. 182), meningitis (p. 185), polio (p. 314), and stroke (p. 327).

- Heart attacks: mostly in older persons (p. 325).

Spanish Name: *LATIDO* (PULSING) Name in Your Area:_____

Latido is a name used in Latin America for a pulsing or 'jumping' in the pit of the stomach. It is really the pulse of the *aorta* or big blood vessel coming from the heart. This pulse can be seen and felt on a person who is very thin and hungry. *Latido* is often a sign of malnutrition (p. 112)—or hunger! Eating nutritious food is the only real treatment (see p. 110).

Spanish Name: *SUSTO* (HYSTERIA, FRIGHT) Name in Your Area:_____

According to Mexican villagers, *susto* is caused by a sudden fright a person has had, or by witchcraft, black magic, or evil spirits. A person with *susto* is very nervous and afraid. He may shake, behave strangely, not be able to sleep, lose weight, or even die.

Possible medical explanations for *susto*:

1. In many people, *susto* is a state of fear or *hysteria,* perhaps caused by the 'power of belief' (see p. 4). For example, a woman who is afraid someone will hex her becomes nervous and does not eat or sleep well. She begins to grow weak and lose weight. She takes this as a sign she has been hexed, so she becomes still more nervous and frightened. Her *susto* gets worse and worse.

2. In babies or small children, *susto* is usually very different. Bad dreams may cause a child to cry out in his sleep or wake up frightened. High fevers from any illness can cause very strange speech and behavior (*delirium*). A child that often looks and acts worried may be malnourished (p. 112). Sometimes early signs of tetanus (p. 182) or meningitis (p. 185) are also called *susto.*

Treatment:

When the *susto* is caused by a specific illness, treat the illness. Help the person understand its cause. Ask for medical advice, if needed.

When the *susto* is caused by fright, try to comfort the person and help him understand that his fear itself is the cause of his problem. Magic cures and home remedies sometimes help.

If the frightened person is breathing very hard and fast, his body may be getting too much air (oxygen)—which may be part of the problem:

EXTREME FRIGHT OR HYSTERIA WITH FAST HEAVY BREATHING (HYPERVENTILATION)

Signs:

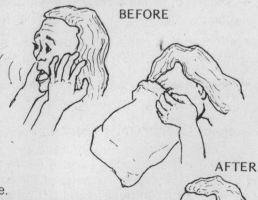

BEFORE

AFTER

- person very frightened
- breathing fast and deep
- fast, pounding heartbeat
- numbness or tingling of face, hands, or feet
- muscle cramps

Treatment:

- Keep the person as quiet as possible.
- Have him put his face in a paper bag and breathe slowly. He should continue breathing the same air for 2 or 3 minutes. This will usually calm him down.
- Explain to him that the problem is not dangerous, and he will soon be all right.

MISUNDERSTANDINGS DUE TO CONFUSION OF NAMES

This page shows 2 examples of misunderstandings that can result when certain names like 'cancer' and 'leprosy' mean one thing to medical workers and something else to villagers. In talking with health workers—and in using this book:

> **Avoid misunderstanding—go by the signs and history of a person's sickness, not the name people give it!**

Spanish Name: *CANCER* (CANCER) Name in Your Area:_____

Mexican villagers use the word *cancer* for any severe infection of the skin, especially badly infected wounds (p. 88) or gangrene (p. 213).

In modern medical language, cancer is not an infection, but an abnormal growth or lump in any part of the body. Common types of cancer that you should watch out for are:

cancer of the skin   breast cancer   cancer of the womb or ovaries
(p. 211)   (p. 279)   (p. 280)

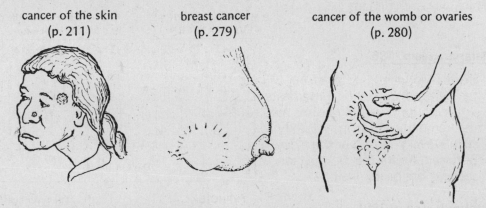

Any hard, painless, slowly growing lump in any part of your body may be cancer. Cancer is often dangerous and may need surgery.

At the first suspicion of cancer seek medical help.

Spanish Name: *LEPRA* (LEPROSY) Name in Your Area:_____

Mexican villagers call any open spreading sore *lepra.* This leads to confusion, because medical workers use this term only for true leprosy (Hansen's disease, p. 191). Sores commonly called *lepra* are:

- impetigo and other skin infections (p. 202)

- sores that come from insect bites or scabies (p. 199)

- chronic sores or skin ulcers such as those caused by poor circulation (p. 213)

- skin cancer (p. 211)

- less commonly, leprosy (p. 191) or tuberculosis of the skin (p. 212)

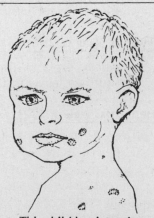

This child has impetigo, not leprosy

CONFUSION BETWEEN DIFFERENT ILLNESSES THAT CAUSE FEVER

Spanish Name: *LA FIEBRE* (THE FEVER) Name in Your Area:_____

Correctly speaking, a *fever* is **a body temperature higher than normal.** But in Latin America, a number of serious illnesses that cause high temperatures are all called *la fiebre*—or 'the fever'.

To prevent or treat these diseases successfully, it is important to know how to tell one from another.

Here are some of the important acute illnesses in which fever is an outstanding sign. The drawings show the **fever pattern** (rise and fall of temperature) that is typical for each disease.

MALARIA—TYPICAL FEVER PATTERN — The solid line shows the rise and fall of temperature.

Malaria: (see p. 186)

Begins suddenly with rising temperature and chills. Fever lasts a few hours. Sweating begins as the temperature drops. Usually strikes every second or third day. Between fevers the sick person seems more or less well.

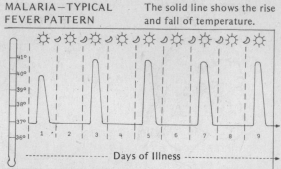

TYPHOID — TYPICAL FEVER PATTERN — The fever goes up a little each day.

Typhoid: (see p. 189)

Begins like a cold. Temperature goes up a little more each day. Pulse relatively slow. Sometimes diarrhea and dehydration. Trembling or delirium (mind wanders). Person very ill.

Typhus: (see p. 190)

Similar to typhoid. Rash similar to that of measles, with tiny bruises.

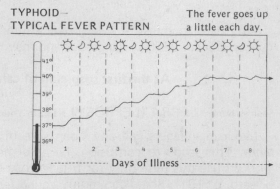

HEPATITIS— TYPICAL FEVER PATTERN — Usually the fever is mild.

Generally the fever drops when the eyes turn yellow.

Hepatitis: (see p. 172)

Person loses appetite. Does not wish to eat or smoke. Wants to vomit (nausea). Eyes and skin turn yellow; urine orange or brown; stools whitish. Sometimes liver becomes large, tender. Mild fever. Person very weak.

Pneumonia: (see p. 171)

Fast, shallow breathing. Temperature rises quickly. Cough with green, yellow, or bloody mucus. May be pain in chest. Person very ill.

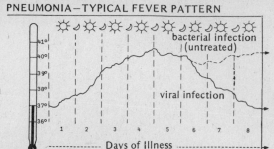

PNEUMONIA—TYPICAL FEVER PATTERN

bacterial infection (untreated)

viral infection

Days of Illness

Rheumatic fever: (see p. 310)

Most common in children and teenagers. Pain in joints. High fever. Often comes after a sore throat. May be pain in the chest with shortness of breath. Or uncontrolled movements of arms and legs.

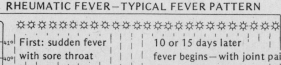

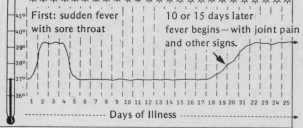

RHEUMATIC FEVER—TYPICAL FEVER PATTERN

First: sudden fever with sore throat

10 or 15 days later fever begins—with joint pain and other signs.

Days of Illness

Brucellosis (undulant fever, Malta fever): (see p. 188)

Begins slowly with tiredness, headache, and pains in the bones. Fever and sweating most common at night. Fever disappears for a few days only to come back again. This may go on for months or years.

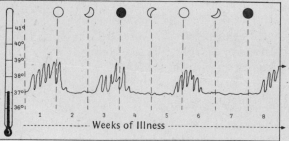

BRUCELLOSIS— TYPICAL FEVER PATTERN

Fever comes in waves. Rises in the afternoon and falls at night.

Weeks of Illness

Childbirth fever: (see p. 276)

Begins a day or more after giving birth. Starts with a slight fever, which often rises later. Foul-smelling vaginal *discharge.* Pain and sometimes bleeding.

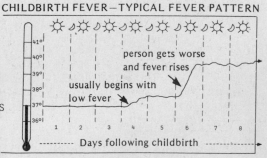

CHILDBIRTH FEVER—TYPICAL FEVER PATTERN

person gets worse and fever rises

usually begins with low fever

Days following childbirth

All of these illnesses can be dangerous. In addition to those shown here, there are many other diseases (especially in *tropical* countries) that may cause similar signs and fevers. These illnesses are not always easy to tell apart. Most are serious or dangerous. When possible—seek medical help.

CHAPTER

3

HOW TO EXAMINE
A SICK PERSON

To find out the needs of a sick person, first you must ask important questions and then examine him carefully. You should look for *signs* and *symptoms* that help you tell how ill the person is and what kind of sickness he may have.

Always examine the person where there is good light, preferably in the sunlight —**never** in a dark room.

There are certain basic things to ask and to look for in anyone who is sick. These include things the sick person feels or reports (symptoms), as well as things **you** notice on examining him (signs). These signs can be especially important in babies and persons unable to talk. In this book the word 'signs' is used for both symptoms and signs.

When you examine a sick person, write down your findings and keep them for the health worker in case he is needed (see p. 44).

QUESTIONS

Start by asking the person about his sickness. Be sure to ask the following:

What bothers you most right now?
What makes you feel better or worse?
How and when did your sickness begin?
Have you had this same trouble before, or has anyone else in your family or neighborhood had it?

Continue with other questions in order to learn the details of the illness.

For example, if the sick person has a pain, ask him:

Where does it hurt? (Ask him to point to the exact place with one finger.)
Does it hurt all the time, or off and on?
What is the pain like? (sharp? dull? burning?)
Can you sleep with the pain?

If the sick person is a baby who still does not talk, look for signs of pain. Notice his movements and how he cries. (For example, a child with an earache sometimes rubs the side of his head or pulls at his ear.)

GENERAL CONDITION OF HEALTH

Before touching the sick person, look at him carefully. Observe how ill or weak he looks, the way he moves, how he breathes, and how clear his mind seems. Look for signs of dehydration (see p. 151) and of shock (p. 77).

Notice whether the person looks well nourished or poorly nourished. Has he been losing weight? When a person has lost weight slowly over a long period of time, he may have a *chronic illness* (one that lasts a long time).

Also note the color of the skin and eyes:

- Paleness, especially of the lips and inside the eyelids, is a sign of anemia (p. 125).
- Bluish skin, especially blueness or darkness of the lips and fingernails, may mean serious problems with breathing (p. 79, 167 and 313) or with the heart (p. 325).
- A grayish-white coloring, with cool, moist skin, often means a person is in shock (p. 77).
- Yellow color (*jaundice*) of the skin and eyes may result from disease in the liver (hepatitis, p. 172 or cirrhosis, p. 328, amebic abscess, p. 145) or gallbladder (p. 329). It may also occur in newborn babies (p. 274).

TEMPERATURE

It is often wise to take a sick person's temperature, even if he does not seem to have a fever. If the person is very sick, take the temperature at least 4 times each day and write it down.

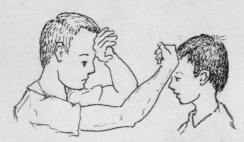

If there is no thermometer, you can get an idea of the temperature by putting the back of one hand on the sick person's forehead and the other on your own or that of another healthy person. If the sick person has a fever, you should feel the difference.

It is important to find out when and how the fever comes, how long it lasts, and how it goes away. This may help you identify the disease. For example:

- Malaria usually causes attacks of a high fever that begin with chills, last a few hours, and come back every 2 or 3 days (p. 186).
- Typhoid causes a fever that rises a little more every day.
- Tuberculosis sometimes causes a mild fever in the afternoon. At night the person often sweats, and the fever goes down.

Note: In newborn babies a temperature that is unusually high **or unusually low** (below 36°) may mean a serious infection (see p. 275).

- To learn about other fever patterns, see p. 26 to 27.
- To learn how to use a thermometer, see the next page.
- To learn what to do for a fever, see p. 75.

How to Use a Thermometer

Every family should have a thermometer. Take the temperature of a sick person 4 times a day and always write it down.

How to read the thermometer (using one marked in degrees *centigrade*—°C):

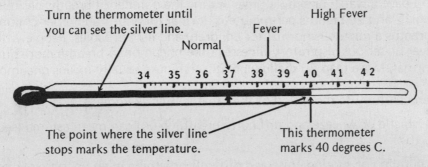

Turn the thermometer until you can see the silver line.

Normal

Fever

High Fever

The point where the silver line stops marks the temperature.

This thermometer marks 40 degrees C.

How to take the temperature:

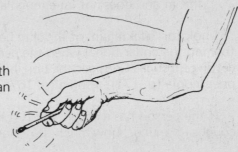

1. Clean the thermometer well with soap and water or alcohol. Shake it hard, with a snap of the wrist until it reads less than 36 degrees.

2. Put the thermometer . . .

under the tongue (keeping the mouth shut)   or   in the armpit if there is danger of biting the thermometer   or   carefully, in the anus of a small child (wet or grease it first)

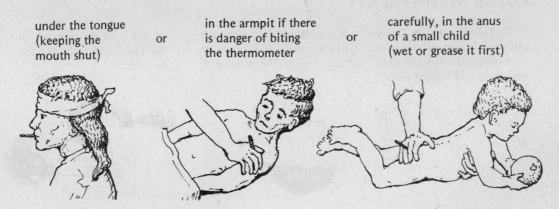

3. Leave it there for 3 or 4 minutes.

4. Read it. (An armpit temperature will read a little lower than a mouth reading; in the anus it will read a little higher.)

5. Wash the thermometer well with soap and water.

BREATHING (RESPIRATION)

Pay special attention to the way the sick person breathes—the depth (deep or shallow), rate (how often breaths are taken), and difficulty. Notice if both sides of the chest move equally when he breathes.

If you have a watch or simple timer, count the number of breaths per minute. Between 12 and 20 breaths per minute is normal for adults and older children. Up to 30 breaths a minute is normal for children, and 40 for babies. People with a high fever or serious respiratory illnesses (like pneumonia) breathe more quickly than normal. More than 40 **shallow** breaths a minute usually means pneumonia.

Listen carefully to the sound of the breaths. For example:

- A whistle or wheeze and difficulty breathing out can mean asthma (see p. 167).

- A gurgling or snoring noise and difficult breathing in an unconscious person may mean the tongue, mucus (slime or pus), or something else is stuck in the throat and does not let enough air get through.

Look for 'sucking in' of the skin between ribs and at the angle of the neck (behind the collar bone) when the person breathes in. This means air has trouble getting through. Consider the possibility of something stuck in the throat (p. 79), pneumonia (p. 171), asthma (p. 167), or bronchitis (mild sucking in, see p. 170).

If the person has a cough, ask if it keeps him from sleeping. Find out if he coughs up mucus, how much, its color, and if there is blood in it.

PULSE (HEARTBEAT)

To take the person's pulse, put your fingers on the wrist as shown. (Do not use your thumb to feel for the pulse.)

If you cannot find the pulse in the wrist, feel for it in the neck beside the voicebox

or put your ear directly on the chest and listen for the heartbeat.

Pay attention to the strength, the rate, and the regularity of the pulse. If you have a watch or timer, count the pulses per minute.

NORMAL PULSE FOR PEOPLE AT REST

adults . . . . from 60 to 80 per minute
children. . . . . .80 to 100
babies . . . . .100 to 140

The pulse gets much faster with exercise and when a person is nervous, frightened, or has a fever. As a general rule, the pulse increases 20 beats per minute for each degree (°C) rise in fever.

When a person is very ill, take the pulse often and write it down along with the temperature and rate of breathing.

It is important to notice changes in the pulse rate. For example:

- A weak, rapid pulse can mean a state of shock (see p. 77).

- A very rapid, very slow, or irregular pulse could mean heart trouble (see p. 325).

- A relatively slow pulse in a person with a high fever may be a sign of typhoid (see p. 189).

EYES

Look at the color of the white part of the eyes. Is it normal, red (p. 219), or yellow? Also note any changes in the sick person's vision.

Have the person slowly move his eyes up and down and from side to side. Jerking or uneven movement may be a sign of brain damage.

Pay attention to the size of the *pupils* (the black 'window' in the center of the eye). If they are very large, it can mean a state of shock (see p. 77). If they are very small, it can mean poison or the effect of certain drugs.

Look at both eyes and note any difference between the two, especially in the size of the pupils:

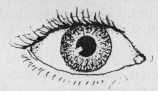 

A difference in the size of the pupils is almost always a medical emergency.

- If the eye with the larger pupil hurts so badly it causes vomiting, the person probably has GLAUCOMA (see p. 222).

- If the eye with the smaller pupil hurts a great deal, the person may have IRITIS, a very serious infection (see p. 221).

- Difference in the size of the pupils of an unconscious person or a person who has had a recent head injury may mean brain damage. It may also mean STROKE (see p. 327).

Always compare the pupils of a person who is unconscious or has had a head injury.

EARS, THROAT AND NOSE

Ears: Always check for signs of pain and infection in the ears—especially in a child with fever or a cold. A baby who cries a lot or pulls at his ear often has an ear infection (p. 309).

Pull the ear gently. If this increases pain, the infection is probably in the tube of the ear (ear canal). Also look for redness or pus inside the ear. A small flashlight or penlight will help. But never put a stick, wire, or other hard object inside the ear.

Find out if the person hears well, or if one side is more deaf than the other. For deafness and ringing of the ears see page 327.

Throat and Mouth: With a torch (flashlight) or sunlight examine the mouth and throat. To do this hold down tongue with a spoon handle or have the person say 'ahhhhh...' Notice if the throat is red and if the tonsils (2 lumps at the back of the throat) are swollen or have spots with pus (see p. 309). Also examine the mouth for sores, inflamed gums, sore tongue, rotten or abscessed teeth and other problems. (Read Chapter 17.)

Nose: Is the nose runny or plugged? (Notice if and how a baby breathes through his nose.) Shine a light inside and look for mucus, pus, blood; also redness, swelling, or bad smell. Check for signs of sinus trouble or hayfever p. 165).

SKIN

It is important to examine the sick person's whole body, no matter how mild the sickness may seem. Babies and children should be undressed completely. Look carefully for anything that is not normal, including:

- sores, wounds or splinters
- rashes or welts
- spots, patches, or any unusual markings
- *inflammation* (sign of infection with redness, heat, pain and swelling)
- swelling or puffiness
- swollen *lymph nodes* (little lumps in the neck, the armpits, or the groin, see p. 88)

- abnormal lumps or masses
- unusual thinning or loss of hair, or loss of its color or shine (p. 112)
- loss of eyebrows (leprosy? p. 191)

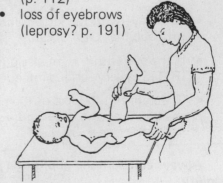

Always examine little children between the buttocks, in the genital area, between the fingers and toes, behind the ears, and in the hair (for lice, ringworm, rashes, and sores).

For identification of different skin problems see page 196 – 198.

THE BELLY (ABDOMEN)

If a person has pain in the belly, try to find out exactly where it hurts.

Learn whether the pain is steady or whether it suddenly comes and goes, like cramps or *colic.*

When you examine the belly, first look at it for any unusual swelling or lumps.

The location of the pain often gives a clue to the cause (see the following page).

First, ask the person to point with one finger where it hurts.

Then, beginning on the opposite side from the spot where he has pointed, press gently on different parts of the belly to see where it hurts most.

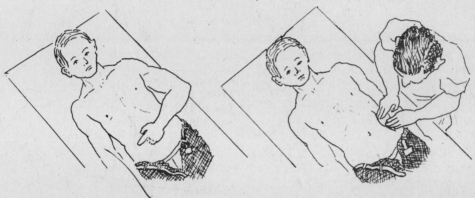

See if the belly is soft or hard and whether the person can relax his stomach muscles. A very hard belly could mean an acute abdomen—perhaps appendicitis or peritonitis (see p. 94).

If you suspect peritonitis or appendicitis, do the test for *rebound pain* described on page 95.

Feel for any abnormal lumps and hardened areas in the belly.

If the person has a constant pain in the stomach, with nausea, and has not been able to move his bowels, put an ear on the belly, like this:

Listen for gurgles in the intestines. If you hear nothing after about 2 minutes, this is a danger sign. (See Emergency Problems of the Gut, p. 93)

A silent belly is like a silent dog. Beware!

These pictures show the areas of the belly that usually hurt when a person has the following problems:

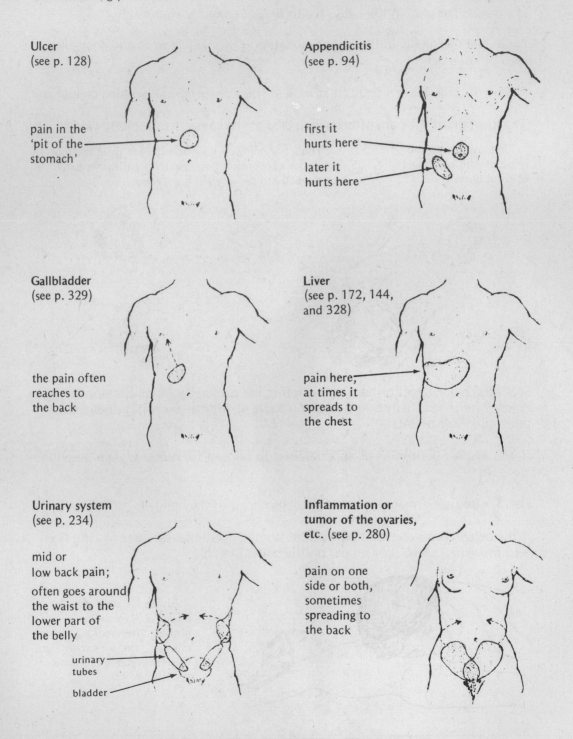

Ulcer
(see p. 128)

pain in the 'pit of the stomach'

Appendicitis
(see p. 94)

first it hurts here

later it hurts here

Gallbladder
(see p. 329)

the pain often reaches to the back

Liver
(see p. 172, 144, and 328)

pain here; at times it spreads to the chest

Urinary system
(see p. 234)

mid or low back pain;

often goes around the waist to the lower part of the belly

urinary tubes

bladder

Inflammation or tumor of the ovaries, etc. (see p. 280)

pain on one side or both, sometimes spreading to the back

Note: For different causes of back pain see p. 173.

MUSCLES AND NERVES

If a person complains of numbness, weakness, or loss of control in part of his body, or you want to test for it: notice the way he walks and moves. Have him stand, sit, or lie completely straight, and carefully compare both sides of his body.

Face: Have him smile, frown, open his eyes wide, and squeeze them shut. Notice any drooping or weakness on one side.

If the problem began more or less suddenly, think of a head injury (p. 91), stroke (p. 327), or Bell's palsy (p. 327).

If it came slowly, it may be a brain tumor. Get medical advice.

Also check for normal eye movement, size of pupils (p. 217), and how well he can see.

Arms and legs: Look for loss of muscle. Notice—or measure—difference in thickness of arms or legs.

Have him squeeze your fingers to compare strength in his hands

and push and pull with his feet against your hand.

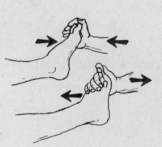

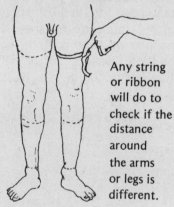

Any string or ribbon will do to check if the distance around the arms or legs is different.

Also have him hold his arms straight out and turn his hands up and down.

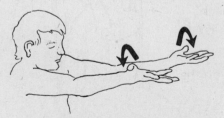

Note any weakness or trembling.

Have him lie down and lift one leg and then the other.

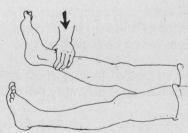

If muscle loss or weakness affects the whole body, suspect malnutrition (p. 112) or a chronic (long-term) illness like tuberculosis.

If muscle loss and weakness is uneven or worse on one side, in children, think first of polio (p. 314); in adults, think of a back problem, a back or head injury, or stroke.

Check for stiffness or tightness of different muscles:

• If the jaw is stiff or will not open, suspect tetanus (p. 182) or a severe infection of the throat (p. 309) or of a tooth (p. 231).

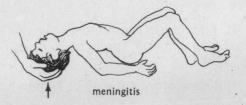

• If the neck or back is stiff and bent backwards, in a very sick child, suspect meningitis. If the head will not bend forward or cannot be put between the knees, meningitis is likely (p. 185).

meningitis

• If a child **always** has some stiff muscles and makes strange or jerky movements, he may be *spastic* (p. 320).

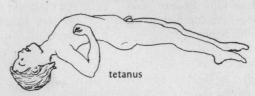

• If strange or jerky movements come suddenly, with loss of consciousness, he may have fits (p. 178). If fits happen often, think of epilepsy. If they happen when he is ill, the cause may be high fever (p. 76) or dehydration (p. 151) or tetanus (p. 182).

tetanus

To test a person's reflexes when you suspect tetanus, see p. 183.

To check for loss of feeling in the hands, feet, or other parts of the body:

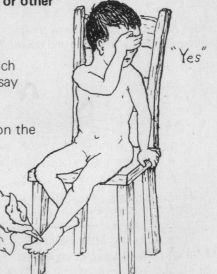

"Yes"

Have the person cover his eyes. Lightly touch or prick the skin in different places. Ask him to say 'yes' when he feels it.

• Loss of feeling in or near spots or patches on the body is probably leprosy (p. 191).

• Loss of feeling in both hands or feet may be due to diabetes (p. 127) or leprosy.

• Loss of feeling on one side only could come from a back problem (p. 174) or injury.

4

HOW TO TAKE CARE
OF A SICK PERSON

Sickness weakens the body. To gain strength and get well quickly special care is needed.

> **The care a sick person receives is frequently the most important part of his treatment.**

Medicines are often not necessary. But good care is always important. The following are the basis of good care:

1. The Comfort of the Sick Person

A person who is sick should rest in a quiet, comfortable place with plenty of fresh air and light. He should keep from getting too hot or cold. If the air is cold or the person is chilled, cover him with a sheet or blanket. But if the weather is hot or the person has a fever, do not cover him at all (see p. 75).

2. Liquids

In nearly every sickness, especially when there is fever or diarrhea, the sick person should drink plenty of liquids: water, tea, juices, broths, etc.

3. Personal Cleanliness

It is important to keep the sick person clean. He should be bathed every day. If he is too sick to get out of bed, wash him with a sponge or cloth and lukewarm water. His clothes, sheets, and covers must also be kept clean. Take care to keep crumbs and bits of food out of the bed.

Lukewarm water

A SICK PERSON SHOULD
BE BATHED EACH DAY

4. Good Food

If the sick person feels like eating, let him. Most sicknesses do not require special diets.

A sick person should drink plenty of liquids and eat body-building and nourishing foods like milk, cheese, chicken, eggs, meat, fish, beans, green vegetables, and fruit (see Chapter 11).

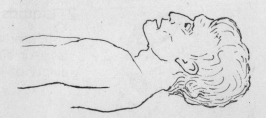

If the person is very weak, give him these same foods, but make them into soups or juices.

Energy foods are also important—for example, porridges of rice, wheat, oatmeal, potato, or cassava. Adding a little sugar and vegetable oil will increase the energy. Also encourage the sick person to drink plenty of sweetened drinks, especially if he will not eat much.

A few problems do require special diets. These are explained on the following pages:

SPECIAL CARE FOR A PERSON WHO IS VERY ILL

1. Liquids

It is extremely important that a very sick person drink enough liquid. If he only can drink a little at a time, give him small amounts often. If he can barely swallow, give him sips every 5 or 10 minutes.

Measure the amount of liquids the person drinks each day. An adult needs to drink 2 liters or more every day and should urinate 3 or 4 times daily. If the person is not drinking or urinating enough, or if he begins to show signs of dehydration (p. 151), encourage him to drink more. He should drink *nutritious* liquids, usually with a little salt added. If he will not drink these, give him Rehydration Drink (see p. 152). If he cannot drink enough of this, and develops signs of *dehydration,* a health worker may be able to give him *intravenous solution.* But the need for this can usually be avoided if the person is urged to take small sips often.

2. Food

If the person is too sick to eat solid foods, give him soups, milk, juices, broths, and other nutritious liquids (see Chapter 11). A porridge of cornmeal, oatmeal, or rice is also good, but should be given together with body-building foods. Soups can be made with egg, beans, or well-chopped meat, fish, or chicken. If the person can eat only a little at a time, he should eat several small meals each day.

3. Cleanliness and Changing Position in Bed

Personal cleanliness is very important for a seriously ill person. He should be bathed every day with warm water. Change the bed clothes daily and each time they become dirty.

A person who is very weak and cannot turn over alone should be helped to change position in bed many times each day. This helps prevent bed sores (see p. 214).

A child who is sick for a long time should be held frequently on his mother's lap.

Frequent changing of the person's position also helps to prevent pneumonia, a constant danger for anyone who is very weak or ill and must stay in bed for a long time. If the person has a fever, begins to cough, and breathes with fast, shallow breaths, he probably has pneumonia (see p. 171).

4. Watching for Changes

You should watch for any change in the sick person's condition that may tell you whether he is getting better or worse. Keep a record of his 'vital signs'. Write down the following facts 4 times a day:

temperature
(how many degrees)

pulse
(beats per minute)

breathing
(breaths per minute)

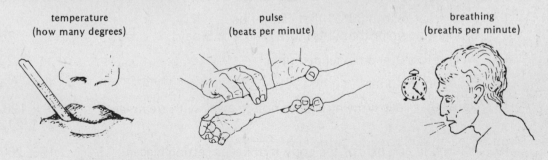

Also write down the amount of liquids the person drinks and how many times a day he urinates and has a bowel movement. Save this information for the health worker or doctor.

It is very important to look for signs that warn you that the person's sickness is serious or dangerous. A list of **Signs of Dangerous Illness** is on the next page. If the person shows any of these signs, **Seek medical help immediately.**

SIGNS OF DANGEROUS ILLNESS

A person who has one or more of the following signs is probably too sick to be treated at home without skilled medical help. His life may be in danger. **Seek medical help as soon as possible.** Until help comes, follow the instructions on the pages indicated.

page

1. Loss of large amounts of blood from anywhere in the body 82, 264, 281

2. Coughing up blood 179

3. Marked blueness of lips and nails (if it is new). .30

4. Great difficulty in breathing; does not improve with rest 167, 325

5. The person cannot be wakened (coma) 78

6. The person is so weak he faints when he stands up 325

7. A day or more without being able to urinate. 234

8. A day or more without being able to drink any liquids 151

9 Heavy vomiting or severe diarrhea that lasts for more than
   one day or more than a few hours in babies 151

10. Black stools like tar, or vomit with blood or feces. 128

11. Strong, continuous stomach pains with vomiting in a person
    who does not have diarrhea or cannot have a bowel movement. 93

12. Any strong continuous pain that lasts for more than 3 days . . . . . . .29 to 38

13. Stiff neck with arched back, with or without a stiff jaw 182, 185

14. More than one fit (convulsions)
    in someone with fever or serious illness. .76, 185

15. High fever (above 39° C) that cannot be
    brought down or that lasts more than 4 or 5 days. 75

16. Weight loss over an extended time. 20

17. Blood in the urine 146, 234

18. Sores that keep growing and do not go away with treatment 191, 196,
                                                                              211, 212

19. A lump in any part of the body that keeps getting bigger 196, 280

20. Problems with pregnancy and childbirth:

    any bleeding during pregnancy 249, 281

    swollen face and trouble seeing in the last months 249

    long delay once the waters have broken and labor has begun 267

    severe bleeding 264

WHEN AND HOW TO LOOK FOR MEDICAL HELP

Seek medical help at the first sign of a dangerous illness. Do not wait until the person is so sick that it becomes difficult or impossible to take him to a health center or hospital.

If a sick or injured person's condition could be made worse by the difficulties in moving him to a health center, try to bring a health worker to the person. But in an emergency when very special attention or an operation may be needed (for example, appendicitis), do not wait for the health worker. Take the person to the health center or the hospital at once.

When you need to carry a person on a stretcher, make sure he is as comfortable as possible and cannot fall out. If he has any broken bones, splint them before moving him (see p. 99). If the sun is very strong, rig a sheet over the stretcher to give shade yet allow fresh air to pass underneath (see the picture on the cover of this book).

WHAT TO TELL THE HEALTH WORKER

For a health worker or doctor to recommend treatment or prescribe medicine wisely, he should see the sick person. If the sick person cannot be moved, have the health worker come to him. If this is not possible, send a responsible person who knows the details of the illness. **Never send a small child or a fool.**

Before sending for medical help, examine the sick person carefully and completely. Then write down the details of his disease and general condition (see Chapter 3).

On the next page is a form on which you can make a PATIENT REPORT. Several copies of this form are at the end of this book. Tear out one of these forms and carefully complete the report, giving all the details you can.

**When you send someone for medical help,
always send a completed information form with him.**

PATIENT REPORT

TO USE WHEN SENDING FOR MEDICAL HELP.

Name of the sick person:_____ Age:_____

Male_____ Female_____ Where is he (she)?_____

What is the main sickness or problem right now?_____

_____

_____

_____

When did it begin?_____

How did it begin?_____

Has the person had the same problem before?_____ When?_____

Is there fever?_____ How high?_____° When and for how long?_____

Pain?_____ Where?_____ What kind?_____

What is wrong or different from normal in any of the following?

Skin:_____ **Ears:**_____

Eyes:_____ **Mouth and throat:**_____

Genitals:_____

Urine: Much or little?_____ Color?_____ Trouble urinating?_____

Describe:_____ Times in 24 hours:_____ Times at night:_____

Stools: Color?_____ Blood or mucus?_____ Diarrhea?_____

Number of times a day :_____ Cramps?_____ Dehydration?_____ Mild or

severe?_____ Worms?_____ What kind?_____

Breathing: Breaths per minute:_____ Deep, shallow, or normal?_____

Difficulty breathing (describe):_____ Cough (describe):_____

_____ Wheezing?_____ Mucus?_____ With blood?_____

Does the person have any of the SIGNS OF DANGEROUS ILLNESS listed on

page 42?_____ Which? (give details)_____.

_____

Other signs:_____

Is the person taking medicine?_____ What?_____

Has the person ever used medicine that has caused hives (or bumps) with itching,

or other allergic reactions?_____ What?_____

The state of the sick person is: Not very serious:_____ Serious:_____

Very serious:_____

On the back of this form write any other information you think may be important.

CHAPTER

5

HEALING WITHOUT MEDICINES

For most sicknesses no medicines are needed. Our bodies have their own defenses, or ways to resist and fight disease. In most cases, these natural defenses are far more important to our health than are medicines.

**People will get well from most sicknesses
—including the common cold and 'flu'—
by themselves, without need for medicines.**

To help the body fight off or overcome a sickness, often all that is needed is to:

keep clean   get plenty of rest   eat well

Even in a case of more serious illness, when a medicine may be needed, **it is the body that must overcome the disease;** the medicine only helps. Cleanliness, rest, and nutritious food are still very important.

Much of the art of health care does not—and should not—depend on use of medications. Even if you live in an area where there are no modern medicines, there is a great deal you can do to prevent and treat most common sicknesses—if you learn how.

Many sicknesses can be prevented or treated without medicines.

If people simply learned how to use **water** correctly, this alone might do more to prevent and cure illnesses than all the medicines they now use . . . and misuse.

HEALING WITH WATER

Most of us could live without medicines. But no one can live without water. In fact, over half (57%) of the human body is water. If everyone living in farms and villages made the best use of water, the amount of sickness and death—especially of children—could probably be cut in half.

For example, correct use of water is basic both in the prevention and treatment of diarrhea. In many areas diarrhea is the most common cause of sickness and death in small children. *Contaminated* (unclean) water is often part of the cause.

An important part of the prevention of diarrhea is to boil water used for drinking or for preparing foods. This is especially important for babies. Babies' bottles and eating utensils should also be boiled. Washing one's hands with soap and water after a bowel movement (shitting) and before eating or handling foods is just as important.

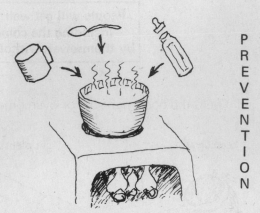

P R E V E N T I O N

T R E A T M E N T

The common cause of death in children with diarrhea is severe *dehydration,* or loss of too much water from the body (see p. 151). By giving a child with diarrhea plenty of water (best with sugar or honey and salt), dehydration can often be prevented or corrected (see Rehydration Drink, p. 152).

Giving lots of liquids to a child with diarrhea is more important than any medicine. In fact, if enough liquid is given, no medicine is usually needed in the treatment of diarrhea.

On the next 2 pages are a number of other situations in which **it is often more important to use water correctly than to use medicines.**

Times When the Right Use of Water
May Do More Good than Medicines

PREVENTION

to prevent	use water	see page
1. diarrhea, worms, gut infections	boil drinking water, wash hands, etc.	135
2. skin infections	bathe often	133
3. wounds becoming infected; tetanus	wash wounds well with soap and water	84, 89

TREATMENT

to treat	use water	see page
1. diarrhea, dehydration	drink plenty of liquids	152
2. illnesses with fever	drink plenty of liquids	75
3. high fever	soak body with cool water	76
4. minor urinary infections (common in women)	drink plenty of water	235
5. cough, asthma, bronchitis, pneumonia, whooping cough	drink a lot of water and breathe hot water vapors (to loosen mucus)	168

to treat	use water	see page
6. sores, impetigo, ringworm of skin or scalp, cradle cap, pimples	scrub with soap and water	201, 202, 205, 211, 215
7. infected wounds, abscesses, boils	hot soaks or compresses	88, 202
8. stiff, sore muscles and joints	hot compresses	102, 173, 174
9. itching, burning, or weeping irritations of the skin	cold compresses	193, 194
10. minor burns	hold in cold water	96
11. sore throat or tonsillitis	gargle hot salt water	309
12. acid, lye, dirt, or irritating substance in eye	flood eye with cool water at once	
13. stuffed up nose	sniff salt water	164
14. constipation, hard stools	drink lots of water (also enemas are safer than laxatives, but do not overuse)	15, 129
15. cold sores or fever blisters	hold ice on blisters for 1 hr. at first sign	232

In each of the above cases (except pneumonia) when water is used correctly, often medicines are not needed. In this book you will find many suggestions for ways of healing without need for medicine. **Use medicines only when absolutely necessary.**

RIGHT AND WRONG USES OF MODERN MEDICINES

Some medicines sold in pharmacies or village stores can be very useful. Others are of no value. Also, people sometimes use the best medicines in the wrong way, so that they do more harm than good. **To be helpful, medicine must be used correctly.**

Many people, including most doctors and health workers, prescribe far more medicines than are needed—and by so doing cause much needless sickness and death.

There is some danger in the use of any medicine.

Some medicines are much more dangerous than others. Unfortunately, people sometimes use very dangerous medicines for mild sicknesses. (I have seen a baby die because his mother gave him a dangerous medicine, chloramphenicol, for a cold.) **Never use a dangerous medicine for a mild illness.**

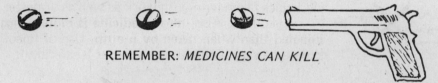

REMEMBER: *MEDICINES CAN KILL*

Guidelines for the use of medicine:

1. Use medicines only when necessary.

2. Know the correct use and precautions for any medicine you use (see the GREEN PAGES).

3. Be sure to use the right dose.

4. If the medicine does not help, or causes problems, stop using it.

5. When in doubt, seek the advice of a health worker.

Note: Some health workers and many doctors give medicines when none is needed, often because they think patients expect medicine and will not be satisfied unless they get some. Tell your doctor or health worker you only want medicine if it is definitely needed. This will save you money and be safer for your health.

Only use a medicine when you are sure it is needed and when you are sure how to use it.

THE MOST DANGEROUS MISUSE OF MEDICINE

Here is a list of the most common and dangerous errors people make in using modern medicines. The improper use of the following medicines causes many deaths each year. BE CAREFUL!

1. Chloramphenicol *(Chloromycetin)* (p. 353)

The popular use of this medicine for simple diarrhea and other mild sicknesses is extremely unfortunate, because it is so risky. Use chloramphenicol only for very severe illnesses, like typhoid (see p. 189). Never give it to newborn infants.

2. Oxytocin *(Pitocin)*, Pituitrin, and Ergonovine *(Ergotrate)* (p. 375)

Unfortunately, some midwives use these medicines to speed up childbirth or 'give strength' to the mother in labor. This practice is very dangerous. It can kill the mother or the child. Use these medicines **only** to control bleeding **after** the child is born (see p. 266).

3. Injections of any medicine

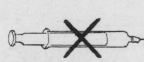

The common belief that injections are usually better than medicine taken by mouth is **not** true. Many times medicines taken by mouth work as well as or better than injections. Also, **most medicine is more dangerous injected than when taken by mouth.** Use of injections should be **very limited** (read Chapter 9 carefully).

4. Penicillin (p. 349)

Penicillin works only against certain types of *infections.* Frequent use of penicillin for sprains, bruises, or any pain or fever is a great mistake. As a general rule, injuries that do not break the skin, even if they make large bruises, have no danger of infection; they do not need to be treated with penicillin or any other antibiotic.

Penicillin is dangerous for some people. Before using it, know its risks and the precautions you must take—see pages 70 and 349.

5. Injections of penicillin with streptomycin (p. 352)
(There are many brand names.)

These medicines are used too much, and often for the wrong thing. They should not be used for colds, for three reasons:

1. They do not work against colds and flu.
2. They can cause serious problems—sometimes deafness or death.
3. Their overuse makes it more difficult to cure tuberculosis or other serious illnesses.

6. Vitamin B₁₂ and liver extract (p. 376)

These medicines do not help anemia or 'weakness' except in rare cases. Also, they have certain risks when injected. They should only be used when a health worker has prescribed them **after testing the blood.** In nearly every case of anemia, iron pills will do more good (see p. 126).

7. Other vitamins (p. 375)

As a general rule, DO NOT INJECT VITAMINS. Injections are more dangerous, more expensive, and usually no more effective than pills.

Unfortunately, many people waste their money on syrups, tonics, and 'elixirs' that contain vitamins. Many lack the most important vitamins (see p. 119). But even when they contain them, it is wiser to buy more and better food. Body-building and protective foods like eggs, meat, fruit, vegetables, and whole grains are rich in vitamins and other nutrients (see p. 110-111). Giving a thin, weak person good food more often will usually help him far more than giving him vitamin and mineral supplements.

> **A person who eats well does not need extra vitamins.**

THE BEST WAY TO GET VITAMINS:

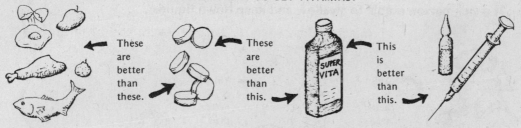

These are better than these. These are better than this. This is better than this.

For more information about vitamins, when they are necessary, and the foods that have them, read Chapter 11, especially pages 111 and 119.

8. Calcium

Injecting calcium into a vein can be extremely dangerous. It can quickly kill someone if not injected **very slowly.** Injecting calcium into the buttocks sometimes causes very serious abscesses or infections.

> **Never inject calcium without first seeking medical advice!**

Note: In Mexico and other countries where people eat a lot of corn tortillas or other foods prepared with lime, it is foolish to use calcium injections or tonics (as is often done to 'give strength' or 'help children grow'). The body gets all the calcium it needs from the lime.

9. 'Feeding' through the veins (Intravenous or 'I.V.' solutions)

In some areas, persons who are anemic or very weak spend their last penny to have a liter of I.V. solution put into their veins. They believe that this will make them stronger or their blood richer. But they are wrong!

Intravenous solution is nothing more than pure water with some salt or sugar in it. It gives less energy than a large candy bar and makes the blood thinner, not richer. It does not help anemia or make the weak stronger.

Also when a person who is not well trained puts the I.V. solution into a vein, there is danger of an infection entering the blood. This can kill the sick person.

Intravenous solution should be used only when a person can take nothing by mouth, or when he is badly dehydrated (see p. 151).

If the sick person can swallow, give him a liter of water with a little sugar and salt (see Rehydration Drink, p. 152). It will do as much for him as injecting a liter of I.V. solution.

For people who are able to eat, nutritious foods do more to strengthen them than any type of I.V. fluid.

If a sick person is able to swallow and keep down liquids . . .

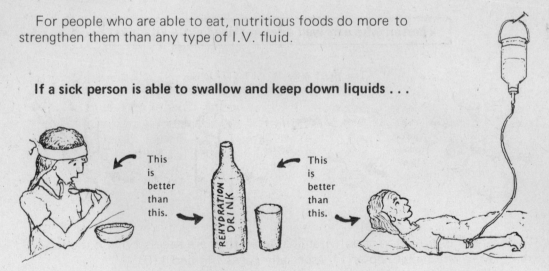

This is better than this.

REHYDRATION DRINK

This is better than this.

10. Laxatives and Purges (p. 368)

EPSOM SALTS

It is always dangerous to give a laxative or purge to a baby or to anyone who is very weak, dehydrated, or has severe pain in his belly. Unfortunately, people often believe that purges bring back health or clean the bad things out of the body. In Chapter 1 it is explained that **purges or strong laxatives nearly always do more harm than good.**

To learn the correct uses of laxatives and enemas, see p. 15.

WHEN SHOULD MEDICINE NOT BE TAKEN?

Many people have beliefs about things they should not do or eat when taking medicines. For this reason they may stop taking a medicine they need. In truth, no medicine causes harm just because it is taken with certain foods—whether pork, chili pepper, guava, oranges, or any other food. But foods with lots of grease or spices can make problems of the stomach or gut worse—whether or not any medicine is being taken (see p. 128). Certain medicines will cause bad reactions if a person drinks alcohol (see metronidazole, p. 359).

There are situations when, without a doubt, it is best **not** to use certain medicines:

1. Pregnant women or women who are breast feeding should avoid all medicines that are not absolutely necessary. (However, they can take vitamins or iron pills without danger.)

2. With newborn children, be very careful when using medicines. Whenever possible look for medical help before giving them any type of medicine. Be sure not to give too much.

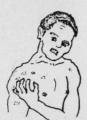

3. A person who has ever had any sort of allergic reaction—hives, itching, etc.—after taking penicillin, ampicillin, a sulfonamide, or other medicines, **should never use that medicine again for the rest of his life** because it would be dangerous (see Dangerous reactions from injections of certain medicines, p. 70).

4. Persons who have ulcers or heartburn should avoid medicines that contain aspirin.

5. There are specific medicines that are harmful or dangerous to take when you have certain illnesses. For example, persons with hepatitis should not be treated with antibiotics or other strong medicines, because their liver is damaged, and the medicines are more likely to poison the body (see p. 172).

6. Persons who are dehydrated or have disease of the kidneys should be especially careful with medicines they take. Do not give more than one dose of a medicine that could poison the body unless (or until) the person is urinating normally. For example, if a child has high fever and is dehydrated (see p. 76), do not give him more than one dose of aspirin until he begins to urinate. **Never give sulfa to a person who is dehydrated.**

ANTIBIOTICS: WHAT THEY ARE AND HOW TO USE THEM

When used correctly, antibiotics are extremely useful and important medicines. They fight certain infections and diseases caused by *bacteria.* Well-known antibiotics are penicillin, tetracycline, streptomycin, and chloramphenicol. In this book the sulfa drugs, or sulfonamides, are also considered as antibiotics.

The different antibiotics work in different ways against specific infections. All antibiotics have dangers in their use, but some are far more dangerous than others. Great care must be taken in the choice and use of antibiotics.

There are many kinds of antibiotics, and each kind is sold under several 'brand names'. This can be confusing. However, the most important antibiotics fall into a few major groups:

antibiotic group (generic name)	examples of brand names	brand names in your area (write in)	see page
PENICILLINS	*Pen-V-K*	_____	349
AMPICILLINS*	*Penbritin*	_____	351
TETRACYCLINES	*Terramycin*	_____	353
SULFONAMIDES	*Gantrisin*	_____	354
STREPTOMYCIN	*Ambistryn*	_____	355
CHLORAMPHENICOL	*Chloromycetin*	_____	353
ERYTHROMYCIN	*Erythrocin*	_____	352

*Note: Ampicillin is a type of penicillin that kills more kinds of bacteria than do ordinary penicillins.

If you have a brand-name antibiotic and do not know to which group it belongs, read the fine print on the bottle or box. For example, if you have some *Paraxin 'S'* but do not know what is in it, read the fine print. It says 'chloramphenicol'.

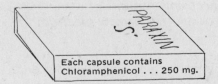

Each capsule contains Chloramphenicol . . . 250 mg.

Look up chloramphenicol in the GREEN PAGES (p. 353). You will find it must be used only for a few very serious illnesses, like typhoid, and is especially dangerous when given to the newborn.

Never use an antibiotic unless you know to what group it belongs, what diseases it fights, and the precautions you must take to use it safely.

Information on the uses, dosage, risks, and precautions for the antibiotics recommended in this book can be found in the GREEN PAGES. Look for the name of the medicine in the alphabetical list at the beginning of those pages.

GUIDELINES FOR THE USE OF *ALL* ANTIBIOTICS

1. If you do not know exactly how to use the antibiotic and what infections it can be used for, do not use it.

2. Use only an antibiotic that is recommended for the infection you wish to treat. (Look for the illness in this book.)

3. Know the risks in using the antibiotic and take all the recommended precautions (see the GREEN PAGES).

4. Use the antibiotic only in the recommended dose—no more, no less. The dose depends on the illness and the age or weight of the sick person.

5. Never use injections of antibiotics if taking them by mouth is likely to work as well. Inject only when absolutely necessary.

6. Keep using the antibiotics until the illness is completely cured, or for at least 2 days after the fever and other signs of infection have gone. (Some illnesses, like tuberculosis and leprosy, need to be treated for many months or years after the person feels better. Follow the instructions for each illness.)

7. If the antibiotic causes a skin rash, itching, difficult breathing, or any serious reactions, the person must stop using it and **never use it again** (see p. 70).

8. **Only use antibiotics when the need is great.** When antibiotics are used too much they begin not to work as well.

GUIDELINES FOR THE USE OF *CERTAIN* ANTIBIOTICS

1. Before you inject penicillin or ampicillin, always have ampules of *Adrenalin* (epinephrine) ready to control an allergic reaction if one occurs (p. 70).

2. For persons who are allergic to penicillin, use another antibiotic such as **erythromycin or a sulfa (see p. 352 and 354).**

3. Do not use tetracycline, or another *broad-spectrum* antibiotic, for an illness that can probably be controlled with penicillin or another *narrow-spectrum* antibiotic (see p. 58).

4. As a rule, use chloramphenicol only for typhoid fever. It is a dangerous drug. **Never** use it for mild illness. And never give it to newborn children (except perhaps for whooping cough, p. 313).

5. Never inject tetracycline or chloramphenicol. They are safer, less painful, and do as much or more good when taken by mouth.

6. Do not give tetracycline to pregnant women after the fourth month or to children under 6 years old (see p. 353).

7. As a general rule, use streptomycin, and products that contain it, only for tuberculosis—and always together with other anti-tuberculosis medicines (see p. 355). Streptomycin in combination with penicillin can be used for deep wounds to the gut, appendicitis, and other specific infections when ampicillin is not available (or is too costly), but should never be used for colds, flu, and common *respiratory* infections.

8. Eating yogurt or curdled milk helps to replace necessary bacteria killed by antibiotics like ampicillin and to return the body's natural balance to normal (see next page).

WHAT TO DO IF AN ANTIBIOTIC DOES NOT SEEM TO HELP

For most common infections antibiotics begin to bring improvement in a day or two. **If the antibiotic you are using does not bring any improvement, it is possible that:**

1. The illness is not what you think. You may be using the wrong medicine. Try to find out more exactly what the illness is—and use the right medicine.

2. The dose of the antibiotic is not correct. Check it.

3. The bacteria have become *resistant* to the antibiotic being used (they no longer are harmed by it). Try another one of the antibiotics recommended for that illness.

4. You may not know enough to cure the illness. Get medical help, especially if the condition is serious or getting worse.

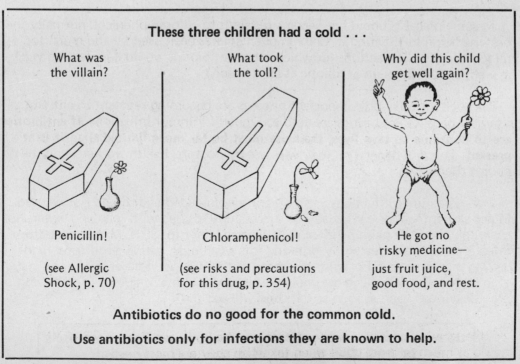

These three children had a cold . . .

What was the villain?	What took the toll?	Why did this child get well again?
Penicillin!	Chloramphenicol!	He got no risky medicine—
(see Allergic Shock, p. 70)	(see risks and precautions for this drug, p. 354)	just fruit juice, good food, and rest.

Antibiotics do no good for the common cold.

Use antibiotics only for infections they are known to help.

IMPORTANCE OF LIMITED USE OF ANTIBIOTICS

The use of all medicines should be limited. But this is especially true of antibiotics, for the following reasons:

1. **Poisoning and reactions.** Antibiotics not only kill bacteria, they can also harm the body, either by poisoning it or by causing allergic reactions. Many people die each year because they take antibiotics they do not need.

2. **Upsetting the natural balance.** Not all bacteria in the body are harmful. Some are necessary for the body to function normally. Antibiotics often kill the good bacteria along with the harmful ones. Babies who are given antibiotics sometimes develop fungus infections of the mouth (thrush, p. 232) or skin (moniliasis, p. 242). This is because the antibiotics kill the bacteria that help keep fungus under control.

For similar reasons, persons who take ampicillin and other broad-spectrum antibiotics for several days may develop diarrhea. Antibiotics may kill some kinds of bacteria necessary for digestion, upsetting the natural balance of bacteria in the gut.

3. **Resistance to treatment.** In the long run, the most important reason the use of antibiotics should be limited, is that WHEN ANTIBIOTICS ARE USED TOO MUCH, THEY BECOME LESS EFFECTIVE.

When attacked many times by the same antibiotic, bacteria become stronger and are no longer killed by it. They become *resistant* to the antibiotic. For this reason, certain dangerous diseases like typhoid are becoming more difficult to treat than they were a few years ago.

In some places typhoid has become resistant to chloramphenicol, normally the best medicine for treating it. Chloramphenicol has been used far too much for minor infections, infections for which other antibiotics would be safer and work as well, or for which no antibiotic at all is needed.

Throughout the world important diseases are becoming resistant to antibiotics —largely because antibiotics are used too much for minor infections. **If antibiotics are to continue to save lives, their use must be far more limited than it is at present.** This will depend on their wise use by doctors, health workers, and the people themselves.

For most minor infections antibiotics are not needed and should not be used. Minor skin infections can usually be successfully treated with soap and water, hot soaks, and perhaps painting them with gentian violet (p. 361). Minor respiratory infections are best treated by drinking lots of liquids, eating good food, and getting plenty of rest. For most diarrheas, antibiotics are not necessary and may even be harmful. What is most important is to drink lots of liquids (p. 155) and provide enough food as soon as the child will eat.

Do not use antibiotics for infections the body can fight successfully by itself. Save them for when they are most needed.

CHAPTER

8

HOW TO MEASURE
AND GIVE MEDICINE

Symbols:

= means: **is equal to** or
          is the same as

+ means: **and** or **plus**

1   +   1   =   2

One   plus   one   equals   two.

How Fractions Are Sometimes Written:

1/2 tablet = half of a tablet =

1 1/2 tablets = one and one-half tablets =

1/4 tablet = one quarter
             or   } of a tablet =
       one-fourth

1/8 tablet = one-eighth of a tablet (dividing it
           into 8 equal pieces and taking 1 piece) =

MEASURING

Medicine is usually weighed in grams (gm.) and milligrams (mg.).

1000 mg. = 1 gm. (one thousand milligrams make one gram)

1 mg. = .001 gm. (one milligram is one one-thousandth part of a gram)

Examples:

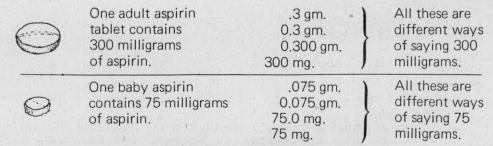

One adult aspirin tablet contains 300 milligrams of aspirin.	.3 gm. 0.3 gm. 0.300 gm. 300 mg.	All these are different ways of saying 300 milligrams.
One baby aspirin contains 75 milligrams of aspirin.	.075 gm. 0.075 gm. 75.0 mg. 75 mg.	All these are different ways of saying 75 milligrams.

Note: In some countries some medicines are still weighed in grains; gr. = grain and
1 gr. = 65 mg. This means a 5 gr. aspirin tablet weighs about 300 mg.

Many times it is important to know how many grams or milligrams are in a medicine.

For example, if you want to give a small piece of adult aspirin to a child, instead of baby aspirin, but you do not know how big a piece to give . . .

read the small print on the labels of each. It says: aspirin: acetylsalicylic acid .3 gm. (acetylsalicylic acid = aspirin)

.3 gm. = 300 mg. and .075 gm. = 75 mg. So, you can see that one adult aspirin weighs 4 times as much as one baby aspirin.

75 mg.
75 mg.
75 mg.
75 mg. } 4 baby aspirin add up to

If you cut the adult aspirin into 4 equal pieces, each quarter = one baby aspirin

300 mg. 1 regular aspirin

So if you cut an adult aspirin into 4 pieces, you can give the child 1 piece in place of a baby aspirin. Both are equal, and the piece of adult aspirin costs less.

CAUTION: Many medicines, especially the antibiotics, come in different weights and sizes. For example, tetracycline may come in 3 sizes of capsules:

250 mg.   100 mg.   50 mg.

Be careful to only give medicine in the recommended amounts. It is very important to check how many grams or milligrams the medicine contains.

For example: If the prescription says: Take tetracycline, 1 capsule or 250 mg. 4 times a day, and you have only 50 mg. capsules, you have to take five 50 mg. capsules 4 times a day (20 a day).

50 mg. + 50 mg. + 50 mg. + 50 mg. + 50 mg. = 250 mg.

MEASURING PENICILLIN

Penicillin is often measured in units.

U. = unit   1,600,000 U. = 1 gm. or 1,000 mg.

Many forms of penicillin (pills and injections) come in doses of 400,000 U.
400,000 U.= 250 mg.

MEDICINE IN LIQUID FORM

Syrups, suspensions, tonics, and other liquid medicines are measured in milliliters:

  ml. = milliliter   1 liter = 1000 ml.

Often liquid medicines are prescribed in tablespoons or teaspoons:

  1 teaspoon (tsp.) = 5 ml.   1 tablespoon (Tbs.) = 15 ml.

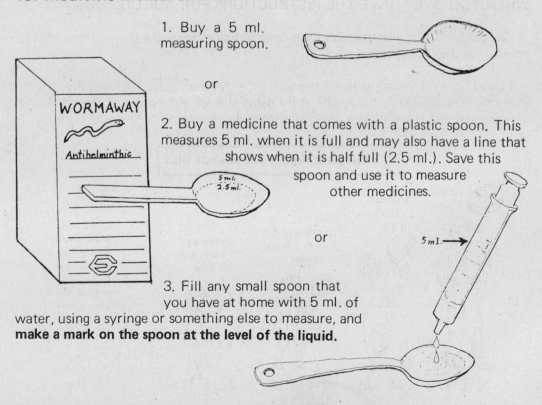

  3 teaspoons =   1 tablespoon

When instructions for a medicine say: Take 1 tsp., this means take 5 ml.

Many of the 'teaspoons' people use hold as much as 8 ml. or as little as 3 ml. **When using a teaspoon to give medicine, it is important that it measure *5 ml.*— No more. No less.**

How to Make Sure that the Teaspoon Used for Medicine Measures 5 ml.

1. Buy a 5 ml. measuring spoon.

                    or

2. Buy a medicine that comes with a plastic spoon. This measures 5 ml. when it is full and may also have a line that shows when it is half full (2.5 ml.). Save this spoon and use it to measure other medicines.

                    or

3. Fill any small spoon that you have at home with 5 ml. of water, using a syringe or something else to measure, and **make a mark on the spoon at the level of the liquid.**

WORMAWAY

Antihelminthic

5 ml.
2.5 ml.

5 ml.➔

HOW TO GIVE MEDICINES TO SMALL CHILDREN

Many medicines that come as pills or capsules also come in syrups or *suspensions* (special liquid form) for children. If you compare the amount of medicine you get, the syrups are usually more expensive than pills or capsules. You can save money by making your own syrup in the following way:

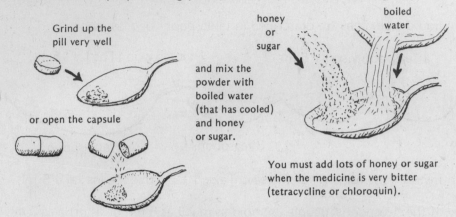

Grind up the pill very well

or open the capsule

and mix the powder with boiled water (that has cooled) and honey or sugar.

honey or sugar

boiled water

You must add lots of honey or sugar when the medicine is very bitter (tetracycline or chloroquin).

When making syrups for children from pills or capsules, **be very careful not to give too much medicine.**

HOW MUCH MEDICINE SHOULD YOU GIVE TO CHILDREN WHEN YOU ONLY HAVE THE INSTRUCTIONS FOR ADULTS?

Generally, the smaller the child, the less medicine he needs. Giving more than needed can be dangerous.

If you have information about the doses for children, follow it carefully. If you do not know the dose, figure it out by using the weight or age of the child. Children should generally be given the following portions of the adult dose:

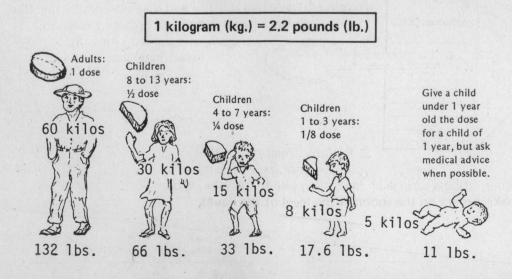

1 kilogram (kg.) = 2.2 pounds (lb.)

Adults: 1 dose

60 kilos

132 lbs.

Children 8 to 13 years: ½ dose

30 kilos

66 lbs.

Children 4 to 7 years: ¼ dose

15 kilos

33 lbs.

Children 1 to 3 years: 1/8 dose

8 kilos

17.6 lbs.

Give a child under 1 year old the dose for a child of 1 year, but ask medical advice when possible.

5 kilos

11 lbs.

HOW TO TAKE MEDICINES

It is important to take medicines more or less at the time recommended. Some medicines should be taken only once a day, but others must be taken more often. If you do not have a clock, it does not matter. If the directions say '1 pill every 8 hours', take 3 a day: one in the morning, one in the afternoon, and one at night. If they say '1 pill every 6 hours', take 4 each day: one in the morning, one at midday, one in the afternoon, and one at night. If the directions are '1 every 4 hours', take 6 a day, allowing more or less the same time between pills.

Whenever you give a medicine to someone else, it is a good idea to write the instructions and also to have the person repeat to you how and when to take the medicine. Make very sure he understands.

To remind people who cannot read when to take their medicine, you can give them a note like this——→

In the blanks at the bottom draw the amount of medicine they should take and carefully explain what it means.——→

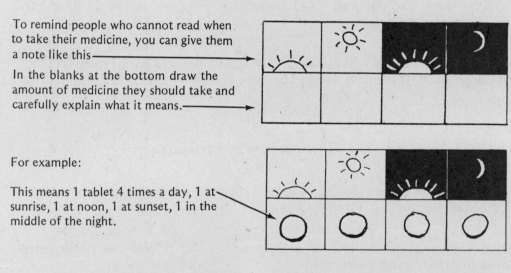

For example:

This means 1 tablet 4 times a day, 1 at sunrise, 1 at noon, 1 at sunset, 1 in the middle of the night.

This means ½ tablet 4 times a day.

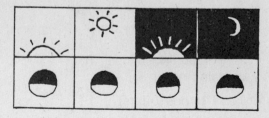

This means 1 capsule 3 times a day.

This means ¼ tablet twice a day.

This means 2 teaspoons twice a day.

WHEN YOU GIVE MEDICINES TO ANYONE . . .

Always write all the following information on the note with the medicine—even if the person cannot read:

- the person's name ——————→
- the name of the medicine ——————→
- what it is for ——————→
- the dosage ——————→

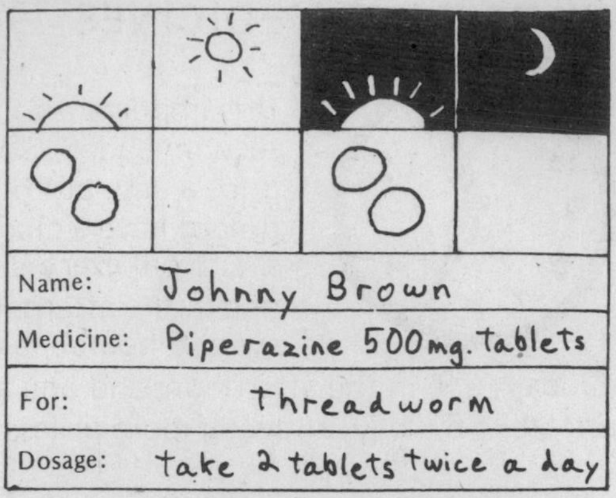

Name:	Johnny Brown
Medicine:	Piperazine 500mg. tablets
For:	threadworm
Dosage:	take 2 tablets twice a day

This information can be put on the same note as the drawing for dosage.

A page of these dosage blanks is included at the end of the book. Cut them out and use them as needed. When you run out, you can make more yourself.

When you give medicine to someone, it is a good idea to keep a record of this same information. If possible, keep a complete Patient Report (see p. 44).

TAKING MEDICINES ON A FULL OR EMPTY STOMACH

Some medicines work best when you take them on an empty stomach—that is, one hour before meals.

Other medicines are less likely to cause upset stomach or heartburn when taken along with a meal or right afterwards.

Take these medicines
1 hour before meals

- penicillin
- ampicillin
- tetracycline

It is better not to drink milk an hour before or after taking tetracycline.

Take these medicines together with or soon after meals:

- aspirin and medicine that contains aspirin
- iron (ferrous sulfate)
- vitamins
- erythromycin
- P.A.S.

Antacids do the most good if you take them when the stomach is empty, 1 or 2 hours after meals and at bedtime.

CHAPTER

9

INSTRUCTIONS AND PRECAUTIONS FOR INJECTIONS

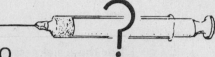

WHEN TO INJECT AND WHEN NOT TO

Injections are not needed often. Most sicknesses that require medical treatment can be treated as well or better with medicines taken by mouth. As a general rule:

> **It is more dangerous to inject medicine than to take it by mouth.**

Injections should be used only when absolutely necessary. Except in emergencies, they should be given only by health workers or persons trained in their use.

The only times medicines should be injected are:

1. When the recommended medicine does not come in a form that can be taken by mouth.

2. When the person vomits often, cannot swallow, or is unconscious.

3. In certain unusual emergencies and special cases (see the next page).

WHAT TO DO WHEN THE DOCTOR PRESCRIBES INJECTIONS

Doctors and other health workers sometimes prescribe injections when they are not needed. After all, they can charge more money for injections. They forget the problems and dangers of giving them in rural areas.

1. If a health worker or healer wants to give you an injection, be sure the medicine is *appropriate* and that he takes all the necessary precautions.

2. If a doctor prescribes injections, explain that you live where no one is well trained to give injections and ask if it would be possible to prescribe a medicine to take by mouth.

3. If a doctor wants to prescribe injections of vitamins, liver extract, or vitamin B_{12}, but has not had your blood tested, tell him you would prefer to see another doctor.

EMERGENCIES WHEN IT IS IMPORTANT TO GIVE INJECTIONS

In case of the following sicknesses, get medical help as fast as you can. If there will be any delay in getting help or in taking the sick person to a health center, inject the appropriate medicine as soon as possible. For details of the doses, consult the pages listed below. Before injecting, know the possible side effects and take the needed precautions.

↓ For these sicknesses	↓ Inject these medicines
Severe pneumonia (p. 171) Infections after childbirth (p. 276) Gangrene (p. 213)	penicillin in high doses (p. 350)

Tetanus (p. 182)	penicillin (p. 349)
	    and tetanus antitoxin (p. 373)
	    and phenobarbital (p. 373)
	    or diazepam (p. 374)

Appendicitis (p. 94)
Peritonitis (p. 94) and bullet wound
    or other puncture wound in the
    belly
	ampicillin in strong doses (p. 351)
	    or penicillin with
	    streptomycin (p. 352)

Poisonous snakebite (p. 105)	snake antivenin (p. 372)
Scorpion sting (in children, p. 106)	scorpion antivenin (p. 372)

Meningitis (p. 185)
    when you do not suspect
    tuberculosis
	ampicillin (p. 351, 352)
	    or penicillin (p. 350) in very high
	    doses

Meningitis (p. 185)
    when you suspect tuberculosis
	ampicillin or penicillin together
	    with streptomycin (p. 351, 352)
	    and if possible other 'anti-
	    tuberculosis' drugs (p. 355)

Vomiting (p. 161) when it
    cannot be controlled
	antihistamines, for example,
	    promethazine (p. 371)

Severe allergic reaction
    allergic shock, (p. 70)
    and severe asthma, (p. 167)
	Adrenalin (p. 370)

The following chronic illnesses generally require injections, but they are rarely emergencies. It is best to consult a health worker for treatment.

Tuberculosis (p. 179, 180)	streptomycin (p. 355) together
	    with INH tablets and PAS tablets
	    (p. 356)

Syphilis (p. 237) Gonorrhea (p. 236)	procaine penicillin in very high doses (p. 350)

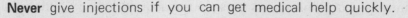

WHEN NOT TO INJECT:

Never give injections if you can get medical help quickly.

Never give an injection for a sickness that is not serious.

Never give injections for a cold or the flu.

Never inject a medicine that is not recommended for the illness you want to treat.

Never inject a medicine unless you know and take all the recommended precautions.

MEDICINES NOT TO INJECT

In general, it is better never to inject the following:

1. Vitamins. Rarely are injected vitamins any better than vitamins taken by mouth. Injections are more expensive and more dangerous. Use vitamin pills or syrups rather than injections. Better still, eat foods rich in vitamins (see p. 111).

2. Liver extract and vitamin B$_{12}$. Do not inject them! Ferrous sulfate pills will do more good for almost all cases of anemia (see p. 376).

3. Calcium. Injected into a vein calcium is extremely dangerous, if not given **very slowly.** An injection in the buttock may cause a large *abscess.* Untrained people should never inject calcium.

4. Penicillin. Nearly all infections that require penicillin can be effectively treated with penicillin taken by mouth. Penicillin is more dangerous when injected. **Use injectable penicillin only for dangerous infections.**

5. Penicillin with streptomycin. As a general rule, avoid this combined medicine. Never use it for colds or the flu (p. 163).

6. Chloramphenicol or tetracycline. These medicines do as much or more good when taken by mouth. Use capsules or syrups rather than injections (p. 353).

7. Intravenous (I.V.) solutions. These should be used only for severe dehydration and given only by someone who is well trained. When not given correctly they can cause dangerous infections or death (p. 52).

8. Intravenous medicines. There is so much danger in injecting any medicine in the vein that only well-trained health workers should do it. However, never inject into a muscle (the buttock) medicine that says 'for intravenous use only'. Also, never inject in the vein medicine that says 'for intramuscular use only'.

RISKS AND PRECAUTIONS

The risks of injecting any medicines are (1) infection caused by germs entering with the needle and (2) allergic or poisonous reactions caused by the medicine.

1. To lower the chance of infection when injecting, take great care that everything is completely clean. It is very important to boil the needle and syringe before injecting. After boiling, do not touch the needle with your fingers or with anything else.

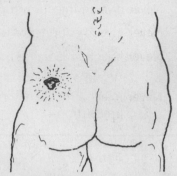

   Never use the same needle and syringe to inject more than one person without boiling it again first. Carefully follow all of the instructions for injecting (see following pages).

An abscess like this one comes from injecting with a needle that has not been well boiled and is not sterile (completely clean and germ-free).

2. It is very important to know what reactions a medicine can produce and to take the recommended precautions before injecting.

   If any of the following signs of allergic or poisonous reaction appear, never give the same or similar medicine again:

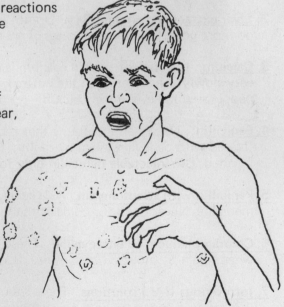

   - hives or a rash with itching

   - swelling anywhere

   - difficulty breathing

   - signs of shock (see p. 70)

   - dizzy spells with nausea (wanting to vomit)

   - problems with vision

   - ringing in the ears or deafness

   - severe back pain

   - difficulty urinating

Hives, or a rash with itching, can appear a few hours or up to several days after getting an injection. If the same medicine is given to the person again, it may cause a very severe reaction or even death (see p. 70).

This child was injected with a needle that was not *sterile* (boiled and completely free of germs).

The dirty needle caused an infection that produced a large, painful abscess (pocket of pus) and gave the child a fever. Finally, the abscess burst as shown in the picture below.

This child was injected for a cold. It would have been far better to give him no medicine at all. Rather than doing good, the injection caused the child suffering and harm.

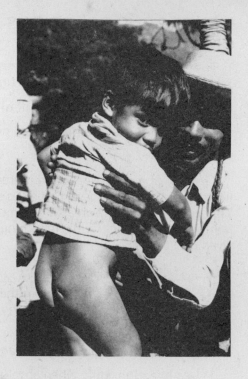

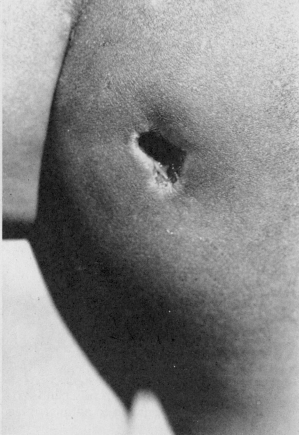

To avoid problems like these:

Inject only when absolutely necessary.

♦ Boil the syringe and needle just before giving the injection and be very careful to keep them completely clean.

♦ Use only the medicine recommended for the disease and be sure it is still in good condition and not spoiled.

♦ Inject in the correct place. (Notice that this child was injected **too low** on the buttock, where it is possible to damage the nerve.)

DANGEROUS REACTIONS FROM INJECTING CERTAIN MEDICINES

The following groups of medicines sometimes produce a dangerous reaction called ALLERGIC SHOCK a short time after injection:

- penicillins (including ampicillin)
- antitoxins that are made from horse serum
  { scorpion antivenin
  { snake antivenin
  { tetanus antitoxin

The risk of a serious reaction is greater in a person who has previously been injected with one of these medicines or with another medicine of the same group. This risk is especially great if the medicine caused an allergic reaction (hives, itching, swelling, or trouble breathing) a few hours or days after the injection was given.

 Rarely, ALLERGIC SHOCK may result from the sting of a wasp or bee or from medicine taken by mouth.

To prevent a serious reaction from an injection:

1. Use injections only when absolutely necessary.

2. Before injecting one of the medicines listed above, always have ready 2 ampules of *Adrenalin* (p. 370) and an ampule of an antihistamine like promethazine (*Phenergan,* p. 371) or diphenhydramine (*Benadryl,* p. 371).

3. Before injecting, always ask if at any other time a similar injection caused itching or other reactions. If the person says yes, do not use this medicine or any other medicine of the same group, either injected or taken by mouth.

4. In very serious cases, like tetanus or snakebite, if there is a good chance that the antitoxin might produce an allergic reaction (if the person suffers from allergies or asthma or has had horse serum before), inject the antihistamine 15 minutes before giving the antitoxin. Diphenhydramine dosage—adults, 3 ml., children, 1 or 2 ml. depending on their size. For Promethazine see p. 371.

5. After injecting any medicine, always stay with the person for 30 minutes to watch for any of the following signs of ALLERGIC SHOCK:

- cool, moist, pale, gray skin (cold sweat)
- weak, rapid pulse or heartbeat
- difficulty breathing
- loss of consciousness

6. If these signs appear, immediately inject *Adrenalin:* adults, ½ ml.; children, ¼ ml. Treat the person for SHOCK (see p. 77). Follow by giving an antihistamine in double the normal dose.

How to Avoid Serious Reactions to a Penicillin Injection

1. For mild to moderate infections:

give penicillin pills

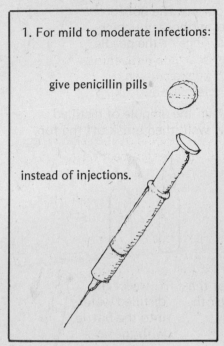

instead of injections.

2. Before injecting ask the person:

"Have you ever had hives, itching, swelling, or trouble breathing after getting an injection of penicillin?"

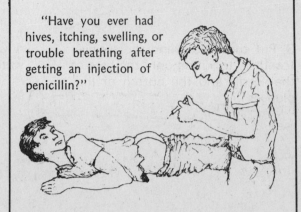

If the answer is yes, do not use penicillin or ampicillin. Use another antibiotic like erythromycin (p. 352) or a sulfonamide (p. 354).

3. Before injecting penicillin:

always have ampules of *ADRENALIN* ready.

4. After injecting:

stay with the person for at least 30 minutes.

5. If the person becomes very pale, his heart beats very fast, he has difficulty breathing, or he starts to faint, immediately inject into a muscle half an ampule of *ADRENALIN* (a quarter of an ampule in small children) and repeat in 10 minutes if necessary.

HOW TO PREPARE A SYRINGE FOR INJECTION

1. Take the syringe apart and boil it and the needle for 15 minutes.

2. Pour out the boiled water without touching the syringe or the needle.

3. Put the needle and the syringe together, touching only the base of the needle and the button of the plunger.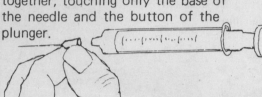

4. Clean the ampule of distilled water well, then break off the top.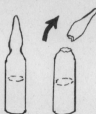

5. Fill the syringe. (Be careful that the needle does not touch the outside of the ampule.)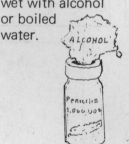

6. Rub the rubber of the bottle with clean cloth wet with alcohol or boiled water.

ALCOHOL

Penicilin 1,000,000

7. Inject the distilled water into the bottle with the powdered medicine.

8. Shake until the medicine dissolves.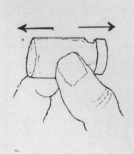

9. Fill the syringe again.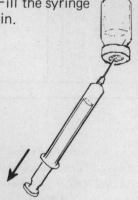

10. Remove all air from the syringe.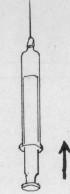

Be very careful not to touch the needle with anything—not even the cotton with alcohol. If by chance the needle touches your finger or something else, boil it again.

WHERE TO GIVE AN INJECTION

It is preferable to inject in the muscle of the buttocks, always in the **upper outer** quarter.

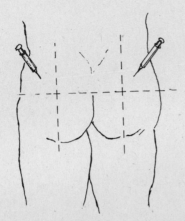

Never inject children under 2 years of age in the buttock. Inject them in the **upper outer** part of the thigh.

HOW TO INJECT

1. Clean the skin with soap and water (or alcohol—but to prevent severe pain, be sure the alcohol is dry before injecting).

2. Put the needle straight in, all the way. (If it is done with one quick movement, it hurts less.)

3. Before injecting, pull back on the plunger. (If blood enters the syringe, take the needle out and put it in somewhere else.)

4. If no blood enters, inject the medicine slowly.

5. Remove the needle and clean the skin again.

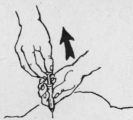

6. After injecting, rinse the syringe and needle at once. Squirt water through the needle and then take the syringe apart and wash it. Boil before using again.

CHAPTER

10

FIRST AID

FEVER

When a person's body temperature is too hot, we say he has a *fever.* Fever itself is not a sickness, but a sign of many different sicknesses. However, **high fever can be dangerous, especially in a small child.**

When a person has a fever:

1. Uncover him completely.

Small children should be undressed completely and left naked until the fever goes down.

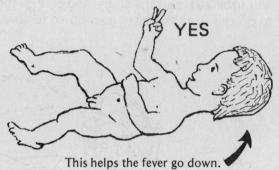

YES

This helps the fever go down.

NO

Never wrap the child in clothing or blankets.

This makes the fever go up.

> **To wrap up a child with fever is dangerous.**

Fresh air or a breeze will not harm a person with fever. On the contrary, a fresh breeze helps lower the fever.

2. Also take aspirin to lower fever (see p. 365). Small children can be given either acetaminophen (paracetamol, p. 366), children's aspirin, or a piece of a regular 5-grain (300 mg.) aspirin tablet.

3. Anyone who has a fever should **drink lots of water,** juices, or other liquids. For small children, especially babies, drinking water should be boiled first (and then cooled).

4. When possible, find and treat the cause of the fever.

Very High Fevers

A very high fever can be dangerous if it is not brought down quickly. It can cause fits (convulsions) or even permanent brain damage (paralysis, mental slowness, epilepsy, etc.). High fever is most dangerous for small children.

When a fever goes very high (over 40°), it must be lowered at once:

1. Strip the person naked.

2. Fan him.

3. Pour cool water over him, or put cloths soaked in cool water on his chest and forehead. Fan the cloths and change them often to keep them cool. Continue to do this until the fever goes down (below 38°).

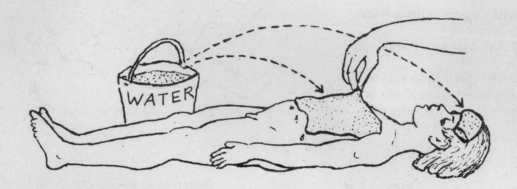

4. Give him plenty of cool water to drink.

5. Give a medicine to bring down fever. Aspirin works well.

Dosage (using 300 mg. adult tablets):

Persons over 12 years: 2 tablets every 4 hours

Children 6 to 12 years: 1 tablet every 4 hours

Children 3 to 6 years: ½ tablet every 4 hours

Children under 3 years: ¼ tablet every 4 hours

If a person with fever cannot swallow aspirin, grind it up, mix it with some water, and put it up the anus as an *enema* or with a syringe without the needle. Some doctors consider acetaminophen (paracetamol) safer than aspirin for small children. For the dosage see p. 366.

If a high fever does not go down soon or if fits (convulsions) begin, continue cooling with water and seek medical help at once.

SHOCK

Shock is a life-threatening condition that develops when the body's blood pressure drops dangerously low. It can result from great pain, a large burn, losing a lot of blood, severe illnesses, dehydration, or severe allergic reaction.

Signs of SHOCK:

- weak, rapid pulse (more than 100 per minute)

- 'cold sweat'; pale, cold, damp skin

- mental confusion, weakness, or loss of consciousness.

What to do to prevent or treat shock:

At the first sign of shock; or if there is risk of shock . . .

- Have the person lie down with his feet higher than his head, like this:

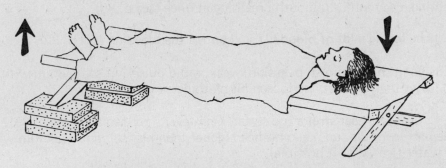

However, if he has a severe head injury put him in a 'half-sitting' position (p. 91).

- If the person feels cold, cover him with a blanket.

- If he is conscious, give him warm water or other lukewarm drinks.

- If he is in pain, give him aspirin or another pain medicine.

- Keep calm and reassure the person.

If the person is unconscious:

- Lay him on his side with his head low, tilted back and to one side (see picture on next page). If he seems to be choking, pull his tongue forward with your finger.

- If he has vomited, clear his mouth immediately. Be sure his head is low, tilted back, and to one side so he does not breathe vomit into his lungs.

- Do not give him anything by mouth until he becomes conscious.

- If you or someone nearby knows how, give intravenous solution (normal saline) at a fast drip.

- Seek medical help fast.

LOSS OF CONSCIOUSNESS

Common causes of loss of consciousness are:

- drunkenness
- a hit on the head (getting knocked out)
- shock (p. 77)
- poisoning (p. 103)

- fainting (from fright, weakness, etc.)
- heat stroke (p. 81)
- stroke (p. 327)
- heart attack (p. 325)

If a person is unconscious and you do not know why, **immediately check each of the following:**

1. Is he **breathing** well? If not, tilt his head way back and pull the jaw and tongue forward. If something is stuck in his throat, pull it out. If he is not breathing, use mouth-to-mouth breathing at once (see p. 80).

2. Is he **losing a lot of blood?** If so, control the bleeding (see p. 82).

3. Is he in **shock** (moist, pale skin; weak, rapid pulse)? If so, lay him with his head lower than his feet and loosen his clothing.

4. Could it be **heat stroke** (no sweat, high fever, hot, red skin, see p. 81)? If so, shade him from the sun, keep his head higher than his feet, and soak him with cold water (ice water if possible).

How to position an unconscious person:

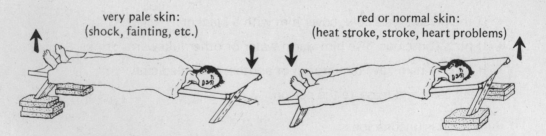

very pale skin:
(shock, fainting, etc.)

red or normal skin:
(heat stroke, stroke, heart problems)

If there is any chance that the unconscious person is badly injured:

It is best not to move him until he becomes conscious. If you have to move him, do so with great care, because if his neck or back is broken, any change of position may cause greater injury.

Look for wounds or broken bones, but move the person as little as possible. Do not bend his back or neck.

Never give anything by mouth to a person who is unconscious.

WHEN SOMETHING GETS STUCK IN THE THROAT

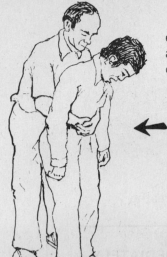

When food or something else sticks in a person's throat and he cannot breathe, **quickly** do this:

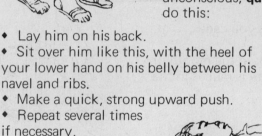

CHOKING

- Stand behind him and wrap your arms around his waist,
- put your fist against his belly above the navel and below the ribs,
- and press into his belly with a **sudden** strong upward jerk.

This forces the air from his lungs and should free his throat. Repeat several times if necessary.

If the person is a lot bigger than you, or is already unconscious, **quickly** do this:

- Lay him on his back.
- Sit over him like this, with the heel of your lower hand on his belly between his navel and ribs.
- Make a quick, strong upward push.
- Repeat several times if necessary.
- If he still cannot breathe, try **mouth-to-mouth breathing** (see next page).

DROWNING

A person who has stopped breathing has only 4 minutes to live! You must **act fast!**

Start mouth-to-mouth breathing at once (see next page)—if possible, even before the drowning person is out of the water, as soon as it is shallow enough to stand.

If you cannot blow air into his lungs, when you reach the shore, quickly put him with his head lower than his feet and push his belly as described above. Then continue mouth-to-mouth breathing at once.

ALWAYS START MOUTH-TO-MOUTH BREATHING AT ONCE before trying to get water out of the drowning person's chest.

WHAT TO DO WHEN BREATHING STOPS: MOUTH-TO-MOUTH BREATHING

Common causes for breathing to stop are:

- something stuck in the throat
- the tongue or thick mucus blocking the throat of an unconscious person
- drowning, choking on smoke, or poisoning
- a strong blow to the head or chest
- a heart attack

A person will die within 4 minutes if he does not breathe.

> **If a person stops breathing,
> begin mouth-to-mouth breathing IMMEDIATELY.**

Do all of the following as quickly as you can:

Step 1: Quickly remove anything stuck in the mouth or throat. Pull the tongue forward. If there is mucus in the throat, quickly try to clear it out.

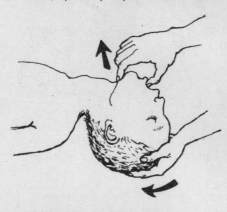

Step 2: Quickly lay the person face up, tilt his head way back, and pull his jaw forward.

Step 3: Pinch his nostrils closed with your fingers, open his mouth wide, cover his mouth with yours, and blow strongly into his lungs so that his chest rises. Pause to let the air come back out and blow again. Repeat about 15 times per minute. With newborn babies, breathe **very gently** about 25 times per minute.

Continue **mouth-to-mouth breathing** until the person can breathe by himself, or until there is no doubt he is dead. Sometimes you must keep it up for an hour or more.

EMERGENCIES CAUSED BY HEAT

Heat Cramps

In hot weather people who work hard and sweat a lot sometimes get painful cramps in their legs, arms, or stomach. These occur because the body lacks salt.

Treatment: Put a teaspoon of salt in a liter of boiled water and drink it.

Heat Exhaustion

Signs: A person who works and sweats a lot in hot weather may become very pale and weak and perhaps feel faint. The skin is cool and moist. The pulse is rapid and weak.

Treatment: Have the person lie down in a cool place, raise his feet, and rub his legs. Give salt water to drink: 1 teaspoon of salt in a liter of water. (Give nothing by mouth while the person is unconscious.)

Heat Stroke

Heat stroke is not common, but is very dangerous. It occurs especially in older people and *alcoholics* during hot weather.

Signs: The skin is red, very hot, and dry. Not even the armpits are moist. The person has a very high fever, sometimes more than 42° C. Often he is unconscious.

Treatment: **The body temperature must be lowered immediately.** Put the person in the shade. Soak him with cold water (ice water if possible) and fan him. Continue until the fever drops. Seek medical help.

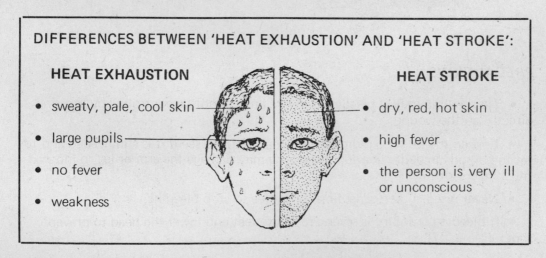

DIFFERENCES BETWEEN 'HEAT EXHAUSTION' AND 'HEAT STROKE':

HEAT EXHAUSTION

- sweaty, pale, cool skin
- large pupils
- no fever
- weakness

HEAT STROKE

- dry, red, hot skin
- high fever
- the person is very ill or unconscious

HOW TO CONTROL BLEEDING FROM A WOUND

1. Raise the injured part.

2. With a clean cloth (or your hand if there is no cloth) press directly on the wound. Keep pressing until the bleeding stops. This may take 15 minutes or sometimes an hour or more.

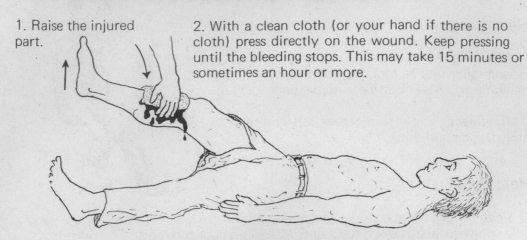

3. If the bleeding cannot be controlled by pressing on the wound, and if the person is losing a lot of blood, do the following:

- ◆ Keep pressing on the wound.

- ◆ Keep the wounded part as high as possible.

- ◆ Tie the arm or leg as close to the wound as possible—between the wound and the body. Tighten enough to control the bleeding.

- ◆ For the tie, use a folded cloth or a wide belt; never use thin rope, string, or wire.

PRECAUTIONS:

- ■ Tie the limb only if bleeding is severe and cannot be controlled by pressing directly on the wound.

- ■ Loosen the tie for a moment every half hour to see if it is still needed and to let the blood circulate. Leaving it too long may damage the arm or leg so much it must be cut off.

- ■ **Never** use dirt, kerosene, lime, or coffee to stop bleeding.

- ■ If bleeding or injury is severe, raise the feet and lower the head to prevent shock (see p. 77).

HOW TO STOP NOSEBLEEDS

1. Sit quietly.

2. Pinch the nose firmly
for 10 minutes or until
the bleeding has stopped.

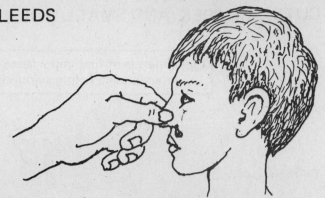

If this does not control the bleeding . . .

Pack the nostril with a wad of cotton,
leaving part of it outside the nose. If
possible, first wet the cotton with
hydrogen peroxide, *Vaseline*, cardon cactus
juice (p. 13), or lidocaine with
epinephrine (p. 367).

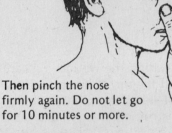

Then pinch the nose
firmly again. Do not let go
for 10 minutes or more.

Leave the cotton in place for a few hours after the bleeding stops; then take it
out very carefully.

If a person's nose bleeds often, smear a little *Vaseline* inside the nostrils twice
a day.

Eating oranges, tomatoes, and other fruits may help to strengthen the veins so
that the nose bleeds less.

In older persons especially, bleeding may
come from the back part of the nose and
cannot be stopped by pinching it. In this
case, have the person hold a cork, corn cob,
or other similar object between his teeth
and, leaning forward, sit quietly and try
not to swallow until the bleeding stops.
(The cork helps keep him from swallowing,
and that gives the blood a chance to clot.)

CUTS, SCRAPES, AND SMALL WOUNDS

> **Cleanliness is of first importance in preventing infection and helping wounds to heal.**

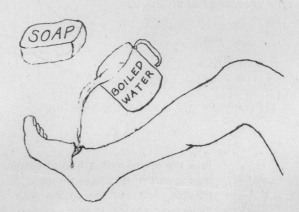

To treat a wound . . .

First, wash your hands very well with soap and water.

Then wash the wound well with soap and boiled water.

When cleaning the wound, be careful to clean out all the dirt. Lift up and clean under any flaps of skin. You can use a clean tweezers or other instruments to remove bits of dirt, but always boil them first to be sure they are sterile.

If possible, squirt out the wound with boiled water in a syringe or suction bulb.

Any bit of dirt that is left in a wound can cause an infection.

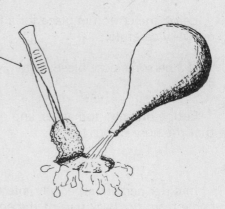

> **NEVER put animal or human feces or mud on a wound. These can cause dangerous infections, such as tetanus.**
>
> **NEVER put alcohol, tincture of iodine, or *Merthiolate* directly into a wound; doing so will only damage the flesh and make healing slower. Use soap and water.**

LARGE CUTS: HOW TO CLOSE THEM

A recent cut that is very clean will heal faster if you bring the edges together so the cut stays closed.

Close a deep cut only if all of the following are true:

- the cut is less than 12 hours old,

- the cut is very clean, and

- it is impossible to get a health worker to close it the same day.

Before closing the cut, wash it very well with boiled water and soap. If possible, squirt it out with a syringe and water. Be absolutely sure that no dirt is left hidden in the cut.

There are two methods to close a cut:

'BUTTERFLY' BANDAGES OF ADHESIVE TAPE

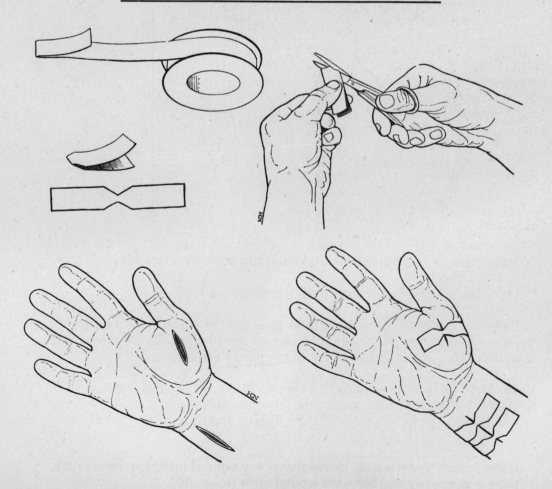

STITCHES OR SUTURES WITH THREAD

To find out if a cut needs stitches see if the edges of the skin come together by themselves. If they do, usually no stitches are needed.

To stitch a wound:

* Boil a sewing needle and a thin thread (nylon or silk is best) for 10 minutes.

* Wash the wound with boiled water and soap, as has been described.

* Wash your hands very well with boiled water and soap.

* Sew the wound like this:

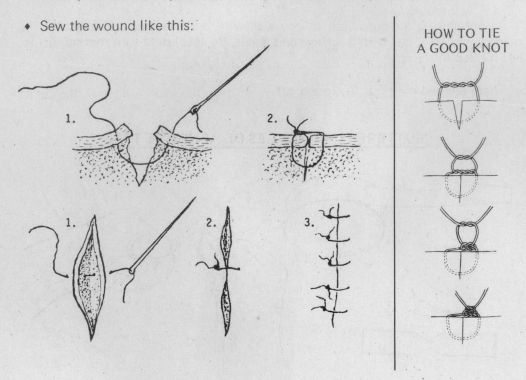

HOW TO TIE
A GOOD KNOT

Make the first stitch in the middle of the cut, and tie it closed (1. and 2.).

Make enough other stitches to close the whole cut (3.).

Leave the stitches in place for 6 to 12 days (on the face 6 days; the body 8 days; the hand or foot 12 days). Then remove the stitches: cut the thread on one side of the knot and pull the knot until the thread comes out.

WARNING: Only close wounds that are very clean and less than 12 hours old. Old, dirty, or infected wounds must be left open. Bites from people, dogs, pigs, or other animals should also be left open. Closing these can cause dangerous infections.

If the wound that has been closed shows any signs of infection, remove the stitches immediately and leave the wound open (see p. 88).

BANDAGES

Bandages are used to help keep wounds clean. For this reason, bandages or pieces of cloth used to cover wounds must always be clean themselves. Cloth used for bandages should be washed and then dried with an iron or in the sun, in a clean, dust-free place.

If possible, cover the wound with a sterile gauze pad before bandaging. These pads are often sold in sealed envelopes in pharmacies.

Or prepare your own sterile gauze or cloth. Wrap it in thick paper, seal it with tape, and bake it for 20 minutes in an oven. Putting a pan of water in the oven under the cloth will keep it from charring.

> **It is better to have no bandage at all than one that is dirty or wet.**

If a bandage gets wet or dirt gets under it, take the bandage off, wash the cut again, and put on a clean bandage.

Examples of bandages:

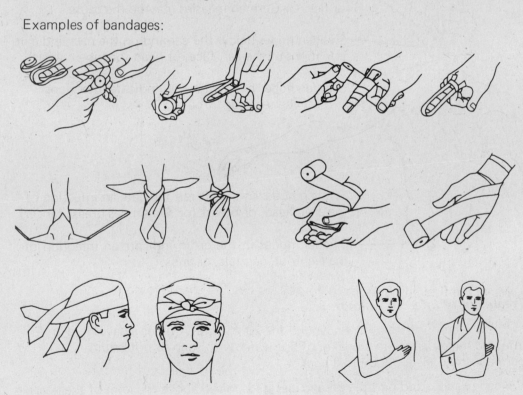

CAUTION:

Be careful that a bandage that goes around a limb is not so tight it cuts off the flow of blood.

Many small scrapes and cuts do not need bandages. They heal best if washed with soap and water and left open to the air. The most important thing is to **keep them clean.**

INFECTED WOUNDS:
HOW TO RECOGNIZE AND TREAT THEM

A wound is infected if:

- it becomes **red, swollen, hot,** and **painful,**

- it has **pus,**

- or if it begins to **smell bad.**

The infection is spreading to other parts of the body if:

- it causes **fever,**

- there is a **red line above the wound,**

- or if the **lymph nodes become swollen and tender.** Lymph nodes—often called 'glands'—are little traps for germs that form small lumps under the skin when they get infected.

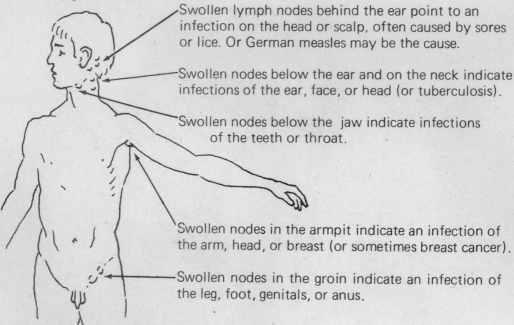

Swollen lymph nodes behind the ear point to an infection on the head or scalp, often caused by sores or lice. Or German measles may be the cause.

Swollen nodes below the ear and on the neck indicate infections of the ear, face, or head (or tuberculosis).

Swollen nodes below the jaw indicate infections of the teeth or throat.

Swollen nodes in the armpit indicate an infection of the arm, head, or breast (or sometimes breast cancer).

Swollen nodes in the groin indicate an infection of the leg, foot, genitals, or anus.

Treatment of infected wounds:

♦ Put hot compresses over the wound for 20 minutes 4 times a day. Hold an infected hand or foot in a bucket of hot water with soap or potassium permanganate (1 teaspoon to a bucket).

♦ Keep the infected part at rest and elevated (raised above the level of the heart).

♦ If the infection is severe or the person has not been vaccinated against tetanus, use an antibiotic like penicillin (see p. 349, 350).

WARNING: If the wound has a bad smell, if brown or gray liquid oozes out, or if the skin around it turns black and forms air bubbles or blisters, this may be gangrene. Seek medical help fast. Meanwhile, follow the instructions for gangrene on p. 213.

WOUNDS THAT ARE LIKELY TO BECOME DANGEROUSLY INFECTED

These wounds are most likely to become dangerously infected:

- dirty wounds, or wounds made with dirty objects

- puncture wounds and other deep wounds that do not bleed much

- wounds made where animals are kept: in corrals, pig pens, etc.

- large wounds with severe mashing or bruising

- bites, especially from pigs, dogs, or people

- bullet wounds

Special care for this type of 'high risk' wound:

1. Wash the wound well with boiled water and soap. **Remove all pieces of dirt, blood clots, and dead or badly damaged flesh.** Squirt out the dirt using a syringe or suction bulb.

2. Soak the wound in water with potassium permanganate (1 teaspoon to a bucket). Then paint the wound with gentian violet or put a little antibiotic ointment into the wound (see p. 361) and cover it with a clean bandage.

3. If the wound is very deep, if it is a bite, or if there is a chance that it still has dirt in it, use an antibiotic. The best is ampicillin, in capsules or, in the most serious cases, injections. If you cannot afford ampicillin, use penicillin, tetracycline, or a sulfa. For dosages, see the GREEN PAGES.

4. **Never** close this type of wound with stitches or 'butterfly' bandages. **Leave the wound open.**

The danger of tetanus is very great in people who have not been vaccinated against this deadly disease. To lower the risk, a person who has not been vaccinated against tetanus should use penicillin or ampicillin immediately after receiving a wound of this type, even if the injury is small.

If a wound of this type is very severe, a person who has not been vaccinated against tetanus should take large doses of penicillin or ampicillin for a week or more. Tetanus antitoxin should also be considered—but be sure to take the necessary precautions in its use (see p. 70).

BULLET, KNIFE, AND OTHER SERIOUS WOUNDS

Danger of infection: Any deep bullet or knife wound runs a high risk of dangerous infection. For this reason an antibiotic, preferably penicillin (p. 349) or ampicillin (p. 351) should be used at once.

Persons who have not been vaccinated against tetanus should perhaps be given an injection of tetanus antitoxin, and be vaccinated against tetanus as well.

If possible, seek medical help.

Bullet Wounds in the Arms or Legs

♦ If the wound is bleeding a lot, control the bleeding as shown on page 82.

♦ If the bleeding is not serious, let the wound bleed for a short while. This will help clean it out.

♦ Wash the wound with boiled water and soap and apply a clean bandage. In the case of a gunshot wound, wash the surface (outside) only. It is usually better not to poke anything into the hole.

♦ Give antibiotics.

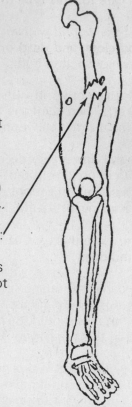

CAUTION:

If there is any possibility that the bullet has hit a bone, the bone may be broken.

Using or putting weight on the wounded limb (standing, for example) might cause a more serious break, like this:

If a break is suspected, it is best to splint the limb and not to use it for several weeks.

When the wound is serious, raise the wounded part higher than the heart and keep the injured person completely still.

This way the wound will heal faster and is less likely to become infected.

YES

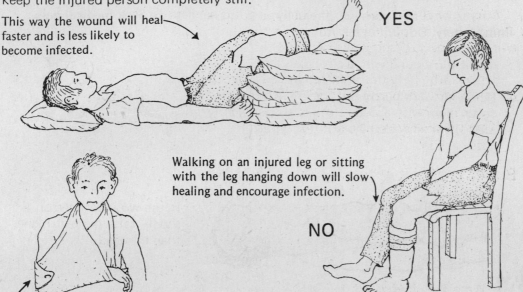

Walking on an injured leg or sitting with the leg hanging down will slow healing and encourage infection.

NO

Make a sling like this to support an arm with a gunshot wound or other serious injury.

Deep Chest Wounds

Chest wounds can be very dangerous. Seek medical help at once.

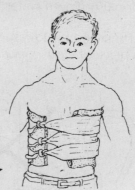

♦ If the wound has reached the lungs and air is being sucked through the hole when the person breathes, cover the wound at once so that no more air enters. Spread *Vaseline* or vegetable fat on a gauze pad or clean bandage and wrap it tightly over the hole like this: ───────▶

♦ Put the injured person in the position in which he feels most comfortable.

♦ If there are signs of shock, give proper treatment (see p. 77).

♦ Give antibiotics and painkillers.

Bullet Wounds in the Head

♦ Cover the wound with a clean bandage.

♦ Place the injured person in a 'half-sitting' position.

♦ Give antibiotics (penicillin).

♦ Seek medical help.

Deep Wounds in the Abdomen

Any wound that goes into the belly or gut is dangerous. **Seek medical help immediately.** But in the meantime:

Cover the wound with a clean bandage.

If the guts are partly outside the wound, cover them with a clean cloth soaked in lightly salted, boiled water. Do not try to push the guts back in.

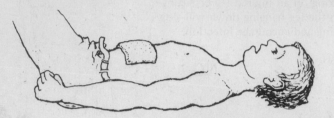

If the wounded person is in shock, raise his feet higher than his head.

Give absolutely nothing by mouth: no food, no drink, not even water.

If the wounded person is thirsty, let him suck on a piece of cloth soaked in water.

Never give an enema, even if the stomach swells up or the injured person does not move his bowels for days. If the gut is torn, an enema or purge can kill him.

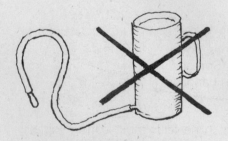

Inject antibiotics (see the following page for instructions).

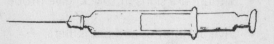

DO NOT WAIT FOR A HEALTH WORKER.

IMMEDIATELY TAKE THE INJURED PERSON TO THE CLOSEST HEALTH CENTER OR HOSPITAL. He will need an operation.

MEDICINE FOR A WOUND THAT GOES INTO THE GUT
(Also for appendicitis or peritonitis)

Until you can get medical help, do the following:

Inject ampicillin (p. 351), 1 gm. (four 250 mg. ampules) every 4 hours.

If there is no ampicillin:

Inject penicillin (crystalline, if possible, p. 350), 5 million units immediately; after that, 1 million units every 4 hours.

Together with the penicillin, give an injection of either: streptomycin (p. 355), 2 ml. (1 gm.), 2 times a day or chloramphenicol, 2 ampules of 250 mg. every 4 hours.

If you cannot obtain these anitbiotics in injectable form, give ampicillin or penicillin by mouth together with chloramphenicol or tetracycline, and very little water.

EMERGENCY PROBLEMS OF THE GUT (ACUTE ABDOMEN)

Acute abdomen is a name given to a number of sudden, severe conditions of the gut for which prompt surgery is often needed to prevent death. Appendicitis, peritonitis, and gut obstruction are examples (see following pages). Often the exact cause of acute abdomen will be uncertain until a surgeon cuts open the belly and looks inside.

> **If a person has continuous severe gut pain with vomiting, but does not have diarrhea, suspect an acute abdomen.**

Acute abdomen:	Less serious illness:
Take to a hospital— surgery may be needed	**Probably can be treated in the home or health center**
• continuous severe pain that keeps getting worse	• pain that comes and goes (cramps)
• constipation and vomiting	• moderate or severe diarrhea
• belly swollen, hard, person protects it	• sometimes signs of an infection, perhaps a cold or sore throat
• severely ill	• he has had pains like this before
	• only moderately ill

> **If a person shows signs of acute abdomen, get him to a hospital as fast as you can.**

Obstructed Gut

An acute abdomen may be caused by something that blocks or 'obstructs' a part of the gut, so that food and stools cannot pass. More common causes are:

- a ball or knot of roundworms (Ascaris, p. 140)
- a loop of gut that is pinched in a hernia (p. 177)
- a part of the gut that slips inside the part below it (intussusception)

Almost any kind of acute abdomen may show some signs of obstruction. Because it hurts the damaged gut to move, it stops moving.

Signs of an obstructed gut:

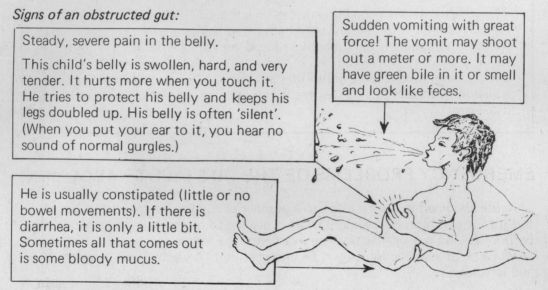

Steady, severe pain in the belly.

This child's belly is swollen, hard, and very tender. It hurts more when you touch it. He tries to protect his belly and keeps his legs doubled up. His belly is often 'silent'. (When you put your ear to it, you hear no sound of normal gurgles.)

Sudden vomiting with great force! The vomit may shoot out a meter or more. It may have green bile in it or smell and look like feces.

He is usually constipated (little or no bowel movements). If there is diarrhea, it is only a little bit. Sometimes all that comes out is some bloody mucus.

Get this person to a hospital **at once.** His life is in danger and surgery may be needed.

Appendicitis, Peritonitis

These dangerous conditions often require surgery. Seek medical help fast.

Appendicitis is an infection of the *appendix,* a finger-shaped sac attached to the large intestine in the lower right-hand part of the belly. An infected appendix sometimes bursts open, causing *peritonitis.*

Peritonitis is an acute, serious infection of the lining of the cavity or bag that holds the gut. It results when the appendix or another part of the gut bursts or is torn.

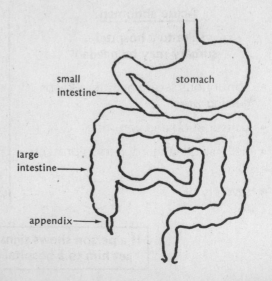

small intestine / stomach / large intestine / appendix

Signs of appendicitis:

- The main sign is a steady pain in the belly that gets worse and worse.

- The pain often begins around the navel ('bellybutton'),

  but it soon moves to the lower right side.

- There may be loss of appetite, vomiting, constipation, or a mild fever.

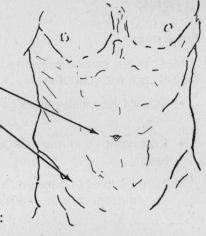

A TEST FOR APPENDICITIS OR PERITONITIS:

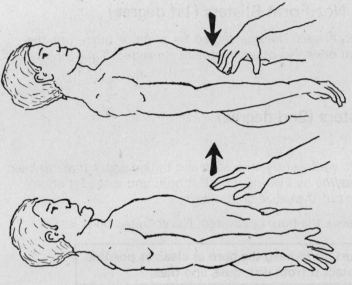

Slowly but forcefully, press on the abdomen a little above the left groin until it hurts a little.

Then quickly remove the hand.

If a very sharp pain *(rebound pain)* occurs when the hand is removed, appendicitis or peritonitis is likely.

If no rebound pain occurs above the left groin, try the same test above the right groin.

IF IT SEEMS THAT A PERSON HAS APPENDICITIS OR PERITONITIS:

- **Seek medical help immediately.** If possible, take the person where he can have surgery.

- **Do not give anything by mouth** and do not give an enema. Only if the person begins to show signs of dehydration, give sips of water or Rehydration Drink (p. 152)—but nothing more.

- The person should rest very quietly in a half-sitting position.

Note: When peritonitis is advanced, the belly becomes hard like a board, and the person feels great pain when his belly is touched even lightly. His life is in danger. Take him to a medical center immediately and on the way give him the medicines indicated at the top of page 93.

BURNS

Prevention:

Most burns can be prevented. Take special care with children:

- ◆ Do not let small babies go near a fire.

- ◆ Keep lamps and matches out of reach.

- ◆ Turn handles of pans on the stove so children cannot reach them.

Minor Burns that Do Not Form Blisters (1st degree)

To help ease the pain and lessen damage caused by a minor burn, put the burned part in cold water **at once.** No other treatment is needed. Take aspirin for pain.

Burns that Cause Blisters (2nd degree)

Do not break blisters.

If the blisters are broken, wash gently with soap and boiled water that has been cooled. Sterilize a little *Vaseline* by heating it until it boils and spread it on a piece of sterile gauze. Then put the gauze on the burn.

If there is no *Vaseline,* leave the burn uncovered. Never smear on grease or butter.

> **It is very important to keep the burn as clean as possible.**
> **Protect it from dirt, dust, and flies.**

If signs of infection appear—pus, bad smell, fever, or swollen lymph nodes—apply compresses of warm salt water (1 teaspoon salt to 1 liter water) 3 times a day. Boil both the water and cloth before use. With great care, remove the dead skin and flesh. You can spread on a little antibiotic ointment such as *Neosporin* (p. 361). In severe cases, consider taking an antibiotic such as penicillin or ampicillin.

Deep Burns (3rd degree) that destroy the skin and expose raw or charred flesh are always serious, as are any burns that cover large areas of the body. Take the person to a health center at once. In the meantime wrap the burned part with a very clean cloth or towel.

If it is impossible to get medical help, treat the burn as described above. If you do not have *Vaseline,* leave the burn in the open air, covering it only with a loose cotton cloth or sheet to protect it from dust and flies. Keep the cloth very clean and change it each time it gets dirty with liquid or blood from the burn. Give penicillin.

Never put grease, fat, hides, coffee, herbs, or feces on a burn.

Special Precautions for Very Serious Burns

Any person who has been badly burned can easily go into *shock* (see p. 77) because of combined pain, fear, and the loss of body fluids from the oozing burn.

Comfort and reassure the burned person. Give him aspirin for the pain and codeine if you can get it. Bathing open wounds in slightly salty water also helps calm pain. Put 1 teaspoon of salt for each liter of boiled (and cooled) water.

Give the burned person plenty of liquid. If the burned area is large (more than twice the size of his hand), make up the following drink:

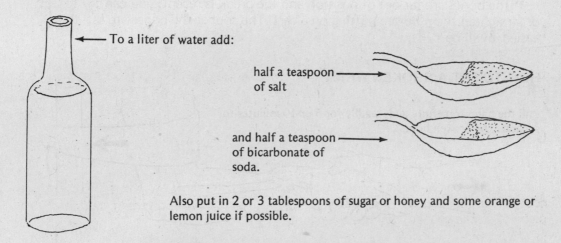

← To a liter of water add:

half a teaspoon → of salt

and half a teaspoon → of bicarbonate of soda.

Also put in 2 or 3 tablespoons of sugar or honey and some orange or lemon juice if possible.

The burned person should drink this as often as possible, especially until he urinates frequently.

It is important for persons who are badly burned to eat foods rich in protein (see p. 110). No type of food needs to be avoided.

Burns around the Joints

When someone is badly burned between the fingers, in the armpit, or at other joints, gauze pads with *Vaseline* on them should be put between the burned surfaces to prevent them from growing together as they heal. Also, fingers, arms, and legs should be straightened completely several times a day while healing. This is painful but helps prevent stiff scars that limit movement.

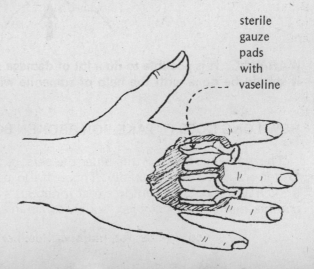

sterile
gauze
pads
with
vaseline

BROKEN BONES (FRACTURES)

When a bone is broken, the most important thing to do is **keep the bone in a fixed position.** This prevents more damage and lets it mend.

Before trying to move or carry a person with a broken bone, keep the bones from moving with splints, strips of bark, or a sleeve of cardboard. Later a plaster cast can be put on the limb at a health center, or perhaps you can make a 'cast' according to local tradition (see p. 14).

Setting broken bones: If the bones seem more or less in the right position, it is better not to move them—this could do more harm than good.

If the bones are far out of position and the break is recent, you can try to 'set' or straighten them before putting on a cast. The sooner the bones are set, the easier it will be.

HOW TO SET A BROKEN WRIST

Pull the hand forcefully and steadily for 5 or 10 minutes to separate the broken bones.

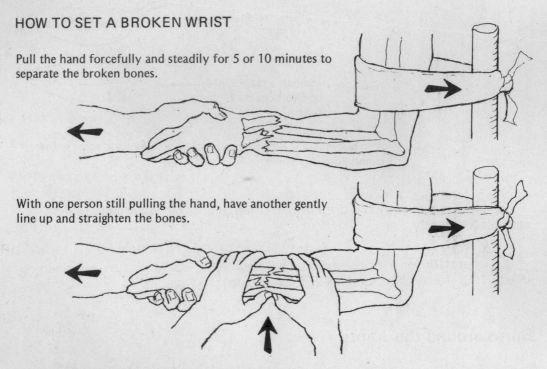

With one person still pulling the hand, have another gently line up and straighten the bones.

WARNING: **It is possible to do a lot of damage while trying to set a bone. Ideally, it should be done with the help of someone with experience. Do not force.**

HOW LONG DOES IT TAKE FOR BROKEN BONES TO HEAL?

The worse the break or the older the person, the longer healing takes. Children's bones mend rapidly. Those of old people sometimes never join. A broken arm should be kept in a cast for about a month, and no force put on it for another month. A broken leg should remain in a cast for about 2 months.

BROKEN THIGH BONE

A broken upper leg often needs special attention. It is best to splint the whole body like this:

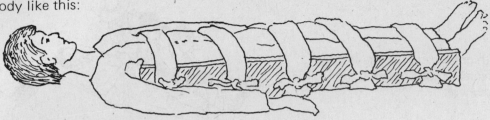

and to take the injured person to a health center at once.

BROKEN NECKS AND BACKS

If there is any chance a person's back or neck has been broken, **be very careful when moving him.** Try not to change his position. If possible, bring a health worker before moving him. If you must move him, do so without bending his back or neck. For instructions on how to move the injured person, see the next page.

BROKEN RIBS

These are very painful, but almost always heal on their own. It is better not to splint or bind the chest. The best treatment is to take aspirin—and rest. It may take months before the pain is gone completely.

A broken rib does not often puncture a lung. But if the person coughs blood or develops breathing difficulties, use antibiotics (penicillin or ampicillin) and seek medical help.

BROKEN BONES THAT BREAK THROUGH THE SKIN (COMPOUND FRACTURES)

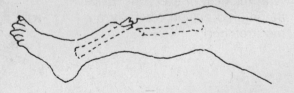

Since the danger of infection is very great in these cases, it is always better to get help from a health worker or doctor in caring for the injury. Clean the wound and the exposed bone very thoroughly with boiled water. **Never put the bone back into the wound until the wound and the bone are absolutely clean.**

Splint the limb to prevent more injury.

If the bone has broken the skin, use an antibiotic immediately to prevent infections: penicillin or ampicillin in high doses (p. 349 and 351).

> *CAUTION:* **Never rub or massage a broken limb or a limb that may possibly be broken.**

HOW TO MOVE A BADLY INJURED PERSON

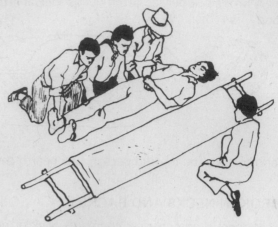

With great care, lift the injured person without bending him anywhere.

Have another person put the stretcher in place.

With the help of everyone, place the injured person carefully on the stretcher.

sand bags

If the neck is injured or broken, put bags of sand or tightly folded clothing on each side of the head to keep it from moving.

DISLOCATIONS
(BONES THAT HAVE COME OUT OF PLACE AT A JOINT)

Three important points of treatment:

- Try to put the bone back into place. **The sooner the better!**

- Keep it bandaged firmly in place so it does not slip out again (about a month).

- Avoid forceful use of the limb long enough for the joint to heal completely (2 or 3 months).

HOW TO SET A DISLOCATED SHOULDER:

Lie down on the floor next to the injured person. Put your bare foot in his armpit and pull his arm slowly downward, at an angle to the body, as shown (1), using steady force for 10 minutes.

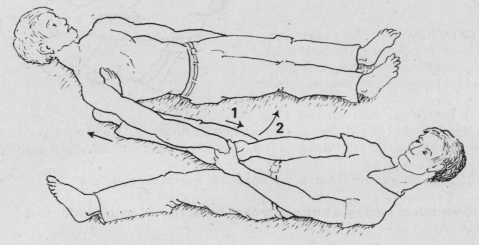

Then swing the arm closer to his body, using your foot to position the bone (2). The shoulder should 'pop' back into place.

After the shoulder is in place, bandage the arm firmly against the body. Keep it bandaged for a month. To prevent the shoulder from becoming completely stiff, older persons should unbandage the arm for a few minutes 3 times a day and, with the arm hanging at the side, move it gently in narrow circles.

In case you cannot put the dislocated limb back in place, look for medical help at once. The longer you wait, the harder it will be to correct.

STRAINS AND SPRAINS
(BRUISING OR TEARING IN A TWISTED JOINT)

Many times it is impossible to know whether a hand or foot is bruised, sprained, or broken. It helps to have an X-ray taken.

But usually, breaks and sprains are treated more or less the same. Keep the joint motionless. Wrap it with something that gives firm support. Serious sprains need at least 3 or 4 weeks to heal. Broken bones take longer.

You can keep the twisted joint in the correct position for healing by using a homemade cast (see p. 14) or an elastic bandage.

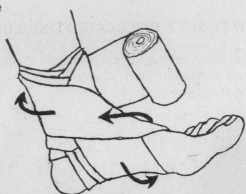

Wrap a twisted ankle as shown here:

CAUTION: If the foot seems very loose or 'floppy' or if the person has trouble moving his toes, look for medical help. Surgery may be needed.

To relieve pain and swelling, keep the sprained part raised high. During the first 24 hours, put ice or cold, wet cloths over the swollen joint. This helps reduce swelling and pain. Also take aspirin.

After 24 hours soak the sprain in hot water several times a day.

Never rub or massage a sprain or broken bone. It does no good and can do more harm.

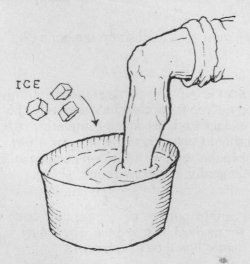

For the first day soak the sprained joint in cold water.

After the first day (24 hours) use hot soaks.

POISONING

Many children die from swallowing things that are poisonous. To protect your children, take the following precautions:

Keep all poisons out of reach of children:

Never keep kerosene, gasoline, or other poisons in cola or soft drink bottles, because children may try to drink them.

SOME COMMON POISONS TO WATCH OUT FOR:

- rat poison
- DDT, lindane, sheep dip, and other insecticides
- medicine (any kind when much is swallowed; take special care with **iron pills)**
- tincture of iodine
- bleach and detergents

- cigarettes
- rubbing or wood alcohol
- poisonous leaves, seeds, or berries
- castor beans
- matches
- kerosene, gasoline, petrol
- lye

Treatment:

If you suspect poisoning, do the following **immediately:**

♦ Make the child vomit. Put your finger in his throat, give him a tablespoon of syrup of ipecac (p. 373), or make him drink water with soap or salt in it.

♦ Have the child drink all he can of milk, beaten eggs, or flour mixed with water. If you have it, give him a tablespoon of powdered charcoal (p. 373). Keep giving him more milk, eggs, or flour and keep him vomiting until the vomit is clear.

CAUTION: Do not make a person vomit if he has swallowed kerosene, gasoline (petrol), or strong acids or corrosive substances (lye).

Cover the person if he feels cold, but avoid too much heat. **If poisoning is severe, look for medical help.**

SNAKEBITE

RATTLESNAKE—
North America,
Mexico, and
Central America

When someone has been bitten by a snake, try to find out if the snake was poisonous or harmless. Their bite marks are different:

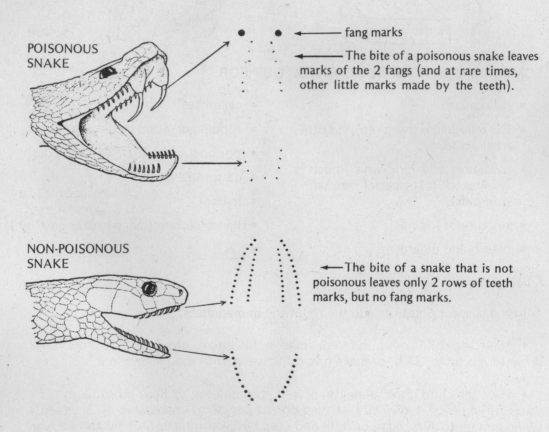

POISONOUS
SNAKE

fang marks

The bite of a poisonous snake leaves marks of the 2 fangs (and at rare times, other little marks made by the teeth).

NON-POISONOUS
SNAKE

The bite of a snake that is not poisonous leaves only 2 rows of teeth marks, but no fang marks.

People often believe that certain harmless snakes are poisonous. Try to find out which of the snakes in your area are truly poisonous and which are not. Contrary to popular opinion, boa constrictors and pythons are not poisonous. Please do not kill non-poisonous snakes, because they do no harm. On the contrary, they kill mice and other pests that do lots of damage. Some even kill poisonous snakes.

Treatment for poisonous snakebite:

1. **Stay quiet; do not move the part that has been bitten.** The more it is moved, the more rapidly the poison will spread through the body. A person who has been bitten on the foot should not walk, not even one step if it can be avoided. Carry him on a stretcher.

2. Tie a cloth around the limb, just above the bite. Do not tie it very tight, and loosen it for a moment every half hour.

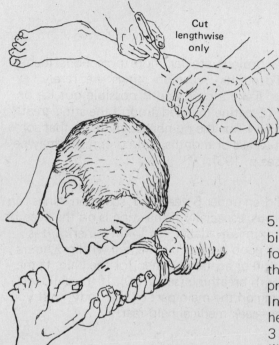

Cut
lengthwise
only

3. With a very clean knife (sterilized in a flame) make a cut into each fang mark: about 1 cm. long and ½ cm. deep.

4. Then suck (and spit out) the poison—for a quarter hour.

Note: If more than a half hour has passed since the bite, do not cut or suck the bite. By then it may do more harm than good.

5. If you can get the right kind of snake-bite antivenin, inject it, being careful to follow the instructions that come with the medicine. Take all precautions to prevent ALLERGIC SHOCK (see p. 70). In order for the antivenin to be of much help, it should be injected not more than 3 hours after the bite. (For some snakes, like cobras, it must be given very quickly.)

Note: Different parts of the world have different kinds of poisonous snakes—which require different antitoxins (antivenins). Find out what antitoxins are available in your area. **Be prepared!**

> **Have snakebite antitoxin ready and study how to use it ahead of time—before someone is bitten!**

6. If you can get ice, wrap pieces in thick cloth and pack these around the limb that was bitten.

7. If signs of infection develop, use penicillin.

Poisonous snakebite is dangerous. Send for medical help—but always do the things explained above **at once.**

Most folk remedies for snakebite do little if any good (see p. 3). Never drink alcohol after a snakebite. It makes things worse!

BITE OF THE BEADED LIZARD (GILA MONSTER) Southern U.S.A. & Mexico

The bite of the beaded lizard is treated just like a poisonous snakebite, except that there are no good antivenins for it. The bite can be very dangerous.

SCORPION STING

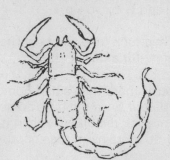

Some scorpions are far more poisonous than others. To adults, scorpion stings are rarely dangerous. Take aspirin and if possible put ice on the sting. (Emetine injected around the sting greatly reduces pain.) For the numbness and pain that sometimes last weeks or months, hot compresses may be helpful (see p. 193).

To children under 5 years old, scorpion stings can be dangerous, especially if the sting is on the head or body. In some countries scorpion antitoxin is available. (In Latin America it is called *Antialacrán,* p. 372). To do much good it must be injected within 2 hours after the child has been stung. Give aspirin or acetaminophen for the pain. If the child stops breathing, use mouth-to-mouth breathing (see p. 80). If the child who was stung is very young or has been stung on the main part of the body, or if you know the scorpion was of a deadly type—seek medical help fast.

BLACK WIDOW AND OTHER SPIDER BITES

The majority of spider bites, including that of the tarantula, are painful but not dangerous. The bite of a few kinds of spiders—such as the 'black widow' and related species—can make an adult quite ill. They can be dangerous for a small child. A black widow bite often causes extreme pain in the stomach muscles. (Sometimes this is confused with appendicitis!)

Give aspirin and look for medical help. The most useful medicines are not found in village stores. (Injection of 10% calcium gluconate, 10 ml., injected intravenously **very slowly** over a 10-minute period, helps to reduce the muscular spasms. Also diazepam, p. 374, may be helpful. If signs of shock develop, treat for allergic shock, p. 70. Injections of cortisone may be needed in children.)

CHAPTER

11

NUTRITION:
WHAT TO EAT TO BE HEALTHY

SICKNESSES CAUSED BY NOT EATING WELL

Good food is needed for a person to grow well, work hard, and stay healthy. Many common sicknesses come from not eating enough of the foods the body needs.

A person who is weak or sick because he does not eat the right foods, or does not eat enough, is said to be poorly nourished—or *malnourished.* He suffers from *malnutrition.*

Poor nutrition is the most common cause of the following health problems:

in children

- failure of a child to grow or gain weight normally (see p. 301)

- slowness in walking, talking, or thinking

- swollen bellies, thin arms and legs

- sadness, lack of energy

- swelling of feet, face, and hands, often with sores or marks on the skin

- thinning or loss of hair, or loss of its color or shine

- dryness of eyes, blindness

in anyone

- weakness and tiredness

- loss of appetite

- anemia

- sores in the corners of the mouth

- painful or sore tongue

- 'burning' or numbness of the feet

Although the following problems may have other causes, they are often caused or made worse by not eating well:

- diarrhea

- ringing or buzzing in the ears

- headache

- bleeding or redness of the gums

- nosebleeds

- stomach discomfort

- dryness and cracking of the skin

- fits or convulsions in small children

- heavy pulsing of the heart (palpitations)

- anxiety (nervous worry) and various nerve or mental problems

- cirrhosis (liver disease)

- frequent infections

Eating right helps the body resist sickness.

Not eating well may be the direct cause of the health problems just listed. But in addition, poor nutrition weakens the body's ability to resist all kinds of diseases, especially infections:

- Poorly nourished children are much more likely to get severe diarrhea, and to die from it, than are children who are well nourished.

- Measles are especially dangerous in children who are malnourished.

- Tuberculosis is more common, and gets worse more rapidly, in those who are malnourished.

- Cirrhosis of the liver, which comes in part from drinking too much alcohol, is more common and worse in persons who are poorly nourished.

- Even minor problems like the common cold are often worse and last longer in persons who are poorly nourished.

Eating right helps the sick get well.

Not only does good food help prevent disease, it also helps the sick body fight disease and become well again. So when a person is sick, nutritious food is especially important.

Unfortunately, some mothers stop giving a child nutritious foods when he is sick or has diarrhea—so the child becomes weaker, cannot fight off the illness, and may die. **Sick children need nutritious food! If a sick child will not eat, encourage him to do so.**

Often the signs of poor nutrition first appear when a person has some other sickness. For example, a child who has had diarrhea for several days may develop swollen hands and feet, a swollen face, purple spots, or peeling sores on his legs. These are signs of malnutrition. The child needs more good food!

During and after any sickness, it is very important to eat nutritious food.

EATING WELL
AND KEEPING
CLEAN
ARE THE
BEST
GUARANTEES
OF GOOD
HEALTH

The patches on this mother's arms are a sign of pellagra, a type of malnutrition. She ate mostly maize and not enough nutritious foods such as beans, eggs, fruit, meat, and dark green vegetables.

Because she was not eating well, her breasts did not produce milk for her baby. As a result, he suffers from extreme malnutrition. The child was 2 years old when this picture was taken. He is very small and thin with a swollen belly, his hair is thin, and probably he will be mentally slow (retarded) for the rest of his life.

To prevent this, mothers and their children must eat better.

FOODS OUR BODIES NEED TO STAY HEALTHY

To be healthy and strong our bodies need a balance of different nutritious foods every day. At every meal we should eat something from each of these four food groups:

1. Body-Building Foods or Proteins:

Proteins are body-building foods. They are necessary for proper growth, for making healthy muscles, brains, and many other parts of our bodies. To grow and be strong **everyone should eat enough protein every day.**

Foods high in protein:

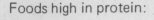

meat	milk
chicken	cheese
eggs	soybeans
fish	insects
seafood	

Foods with some protein:

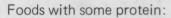

beans	groundnuts (peanuts)
peas	dark green leafy vegetables
lentils	cereals (wheat, oats, millet, etc.)
nuts	

2. Energy Foods or Carbohydrates: Sugars and Starches:

Starches and sugars are energy foods. They are like wood for our fires. The harder a person works, the more energy foods he needs. But a diet of these foods alone, without proteins, makes our bodies weak.

Starches:

maize (corn)
cereals (wheat, rice, oats, millet, sorghum)
noodles (pasta)
potatoes
sweet potatoes, yams
squash
cassava (manioc)
plantain (cooking bananas)
taro (eddo, poi)

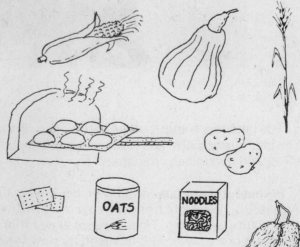

Sugars:

sugar	fruit
honey	sweet ripe banana
raw sugar, molasses	milk

3. Energy Storage Foods: Fats and Oils:

Fat is a concentrated form of stored energy. Our bodies change fat into sugar when more energy is needed. To eat a lot of fat can be harmful, but eating some fat or oil with each meal is healthy.

Foods high in fat:

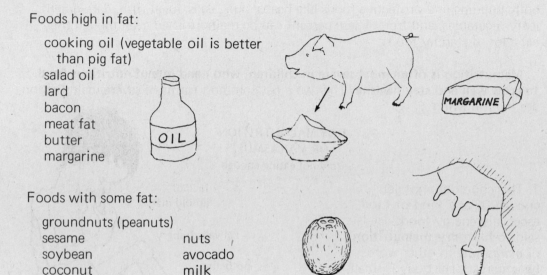

cooking oil (vegetable oil is better than pig fat)
salad oil
lard
bacon
meat fat
butter
margarine

Foods with some fat:

groundnuts (peanuts)
sesame   nuts
soybean   avocado
coconut   milk

4. Protective Foods: Those Rich in Vitamins and Minerals:

Vitamins are protective foods. They help our bodies work properly. We become sick if we do not eat foods with all the necessary vitamins.

Minerals are needed for making healthy blood, bones, and teeth.

Foods rich in vitamins and minerals:

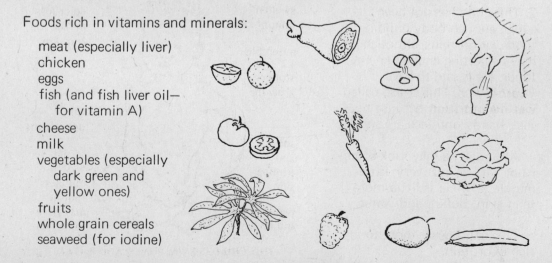

meat (especially liver)
chicken
eggs
fish (and fish liver oil—
     for vitamin A)
cheese
milk
vegetables (especially
     dark green and
     yellow ones)
fruits
whole grain cereals
seaweed (for iodine)

WHAT IT MEANS TO EAT RIGHT

To eat right means **to eat enough.** But it also means **to eat a balance of the different foods the body needs.** To be healthy, a person needs to eat enough foods from each of the food groups just described. Many people get large amounts of starchy energy foods like rice, maize, cassava, or plantain, but not enough body-building and protective foods like beans, nuts, eggs, meat, fish, dark green leafy vegetables, and fruit. These persons can be malnourished even though they eat a lot of starchy foods.

Malnutrition is often most severe in children, who need lots of nutritious food to grow well and stay healthy. The two most common forms of severe malnutrition are the following:

DRY MALNUTRITION OR MARASMUS
—from not eating enough—

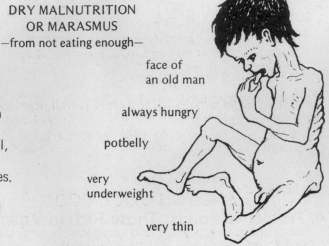

1. This child does not get enough of any kind of food, especially energy foods. He is said to have **dry malnutrition** or *marasmus.* In other words, he is starved. His body is small, very thin, and wasted. He is little more than skin and bones.

face of an old man

always hungry

potbelly

very underweight

very thin

This child needs more food —especially energy foods.

THIS CHILD IS JUST *SKIN* AND *BONES*.

WET MALNUTRITION OR KWASHIORKOR
—from not eating enough protein—

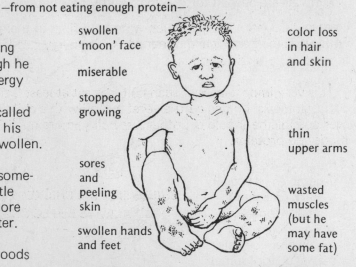

2. This child has not been eating enough body-building foods, or proteins, although he may be getting enough energy foods. He is said to have *kwashiorkor.* This is also called **wet malnutrition** because his feet, hands, and face are swollen.

Although he may look somewhat fat, he has very little muscle left. He is little more than skin, bones, and water.

This child needs more foods rich in protein.

swollen 'moon' face

miserable

stopped growing

sores and peeling skin

swollen hands and feet

color loss in hair and skin

thin upper arms

wasted muscles (but he may have some fat)

THIS CHILD IS *SKIN*, *BONES*, AND *WATER*.

Kwashiorkor often first appears when a child has diarrhea or another infection. It is seen most often in babies who stopped breast feeding and who are given foods made with rice, corn, sugar, or other energy foods, without enough milk or other protein-rich food.

Because of swelling, and because he may even have some fat, the child with kwashiorkor may look plump rather than thin. But his muscles are wasted, and if you look at his upper arms, you will find them surprisingly thin.

Neither kwashiokor nor marasmus develops all at once. A child may already be fairly malnourished and still show few signs. A good way to check if a child is poorly nourished is to measure the distance around his upper arm.

Checking for Malnutrition: The Sign of the Upper Arm:

less than 13 cm.

After 1 year of age, any child whose upper arm measures less than 13 cm. around is malnourished—no matter how 'fat' his feet, hands, and face may look. If the arm measures less than 12 cm., he is severely malnourished.

Another good way to tell if a child is well nourished or poorly nourished is to weigh him once a month. A healthy, well-nourished child gains weight regularly. The weighing of children and the use of the Road to Health Chart is discussed fully in Chapter 21, page 297.

GETTING ENOUGH GOOD FOOD

Some children are weak and underweight and begin to swell or show other signs of 'wet' malnutrition even though they are getting some milk and other body-building foods. This is often because they are not getting enough energy foods ,so they 'burn up' the protein they should be using to grow and make their bodies strong.

Certain bulky foods like plantains (cooked green bananas) and roots (yams, cassava, taro, etc.) have so much water and fiber in them that the child gets full without getting enough food to meet his energy needs. His belly cannot hold more, but he is still starving.

It is very important that such children eat at least 3 times a day, **and also snack between meals.** Mixing a little vegetable oil with a child's food also helps. Whenever possible he should eat other less bulky, more nutritious foods—both energy foods and proteins.

CHILDREN, LIKE CHICKENS,
SHOULD ALWAYS BE PECKING.

Prevention and treatment of malnutrition:

Both marasmus and kwashiorkor can be prevented or treated by eating a balance of nutritious foods and by eating enough. For babies, breast milk is the best complete food. Breast feeding should be continued as long as possible. Some mothers breast feed their babies for 2 years or longer. After the first 4 to 6 months the baby should begin to get other nutritious foods in addition to breast milk. This is discussed more fully on page 122.

Children with kwashiorkor need extra protein. Powdered nonfat milk, if available, often works well. It should be mixed with a small amount of honey or sugar and cooking oil if the child is not getting enough energy foods (see p. 110 and 121). Eggs, chicken, meat, and fish are high in protein, but expensive. Beans, peas, lentils, and groundnuts (peanuts) also have protein, and are cheaper. To be easily digested, the beans should have their skins peeled off and be well cooked and mashed. Soybeans are very high in protein, and a flour made from them can be mixed with other foods such as rice, wheat, peanuts, or sesame to increase the protein content.

Other forms of malnutrition:

Among poor people the most common forms of malnutrition are due either to hunger (marasmus) or lack of protein (kwashiorkor). However, other forms of malnutrition may result when certain vitamins and minerals are missing from the foods people eat. For example:

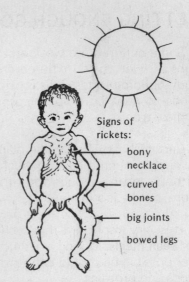

Signs of rickets:

bony necklace

curved bones

big joints

bowed legs

SUNLIGHT IS THE BEST PREVENTION AND TREATMENT OF RICKETS.

• Young children who eat no yellow or dark green fruits and vegetables, or other foods rich in vitamin A may develop night blindness, dry eyes, and eventually go blind (see p. 226).

• Children who do not drink milk and whose skin is almost never exposed to the sunlight may become bowlegged and develop other bone deformities (rickets). While this problem can be corrected by giving the child milk and vitamin D (found in fish liver oil), the easiest and cheapest form of prevention and treatment is to be sure sunlight reaches the child's skin.

• Persons who do not eat enough foods with iron, such as eggs, dark green leafy vegetables, or meat, may develop anemia (see p. 125).

• A number of skin problems (p. 208), sores on the lips and mouth (p. 232), or bleeding gums may come from not eating fruits, vegetables, and other foods containing certain vitamins (see p. 111).

These and other problems related to nutrition are discussed more fully in this and other chapters.

WAYS OF EATING BETTER WHEN YOU DO NOT HAVE MUCH MONEY OR LAND

There are many reasons for hunger and poor nutrition. One reason is poverty. In many parts of the world a few people own most of the wealth and the land. They may grow crops like coffee or tobacco, which they sell to make more money, but which have no nutritional value. Or the poor may farm small plots of borrowed land, while the owners take a big share of the harvest. **The problem of hunger and poor nutrition will never be completely solved until people learn to share with each other fairly.**

But there are many things poor persons can do to eat better at low cost—and by eating well gain strength to stand up for their rights. On pages w13 and w14 of "Words to the Village Health Worker" you will find several suggestions for achieving better nutrition. These include improved use of land through **rotating crops, contour ditches,** and **irrigation;** also **breeding fish, beekeeping,** improved **grain storage,** and planting **family gardens.** If the whole village or a group of families works together on some of these things, a lot can be done to improve nutrition.

When considering the question of food and land, it is important to remember that **a given amount of land can feed only a certain number of persons.** If the amount of land and other resources your family has is limited, it is wise to plan ahead and only have the number of children that you can feed well. More children may mean more hands to do work, but it does not necessarily mean more land to work.

Hungry children do not work well, and many of them die.

Small family size is becoming increasingly important for good nutrition. Think about this and plan ahead. A discussion of the balance between people and land is found on page w16. For a discussion of family planning, see Chapter 20.

When money is limited, it is important to use it wisely. This means cooperation and looking ahead. Too often the father of a poor family will spend the little bit of money he has on alcohol and tobacco rather than on buying nutritious food, a hen to lay eggs, or something to improve the family's health. Men who drink together would do well to get together sometime when they are sober, to discuss these problems and look for a healthy solution.

Also, mothers sometimes buy sweets or soft drinks (fizzy drinks) for their children when they could spend the same money buying eggs, milk, or other nutritious foods. This way their children could become more healthy for the same amount of money.

NO
YES

IF YOU HAVE A LITTLE MONEY AND WANT TO HELP YOUR CHILD GROW STRONG:

DO NOT BUY HIM A SOFT DRINK OR SWEETS— BUY HIM A COUPLE OF EGGS.

Better Foods at Low Cost:

Many of the world's people eat a lot of starchy foods, or carbohydrates, and not enough foods rich in protein, vitamins, and minerals. This is because most of these 'better' foods cost so much. Animal protein like milk and meat is very nutritious, but also expensive. Animals also require more land for the amount of protein they provide.

Most people cannot afford much food from animals. In fact, a poor family can usually get more protein and good nutrition if they **grow or buy plant foods high in protein, like beans, peas, lentils, groundnuts, and dark green leafy vegetables, rather than expensive animal foods like meat and fish.**

> **People can be strong and healthy when most of their protein comes from plants.**

However, it is wise to eat a little animal protein with most meals. This is because even plants high in protein often do not have all of the different proteins the body needs.

Try to **eat a variety of plant foods** rather than mostly one or two. Different plants supply the body with different proteins, vitamins, and minerals. For example, beans and maize together meet the body's needs much better than either beans or maize alone. And if other vegetables and fruits are added, this is even better.

Here are some suggestions for getting more proteins, vitamins, and minerals at low cost.

1. **Breast milk.** This is the cheapest, healthiest, and most complete food for a baby. The mother can eat plenty of plant protein and turn it into the perfect baby food—breast milk. Breast feeding is not only best for the baby, it saves money!

2. **Eggs and chicken.** In many places eggs are one of the cheapest and best forms of animal protein. They can be mixed with foods given to babies who cannot get breast milk. Or they can be given along with breast milk as the baby grows older.

Eggshells, ground up and mixed with food, can provide needed calcium for pregnant women who develop sore, loose teeth or muscle cramps.

Chicken is a good, often fairly cheap form of animal protein—especially if the family raises its own chickens.

3. **Liver, heart, kidney, and blood.**
These are especially high in protein,
vitamins, and iron (for anemia) and
are often cheaper than other meat.
Also **fish** is often cheaper than other
meat, but is just as nutritious.

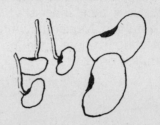

4. **Beans and other legumes** (peas,
lentils, etc.) are a good cheap source
of protein, especially **soybeans.** If
allowed to sprout before cooking and
eating, they are higher in vitamins.
Baby food can be made from beans by
cooking them well, peeling off their
skins, and mashing them.

Beans, peas, and other legumes are
not only a low-cost form of protein.
Growing these crops makes the
soil richer so that other crops will
grow better afterwards. For this
reason, crop rotation is a good idea
(see p. w13).

5. **Dark green leafy vegetables** have a
modest amount of protein, some iron,
and a lot of vitamin A. The leaves of
sweet potatoes, beans and peas,
pumpkins and squash, and baobab are
especially nutritious. They can be
dried, powdered, and mixed with
babies' gruel to add to the protein and
vitamin content.

Light green leafy vegetables like
lettuce and cabbage contain very little
protein or vitamins. In terms of
nutritional value, they are not worth
growing.

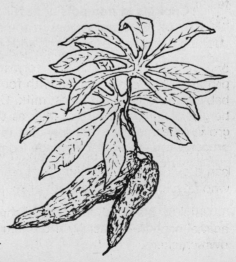

6. **Cassava leaves** contain 7 times
as much protein and more vitamins
than the root. If eaten together with
the root, they have more food value—at
no additional cost. The young leaves are best.

7. **Dried maize (corn).** When soaked in lime before cooking, as is the custom in much of Latin America, maize is richer in calcium. Soaking in lime also allows more of the vitamins (niacin) and protein to be used by the body.

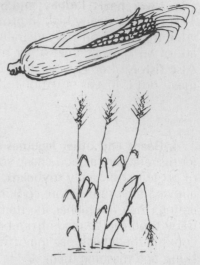

8. **Rice, wheat, and other grains** are more nutritious if their inner skins are not removed during milling. Moderately milled rice and whole wheat contain more vitamins than the white, over-milled product.

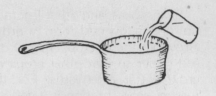

9. **Cook vegetables, rice, and other foods in little water.** And do not overcook. This way fewer vitamins and proteins are lost. Be sure to drink the leftover water, or use it for soups.

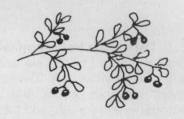

10. Many **wild fruits and berries** are rich in vitamin C as well as natural sugars. They can provide a good vitamin and food supplement. (Be sure to eat only those which are not poisonous.)

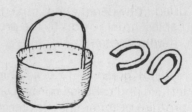

11. **Cooking in iron pots** or putting a piece of old iron or rusty horseshoes in the pan when cooking beans and other foods adds iron to food and helps prevent anemia.

12. In some countries **low-cost infant food preparations** are available, made from different combinations of soybean, cotton seed, skim milk, or dried fish. Some taste better than others, but most are balanced protein foods. When mixed with gruel, cooked cereal, or other baby food, they add to its nutrition content—at low cost.

INCAP-ARINA

WHERE TO GET VITAMINS:
IN PILLS, INJECTIONS, SYRUPS—OR IN FOODS?

Anyone who eats well gets all the vitamins he needs. It is always better to eat well than to buy vitamin pills, injections, syrups, or tonics.

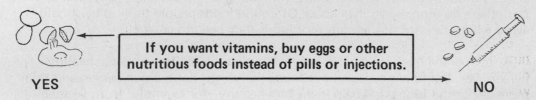

YES

If you want vitamins, buy eggs or other nutritious foods instead of pills or injections.

NO

Sometimes nutritious foods are scarce. If a person is already poorly nourished, he should eat as well as he can and perhaps take vitamins besides.

In almost all cases vitamins taken by mouth work as well as injections, cost less, and are not as dangerous. **Do not inject vitamins! It is better to swallow them—preferably in the form of nutritious foods.**

If you buy vitamin preparations, be sure they have all the vitamins and minerals commonly lacking in a high carbohydrate diet. These are:

Niacin (niacinamide)

Vitamin B_1 (thiamine)

Vitamin B_2 (riboflavin)

Iron (ferrous sulfate, etc.)—especially for pregnant women and persons with anemia

In addition, certain people need extra:

Folic Acid (folicin), for pregnant women

Vitamin A

Vitamin C
  (ascorbic acid) } for small children

Vitamin D

Vitamin B_6 (pyridoxine), for small children and persons taking medicine for tuberculosis

Calcium, for children and nursing mothers who do not get enough calcium in foods such as milk and cheese, or foods prepared with lime

THINGS TO AVOID IN OUR DIET

A lot of people believe that there are many kinds of foods that will hurt them or that they should not eat when they are sick. They may think of some kinds of foods as 'hot' and others as 'cold', and not permit hot foods for 'hot' sicknesses or cold foods for 'cold' sicknesses. Or they may believe that many different foods are bad for a mother with a newborn child. Some of these beliefs are reasonable but others do more harm than good. Often the foods people think they should avoid when they are sick are the very foods they need to get well.

A sick person has even greater need for body-building foods than a healthy person. We should worry less about foods that might harm a sick person and think more about the foods that help make him healthy—for example: fruit, vegetables, milk, meat, eggs, and fish. As a general rule:

> **The same foods that are good for us when we are healthy are good for us when we are sick.**

Also, the things that harm us when we are healthy do us even more harm when we are sick. Avoid these things:

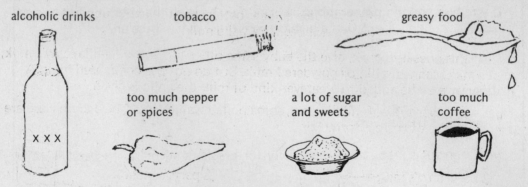

alcoholic drinks   tobacco   greasy food

too much pepper   a lot of sugar   too much
or spices   and sweets   coffee

■ Alcohol causes or makes worse diseases of the liver, stomach, and nerves. It also causes social problems.

■ Smoking can cause chronic (long-term) coughing or lung cancer and other problems (see p. 149). Smoking is especially bad for people with lung diseases like tuberculosis, asthma, and bronchitis.

■ Too much greasy food, hot spices, or coffee can cause stomach ulcers and other problems of the digestive tract.

■ Too much sugar and sweets spoils the appetite, rots the teeth, can cause heart problems, and may be part of the cause of intestinal cancer. However, some sugar may help give needed energy to a very sick person or poorly nourished child.

A few diseases require not eating certain other foods. For example, people with high blood pressure, certain heart problems, or swollen feet should use little or no salt. Too much salt is not good for anyone. Stomach ulcers and diabetes also require special diets (see p. 127 and 128).

THE BEST DIET FOR SMALL CHILDREN

THE FIRST 4 TO 6 MONTHS OF LIFE:

> **For the first 4 months give the baby mother's milk and nothing else.**

Breast milk is the best and purest food for babies. It is better than any baby food or formula you can buy. If you give the baby only breast milk during the first 4 to 6 months, this helps protect him against diarrhea and many infections.

If the mother's breasts do not make enough milk:

♦ The mother should drink a lot of water or other liquids. The more liquid she drinks the more milk she will produce.

♦ The mother should eat better. Foods with proteins and vitamins—beans, dark green leafy vegetables, meat, milk, cheese, and eggs—will help her make more milk for her baby.

If the mother's breasts do not give any milk:

♦ Have her drink a lot of liquids and eat better. Let the baby suck her breasts often. Sometimes her breasts will begin to make milk.

♦ If this does not work, give the baby some other type of milk—like cow's milk, goat's milk, canned milk, or powdered milk. But do not use condensed milk. A little sugar may be added to whatever kind of milk the child is given.

Note: Whatever type of milk is used, some boiled water should be added. Here are two examples of correct formulas:

#1.

2 parts cow's milk
1 part boiled water
1 teaspoon sugar

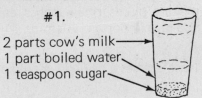

#2.

2 parts canned evaporated milk
3 parts boiled water
1 teaspoon sugar

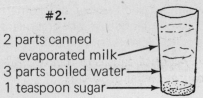

If non-fat milk is used, add a tablespoon of cooking or vegetable oil to the formula.

♦ Always boil the milk and water. **It is safer to feed the baby with a cup and spoon than to use a baby bottle.** Baby bottles and nipples are difficult to keep clean and cause many infections, including diarrhea (see p. 154). If a bottle is used, both it and the nipple should be boiled each time before the baby is fed.

♦ If there is not enough money to buy milk for the child, make a porridge from rice, cornmeal, or other cereal. Always add to this some skinned beans, eggs, meat, chicken, or other protein. These should be well mashed and given as a liquid.

> *WARNING:* **Cornmeal or rice water alone is not nutritious enough for a baby. The child will not grow properly or walk or speak on time. He will get sick easily and may die. THE BABY MUST HAVE SOME FORM OF PROTEIN.**

FROM 4 MONTHS TO 1 YEAR OF AGE:

1. Continue to give the baby breast milk, if possible until he reaches 2 years of age.

2. When the baby is between 4 and 6 months old, start giving him other foods as well. These foods need to be well cooked and mashed. Inexpensive, nutritious feedings can be made by combining at least 1 food from each group.

Animal protein	Vegetable protein	Carbohydrates	Fats
boiled or powdered milk	beans	cornmeal	any local cooking oil
eggs	lentils or peas	rice	
meat	groundnuts (peanuts)	wheat or oats	
chicken	soybeans	cooked potatoes	
cheese	nuts	noodles	
fish	dark green leafy vegetables	squash	

Here are some examples of balanced feedings using foods from each group:

Feeding 1	**Feeding 2**
4 spoons cornmeal	4 spoons cooked rice
1 spoon cooked beans	2 spoons well-cooked young string beans
1 spoon powdered milk	1 cooked egg
½ spoon cooking oil	½ spoon cooking oil

Children older than 4 to 6 months should also be given **juices and fruits** rich in vitamins, such as oranges, tomatoes, papayas, melons, plums, ripe bananas, and cooked mangoes. Dark green leafy vegetables also give important vitamins. They should be well cooked and mashed.

Children younger than 1 year should eat at least 5 times a day and should also 'snack' in between meals.

CAUTION: The time when children are most likely to become malnourished is between 6 months and 1 year old. If they are very pale and thin with a big belly, have swollen feet or face, have large, peeling sores on their skin, eat dirt, or fail to grow and gain weight normally, **they must eat better!**

For children of this age to be healthy we should:

KEEP FEEDING THEM BREAST MILK,

FEED THEM OTHER NUTRITIOUS FOODS ALSO,

BOIL THE WATER THEY DRINK, AND

KEEP THE CHILDREN AND THEIR SURROUNDINGS CLEAN.

ONE YEAR AND OLDER:

After a child is 1 year old, he can eat the same foods as adults, but should also drink milk whenever possible.

Try to give the child foods with plenty of proteins, vitamins, iron, and minerals (as shown on p. 110 and 111) every day, so that he will grow up strong and healthy.

Children and candy: Do not accustom small children to eating candy and sweets or drinking soft drinks (colas). When they have too many sweets, they no longer want the foods that are better for them. Also, sweets are bad for their teeth.

However, when food supply is limited, adding a little sugar and vegetable oil to milk or other food may allow children to make fuller use of the protein in the food they get.

THE BEST DIET FOR CHILDREN

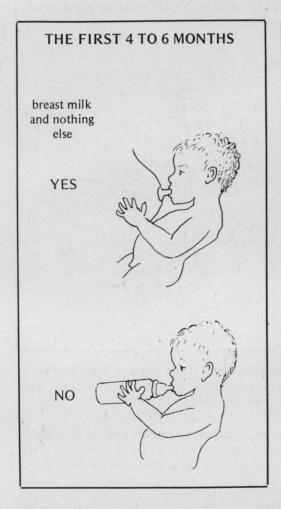

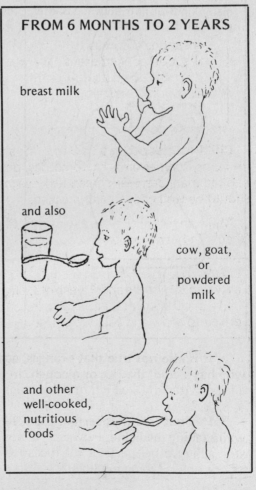

HARMFUL IDEAS ABOUT DIET

1. The diet of mothers after giving birth:

In many areas there is a dangerous popular belief that a woman who has just had a baby should not eat certain foods. This folk diet—which forbids the new mother some of the most nutritious foods and permits her to eat little more than cornmeal, noodles, or rice soup—makes the mother weak and anemic. It may even cause her death, by lowering her resistance to hemorrhage and infection.

> **After giving birth a mother needs to eat the most nutritious foods she can get.**

In order to fight infections or bleeding and to produce enough milk for her child, **a new mother should eat plenty of body-building foods like beans, eggs, chicken, milk products, meat, fish, fruits, and vegetables.** None of these foods will harm her; all bring better health.

Here is a healthy mother who ate many kinds of nutritious foods after giving birth:

Here lies a mother who was afraid to eat nutritious foods after giving birth:

2. It is also not true that oranges, guavas, or other fruits are bad for a person who has a cold, the flu, or a cough. In fact, fruits like oranges and tomatoes have a lot of vitamin C, which may help fight colds and other infections.

3. It is not true that certain foods like pork, spices, or guavas cannot be eaten while taking medicine. However, eating fat or spices when one has a disease of the stomach or other parts of the digestive system may make things worse—whether or not one is taking medicines.

HEALTH PROBLEMS RELATED TO WHAT PEOPLE EAT

Special diets are the best prevention and treatment for certain diseases. Here are some of these diseases:

ANEMIA

A person with anemia has thin blood. This happens when blood is lost or destroyed faster than his body can replace it. Blood loss from large wounds, bleeding ulcers, or dysentery can cause anemia. So can the monthly bleeding (menstrual period) of women, if they do not eat the foods their bodies need.

A diet lacking meat, dark green leafy vegetables, and other foods rich in iron can cause anemia or make it worse.

In children anemia can come from not eating foods rich in iron. It can also come from breast feeding or bottle feeding a baby after 6 months without giving other foods, too. Common causes of severe anemia in children are hookworm infection (see p. 142), chronic diarrhea, and dysentery.

Malaria, which destroys red blood cells, can also cause anemia.

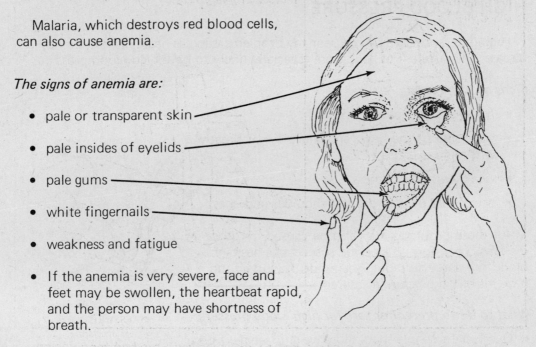

The signs of anemia are:

- pale or transparent skin

- pale insides of eyelids

- pale gums

- white fingernails

- weakness and fatigue

- If the anemia is very severe, face and feet may be swollen, the heartbeat rapid, and the person may have shortness of breath.

- Children and women who like to eat dirt are usually anemic.

Treatment and prevention of anemia:

- **Eat foods rich in iron.** Meat, fish, chicken, and eggs are high in iron. Liver is especially high. Dark green leafy vegetables, beans, peas, and lentils also have some iron.

• If foods rich in iron are hard to get, or if the anemia is severe, the person should take iron (ferrous sulfate pills, p. 376). This is especially important for pregnant women who are anemic. For nearly all cases of anemia, ferrous sulfate tablets are much better than liver extract or vitamin B$_{12}$. As a general rule, **iron should be given by mouth, not injected,** because iron injections are dangerous.

• If the anemia is caused by dysentery (diarrhea with blood), hookworm, malaria, or another disease, this should also be treated.

• If the anemia is severe or does not get better, seek medical help. This is especially important for a pregnant woman.

Many women are anemic. This is often because they do not eat enough foods rich in iron to replace the blood they lose during menstrual periods or with childbirth. Anemic women run a greater risk of miscarriage and of dangerous bleeding in childbirth. For this reason it is very important that women eat beans, dark green vegetables, and as much meat, chicken, and eggs as possible, especially during pregnancy. Family planning—allowing 2 to 3 years between pregnancies—lets the woman regain strength and make new blood (see Chapter 20).

HIGH BLOOD PRESSURE

High blood pressure can cause many problems, such as heart disease, kidney disease, and stroke. Fat people are especially likely to have high blood pressure.

Signs of high blood pressure:

- frequent headaches
- pounding of the heart and shortness of breath with mild exercise
- weakness and dizziness
- occasional pain in the left shoulder and chest

All these problems may also be caused by other diseases. Therefore, if a person suspects he has high blood pressure, he should see a health worker and have his blood pressure measured.

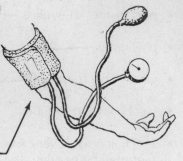

A BLOOD PRESSURE CUFF for measuring blood pressure

What to do to prevent or care for high blood pressure:

• Overweight people should lose weight (see next page).

• Fatty foods, especially pig fat, and foods with a lot of sugar or starch should be avoided. Always use vegetable oil instead of pig fat.

• Food should be prepared and eaten with little or no salt.

• When the blood pressure is very high, the health worker may give medicines to lower it. Many people can lower their blood pressure by losing weight if they are fat (next page), and by learning to relax.

FAT PEOPLE

To be very fat is not healthy. Too much fat helps cause high blood pressure, heart disease, stroke, gallstones, diabetes, arthritis in legs and feet, and other problems.

Fat people should lose weight by:

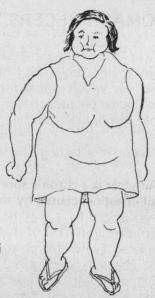

* not eating greasy, fatty, or oily foods.
* not eating sugar or sweet foods.
* getting more exercise.
* **not eating so much** of anything, especially starchy foods, like corn, bread, potatoes, rice, pasta, cassava, etc. Fat people should not eat more than one piece of bread, tortilla, or chapati with each meal. However, they can eat more fruit, vegetables, and lean meat.

> **To lose weight, eat only half of what you now eat.**

DIABETES

Persons with diabetes have too much sugar in their blood.

The signs of diabetes are:

* continual thirst
* urinating often and a lot
* unexplained tiredness
* itching and long-term skin infections

And in severe cases:

* weight loss
* numbness or pain in the hands or feet
* sores on the feet that do not heal
* loss of consciousness

All of these signs may be caused by other diseases, too. In order to find out whether a person has diabetes, his urine should be tested to see if there is sugar in it. One way of testing the urine is to taste it. If it tastes sweet to you, have 2 other persons taste it. Have them also taste 3 other people's urine. If everyone agrees that the same person's urine is sweeter, he is probably diabetic.

Another way of testing the urine is to use special paper strips (for example, *Uristix*). If these change color when dipped in the urine, it has sugar in it.

When a person gets diabetes after he is 40 years old, it can often be best controlled without medicines, by eating correctly. **The diabetic person's diet is very important and must be followed carefully for life.**

The diabetic diet: Fat people with diabetes should lose weight until their weight is normal. **Diabetics must not eat any sugar or sweets.** They should eat foods high in protein (eggs, fish, beans, dark green leafy vegetables, nuts, lean meat, etc.) and low in starch.

Some diabetic persons—especially the young—need special medicine (insulin).

STOMACH ULCERS, HEARTBURN, AND ACID INDIGESTION

Acid indigestion and 'heartburn' often come from eating too much heavy or greasy food or from drinking too much alcohol. These make the stomach produce extra acid, which causes discomfort or a 'burning' feeling in the stomach or mid-chest. Some people mistake the chest pain called 'heartburn' for a heart problem rather than indigestion.

Frequent or lasting acid indigestion is a warning sign of an ulcer.

An ulcer is a chronic sore in the stomach or small intestine, caused by too much acid. It can be recognized by a chronic, dull (sometimes sharp) pain in the pit of the stomach. Often the pain lessens when the person eats food or drinks milk. The pain gets worse 2 or 3 hours after eating, if the person misses a meal, or after he drinks alcohol or eats fatty or spicy foods. Pain is often worse at night.

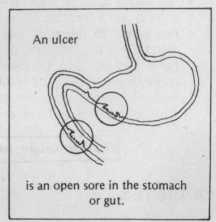

An ulcer

is an open sore in the stomach or gut.

If the ulcer is severe, it can cause vomiting, sometimes with blood. Stools with blood from an ulcer are usually black, like tar.

Prevention and treatment:

• Eat foods that heal ulcers instead of those which irritate them:

These cure ulcers:	These do no harm:	These make ulcers worse:
boiled milk	boiled or poached eggs	alcoholic drinks
cheese	saltine crackers	coffee
cream	plain noodle soup	cigarettes
oats	boiled potatoes	spices and pepper
bananas	squash	carbonated drinks
	pancakes	(soda pop, colas)
	ripe bananas	greasy food

• Milk is one of the best medicines for ulcers or acid indigestion. If the ulcer is severe, drink a glass of milk every hour for the first few days and eat only things listed in the first column above (those which cure ulcers). In a few days, when the pain lessens, begin eating things in the center column (those which do no harm). For a few months, it is a good idea to drink some milk with each meal and also in mid-morning, in the afternoon, and again before going to bed (6 times a day).

• Antacids, such as milk of magnesia or magnesium and aluminum hydroxide (p. 367), also help fight stomach acid and cure ulcers. If pain is severe, an antispasmodic may help (see p. 367).

• Even after the ulcer is cured the person should never eat any of the things in the right-hand column above (those which make ulcers worse), as these may cause the ulcer to return. If possible, he should keep taking antacids or milk at bedtime.

THESE TWO MEN HAD STOMACH ULCERS

This man ate these foods:

This man ate, smoked, and drank these:

and got well.

and got worse.

It is important to cure an ulcer early. Otherwise it may lead to dangerous bleeding or peritonitis. Ulcers usually get better if the person is careful with what he eats and drinks. Anger, tension, and nervousness make ulcers worse. Learning to relax and keep calm will help. Continued care is necessary to prevent the ulcer from returning.

Better still, **avoid ever getting an ulcer by eating wisely, not drinking much, and not smoking.**

CONSTIPATION

A person who has hard stools and has not had a bowel movement for 2 or more days is said to be constipated. Constipation is often caused by a poor diet (especially not eating enough fruits, green vegetables, or foods with natural fiber) or by lack of exercise.

Drinking more water and eating more fruits, vegetables, and foods with natural fiber like cassava or wheat bran is better than using laxatives. Older people may need to walk or exercise more in order to have regular bowel movements.

A person who has not had a bowel movement for 3 or more days, if he does not have a sharp pain in his stomach, can take a mild salt laxative like milk of magnesia. **But do not take laxatives often.**

> **Never use strong laxatives or purgatives—
> especially if there is stomach pain.**

GOITER (A SWELLING OR MASS ON THE THROAT)

A goiter is a swelling or large mass on the throat that results from abnormal growth of a gland called the thyroid.

Most goiters are caused by a lack of iodine in the diet. Also, a lack of iodine in a pregnant woman's diet sometimes causes babies to die or be born mentally slow and/or deaf (cretinism, p. 318). This can happen even though the mother does not have a goiter.

How to prevent or cure a goiter and prevent cretinism:

Everyone living in areas where people get goiters should use **iodized salt.** Use of iodized salt prevents the common kind of goiter and will help many goiters go away. (Old, hard goiters can only be removed by surgery, but this is not usually necessary.)

If it is not possible to get iodized salt, use tincture of iodine. Put 1 drop in a glass of water each day and drink. BE CAREFUL: Too much tincture of iodine is poisonous. Drink only 1 drop a day. Keep the bottle where children cannot reach it. Iodized salt is much safer.

Most home cures for goiter do not do any good. However, eating crab and other seafood can do some good because they contain iodine. Mixing a little seaweed with food also adds iodine. But the easiest way is to use **iodized salt.**

HOW TO KEEP FROM GETTING A GOITER

NEVER use regular salt.

IODIZED SALT
costs only a little more
than other salt and
is much better.

ALWAYS use iodized salt.

ORDINARY SALT

IODIZED SALT

Note: If a person with a goiter trembles a lot, is very nervous, and has eyes that bulge out, this may be a different kind of goiter (toxic goiter). Seek medical advice.

CHAPTER

12
PREVENTION:
HOW TO AVOID MANY SICKNESSES

An ounce of prevention is worth a pound of cure! If we all took more care to **eat well,** to **keep ourselves, our homes, and our villages clean,** and to **be sure that our children are vaccinated,** we could stop most sicknesses before they start.

CLEANLINESS—AND PROBLEMS THAT COME FROM LACK OF CLEANLINESS

Cleanliness is of great importance in the prevention of many kinds of infections —infections of the gut, the skin, the eyes, the lungs, and the whole body. Personal cleanliness (or *hygiene*) and public cleanliness (or *sanitation*) are both important.

Many common infections of the gut are spread from one person to another because of poor hygiene and poor sanitation. Germs and worms (or their eggs) are passed by the thousands in the *stools* or *feces* (shit) of infected persons. These are carried from the feces of one person to the mouth of another by dirty fingers or *contaminated* food or water. Diseases that are spread or *transmitted* from *feces-to-mouth* in this way, include:

- intestinal worms (several types)

- diarrhea and dysentery (caused by amebas and bacteria)

- hepatitis, typhoid fever, and cholera

- certain other diseases, like polio, are sometimes spread this same way

The way these infections are transmitted can be very direct.

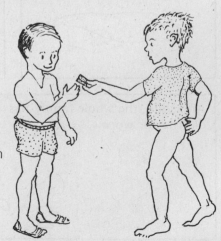

For example: A child who has worms and who forgot to wash his hands after his last bowel movement, offers his friend a cracker. His fingers, still dirty with his own stool, are covered with hundreds of tiny worm eggs (so small they cannot be seen). Some of these worm eggs stick to the cracker. When his friend eats the cracker, he swallows the worm eggs, too.

Soon the friend will also have worms. His mother may say this is because he ate sweets. But no, it is because he ate shit!

Many times pigs, dogs, chickens, and other animals spread intestinal disease and worm eggs. For example:

A man with diarrhea or worms has a bowel movement behind his house.

A pig eats his stool, dirtying its nose and feet.

Then the pig goes into the house.

In the house a child is playing on the floor. In this way, a bit of the man's stool gets on the child, too.

Later the child starts to cry, and the mother takes him in her arms.

Then the mother prepares food, forgetting to wash her hands after handling the child.

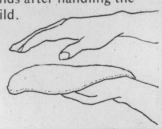

The family eats the food.

And soon, the whole family has diarrhea or worms.

Many kinds of infections, as well as worm eggs, are passed from one person to another in the way just shown.

If the family had taken **any** of the following precautions, the spread of the sickness could have been prevented:

- if the man had used a latrine or out-house,
- if the family had not let the pigs come into the house,
- if they had not let the child play where the pig had been,
- if the mother had washed her hands after touching the child and before preparing food.

If there are many cases of diarrhea, worms, and other intestinal parasites in your village, people are not being careful enough about cleanliness. If many children die from diarrhea, it is likely that poor nutrition is also part of the problem. **To prevent death from diarrhea, both cleanliness and good nutrition are important** (see p. 154 and Chapter 11).

BASIC GUIDELINES OF CLEANLINESS

PERSONAL CLEANLINESS (HYGIENE):

1. Always wash your hands with soap when you get up in the morning, after having a bowel movement, and before eating.

2. Bathe often—every day when the weather is hot. Bathe after working hard or sweating. Frequent bathing helps prevent skin infections, dandruff, pimples, itching, and rashes. Sick persons, including babies, should be bathed daily.

3. In areas where hookworm is common, do not go barefoot or allow children to do so. Hookworm infection causes severe anemia. These worms enter the body through the soles of the feet (see p. 142).

YES   NO

4. Brush your teeth every day and after each time you eat sweets. If you do not have a toothbrush and toothpaste, rub your teeth with salt and baking soda (see p. 230).

CLEANLINESS IN THE HOME:

1. Do not let pigs come into the house or places where children play.

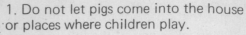

2. Do not let dogs lick children or climb up on beds. Dogs, too, can spread disease.

3. If children or animals have a bowel movement near the house, clean it up at once. Teach them to use a latrine or at least to go farther from the house.

4. Hang or spread sheets and blankets in the sun often. If there are bedbugs, pour boiling water on the cots and wash the sheets and blankets—all on the same day.

5. De-louse the whole family often (see p. 200). Lice and fleas carry many diseases. Dogs and other animals that carry fleas should not come into the house.

6. Do not spit on the floor. Spit can spread disease. When you cough or sneeze, cover your mouth with your hand or a cloth or handkerchief.

7. Clean house often. Sweep and wash the floors, walls, and beneath furniture. Fill in cracks and holes in the floor or walls where roaches, bedbugs, and scorpions can hide.

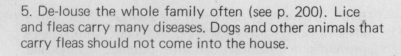

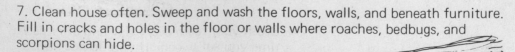

CLEANLINESS IN EATING AND DRINKING:

1. Ideally all water that does not come from a pure water system should be boiled before drinking. This is especially important for small children and at times when there is a lot of diarrhea or cases of typhoid, hepatitis, or cholera. Water from holes or rivers, even when it looks clean, may spread disease if it is not boiled before use.

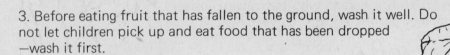

2. Do not let flies and other insects land or crawl on food. These insects carry germs and spread disease. Do not leave food scraps or dirty dishes lying around, as these attract flies and breed germs. Protect food by keeping it covered or in boxes or cabinets with wire screens.

3. Before eating fruit that has fallen to the ground, wash it well. Do not let children pick up and eat food that has been dropped —wash it first.

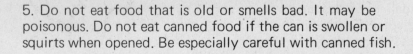

4. Only eat meat that is well cooked. Be careful that roasted meat, especially pork, does not have raw parts inside. Raw pork carries dangerous diseases.

5. Do not eat food that is old or smells bad. It may be poisonous. Do not eat canned food if the can is swollen or squirts when opened. Be especially careful with canned fish.

6. People with tuberculosis, flu, colds, or other infectious diseases should eat separately from others. Plates and utensils used by sick people should be boiled before being used by others.

HOW TO PROTECT YOUR CHILDREN'S HEALTH:

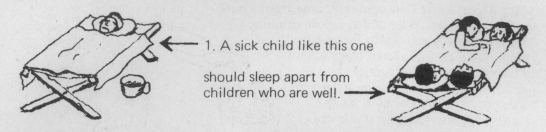

1. A sick child like this one

should sleep apart from children who are well.

Sick children or children with sores, itchy skin, or lice should always sleep separately from those who are well. Children with infectious diseases like whooping cough, measles, or the common cold should sleep in separate rooms, if possible, and should not be allowed near babies or small children.

2. Protect children from tuberculosis. People with long-term coughing or other signs of tuberculosis should cover their mouths whenever they cough. They should **never** sleep in the same room with children. They should see a health worker and be treated as soon as possible.

Children living with a person who has tuberculosis should be vaccinated against TB (B.C.G. Vaccine).

3. Bathe children, change their clothes, and cut their fingernails often. Germs and worm eggs often hide beneath long fingernails.

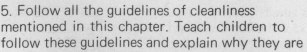

4. Treat children who have infectious diseases as soon as possible, so that the diseases are not spread to others.

5. Follow all the guidelines of cleanliness mentioned in this chapter. Teach children to follow these guidelines and explain why they are important. Encourage children to help with projects that make the home or village a healthier place to live.

6. **Be sure children get enough good food.** Good nutrition helps protect the body against many infections. A well-nourished child will usually resist or fight off infections that can kill a poorly nourished child (read Chapter 11).

PUBLIC CLEANLINESS (SANITATION):

1. Keep wells and public water holes clean. Do not let animals go near where people get drinking water. If necessary, put a fence around the place to keep animals out.

Do not defecate (shit) or throw garbage near the water hole. Take special care to keep rivers and streams clean upstream from any place where drinking water is taken.

2. Burn all garbage that can be burned. Garbage that cannot be burned should be buried in a special pit or place far away from houses and the places where people get drinking water.

3. Build latrines (out-houses, toilets) so pigs and other animals cannot reach the human waste. A deep hole with a little house over it works well.

Here is a drawing of a simple out-house that is easy to build.

It helps to throw a little lime, dirt, or ashes in the hole after each use to reduce the smell and keep flies away.

Out-houses should be built at least 20 meters from homes or the source of water.

If you do not have an out-house, go far away from where people bathe or get drinking water. Teach your children to do the same.

> **Use of latrines helps prevent many sicknesses.**

Ideas for better latrines are found on the next pages. Also latrines can be built to produce good fertilizer for gardens. For plans write to I.T.D.G. or V.I.T.A. (see p. 390).

BETTER LATRINES:

The latrine or out-house shown on the previous page is very simple and costs almost nothing to make. But it is open at the top and lets in flies.

Closed latrines are better because the flies stay out and the smell stays in. A closed latrine has a platform or slab with a hole in it and a lid over the hole. The slab can be made of wood or cement. Cement is better because the slab fits more tightly and will not rot.

One way to make a cement slab:

1. Dig a shallow pit, about 1 meter square and 7 cm. deep. Be sure the bottom of the pit is level and smooth.

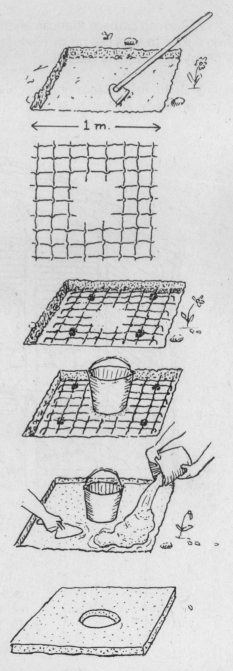

2. Make or cut a wire mesh or grid 1 meter square. The wires can be ¼ to ½ cm. thick and about 10 cm. apart. Cut a hole about 25 cm. across in the middle of the grid.

3. Put the grid in the pit. Bend the ends of the wires, or put a small stone at each corner, so that the grid stands about 3 cm. off the ground.

4. Put an old bucket in the hole in the grid.

5. Mix cement with sand, gravel, and water and pour it until it is about 5 cm. thick. (With each shovel of cement mix 2 shovels of sand and 3 shovels of gravel.)

6. Remove the bucket when the cement is beginning to get hard (about 3 hours). Then cover the cement with damp cloths, sand, hay, or a sheet of plastic and keep it wet. Remove slab after 3 days.

To make the closed latrine, the slab should be placed over a round hole in the ground. Dig the hole a little less than 1 meter across and between 1 and 2 meters deep.

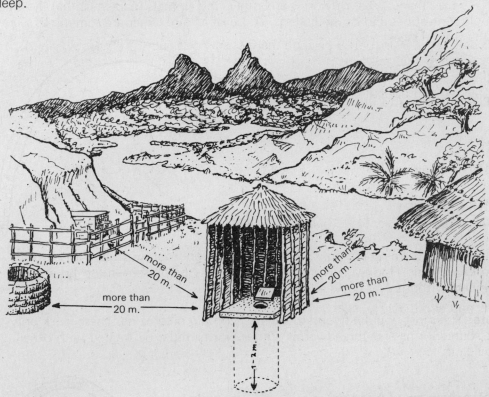

To be safe, the latrine should be at least 20 meters from all houses, wells, springs, rivers, or streams. If it is anywhere near where people go for water, be sure to put the latrine **downstream.**

Keep your latrine clean. Wash the slab often. Teach children and others not to get it dirty.

Be sure the hole in the slab has a cover and that the cover is kept in place. A simple cover can be made of wood.

If you prefer to sit when you use the latrine, you can make a cement seat like this:

You will have to make a mold or you can use 2 buckets of different sizes, one inside the other.

WORMS AND OTHER INTESTINAL PARASITES

There are many types of worms and other tiny animals (parasites) that live in people's intestines and cause diseases. Those which are larger are sometimes seen in the stools (feces):

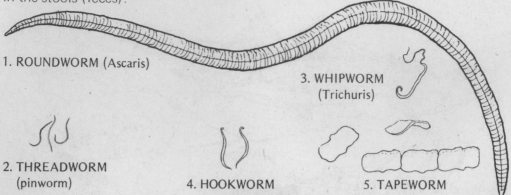

1. ROUNDWORM (Ascaris)

3. WHIPWORM (Trichuris)

2. THREADWORM (pinworm)

4. HOOKWORM

5. TAPEWORM

The only worms commonly seen in the stools are roundworms, threadworms, and tapeworms. Hookworms and whipworms may be present in the gut in large numbers without ever being seen in the stools.

Note: The most popular 'worm medicines' contain piperazine. These work only for roundworms and threadworms. Other worms must be treated with other medicines.

Roundworm (Ascaris):

20 to 30 cm. long. Color: pink or white.

How they are spread:

Feces-to-mouth. Through lack of cleanliness, the roundworm eggs pass from one person's stools to another person's mouth.

Effect on health:

Once the eggs are swallowed, young worms hatch and enter the bloodstream; this may cause general itching. The young worms then travel to the lungs, sometimes causing a dry cough or, at worst, pneumonia with coughing of blood. The young worms are coughed up, swallowed, and reach the intestines, where they grow to full size.

Many roundworms in the intestines may cause discomfort, indigestion, and weakness. Children with many roundworms often have very large, swollen bellies. Rarely, roundworms may cause asthma, fits, or a dangerous obstruction or blockage in the gut (see p. 94). When the child has a fever, the worms sometimes come out in the stools or crawl out through the mouth or nose. Occasionally they crawl into the airway and cause gagging.

Prevention:

Use latrines, wash hands before eating or handling food, protect food from flies, and follow the guidelines of cleanliness described in the first part of this chapter.

Treatment:

One dose of piperazine will usually get rid of roundworms. For dosage, see page 363. Some home remedies work fairly well. For a home remedy using papaya see page 13.

Threadworm (Pinworm, Enterobius):

1 cm. long. Color: white. Very thin and threadlike.

How they are transmitted:

These worms lay thousands of eggs just outside the anus (ass hole). This causes itching, especially at night. When a child scratches, the eggs stick under his nails, and are carried to food and other objects. In this way they reach his own mouth or the mouths of others, causing new infections of threadworms.

Effect on health:

These worms are not dangerous. Itching may disturb the child's sleep.

Treatment and Prevention:

- A child who has pinworms should wear tight diapers or pants while sleeping to keep him from scratching his anus.

- Wash the child's hands and buttocks (anal area) when he wakes up and after he has a bowel movement. Always wash his hands before he eats.

- Cut his fingernails very short.

- Change his clothes and bathe him often—wash the buttocks and nails especially well.

- Put *Vaseline* in and around his anus at bedtime to help stop itching.

- Give him a worm medicine that contains piperazine. For dosage, see page 363. When one child is treated for these worms, it is wise to treat the whole family at the same time.

- Cleanliness is the best prevention for threadworms. Even if medicine gets rid of the worms, they will be picked up again if care is not taken with personal hygiene. Pinworms only live for about 6 weeks. **By carefully following the guidelines of cleanliness, most of the worms will be gone within a few weeks, even without medicine.**

Whipworm (Trichuris, Trichocephalus):

3 to 5 cm. long. Color: pink or gray.

This worm, like the roundworm, is passed from the feces of one person to the mouth of another person. Usually this worm does little harm, but it may cause diarrhea. In children it occasionally causes part of the intestines to come out of the anus (*prolapse* of the *rectum*).

Prevention: The same as for roundworm.

Treatment: If the worms cause a problem, give thiabendazole or mebendazole. For dosage, see pages 363 and 364. For prolapse of the rectum, turn the child upside down and pour cool water on the intestine. This should make it pull back in.

Hookworm:

1 cm. long. Color: red.

Hookworms cannot usually be seen in the feces. A stool analysis is needed to prove that they are there.

How hookworms are spread:

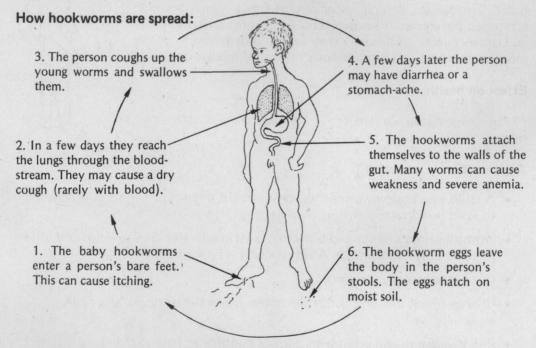

3. The person coughs up the young worms and swallows them.

2. In a few days they reach the lungs through the bloodstream. They may cause a dry cough (rarely with blood).

1. The baby hookworms enter a person's bare feet. This can cause itching.

4. A few days later the person may have diarrhea or a stomach-ache.

5. The hookworms attach themselves to the walls of the gut. Many worms can cause weakness and severe anemia.

6. The hookworm eggs leave the body in the person's stools. The eggs hatch on moist soil.

Hookworm infection can be one of the most damaging diseases of childhood. Any child who is anemic, very pale, or eats dirt may have hookworms. If possible, his stools should be analyzed.

Treatment: Use thiabendazole, mebendazole, tetrachloroethylene (T.C.E.), or bephenium. For dosage and precautions, see pages 363 and 364. Treat anemia by eating foods rich in iron and if necessary by taking iron pills (p. 125).

> *Prevent hookworm:* **Build and use latrines.**
> **Do not let children go barefoot.**

Tapeworm:

In the intestines tapeworms grow several meters long. But the small, flat, white pieces (segments) found in the feces are usually about 1 cm. long. Occasionally a segment may crawl out by itself and be found in the underclothing.

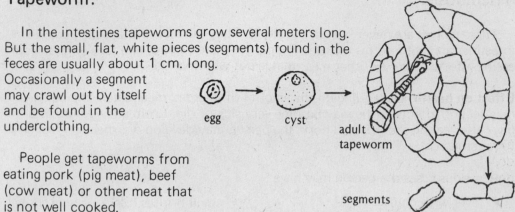

egg → cyst → adult tapeworm

segments

People get tapeworms from eating pork (pig meat), beef (cow meat) or other meat that is not well cooked.

Prevention: **Be careful that all meat is well cooked, especially pork.** Make sure no parts in the center of roasted meat are still raw.

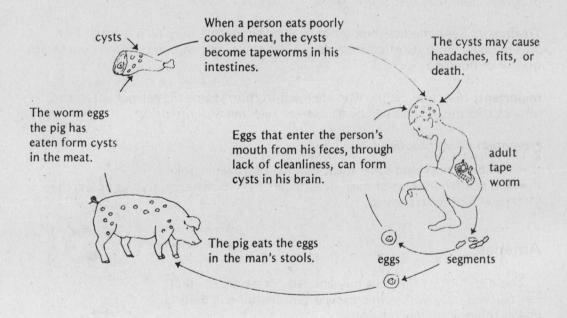

cysts

When a person eats poorly cooked meat, the cysts become tapeworms in his intestines.

The cysts may cause headaches, fits, or death.

The worm eggs the pig has eaten form cysts in the meat.

Eggs that enter the person's mouth from his feces, through lack of cleanliness, can form cysts in his brain.

adult tape worm

The pig eats the eggs in the man's stools.

eggs   segments

Effect on health: Tapeworms in the intestines sometimes cause mild stomachaches, but few other problems.

The greatest danger exists when the *cysts* (small sacs containing baby worms) get into a person's brain. This happens when the eggs pass from his stools to his mouth. For this reason, **anyone with tapeworms must follow the guidelines of cleanliness carefully—and get treatment as soon as possible.**

Treatment: Take niclosamide (*Yomesan,* see p. 364), dichlorophen (*Antiphen,* p. 364), or quinacrine (mepacrine, *Atabrine,* p. 359). Follow instructions carefully.

Trichinosis:

These worms are never seen in the stools. They burrow through the person's intestines and get into his muscles. People get these worms, like tapeworms, from eating infected pork or other meat that is not well cooked.

Effect on health: Depending on the amount of infected meat eaten, the person may feel no effects, or he may become very sick or die. From a few hours to 5 days after eating the infected pork, the person may develop diarrhea and feel sick to his stomach.

In serious cases the person may have:

- fever with chills
- muscle pain
- swelling around the eyes and sometimes swelling of the feet
- small bruises (black or blue spots) on the skin
- bleeding in the whites of the eyes

Severe cases may last 3 or 4 weeks.

Treatment: Seek medical help at once. Thiabendazole may help a little. For dosage, see p. 363. (Cortico-steroids may also help, but should be given by a health worker or doctor.)

Important: If several people who ate meat from the same pig get sick afterward, suspect trichinosis. This can be dangerous; seek medical attention.

Prevention of trichinosis:

- Only eat pork and other meat that has been well cooked.
- Do not feed scraps of meat or leftovers from butchering to pigs unless they have first been cooked.

Ameba as seen under microscope

Amebas:

These are not worms, but tiny animals—or parasites—that can be seen only with a *microscope* (an instrument that makes things look much bigger).

Microscope

How they are transmitted:

The stools of infected people have millions of these tiny parasites. Because of poor sanitation, they get into the source of drinking water or into food, and other people become infected.

Signs of infection with amebas:

Many healthy people have amebas without becoming sick. However, amebas are a common cause of severe diarrhea or *dysentery* (diarrhea with blood)—especially in persons already weakened by other sickness or poor nutrition. Less commonly, amebas cause painful, dangerous abscesses in the liver.

Typical amebic dysentery consists of:

- diarrhea that comes and goes—sometimes alternating with constipation
- cramps in the belly and a need to have frequent bowel movements, even when little or nothing—or just mucus—comes out
- many loose (but usually not watery) stools with lots of mucus, sometimes stained with blood
- in severe cases, much blood; the person may be very weak and ill
- usually there is no fever

Diarrhea with blood may be caused by either amebas or bacteria. However, bacterial dysentery (Shigella) begins more suddenly, the stools are more watery, and there is almost always fever (p. 158). As a general rule:

> **Diarrhea + blood + fever = bacterial infection (Shigella)**
> **Diarrhea + blood + no fever = amebas**

Occasionally bloody diarrhea has other causes. To be sure of the cause, a *stool analysis* may be necessary.

Sometimes amebas get into the liver and form an **abscess** or pocket of pus. This causes tenderness or pain in the right upper belly. Pain may extend into the right chest and is worse when the person walks. (Compare this with gallbladder pain, p. 329; hepatitis, p. 172; and cirrhosis, p. 328.) If the person with these signs begins to cough up a brown liquid, an amebic abscess is draining into his lung.

Treatment:

- If possible get medical help and a stool analysis.
- Mild gut infection with amebas can be treated with tetracycline, alone or with diiodohydroxyquin (for dosage, length of treatment, and precautions, see p. 353 and 359).
- For severe dysentery or amebic abscess, take tetracycline together with metronidazole (for dosage, see p. 359). If metronidazole is not available, use chloroquine (see p. 357).

Prevention: Make and use latrines, protect the source of drinking water, and follow the guidelines of cleanliness. Eating well and avoiding fatigue and drunkenness are also important in preventing amebic dysentery.

Giardia:

The giardia, like the ameba, is a microscopic parasite that lives in the gut and is a common cause of diarrhea, especially in children. The diarrhea may be *chronic* or intermittent (may come and go).

A person who has yellow, bad-smelling diarrhea that is frothy (full of bubbles) but without blood or mucus, probably has giardia. The belly is swollen with gas and uncomfortable, there are mild intestinal cramps, and the person farts a lot. There is usually no fever.

Giardia as seen under a microscope

Giardia infections often clear up by themselves. Good nutrition helps. Severe cases are best treated with metronidazole (for dosage, see p. 359). Quinacrine (*Atabrine*, p. 359) is cheaper but does not work as well.

BLOOD FLUKES (SCHISTOSOMIASIS, BILHARZIA):

This infection, caused by a kind of worm that gets into the bloodstream, occurs only in certain parts of the world. It is common in much of Africa, the Middle East, and parts of Latin America. In areas where the disease is known to occur, **any person who has blood in his urine should have his urine checked** under a microscope to see if it has fluke eggs.

Signs:

- **The most common sign is blood in the urine,** especially when passing the last drops.
- Pain may occur in the lower belly and between the legs; it is usually worst at the end of urinating. Low fever and itching may occur.
- After months or years, the kidneys may be badly damaged—causing general swelling and death.

Treatment:

Good nutrition is important. In areas where the disease is very common, often only severely ill persons are treated. Give niridazole (for dosage, see p. 365). Medicine should be given under direction of an experienced health worker.

Prevention:

Blood flukes are not spread directly from person to person. Part of their life they must live inside a certain kind of small water snail.

SNAIL, REAL SIZE

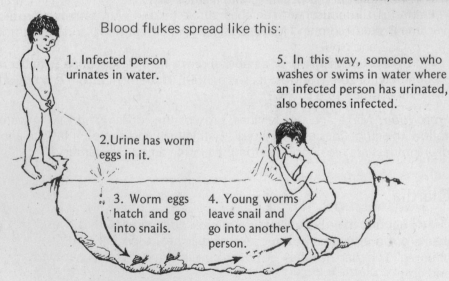

Blood flukes spread like this:

1. Infected person urinates in water.

2. Urine has worm eggs in it.

3. Worm eggs hatch and go into snails.

4. Young worms leave snail and go into another person.

5. In this way, someone who washes or swims in water where an infected person has urinated, also becomes infected.

To prevent schistosomiasis, cooperate with programs to kill snails and treat infected persons. But most important: **Everyone should learn to urinate in latrines and NEVER URINATE IN OR NEAR WATER.**

Note: Another kind of blood fluke infects the gut and causes bloody diarrhea. Stools are infected with worm eggs. So, once again, it is important to use latrines and never to defecate near drinking water or where people bathe.

VACCINATIONS (IMMUNIZATIONS)—
SIMPLE, SURE PROTECTION

Vaccines give protection against many dangerous diseases. If health workers do not vaccinate in your village, take your children to the nearest health center to be vaccinated. It is better to take them for vaccinations while they are healthy, than to take them for treatment when they are sick or dying. Vaccinations are usually given free.

The most important vaccines for children are:

1. D.P.T., for diphtheria, whooping cough (pertussis), and tetanus. For full protection, the child needs three injections: first at 2 months old, the second at 3 months, and the third a year later. (Different countries use different schedules.)

2. POLIO (infantile paralysis). The child needs drops in the mouth once each month for 3 months. In some countries, polio vaccine is first given shortly after birth; in other countries, when the baby is 2 months old. It is best not to breast feed the baby for 2 hours before or after giving the drops.

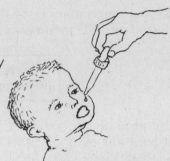

POLIO VACCINE—
The drops taste sweet.

3. B.C.G., for tuberculosis. A single injection is given into the skin of the **right** shoulder. Children can be vaccinated at birth or anytime afterwards. Early vaccination is especially important if any member of the household has tuberculosis. The vaccine makes a sore and leaves a scar.

4. MEASLES. One injection only, given no younger than 9 to 15 months of age, depending on the country.

5. TETANUS. For adults and children over 12 years old, the most important vaccine is for tetanus (lockjaw). One injection every month for 3 months, another after a year, and then one every 10 years. Everyone should be vaccinated against tetanus—especially pregnant women, so that their babies will be protected against tetanus of the newborn (see p. 182 and 250).

6. SMALL POX. This vaccination, put on the **left** shoulder, leaves a round scar. Thanks to world-wide vaccination in the past, small pox no longer exists. So vaccination against it is now not needed.

In some places there are also vaccinations for cholera, yellow fever, typhus, mumps, and German measles. The World Health Organization is also working to develop vaccines for leprosy and malaria.

WARNING: Vaccines spoil easily and then do not work. Measles and B.C.G. must be kept **frozen**. D.P.T. and Tetanus cold (4° to 8° C.) but **never frozen**. Good D.P.T. remains cloudy at least 1 hour after shaking. If it becomes clear within 1 hour, it is spoiled.

> **Vaccinate your children on time.**
> **Be sure they get the complete series of each vaccine they need.**

OTHER WAYS TO PREVENT SICKNESS AND INJURY

In this chapter we have talked about ways to prevent intestinal and other infections through **hygiene, sanitation,** and **vaccination.** All through this book you will find suggestions for the prevention of sickness and injury—from building healthy bodies by eating nutritious foods to the wise use of home remedies and modern medicines.

The **Introduction to the Village Health Worker** gives ideas for getting people working together to change the conditions that cause poor health.

In the remaining chapters, as specific health problems are discussed, you will find many suggestions for their prevention. By following these suggestions you can help make your home and village healthier places to live.

Keep in mind that one of the best ways to prevent serious illness and death is early and sensible treatment.

> **Early and sensible treatment is an important part of preventive medicine.**

Before ending this chapter, I would like to mention a few aspects of prevention that are touched on in other parts of the book, but deserve special attention.

Habits that Affect Health

Some of the habits that people have not only damage their own health but in one way or another harm those around them. Many of these habits can be broken or avoided—but the first step is to understand why breaking these habits is so important.

DRINKING:

If alcohol has brought much joy to man, it has also brought much suffering—especially to the women and children of men who drink. A little alcohol now and then may do no harm. But too often a little leads to a lot. In much of the world, heavy or excessive drinking is one of the underlying causes of major health problems—even for those who do not drink. Not only can drunkenness harm the health of those who drink (through diseases such as cirrhosis of the liver, p. 328), but it also hurts the family and community in many ways. Through loss of judgment when drunk—and of self-respect when sober—it leads to much unhappiness, waste, and violence, often affecting those who are loved most.

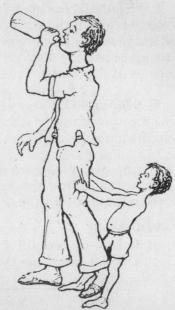

How many fathers have spent their last money on drink when their children were hungry? How many sicknesses result because a man spends the little bit of extra money he earns on drink rather than on improving his family's living conditions? How many persons, hating themselves because they have hurt those they love, take another drink—to forget?

Once a man realizes that alcohol is harming the health and happiness of those around him, what can he do? First, he must admit that his drinking is a problem. He must be honest with himself and with others. Some individuals are able to simply decide to stop drinking. More often people need help and support—from family, friends, and others who understand how hard it may be to give up this habit. People who have been heavy drinkers and have stopped are often the best persons to help others do the same.

Drinking is not so much a problem of individuals as of a whole community. A community that recognizes this can do much to encourage those who are willing to make changes. If you are concerned about the misuse of alcohol in your community, help organize a meeting to discuss these problems and decide what actions to take.

> **Many problems can be resolved when people work together and give each other help and support.**

SMOKING:

There are many reasons why smoking is dangerous to your own and your family's health.

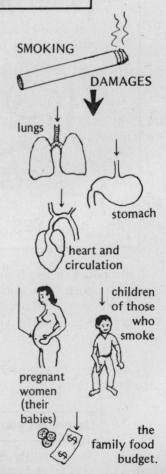

SMOKING DAMAGES

lungs

stomach

heart and circulation

children of those who smoke

pregnant women (their babies)

the family food budget.

1. Smoking increases the risk of cancer of the lungs and lips. (The more you smoke, the greater the chance of dying of cancer.)

2. Smoking causes serious diseases of the lungs, including chronic bronchitis and emphysema (and is deadly for persons who already have these conditions or have asthma).

3. Smoking can help cause stomach ulcers or make them worse.

4. Children whose parents smoke have more cases of pneumonia and other respiratory illness than children whose parents do not smoke.

5. Smoking increases your chance of suffering or dying from heart disease or stroke.

6. Babies of mothers who smoked during pregnancy are smaller and develop more slowly than babies whose mothers did not smoke.

(turn page)

7. Parents, teachers, health workers, and others who smoke set an unhealthy example for children and young people, increasing the likelihood that they too will begin smoking.

8. Also, smoking costs money. It looks like little is spent, but it adds up to a lot. In poorer countries, many of the poorest persons spend more on tobacco than the country spends per person on its health program. **If money spent on tobacco were spent for food instead, children and whole families could be healthier.**

> **Anyone interested in the health of others should not smoke, and should encourage others not to smoke.**

CARBONATED DRINKS (soft drinks, soda pop, Coke, fizzy drinks, colas):

In some areas these drinks have become very popular. Often a poor mother will buy carbonated drinks for a child who is poorly nourished, when the same money could be better used to buy 2 eggs or other nutritious food.

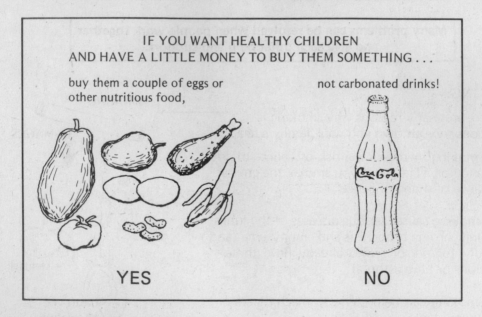

IF YOU WANT HEALTHY CHILDREN
AND HAVE A LITTLE MONEY TO BUY THEM SOMETHING . . .

buy them a couple of eggs or other nutritious food,

not carbonated drinks!

YES

NO

Carbonated drinks have no nutritional value apart from sugar. And for the amount of sugar they contain, they are very expensive. Children who are given a lot of carbonated drinks and other sweet things often begin to get cavities and rotten teeth at an early age. Carbonated drinks are especially bad for persons with acid indigestion or stomach ulcer.

Natural drinks you make from fruits are healthier and often much cheaper than carbonated drinks.

> **Do not get your children used to drinking carbonated drinks.**

CHAPTER

13 SOME VERY COMMON SICKNESSES

DEHYDRATION

Most children who die from diarrhea die because they do not have enough water left in their bodies. This lack of water is called dehydration.

Dehydration results when the body loses more liquid than it takes in. This can happen with severe diarrhea, especially when there is vomiting as well. It can also happen in very serious illness, when a person is too sick to take much food or liquid.

People of any age can become dehydrated, but **dehydration develops more quickly and is most dangerous in small children.**

> **Any child with watery diarrhea is in danger of dehydration.**

It is important that everyone—especially mothers—know the signs of dehydration and how to prevent and treat it.

Signs of dehydration:

- little or no urine; the urine is dark yellow
- sudden weight loss
- dry mouth
- sunken, tearless eyes
- sagging in of the 'soft spot' in infants
- loss of elasticity or stretchiness of the skin

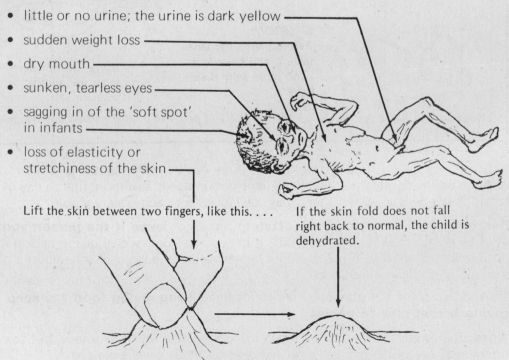

Lift the skin between two fingers, like this. . . .

If the skin fold does not fall right back to normal, the child is dehydrated.

Very severe dehydration may cause rapid, weak pulse (see Shock, p. 77), fast, deep breathing, fever, or fits (convulsions, p. 178).

Prevention and treatment of dehydration:

♦ A dehydrated person should drink large amounts of liquids: water, tea, soup, etc. But **do not wait for dehydration to begin.**

♦ Dehydration can usually be prevented if a person with diarrhea, with or without vomiting, is given plenty of liquids or Rehydration Drink from the very first. This is especially important for small children with watery stools.

♦ Especially useful in the prevention and treatment of dehydration is the following Rehydration Drink:

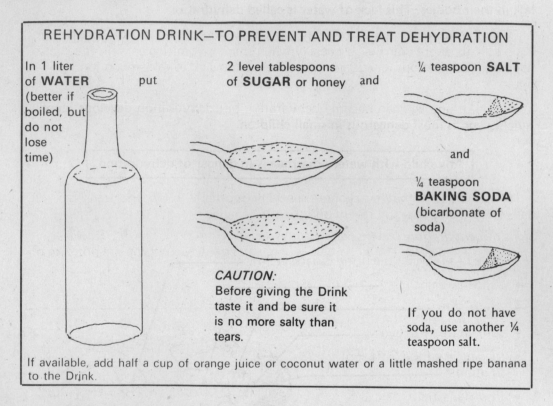

REHYDRATION DRINK—TO PREVENT AND TREAT DEHYDRATION

In 1 liter of **WATER** (better if boiled, but do not lose time)   put   2 level tablespoons of **SUGAR** or honey   and   ¼ teaspoon **SALT**

and

¼ teaspoon **BAKING SODA** (bicarbonate of soda)

CAUTION:
Before giving the Drink taste it and be sure it is no more salty than tears.

If you do not have soda, use another ¼ teaspoon salt.

If available, add half a cup of orange juice or coconut water or a little mashed ripe banana to the Drink.

Give the dehydrated person sips of this drink every 5 minutes, day and night, until he begins to urinate normally. A large person needs 3 or more liters a day. A small child needs at least 1 liter a day, or 1 glass for each watery stool.

Keep giving Rehydration Drink **often** in small sips, **even if the person vomits**. (Not all of the drink will be vomited). If dehydration gets worse or the person does not urinate within 4 to 6 hours, find a health worker who can give liquid in a vein (intravenous solution).

When you give Rehydration Drink for diarrhea, **keep giving food** and **keep giving breast milk to babies**.

Note: Rehydration Drink can be made using raw sugar or bee's honey, but some honey may cause allergic reactions. In some countries small envelopes of "Rehydration Salts" are available for mixing with water (usually 1 liter). These contain a simple sugar (glucose) along with salt, soda, and potassium (see p. 368). This drink is possibly better for children who are badly malnourished or dehydrated. But in most cases, it is wise if mothers learn to make the Drink from local sugar and salt. Adding orange juice, coconut water or banana provides potassium.

DIARRHEA AND DYSENTERY

When a person has loose or watery stools, he has *diarrhea.* If mucus and blood can be seen in the stools, he has *dysentery.*

Diarrhea can be mild or serious. It can be *acute* (sudden and severe) or *chronic* (lasting many days).

Diarrhea is more common and more dangerous in young children, especially those who are poorly nourished.

This child is well nourished. He is less likely to get diarrhea. If he gets it he usually will get well again quickly.

This child is poorly nourished. He is more likely to get diarrhea —and there is a much greater chance he will die from it.

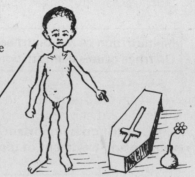

Diarrhea has many causes. Sometimes special treatment is needed. However, **most diarrhea can be treated successfully in the home,** even if you are not sure of the exact cause or causes.

THE MAIN CAUSES OF DIARRHEA:

poor nutrition (p. 154) This weakens the child and makes diarrhea from other causes more frequent and worse.

virus infection or 'intestinal flu' (diarrhea usually mild)

an infection of the gut caused by bacteria (p. 131), amebas (p. 144), or giardia (p. 145)

worm infections (p. 140 to 144)

infections outside the gut (ear infections, p. 309; tonsillitis, p. 309; measles, p. 311; urinary infections, p. 234)

malaria (*falciparum* type—in parts of Africa, Asia, and the Pacific, p. 186)

food poisoning (spoiled food, p. 135)

inability to digest milk (mainly in severely malnourished children and certain adults)

difficulty babies have digesting foods that are new to them

allergies to certain foods (seafood, crayfish, etc., p. 166); occasionally babies are allergic to cow's milk or other milk

side effects produced by certain medicines, such as ampicillin or tetracycline (p. 58)

laxatives, purges, irritating or poisonous plants, certain poisons

eating too much unripe fruit or heavy, greasy foods

Preventing diarrhea:

Although diarrhea has many different causes, the most common are **infection** and **poor nutrition. With good hygiene and good food, most diarrhea could be prevented.** And if treated correctly, fewer children who get diarrhea would die.

Children who are poorly nourished get diarrhea and die from it far more often than those who are well nourished. Yet diarrhea itself can be part of the cause of malnutrition. And if malnutrition already exists, diarrhea rapidly makes it worse.

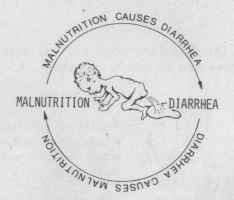

> **Malnutrition causes diarrhea.**
> **Diarrhea causes malnutrition.**

This results in a vicious circle, in which each makes the other worse. For this reason, **good nutrition is important in both the prevention and treatment of diarrhea.**

THE 'VICIOUS CIRCLE' OF MALNUTRITION AND DIARRHEA TAKES MANY CHILDREN'S LIVES.

> **Prevent diarrhea by preventing malnutrition.**
> **Prevent malnutrition by preventing diarrhea.**

To learn about the kinds of foods that help the body resist or fight off different illnesses, including diarrhea, read Chapter 11.

The prevention of diarrhea depends both on **good nutrition** and **cleanliness.** Many suggestions for personal and public cleanliness are given in Chapter 12. These include the use of **latrines,** the importance of **clean water,** and the **protection of foods** from dirt and flies.

Here are some other important suggestions for preventing diarrhea in babies:

◆ **Breast feed rather than bottle feed babies.** Give only breast milk for the first 4 months. Breast milk helps babies resist the infections that cause diarrhea. If it is not possible to breast feed a baby, feed him with a cup and spoon. **Do not use a baby bottle** because it is harder to keep clean and more likely to cause an infection.

◆ When you begin to give the baby new or solid foods, start by giving him just a little, and mashing it well. He has to learn how to digest new foods, and if he starts with too much at one time, he may get diarrhea.

BREAST FEEDING HELPS PREVENT DIARRHEA

◆ Keep the baby clean—and in a clean place. Try to keep him from putting dirty things in his mouth.

◆ Do not give babies unnecessary medicines.

Treatment of diarrhea:

For most cases of diarrhea no medicine is needed. If the diarrhea is severe, the biggest danger is **dehydration.** If the diarrhea lasts a long time, the biggest danger is **malnutrition.** So the most important part of treatment has to do with giving **enough liquids** and **good food.** No matter what the cause of diarrhea, always take care with the following:

1. PREVENT OR CONTROL DEHYDRATION. A person with watery diarrhea must drink large amounts of liquids. If diarrhea is severe or there are signs of dehydration, give him Rehydration Drink (p. 152). Even if he does not want to drink, gently insist that he do so. Have him take several swallows every few minutes.

2. MEET NUTRITIONAL NEEDS. **A person with diarrhea needs food as soon as he will eat.** This is especially important in small children or persons who are already poorly nourished.

- A baby with diarrhea should go on breast feeding.

- A small or underweight child, or anyone who is thin and weak, should get plenty of body-building foods (proteins) and energy foods all the time he has diarrhea—and also when he gets well. If he stops eating because he is too sick or is vomiting, he should eat again as soon as he can. **Although giving food may cause more frequent stools at first, it can save his life.**

- If a child who is underweight has diarrhea that lasts for many days or keeps coming back, give him more food rich in protein. Often no other treatment is needed.

- When an older child or adult who is **well nourished** has a severe case of acute diarrhea, he may recover more quickly on a liquid diet of teas, broths, or Rehydration Drink. But if the diarrhea lasts more than 1 day, he should begin taking food.

FOODS FOR A PERSON WITH DIARRHEA

When the person is vomiting or feels too sick to eat, he should drink:	As soon as the person is able to eat, in addition to giving the drinks listed at the left, he should eat a balanced selection of the following foods or similar ones:	
	energy foods	**body-building foods**
teas	ripe or cooked bananas	milk (sometimes this causes
rice water	crackers	problems, see the next
chicken, meat, egg, or bean broth	rice	page)
	oatmeal or other well-cooked grain	chicken (boiled or roasted)
Kool-Aid or similar sweetened drinks	fresh maize (well cooked and mashed)	eggs (boiled)
REHYDRATION DRINK	potatoes	meat, well cooked, without fat or grease
Breast milk	applesauce (cooked)	beans, lentils, or peas (well cooked and mashed)
	papaya	fish (well cooked)

DO NOT EAT OR DRINK		
fatty or greasy foods	beans cooked in fat	alcoholic drinks
most raw fruits	highly seasoned food	any kind of laxative or purge

Diarrhea and milk:

Breast milk is the best food for babies. Keep giving breast milk when the baby has diarrhea. It does not cause diarrhea and will help the baby get better quickly.

Cow's milk, dry skim milk, and canned milk can be good sources of protein for children who have diarrhea. However, if the child is badly malnourished, he may have trouble digesting the milk, and this may cause even more diarrhea. If this happens, try giving less milk and mixing it with other foods. But remember: **a poorly nourished child with diarrhea must have enough protein,** so if less milk is given, well-cooked and mashed foods such as chicken, egg yolk, meat, fish, or beans should be added. Beans are easier to digest if their skins have been taken off and they are boiled and mashed. They should not be cooked in fat.

As the child gets better, he will usually be able to drink more milk without getting diarrhea.

Medicines for diarrhea:

For most cases of diarrhea no medicines are needed. But in certain cases, using the right medicine can be important. However, many of the medicines commonly used for diarrhea do little or no good. Some are actually harmful:

GENERALLY IT IS BETTER NOT TO USE THE FOLLOWING MEDICINES IN THE TREATMENT OF DIARRHEA:

'Anti-diarrhea' medicines with kaolin and pectin (such as *Kaopectate*, p. 369) make diarrhea thicker and less frequent, but they do not correct dehydration or control infection. Some anti-diarrhea medicines, like diphenoxylate *(Lomotil)* may even make infections last longer.

'ANTI-DIARRHEA MEDICINES' ACT LIKE PLUGS. THEY KEEP IN THE INFECTED MATERIAL THAT NEEDS TO COME OUT.

'Anti-diarrhea' mixtures containing neomycin or streptomycin should not be used, as these may irritate the gut and do more harm than good.

Antibiotics like ampicillin and tetracycline are useful in some cases of diarrhea. But they themselves sometimes cause diarrhea, especially in small children. If, after taking these antibiotics for more than 2 or 3 days, diarrhea gets worse rather than better, stop taking them—the antibiotics may be the cause.

Chloramphenicol has certain dangers in its use (see p. 354) and should never be used for mild diarrhea or given to babies less than 1 month old.

Laxatives and purges should never be given to persons with diarrhea. They will make it worse and increase the danger of dehydration.

Special treatment in different cases of diarrhea:

While most cases of diarrhea can be treated by giving plenty of liquids and nutritious food, sometimes special treatment is needed.

In considering treatment, keep in mind that some cases of diarrhea, especially in small children, are caused by **infections outside the gut.** Always check for **infections of the ears,** the **throat,** and the **urinary system.** If found, these infections should be treated. Also look for signs of **measles.**

If the child has mild diarrhea together with signs of a cold, the diarrhea is probably caused by a virus, or 'intestinal flu', and no special treatment is called for. Give lots of liquids.

In certain difficult cases of diarrhea, analysis of the stools or other tests may be needed to know how to treat it correctly. But usually you can learn enough from asking specific questions, seeing the stools, and looking for certain signs. Here are some guidelines for treatment according to signs.

1. **Sudden, mild diarrhea. No fever.** (Upset stomach? 'Intestinal flu'?)

♦ Drink lots of liquids. Usually no special treatment is needed. For a 'plug', a mixture of kaolin and pectin, such as *Kaopectate,* can be used, but it is never necessary and does not help either to correct dehydration or get rid of infection— so why waste money buying it? It should not be given to persons who are very ill, or to small children. (For dosage, see p. 369.)

♦ If severe colic (painful cramps) is a problem, an antispasmodic like belladonna may help. (For precautions and dosage, see p. 367.)

2. **Diarrhea with vomiting.** (Many causes)

♦ If a person with diarrhea is also vomiting, the danger of dehydration increases, especially in small children. It is very important to give the Rehydration Drink (p. 152), tea, a cola drink, or whatever liquids he will take. Give sips every 5 to 10 minutes. If vomiting does not stop soon, you can use medicines like promethazine (p. 371) or phenobarbital (p. 373).

♦ If you cannot control the vomiting or if the dehydration gets worse, seek medical help fast.

3. **Diarrhea with mucus and blood. Often chronic. No fever.** (Possibly amebic dysentery. For more details, see page 144.)

♦ Use tetracycline (p. 353), metronidazole (p. 359), or best, both together. Take the medicine according to the recommended dose. If the diarrhea continues after treatment, seek medical advice.

4. **Acute diarrhea with fever, with or without blood.** (Bacterial dysentery? Typhoid? Malaria?)

◆ If the person with diarrhea has a fever lasting more than 6 hours after beginning treatment for dehydration, and seems very ill, give ampicillin if possible (p. 351). If not, give tetracycline (p. 353).

◆ If the persons's condition is very poor or he is not improving with ampicillin or tetracycline, seek medical help. If there are signs of typhoid fever (see p. 189), give chloramphenicol (p. 353) in the recommended dose.

◆ In areas where the *falciparum* type of malaria is common, it is a good idea that persons with diarrhea and fever also be treated with chloroquine (see p. 357), especially if they have a large spleen.

5. **Yellow, bad-smelling diarrhea with bubbles or froth, without blood or mucus.** (Giardia? See p. 145.)

◆ This may be caused by microscopic parasites called Giardia or perhaps by malnutrition. In either case, plenty of liquid, nutritious food, and rest are often the only treatment needed. Severe giardia infections can be treated with metronidazole (p. 359). Mepacrine *(Atabrine)* is cheaper, but less effective.

6. **Chronic diarrhea (diarrhea that lasts a long time or keeps coming back).**

◆ This is most commonly due to malnutrition, less commonly to a chronic infection such as that caused by amebas. See that the child eats more nutritious food, especially foods rich in proteins (p. 110). If the diarrhea still continues, seek medical help.

7. **Diarrhea like rice water.** (Cholera?)

◆ 'Rice water' stools are a sign of cholera. In countries where this dangerous disease occurs, cholera often comes in *epidemics* (striking many people at once) and is usually worse in older children and adults. Dehydration is extreme, especially if there is vomiting also. Treat the dehydration continuously and either give twice the usual dose of tetracycline (p. 353) or give the normal dose of chloramphenicol (p. 353). Cholera should be reported to the health authorities. Seek medical help.

A 'cholera bed' like this can be made for persons with very severe diarrhea. Watch how much liquid the person is losing and be sure he is given an even larger amount of Rehydration Drink.

sleeve made of plastic sheet

Care of Babies with Diarrhea

Diarrhea is especially dangerous in babies and small children. Often no medicine is needed, but special care must be taken because a baby can die very quickly of dehydration.

♦ Continue breast feeding and also give sips of Rehydration Drink.

♦ If vomiting is a problem, give breast milk often, but only a little at a time. Also give Rehydration Drink in small sips every 5 to 10 minutes (see Vomiting, p. 161).

AND ALSO
REHYDRATION DRINK

♦ If there is no breast milk, try giving frequent small feedings of some other milk or milk substitute (like milk made from soybeans) **mixed to half normal strength with boiled water.** If milk seems to make the diarrhea worse, give some other protein (mashed chicken, eggs, lean meat, or skinned mashed beans, mixed with honey, sugar, or well-cooked rice or another carbohydrate, and boiled water).

♦ If the child is younger than 1 month, try to find a health worker before giving any medicine. If there is no health worker and the child is very sick, give him an 'infant syrup' that contains ampicillin: half a teaspoon 4 times daily (see p. 351). It is better not to use other antibiotics.

When to Seek Medical Help in Cases of Diarrhea

Diarrhea and dysentery can be very dangerous—especially in small children. **In the following situations you should get medical help:**

- if diarrhea lasts more than 4 days and is not getting better—or more than 1 day in a small child with severe diarrhea

- if the person is dehydrated and getting worse

- if the child vomits everything he drinks, or drinks nothing

- if the child begins to have fits, or if the feet and face swell

- if the person was very sick, weak, or malnourished before the diarrhea began (especially a little child or a very old person)

- if there is much blood in the stools, this can be dangerous even if there is little diarrhea (see gut obstruction, p. 94)

THE CARE OF A PERSON WITH ACUTE DIARRHEA

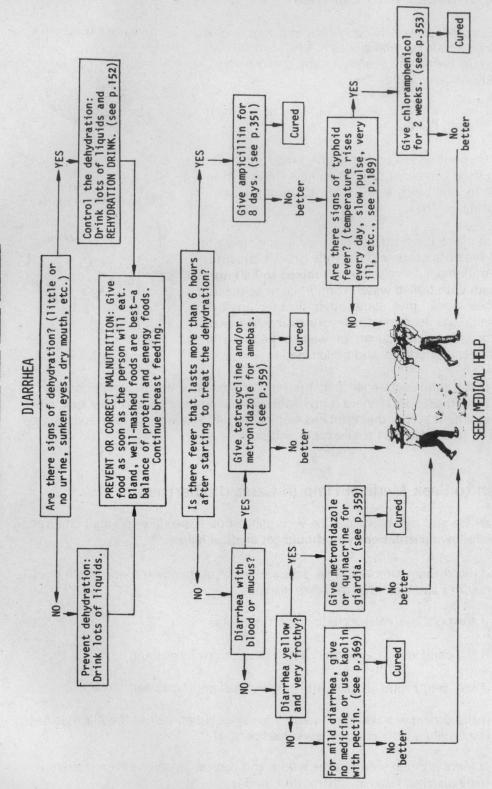

DIARRHEA

Are there signs of dehydration? (little or no urine, sunken eyes, dry mouth, etc.)

- **NO** → Prevent dehydration: Drink lots of liquids.
- **YES** → Control the dehydration: Drink lots of liquids and REHYDRATION DRINK. (see p.152)

PREVENT OR CORRECT MALNUTRITION: Give food as soon as the person will eat. Bland, well-mashed foods are best—a balance of protein and energy foods. Continue breast feeding.

Is there fever that lasts more than 6 hours after starting to treat the dehydration?

- **YES** → Give ampicillin for 8 days. (see p.351)
  - **Cured**
  - **No better** → Are there signs of typhoid fever? (temperature rises every day, slow pulse, very ill, etc., see p.189)
    - **YES** → Give chloramphenicol for 2 weeks. (see p.353)
      - **Cured**
      - **No better** → SEEK MEDICAL HELP
    - **NO** → SEEK MEDICAL HELP

- **NO** → Diarrhea with blood or mucus?
  - **YES** → Give tetracycline and/or metronidazole for amebas. (see p.359)
    - **Cured**
    - **No better** → SEEK MEDICAL HELP
  - **NO** → Diarrhea yellow and very frothy?
    - **YES** → Give metronidazole or quinacrine for giardia. (see p.359)
      - **Cured**
      - **No better** → SEEK MEDICAL HELP
    - **NO** → For mild diarrhea, give no medicine or use kaolin with pectin. (see p.369)
      - **Cured**
      - **No better** → SEEK MEDICAL HELP

SEEK MEDICAL HELP

VOMITING

Many people, especially children, have an occasional 'stomach upset' with vomiting. Often no cause can be found. There may be mild stomach or gut ache or fever. This kind of simple vomiting usually is not serious and clears up by itself.

Vomiting is one of the signs of many different problems, some minor and some quite serious, so it is important to examine the person carefully. Vomiting often comes from a problem in the stomach or guts, such as: an infection (see diarrhea, p. 153), poisoning from spoiled food (p. 135), or 'acute abdomen' (for example, appendicitis or something blocking the gut, p. 94). Also, almost any sickness with high fever or severe pain may cause vomiting, especially malaria (p. 186), hepatitis (p. 172), tonsillitis (p. 309), earache (p. 309), meningitis (p. 185), urinary infection (p. 234), gallbladder pain (p. 329) or migraine headache (p. 162).

Danger signs with vomiting—seek medical help quickly!

- dehydration that increases and that you cannot control, (p. 152)
- severe vomiting that lasts more than 24 hours
- violent vomiting, especially if vomit is dark green, brown, or smells like feces (signs of obstruction, p. 94)
- constant pain in the gut, especially if the person cannot defecate (shit) or if you cannot hear gurgles when you put your ear to the belly (see acute abdomen: obstruction, appendicitis, p. 94)
- vomiting of blood (ulcer, p. 128; cirrhosis, p. 328)

To help control simple vomiting:

- Eat nothing while vomiting is severe.
- Sip a cola drink or ginger ale. Some herbal teas, like camomile, may also help.
- For dehydration give small frequent sips of cola, tea, or Rehydration Drink (p. 152).
- If vomiting does not stop soon, use a vomit-control medicine like promethazine (p. 371), diphenhydramine (p. 371), or phenobarbital (p. 373).

Most of these come in pills, syrups, injections, and suppositories (soft pills you push up the *anus*). Tablets or syrup can also be put up the anus. Grind up the tablet in a little water. Put it in with an enema set or syringe without a needle.

When taken by mouth, the medicine should be swallowed with very little water and nothing else should be swallowed for 5 minutes. Never give more than the recommended dose. Do not give a second dose until dehydration has been corrected and the person has begun to urinate. If severe vomiting and diarrhea make medication by mouth or anus impossible, give an injection of 1 of these vomit-control medicines. Promethazine may work best. Take care not to give too much.

HEADACHES AND MIGRAINES

SIMPLE HEADACHE can be helped by rest and aspirin. It often helps to put a cloth soaked in hot water on the back of the neck and to massage (rub) the neck and shoulders gently. Some other home remedies also seem to help.

Headache is common with any sickness that causes fever. If headache is severe, check for signs of meningitis (p. 185).

Headaches that keep coming back may be a sign of a chronic illness or poor nutrition. It is important to eat well and get enough sleep. If the headaches do not go away, seek medical help.

For simple or nervous headache, folk cures sometimes work as well as modern medicine.

Mexican folk cure

aspirin

A **MIGRAINE** is a severe throbbing headache often on one side of the head only. Migraine attacks may come often, or months or years apart.

A typical migraine begins with blurring of vision, seeing strange spots of light, or numbness of one hand or foot. This is followed by severe headache, which may last hours or days. Often there is vomiting. Migraines are very painful, but not dangerous.

TO STOP A MIGRAINE, DO THE FOLLOWING AT THE FIRST SIGN:

+ Take 2 aspirins with a cup of strong coffee or strong black tea.

+ Lie down in a dark, quiet place. Do your best to relax. Try not to think about your problems.

+ For especially bad migraine headaches, obtain pills of ergotamine with caffeine (*Cafergot,* p. 366). Take 2 pills at first and 1 pill every 30 minutes until the pain goes away. Do not take more than 6 pills in 1 day.

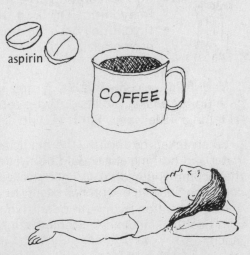

aspirin

COFFEE

COLDS AND THE FLU

Colds and the flu are common virus infections that may cause runny nose, cough, sore throat, and sometimes fever or pain in the joints. There may be mild diarrhea, especially in young children.

Colds and the flu almost always go away without medicine. **Do not use penicillin, tetracycline, or other antibiotics,** as they will not help at all and may cause harm.

♦ Drink plenty of water and get enough rest.

♦ Aspirin (p. 365) or acetaminophen (p. 366) helps lower fever and relieve body aches and headaches. More expensive 'cold tablets' are no better than aspirin. So why waste your money?

♦ No special diet is needed. However, fruit juices, especially orange juice or lemonade, are helpful.

For treating coughs and stuffy noses that come with colds, see the next pages.

If a cold or the flu lasts more than a week, or if the person has fever, coughs up a lot of *phlegm* (mucus with pus), has shallow fast breathing or chest pain, he could be developing bronchitis or pneumonia (see p. 170 and 171). An antibiotic may be called for. The danger of a cold turning into pneumonia is greater in old people and those who have lung problems like chronic bronchitis.

Sore throat is often part of a cold. No special medicine is needed, but it may help to gargle with warm water. However, if the sore throat begins suddenly, with high fever, it could be a strep throat. Special treatment is needed (see p. 309).

Prevention of colds:

♦ Getting enough sleep and eating well helps prevent colds. Eating oranges, tomatoes, and other fruit containing vitamin C may also help.

♦ Contrary to popular belief, colds do not come from getting cold or wet. A cold is 'caught' from others who have the infection and sneeze the virus into the air.

♦ To keep from giving his cold to others, the sick person should eat and sleep separately—and take special care to keep far away from small babies. He should cover his nose and mouth when he coughs or sneezes.

♦ To prevent a cold from leading to earache (p. 309), **do not blow your nose—just wipe it.** Teach children to do the same.

STUFFY AND RUNNY NOSES

A stuffy or runny nose can result from a cold or allergy (see next page). A lot of mucus in the nose may cause ear infections in children or sinus problems in adults.

To help clear a stuffy nose, do the following:

1. In little children, carefully suck the mucus out of the nose with a suction bulb or syringe **without a needle,** like this:

2. Older children and adults can put a little salt water into their hand and sniff it into the nose. This helps to loosen the mucus.

3. Breathing hot water vapor as described on page 168, helps clear a stuffy nose.

4. Wipe a runny or stuffy nose, but **do not blow it.** Blowing the nose may lead to earache and sinus infections.

5. Persons who often get earaches or sinus trouble after a cold can help prevent these problems by using *decongestant* nose drops like phenylephrine (p. 369). After sniffing a little salt water, put the drops in the nose like this:

With the head sideways, put 2 or 3 drops in the lower nostril. Wait a couple of minutes and then do the other side.

CAUTION: Use decongestant drops no more than 3 times a day, for **no more than 3 days.**

A decongestant syrup (with phenylephrine or something similar) may also help.

Prevent ear and sinus infections—wipe but do not blow your nose.

SINUS TROUBLE (SINUSITIS)

Sinusitis is an acute or chronic (long-term) inflammation of the sinuses or hollows in the bone that open into the nose.

Signs:

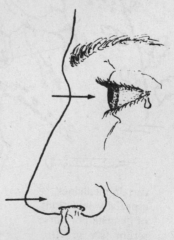

- Pain in the face above and below the eyes, here (It hurts more when you tap lightly just over the bones, or when the person bends over.)

- Thick mucus or pus in the nose, perhaps with a bad smell. The nose is often stuffy.

- Fever (sometimes).

Treatment:

- Sniff a little salt water into the nose (see p. 164).

- Put hot compresses on the face.

- Use decongestant nose drops such as phenylephrine (*Neo-synephrine,* p. 369).

- Use an antibiotic such as tetracycline (p. 353), ampicillin (p. 351), or penicillin (p. 349).

- If the person does not get better, seek medical help.

Prevention:

When you get a cold and a stuffy nose, try to keep your nose clear. Follow the instructions on page 164.

HAY FEVER (ALLERGIC RHINITIS)

Runny nose and itchy eyes can be caused by an allergic reaction to something in the air that a person has breathed in (see the next page). It is often worse at certain times of year.

Treatment:

Use an antihistamine such as chlorpheniramine (p. 371). Dimenhydrinate (*Dramamine,* p. 372), usually sold for motion sickness, also works.

Prevention:

Find out what things cause this reaction (for example: dust, chicken feathers, *pollen,* mold) and try to avoid them.

ALLERGIC REACTIONS

An allergy is a disturbance or reaction that affects only certain persons when things they are sensitive or allergic to are . . .

- breathed in
- eaten
- injected
- or touch the skin

Allergic reactions, which can be mild or very serious, include:

- itching rashes, lumpy patches or *hives* (p. 203)
- runny nose and itching or burning eyes (hay fever, p. 165)
- irritation in the throat, difficulty breathing, or asthma (see next page)
- allergic shock (p. 70)
- diarrhea (in children allergic to milk—a rare cause of diarrhea, p. 153)

An allergy is not an infection and cannot be passed from one person to another. However, children of allergic parents also tend to have allergies.

Often allergic persons suffer more in certain seasons—or whenever they come in touch with the substances that bother them. Common causes of allergic reactions are:

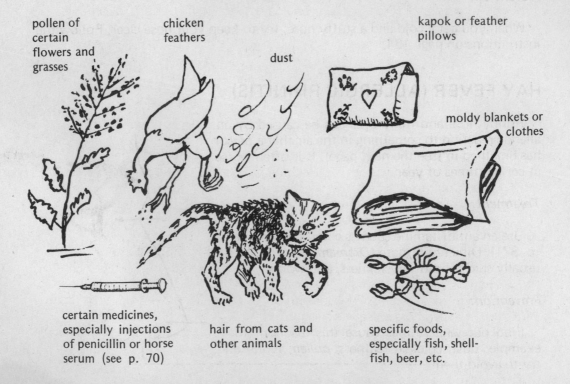

pollen of certain flowers and grasses

chicken feathers

dust

kapok or feather pillows

moldy blankets or clothes

certain medicines, especially injections of penicillin or horse serum (see p. 70)

hair from cats and other animals

specific foods, especially fish, shell-fish, beer, etc.

ASTHMA

A person with asthma has fits or attacks of difficult breathing. Listen for a hissing or wheezing sound, especially when breathing out. When he breathes in, the skin behind his collar bones and between his ribs may suck in as he tries to get air. If the person cannot get enough air, his nails and lips may turn blue, and his neck veins may swell. Usually there is no fever.

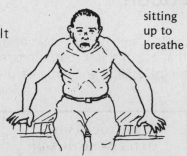

sitting up to breathe

Asthma often begins in childhood and may be a problem for life. It is not *contagious,* but is more common in children with relatives who have asthma. It is generally worse during certain months of the year or at night. Persons who have had asthma for years may develop emphysema (see p. 170).

An asthma attack may be caused by eating or breathing things to which the person is allergic (see p. 166). In children asthma often starts with a common cold. In some persons nervousness or worry also plays a part in bringing on an asthma attack.

Treatment:

◆ If asthma gets worse inside the house, the person should go outside to a place where the air is cleanest. Remain calm and be gentle with the person. Reassure him.

◆ Give a lot of liquids. This loosens mucus and makes breathing easier. Breathing water vapor may also help (see p. 168).

◆ For mild attacks give ephedrine or theophylline (see p. 370).

◆ If the asthma attack is especially bad, inject *Adrenalin.* Adults: ½ ampule; children ¼ ampule. You can repeat the dose every half hour, as needed up to 3 times. For precautions, see p. 370.

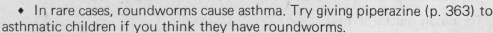

Inject *Adrenalin* just under the skin.

◆ If the person has a fever, or if the attack lasts more than 3 days, give tetracycline capsules (p. 353) or erythromycin (p. 352).

◆ In rare cases, roundworms cause asthma. Try giving piperazine (p. 363) to asthmatic children if you think they have roundworms.

◆ **If the person does not get better, seek medical help.**

Prevention:

A person with asthma should avoid eating or breathing things that bring on attacks. The house or work place should be kept clean. Do not let chickens or other animals inside. Put bedding out to air in the sunshine. Sometimes it helps to sleep outside in the open air. Persons with asthma may improve when they move to a different area where the air is cleaner.

If you have asthma do not smoke—smoking damages your lungs even more.

COUGH

Coughing is not a sickness in itself, but is a sign of many different sicknesses that affect the throat, lungs, or *bronchi* (the network of air tubes going into the lungs). Below are some of the problems that cause different kinds of coughs:

DRY COUGH WITH LITTLE OR NO PHLEGM:	COUGH WITH MUCH OR LITTLE PHLEGM:	COUGH WITH A WHEEZE OR WHOOP AND TROUBLE BREATHING:
cold or flu (p. 163) worms—when passing through the lungs (p. 140) measles (p. 311) smoker's cough (smoking, p. 149)	bronchitis (p. 170) pneumonia (p. 171) asthma (p. 167)	asthma (p. 167) whooping cough (p. 313) diphtheria (p. 313) heart trouble (p. 325)

CHRONIC OR PERSISTENT COUGH:	COUGHING UP BLOOD:
tuberculosis (p. 179) smoker's or miner's cough (p. 149) asthma (repeated attacks, p. 167) chronic bronchitis (p. 170) emphysema (p. 170)	tuberculosis (p. 179) pneumonia (yellow, green, or blood-streaked phlegm, p. 171) severe worm infection (p. 140)

Coughing is the body's way of cleaning the breathing system and getting rid of phlegm (mucus with pus) and germs in the throat or lungs. So when a cough produces phlegm, **do not take medicine to stop the cough, but rather do something to help loosen and bring up the phlegm.**

Treatment for cough:

1. **To loosen mucus** and ease any kind of cough, **drink lots of water.** This works better than any medicine. (However, potassium iodide may help. See page 370.)

Also **breathe hot water vapors.** Sit on a chair with a bucket of very hot water at your feet. Place a sheet over your head and cover the bucket to catch the vapors as they rise. Breathe the vapors deeply for 15 minutes. Repeat several times a day. Some people like to add mint or eucalyptus leaves or *Vaporub,* but hot water works just as well alone.

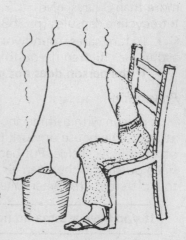

2. **For all kinds of cough,** especially a dry cough, the following cough syrup can be given:

Mix:

| 1 part honey | 1 part lemon juice | 1 part gin or rum |

Take a teaspoonful every 2 or 3 hours. For little children and people who have difficulty in breathing, leave out the alcohol.

3. **For a severe dry cough that does not let you sleep,** you can take a syrup with codeine (p. 369), or a mixture of chloral hydrate (p. 369). Tablets of aspirin with codeine (or even aspirin alone) also help. If there is a lot of phlegm or wheezing, do not use codeine.

4. **For a cough with wheezing** (difficult, noisy breathing), see Asthma (p. 164), Chronic Bronchitis (p. 170), and Heart Trouble (p. 325).

5. **Try to find out what sickness is causing the cough and treat that.** If the cough lasts a long time, if there is blood, pus, or smelly phlegm in it, or if the person is losing weight or has continual difficulty breathing, see a health worker.

6. **If you have any kind of a cough, do not smoke.** Smoking damages the lungs.

To prevent a cough, do not smoke.
To cure a cough, treat the illness that causes it—and do not smoke.
To calm a cough, and loosen phlegm, drink lots of water—and do not smoke.

HOW TO DRAIN MUCUS FROM THE LUNGS (POSTURAL DRAINAGE):

When a person who has a bad cough is very old or weak and cannot get rid of the sticky mucus or phlegm in his chest, it will help if he drinks a lot of water. Also do the following:

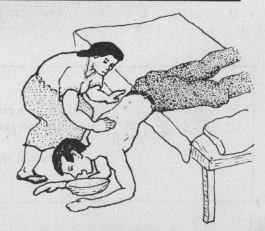

◆ First, have him breathe hot water vapors to loosen the mucus.

◆ Then have him lie partly on the bed, with his head and chest hanging over the edge. Pound him lightly on the back. This will help to bring out the mucus.

BRONCHITIS

Bronchitis is an infection of the bronchi or tubes that carry air to the lungs. It causes a noisy cough, often with mucus or phlegm. Bronchitis is usually caused by a virus, so antibiotics do not generally help. **Use antibiotics only if the bronchitis lasts more than a week** and is not getting better, if the person shows signs of **pneumonia** (see the following page), or if he already has a **chronic lung problem.**

CHRONIC BRONCHITIS:

Signs:

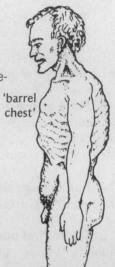

'barrel chest'

• A cough, with mucus that lasts for months or years. Sometimes the cough gets worse, and there may be fever. A person who has this kind of cough, but does not have another long-term illness such as tuberculosis or asthma, probably has chronic bronchitis.

• It occurs most frequently in older persons who have been heavy smokers.

• It can lead to *emphysema,* a very serious and incurable condition of the lungs. A person with emphysema has a hard time breathing, especially with exercise, and his chest becomes big 'like a barrel'.

Emphysema can result from chronic asthma or chronic bronchitis.

Treatment:

♦ Stop smoking.

♦ Take an anti-asthma medicine with ephedrine or theophylline (p. 370).

♦ Persons with chronic bronchitis should use ampicillin or tetracycline every time they have a cold or 'flu' with a fever.

♦ If the person has trouble coughing up sticky phlegm, have him breathe hot water vapors (p. 168) and then help him with postural drainage (see p. 169).

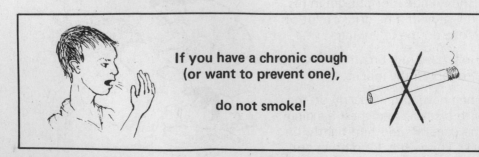

If you have a chronic cough (or want to prevent one),

do not smoke!

PNEUMONIA

Pneumonia is an acute infection of the lungs. It often occurs after other respiratory illnesses such as measles, whooping cough, flu, bronchitis, asthma—or any very serious illness.

Signs:

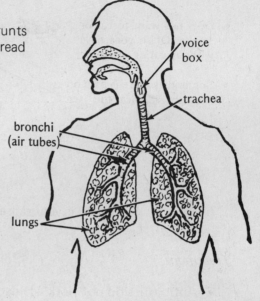

- Sudden chills and then high fever.

- Rapid, shallow breathing, with little grunts or sometimes wheezing. The nostrils may spread with each breath.

- Fever (sometimes newborns and old or very weak persons have severe pneumonia with little or no fever).

- Cough (often with yellow, greenish, rust-colored, or slightly bloody mucus).

- Chest pain (sometimes).

- The person looks very ill.

- Cold sores often appear on the face or lips (p. 232).

A very sick child who takes more than 50 **shallow** breaths a minute probably has pneumonia.

(If breathing is rapid and **deep,** check for dehydration, p. 151 or hyperventilation, p. 24.)

Treatment:

- For pneumonia, treatment with antibiotics can make the difference between life and death. Give penicillin (p. 349) or sulfonamide tablets (p. 354). In serious cases, inject procaine penicillin (p. 350), adults: 400,000 units (250 mg.) 2 or 3 times a day or ampicillin (p. 351), 500 mg., 4 times a day. Give small children ¼ to ½ the adult dose. In children under 6, ampicillin is usually best.

- Give aspirin or acetaminophen (p. 365) to lower the temperature and lessen the pain.

- Give plenty of liquids. If the person will not eat, give him liquid foods or Rehydration Drink (see p. 152).

- Ease the cough and loosen the mucus by giving the person plenty of water and having him breathe hot water vapors (see p. 168). Postural drainage may also help (see p. 169).

- If the person is wheezing, an anti-asthma medicine with theophylline or ephedrine may help.

HEPATITIS

Hepatitis is a virus infection that harms the liver. Even though in some places people call it 'the fever' (see p. 25), hepatitis often causes little or no rise in temperature. The disease is usually mild in small children and more serious in older persons.

Signs:

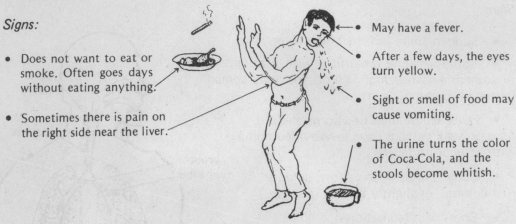

- Does not want to eat or smoke. Often goes days without eating anything.

- Sometimes there is pain on the right side near the liver.

- May have a fever.

- After a few days, the eyes turn yellow.

- Sight or smell of food may cause vomiting.

- The urine turns the color of Coca-Cola, and the stools become whitish.

In general, the person is very sick for 2 weeks and remains very weak for 1 to 3 months after.

Treatment:

- Antibiotics do not work against hepatitis. In fact some medicines will cause added damage to the sick liver. **Do not use medicines.**
- The sick person should rest and drink lots of liquids. If he refuses most food, give him orange juice, papaya, and other fruit, plus broth with chicken or other proteins (p. 110). It may help to take vitamins.
- To control vomiting, see p. 161.
- When the sick person can eat, give a balance of energy foods and protein. Beans, meat, chicken, and boiled eggs are good. Avoid lard and fatty foods. **Do not drink any alcohol** for a long time afterward.

Prevention:

- The hepatitis virus passes from the stool of one person to the mouth of another by way of contaminated water or food. To prevent others from getting sick, it is very important to bury or burn the sick person's stools and to keep him very clean. The person providing care should wash his hands well after each time he goes near the sick person.
- Small children often have hepatitis without any signs of sickness, but they can spread the disease to others. It is very important that everyone in the house follow all the guidelines of cleanliness with great care (see pages 133 to 139).

WARNING: Hepatitis can also be transmitted by giving injections with needles that are not sterile (not well boiled). **Always boil needles and syringes before each use.**

ARTHRITIS (PAINFUL, INFLAMED JOINTS)

Most chronic joint pain, or arthritis, in older people cannot be cured completely. However, the following offer some relief:

♦ **Rest.** If possible, avoid hard work and heavy exercise that bother the painful joints. If the arthritis causes some fever, it helps to take naps during the day.

♦ **Place hot compresses** (cloths soaked in hot water) on the painful joints (see p. 195).

♦ **Aspirin** helps relieve pain; the dose for arthritis is higher than that for calming other pain. Take 3 tablets, 4 to 6 times a day. If your ears begin to ring, take less. To avoid stomach problems caused by aspirin, take it with food, milk, bicarbonate of soda, or plenty of water.

♦ It is important to do simple **exercises** to help maintain or increase the range of motion in the painful joints.

If only one joint is swollen and feels hot, it probably is infected —especially if there is fever. Use an antibiotic such as penicillin (see p. 349) and if possible see a health worker.

Painful joints in young people and children may be a sign of other serious illness, such as rheumatic fever (p. 310) or tuberculosis (p. 179).

BACK PAIN

Back pain has many causes. Here are some:

Chronic upper back pain with cough and weight loss may be TB of the lungs (p. 179).

Mid back pain in a child may be TB of the spine, especially if the backbone has a hump or lump.

Low back pain that is worse the day after heavy lifting or straining may be a sprain.

Severe low back pain that first comes suddenly when lifting or twisting may be a *slipped disc*,

especially if one leg or foot becomes painful or numb and weak. This can result from a pinched nerve.

Standing or sitting wrong, with the shoulders drooped, is a common cause of backache.

In older people, chronic back pain is often arthritis.

Pain in the upper right back may be from a gallbladder problem (p. 329).

Acute (or chronic) pain here may be a urinary problem (p. 234).

Low backache is normal for some women during menstrual periods or pregnancy (p. 248).

Very low back pain sometimes comes from problems in the uterus, ovaries, or rectum.

Treatment and prevention of back pain:

• If back pain has a cause like TB, a urinary infection, or gallbladder disease, treat the cause. Seek medical help if you suspect a serious disease.

• Simple backache, including that of pregnancy, can often be prevented or made better by:

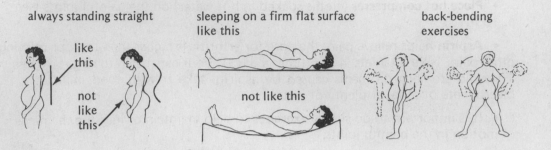

always standing straight

like this

not like this

sleeping on a firm flat surface like this

not like this

back-bending exercises

• Aspirin and hot soaks (p. 195) help calm most kinds of back pain.

• For low back pain that comes from lifting or straining, quick relief can sometimes be brought like this:

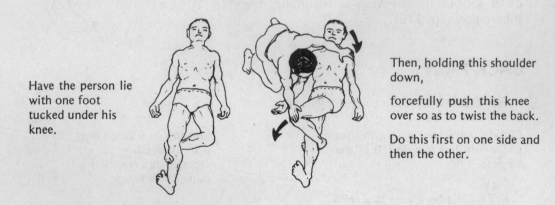

Have the person lie with one foot tucked under his knee.

Then, holding this shoulder down,

forcefully push this knee over so as to twist the back.

Do this first on one side and then the other.

CAUTION: Do not try this if the back pain is from a fall or injury.

• If back pain from lifting or twisting is sudden and severe with knife-like pain when you bend over, if the pain goes into the leg(s), or if a foot becomes numb or weak, this is serious. A nerve coming from the back may be 'pinched' by a slipped disc (pad between the bones of the back). It is best to rest flat on your back for a few days. It may help to put something firm under the knees and mid back.

• Take aspirin and use hot soaks. If pain does not begin to get better in a few days, seek medical advice.

VARICOSE VEINS

Varicose veins are veins that are swollen, twisted, and often painful. They are often seen on the legs of older people and of women who are pregnant or who have had many children.

Treatment:

There is no medicine for varicose veins. But the following will help:

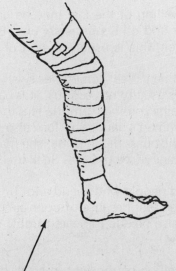

• Do not spend much time standing or sitting with your feet down. If you have no choice but to sit or stand for long periods, try to lie down with your feet up for a few moments every half hour. Also, sleep with your feet up (on pillows).

• Use elastic stockings (support hose) or elastic bandages to help hold in the veins. Be sure to take them off at night.

• Taking care of your veins in this way will help prevent chronic sores or *varicose ulcers* on the ankles (p. 213).

PILES (HEMORRHOIDS)

Piles or hemorrhoids are varicose veins of the anus or rectum, which feel like little lumps or balls. They may be painful, but are not dangerous. They frequently appear during pregnancy and may go away afterwards.

If a hemorrhoid begins to bleed and does not stop, the bleeding can sometimes be controlled by removing the clot that is inside the swollen vein. Tweezers like these can be used after they have been sterilized by boiling.

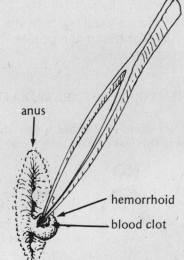

anus

hemorrhoid

blood clot

• Certain bitter plant juices (witch hazel, cactus, etc.) dabbed on hemorrhoids help shrink them. So do hemorrhoid *suppositories* (p. 375).

• Piles may be caused in part by constipation. It helps to eat plenty of fruit or food with a lot of fiber, like cassava or bran.

• Very large hemorrhoids may require an operation. Get medical advice.

SWELLING OF THE FEET
AND OTHER PARTS OF THE BODY

Swelling of the feet may be caused by a number of different problems, some minor and others more serious. But if the face or other parts of the body are also swollen, this is usually a sign of serious illness.

Women's feet sometimes swell during the last three months of pregnancy. This is usually not serious. It is caused by the weight of the child that presses on the veins coming from the legs in a way that limits the flow of blood. However, if the woman's hands and face also swell, she feels dizzy, has problems seeing, or does not pass much urine, she may be suffering from poisoning or *toxemia* of pregnancy (see p. 249). Seek medical help fast.

Old people who spend a lot of time sitting or standing in one place often get swollen feet because of poor circulation. However, swollen feet in older persons may also be due to heart trouble (p. 325) or, less commonly, kidney disease (p. 234).

Swelling of the feet in small children may result from anemia (p. 125) or malnutrition (p. 107). In severe cases the face and hands may also become swollen (see Kwashiorkor, p. 112).

Treatment:

To reduce swelling, treat the sickness that causes it. Use little or no salt in food. Herbal teas that make people urinate a lot usually help (see corn silk, p. 12). Also do the following:

WHEN YOUR FEET ARE SWOLLEN:

Do not spend time sitting with your feet down. This makes them swell more.

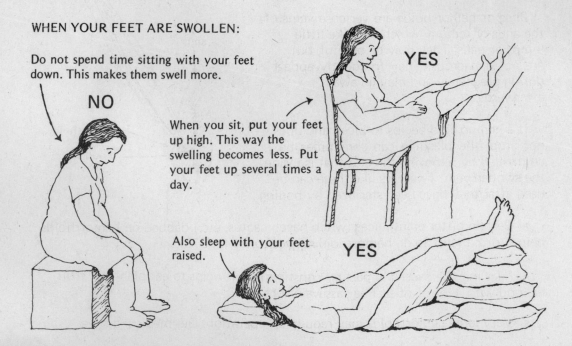

NO

YES

When you sit, put your feet up high. This way the swelling becomes less. Put your feet up several times a day.

Also sleep with your feet raised.

YES

HERNIA (RUPTURE)

A hernia is an opening or tear in the muscles covering the belly. This permits a loop of gut to push through and form a lump under the skin. Hernias usually come from lifting something heavy, or straining (as during childbirth). Some babies are born with a hernia (see p. 317). In men, hernias are common in the groin. Swollen lymph nodes (p. 88) may also cause lumps in the groin. However . . .

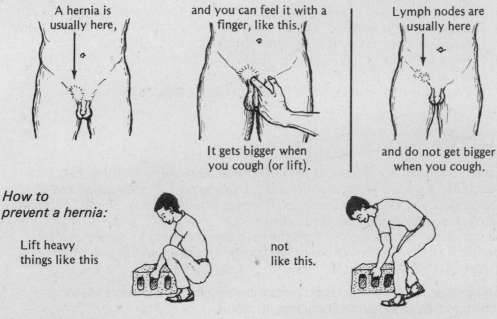

A hernia is usually here,

and you can feel it with a finger, like this.

It gets bigger when you cough (or lift).

Lymph nodes are usually here

and do not get bigger when you cough.

How to prevent a hernia:

Lift heavy things like this

not like this.

How to live with a hernia:

+ Avoid lifting heavy objects.

+ Make a truss to hold the hernia in.

PLAN FOR A SIMPLE TRUSS:

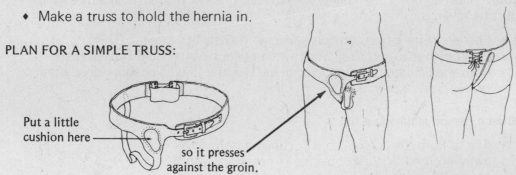

Put a little cushion here

so it presses against the groin.

CAUTION: If a hernia suddenly becomes large or painful, try to make it go back in by lying with the feet higher than the head and pressing gently on the bulge. If it will not go back, seek medical help.

If the hernia becomes very painful and causes vomiting, and the person cannot have a bowel movement, this can be very dangerous. Surgery may be necessary. Seek medical help fast. In the meantime, treat as for Appendicitis (p. 95).

FITS (CONVULSIONS)

We say a person has a fit when he suddenly loses consciousness and makes strange, jerking movements (convulsions). Fits come from a problem in the brain. In small children common causes of fits are **high fever** and **severe dehydration.** In very ill persons, the cause may be **meningitis, malaria of the brain,** or **poisoning.** A person who often has fits may have epilepsy.

- Try to figure out the cause of a fit and treat it, if possible.
- If the child has a high fever, lower it at once with cool water (see p. 76).
- If the child is dehydrated, give an enema of Rehydration Drink **slowly.** Send for medical help. Give nothing by mouth during a fit.
- If there are signs of meningitis (p. 185), begin treatment at once and seek medical help.
- If you suspect cerebral malaria (p. 358), inject chloroquine (p. 357).

EPILEPSY

Epilepsy causes fits in people who otherwise seem fairly healthy. Fits may come hours, days, weeks, or months apart. In some persons they cause loss of consciousness and violent movements. The eyes often roll back. In mild types of epilepsy the person may suddenly 'blank out' a moment, make strange movements, or behave oddly. Epilepsy is more common in some families (inherited). Or it may come from brain damage at birth, high fever in infancy, or tapeworm cysts in the brain (p. 143).

Epilepsy is not an infection and cannot be 'caught'. It is often a life-long problem. However, infants sometimes get over it.

Medicines to prevent epileptic fits:

Note: These do not 'cure' epilepsy; they help prevent fits. Often the medicine must be taken for life.

- Phenobarbital often controls epilepsy. It costs little (see p. 373).
- Diphenylhydantoin may work when phenobarbital does not. Sometimes both medicines are needed together. Use the lowest possible dose that prevents fits (see p. 374).

When a person is having a fit:

- Try to keep the person from hurting himself: move away all hard or sharp objects. If necessary, put a corn cob or padded piece of wood between his teeth to prevent him from biting his tongue.
- After the fit the person may be dull and sleepy. Let him sleep.
- If fits last a long time, inject diazepam (*Valium*) or phenobarbital. For dosages see p. 370 to 374. If the fit still has not stopped after 15 minutes, give a second dose.

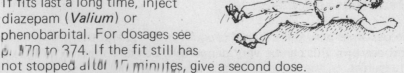

CHAPTER

14

SERIOUS ILLNESSES THAT NEED SPECIAL MEDICAL ATTENTION

The diseases covered in this chapter are often difficult or impossible to cure without medical help. Many need special medicines that are difficult to get in rural areas. Home remedies will not cure them. If a person has one of these illnesses, *THE SOONER HE GETS MEDICAL HELP, THE BETTER HIS CHANCE OF GETTING WELL.*

CAUTION: Many of the illnesses covered in other chapters may also be serious and require medical assistance. See the **Signs of dangerous illness,** p. 42.

TUBERCULOSIS (TB, CONSUMPTION)

Tuberculosis of the lungs is a *chronic* (long-lasting), *contagious* (easily spread) disease that anyone can get. But it most often strikes persons between 15 and 35 years of age—especially those who are weak, are poorly nourished, or live with someone who has the disease.

Tuberculosis is curable. Yet thousands die needlessly from this disease every year. Both for prevention and cure, it is very important to **treat tuberculosis early.** Therefore, you should **know the signs of tuberculosis and be on the lookout for them.**

Most frequent signs of TB:

- Chronic cough, especially just after waking up.
- Mild fever in the afternoon and sweating at night.
- There may be pain in the chest or upper back.
- Chronic loss of weight and increasing weakness.

In serious or advanced cases:

- Coughing up blood (usually a little, but in some cases a lot).
- Pale, waxy skin.
- Voice grows hoarse (very serious).

Tuberculosis is usually only in the lungs. But it can affect any part of the body. In young children it may cause meningitis (see p. 185). For skin problems from TB, see p. 212.

If you think you might have tuberculosis:

Seek medical help. At the first sign of tuberculosis, go to a health center where the workers can give you a skin test, take an X-ray, and examine the stuff you cough up (*phlegm* or *sputum*) to see if you have TB or not. Many governments give the medicines free. Ask at the nearest health center. You will probably be given 2 or 3 of the following:

- Streptomycin injections (p. 355)
- Isoniazid (I.N.H.) pills (p. 356)
- P.A.S. (aminosalicylic acid) pills (p. 356)

- Thiacetazone (p. 356)
- Ethambutol pills (p. 356)

It is very important to take the medicines as directed. At least 2 must be taken at the same time. (For the risks and precautions in the use of these medicines, see p. 355 to 356.)

Continue taking the medicines until the health worker tells you that you are cured. Do not stop taking the medicines just because you feel better. **To cure tuberculosis completely usually takes from 1 to 2 years.**

Eat as well as possible: plenty of foods rich in proteins and vitamins, as well as energy foods (p. 110 to 111).

Rest is important. You should stop working and take it easy until you begin to get better. From then on, try not to work so hard that you become tired or breathe with difficulty. Try to always get enough rest and sleep.

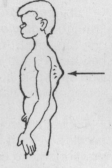

Tuberculosis in any other part of the body is treated the same as TB of the lungs. For children with severe tuberculosis of the backbone, surgery may be needed to prevent paralysis.

TB of
the backbone

Tuberculosis is very contagious. Persons who live in the same house with someone who has TB, especially children, run a great risk of catching the disease.

If someone in the house has TB:

- If possible, see that the whole family is tested for TB.
- Have the children vaccinated against TB.
- Everyone, especially the children, should eat plenty of nutritious food (see p. 110).
- The person who has TB should eat and sleep separately from the children, if possible in a different room, as long as he has any cough at all.
- A person with TB should be careful to cover his mouth when coughing and should never spit on the floor.
- Take a child to a health center at the first suspicion of TB or if he gets a cough that lasts more than 2 weeks.
- Treat TB at once. A person who no longer has TB will not spread it.

Early and full treatment is a key part of prevention.

RABIES

Rabies comes from the bite of a rabid or 'mad' animal, usually a rabid dog, cat, fox, wolf, skunk, or jackal. Bats and other animals may also spread rabies.

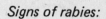

Signs of rabies:

In the animal:

- Acts strangely—sometimes sad, restless, or irritable.
- Foaming at the mouth, cannot eat or drink.
- Sometimes the animal goes wild (mad) and may bite anyone or anything nearby.
- The animal dies within 5 to 7 days.

Signs in people:

- Pain and tingling in the area of the bite.
- Pain and difficulty swallowing. A lot of thick, sticky saliva.
- Fits of anger between periods of calm.
- As death nears, fits (convulsions) and paralysis.

If you have any reason to believe an animal that has bitten someone has rabies:

- Tie or cage the animal for a week.
- Clean the bite well with soap, water, and hydrogen peroxide. Do not close the wound; leave it open.
- If the animal dies before the week is up (or if it was killed or cannot be caught), take the bitten person at once to a health center where he can be given a series of anti-rabies injections.

The first symptoms of rabies appear from 10 days up to 2 years after the bite (usually within 3 to 7 weeks). Treatment must begin before the first signs of the sickness appear. Once the sickness begins, no treatment known to medical science can save the person's life.

Prevention:

- Kill and bury (or cage for one week) any animal suspected of having rabies.
- Cooperate with programs to vaccinate dogs.
- Keep children far away from any animal that seems sick or acts strangely.

> **Take great care in handling any animal that seems sick or acts strangely. Even if it does not bite anyone, its saliva can cause rabies if it gets into a cut or scratch.**

TETANUS (LOCKJAW)

Tetanus results when a germ that lives in the feces of animals or people enters the body through a wound. Deep or dirty wounds are especially dangerous.

Wounds very likely to cause tetanus:

animal bites, especially those of dogs and pigs

gunshot and knife wounds

holes made with dirty needles

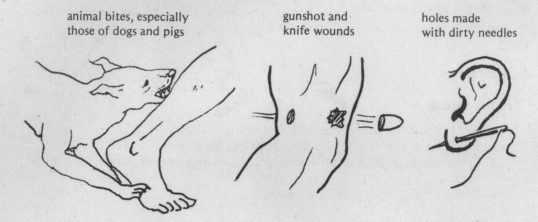

injuries caused by barbed wire

puncture wounds from thorns, splinters, or nails

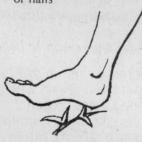

Causes of tetanus in the newborn child:

Tetanus germs enter through the *umbilical cord* of a newborn baby because of lack of cleanliness or failure to take other simple precautions. The chance of tetanus is greater . . .

WHEN THE CORD IS CUT A LONG WAY FROM THE BODY, LIKE THIS, THE CHANCE OF TETANUS IS GREATER.

- when the cord has been cut with an instrument that has not been boiled and kept completely clean or

- when the cord has not been cut **close** to the body (see p. 262) or

- when the newly cut cord is tightly covered or is not kept dry.

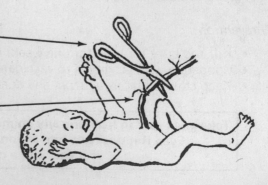

Signs of tetanus:

- An infected wound (sometimes no wound can be found).

- Discomfort and difficulty in swallowing.

- The jaw gets stiff (lockjaw), then the muscles of the neck and other parts of the body.

- Painful *convulsions* (sudden tightening) of the jaw and finally of the whole body. Moving or touching the person may trigger sudden *spasms* like this:

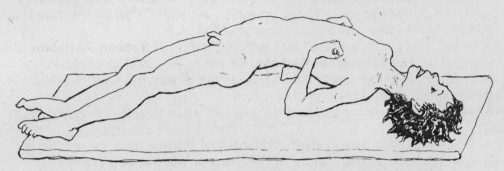

Sudden noise or bright light may also bring on these spasms.

In the newborn, the first signs of tetanus generally appear 3 to 10 days after birth. The child begins to cry continuously and is unable to suck. Often the umbilical area is dirty or infected. After several hours or days, lockjaw and the other signs of tetanus begin.

It is very important to start treating tetanus at the first sign. If you suspect tetanus (or if a newborn child cries continuously or stops nursing), make this test:

TEST OF KNEE REFLEXES

With the leg hanging freely, tap the knee with a knuckle just below the kneecap.

If the leg jumps just a little bit, the reaction is normal.

If the leg jumps high, this indicates a serious illness like tetanus (or perhaps meningitis or poisoning with certain medicines or rat poison).

This test is especially useful when you suspect tetanus in a newborn baby.

What to do when there are signs of tetanus:

Tetanus is a deadly disease. Seek medical help at the first sign. If there is any delay in getting help, do the following things:

♦ Examine the whole body for infected wounds or sores. Often the wound will contain pus. Open the wound and wash it with soap and boiled water; completely remove all dirt, pus, thorns, splinters, etc.; flood the wound with hydrogen peroxide if you have any.

♦ Inject 1 million units of procaine penicillin at once and repeat every 12 hours (p. 350). (For newborn babies crystalline penicillin is better.) If there is no penicillin, use another antibiotic, like tetracycline.

♦ If you can get it, inject 40,000 to 50,000 units of **Tetanus Antitoxin** or 5,000 units of **Human Immune Globulin.** Be sure to follow all the precautions (see p. 70). Human Immune Globulin has less risk of severe allergic reaction, but is more expensive and harder to obtain.

♦ As long as the person can swallow, give nutritious liquids in frequent, small sips.

♦ To control convulsions, inject phenobarbital (for the dose, see p. 374) or diazepam (*Valium,* p. 374), adults: 10 to 20 mg. to start with, and more as necessary.

♦ Touch and move the person as little as possible. Avoid noise and bright light.

♦ If necessary, use a *catheter* (rubber tube) connected to a syringe to suck the mucus from the nose and throat. This helps clear the airway.

How to prevent tetanus:

Even in the best hospitals, half of the people with tetanus die. It is much easier to prevent tetanus than to treat it.

♦ **Vaccination:** This is the surest protection against tetanus. Both children and adults should be vaccinated. Vaccinate your whole family at the nearest health center (see p. 147). **Vaccinating pregnant women against tetanus will prevent tetanus in newborn infants** (see p. 250).

♦ When you have a wound, especially a dirty or deep wound, clean and take care of it in the manner described on page 89.

♦ If the wound is very big, deep, or dirty, seek medical help. If you have not been vaccinated against tetanus, take penicillin. Also consider getting an injection of tetanus antitoxin.

♦ In newborn babies, cleanliness is very important to prevent tetanus. The instrument used to cut the umbilical cord should be sterilized (see p. 262); the cord should be cut short, and the umbilical area kept clean and dry.

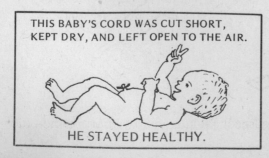

THIS BABY'S CORD WAS CUT SHORT, KEPT DRY, AND LEFT OPEN TO THE AIR.

HE STAYED HEALTHY.

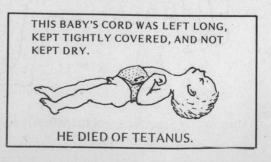

THIS BABY'S CORD WAS LEFT LONG, KEPT TIGHTLY COVERED, AND NOT KEPT DRY.

HE DIED OF TETANUS.

MENINGITIS

This is a very serious infection of the brain, more common in children. It may begin as a *complication* of another illness, such as measles, mumps, whooping cough, or an ear infection. Children of mothers who have tuberculosis sometimes get tubercular meningitis in the first few months of life.

Signs:

- Fever.

- Severe headache.

- Stiff neck. The child looks very ill, and lies with his head and neck bent back, like this:——————————

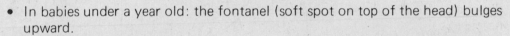

- The back is too stiff to put the head between the knees.

- In babies under a year old: the fontanel (soft spot on top of the head) bulges upward.

- Vomiting is common.

- The child is very sleepy.

- Sometimes there are fits (convulsions) or strange movements.

- The child often gets worse and worse until he loses consciousness.

- Tubercular meningitis develops slowly, over days or weeks. Other forms of meningitis come on more quickly, in hours or days.

Treatment:

Get medical help fast—every minute counts! If possible take the person to a hospital. Meanwhile:

- Inject ampicillin, 500 mg. every 4 hours (see p. 351) or crystalline penicillin, 1,000,000 U. every 4 hours (see p. 350).

- If there is high fever (more than 40°), lower it with wet cloths and aspirin or acetaminophen (see p. 365 to 366).

- If the mother has tuberculosis or if you have any other reason to suspect that the child has tubercular meningitis, inject him with 0.2 ml. of streptomycin for each 5 kilos he weighs and get medical help at once. Also, use ampicillin or penicillin in case the meningitis is not from TB.

Prevention:

For prevention of tubercular meningitis, newborn babies of mothers with tuberculosis should be vaccinated with B.C.G. at birth. Dose for the newborn is 0.05 ml. (half the normal dose of 0.1 ml.). For other suggestions on prevention of TB, see pages 179 to 180.

MALARIA

Malaria is an infection of the blood that causes chills and high fever. Malaria is spread by mosquitos. The mosquito sucks up the malaria parasites in the blood of an infected person and injects them into the next person it bites.

Signs of malaria:

- The typical attack strikes every 2 or 3 days and lasts several hours. It has 3 stages:

1. It begins with chills— and often headache. The person shivers or shakes for 15 minutes to an hour.

2. Chills are followed by fever, often 40° or more. The person is weak, flushed (red skin), and at times delirious (not in his right mind). The fever lasts several hours.

3. Finally the person begins to sweat, and his temperature goes down. After an attack, the person feels weak, but more or less OK.

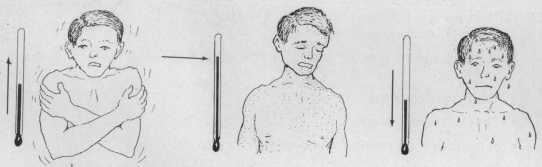

- Usually malaria causes fevers every 2 or 3 days (depending on the kind of malaria), but in the beginning it may cause fever daily. Also, in small children and persons who have had malaria before, the fever pattern may not be regular or typical. For this reason anyone who suffers from unexplained fevers should have his blood tested for malaria.

- Chronic malaria often causes a large *spleen* and anemia.

Analysis and treatment:

- If you suspect malaria or suffer from repeated fevers, go to a health center for a blood test.

- If there is no health center nearby, take chloroquine or whatever medicine is known to work best in your area. Using chloroquine tablets with 150 mg. of base, adults should take 4 tablets once a day for 3 days. For the children's dosage, see p. 358.

- If you get better with chloroquine, but after several days the fevers start again, you may need a different medicine, like primaquine. Get advice from the nearest health center.

- If a person who possibly has malaria begins to have fits or other signs of meningitis (p. 185) he may have *cerebral* malaria. If possible inject chloroquine at once (see p. 357).

HOW TO AVOID MALARIA:

Malaria is a problem in many of the hot or tropical parts of the world. If everyone cooperates, it can be controlled. All these control measures should be practiced at once.

1. Avoid mosquitos. Sleep where there are no mosquitos or underneath a sheet.

Cover the baby's cradle with a mosquito netting or a thin cloth.

2. Cooperate with the malaria control workers when they come to your village. Tell them if anyone in the family has had fevers and let them take blood for testing.

3. If you suspect malaria, get treatment quickly. After you have been treated, mosquitos that bite you will not pass malaria on to others.

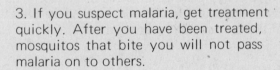

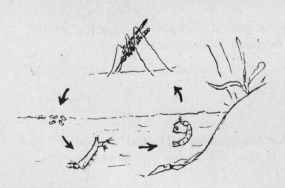

4. Destroy mosquitos and their *larvae* (young). Mosquitos breed in standing water. Clear the neighborhood of ponds, pits, old cans, or broken pots that collect water. Drain or put a little oil on pools or marshes where mosquitos breed. Organize children to fill the cut off tops of bamboo poles (of fences, etc.) with sand.

5. Malaria can also be prevented, or its effects greatly reduced, by taking different doses of anti-malaria medicines on a regular schedule. For more information about this, see pages 357 to 358.

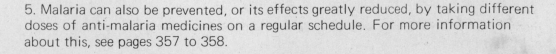

BRUCELLOSIS (UNDULANT FEVER, MALTA FEVER)

PREVENT BRUCELLOSIS:

NEVER DRINK
UNBOILED MILK

This is a disease that comes from drinking fresh milk from infected cows or goats. It may also enter the body through scrapes or wounds in the skin of persons who work with sick cattle, goats, or pigs.

Signs:

- Brucellosis may start with fever and chills, but it often begins very gradually, with increasing tiredness, weakness, loss of appetite, headache, stomach-ache, and sometimes joint pains.

- The fevers may be mild or severe. Typically, these begin with afternoon chills and end with sweating in the early morning. In chronic brucellosis, the fevers may stop for several days and then return. Without treatment, brucellosis may last for years.

- There may be swollen lymph nodes (see p. 88).

Treatment:

- If you suspect brucellosis, get medical advice, because it is easy to confuse this disease with others, and the treatment is long and expensive.

- Treat with tetracycline, adults: two 250 mg. capsules 4 times a day for 15 to 21 days. For precautions see page 353.

Prevention:

- **Drink only cow's or goat's milk that has been boiled or pasteurized.** In areas where brucellosis is a problem, it is safer not to eat cheese made from unboiled milk.

- Be careful when handling cattle, goats, and pigs, especially if you have any cuts or scrapes.

- Cooperate with livestock inspectors who check to be sure your animals are healthy.

TYPHOID FEVER

Typhoid is an infection of the gut that affects the whole body. It is spread from *feces-to-mouth* in contaminated food and water and often comes in *epidemics* (many people sick at once).

Of the different infections sometimes called 'the fever' (see p. 25), typhoid is one of the most dangerous.

Signs:

First week:

- It begins like a cold or flu.
- Headache and sore throat.
- The fever rises a little more each day until it reaches 40° or more.
- Pulse is often relatively slow for the amount of fever present. Take the pulse and temperature every half hour. **If the pulse gets slower when the fever goes up, the person probably has typhoid** (see p. 26).
- Sometimes there is vomiting, diarrhea, or constipation.

1st day   37½° C

2nd day   38°

3rd day   38½°

4th day   39°

5th day   39½°

6th day   40°

Second week:

- High fever, pulse relatively slow.
- A few pink spots may appear on the body.
- Trembling.
- Delirium (person does not think clearly or make sense).
- Weakness, weight loss, dehydration.

Third week:

- If there are no complications, the fever and other symptoms slowly go away.

Treatment:

- Seek medical help.
- Give chloramphenicol (see p. 353), adults: 3 capsules of 250 mg. 4 times a day. If there is no chloramphenicol, use ampicillin. If there is no ampicillin either, use tetracycline.
- Lower the fever with cool wet cloths (see p. 76).
- Give plenty of liquids: soups, juices, and Rehydration Drink to avoid dehydration (see p. 152).
- Give nutritious foods, in liquid form if necessary.
- The person should stay in bed until the fever is completely gone.
- If the person shits blood or develops signs of peritonitis (p. 94) or pneumonia (p. 171), he should be sent to a hospital at once.

Prevention of typhoid:

♦ To prevent typhoid, care must be taken to avoid contamination of water and food by human feces. Follow the guidelines of personal and public hygiene in Chapter 12. Make and use latrines. Be sure latrines are a safe distance from where people get drinking water.

♦ Cases of typhoid often appear after a flood or other disaster, and special care must be taken with cleanliness at these times. Be sure drinking water is clean. If there are cases of typhoid in your village, all drinking water should be boiled. Look for the cause of contaminated water or food.

♦ To avoid the spread of typhoid, a person who has the disease should stay in a separate room. No one else should eat or drink from the dishes he uses. His stools should be burned or buried in deep holes. Persons who care for him should wash their hands right afterwards.

♦ After recovering from typhoid, some persons still carry the disease and can spread it to others. For this reason anyone who has had typhoid should be extra careful with personal cleanliness and should not work in restaurants or where food is handled. Sometimes ampicillin is effective in treating typhoid carriers.

TYPHUS

Typhus is an illness similar to but different from typhoid. The infection is transmitted by bites of:

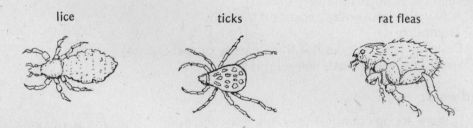

lice   ticks   rat fleas

Signs:

● Typhus begins like a bad cold. After a week or more fever begins, with chills, headache, and pain in the muscles and chest.

● After a few days of fever a typical rash appears, first on the main part of the body, then the arms and legs, but not the face. The rash looks like many tiny bruises.

● The fever lasts 2 weeks or more. Typhus is usually mild in children and very severe in old people. An epidemic form of typhus is especially dangerous.

● In typhus spread by ticks, there is often a large painful sore at the point of the bite, and the lymph nodes nearby are swollen and painful.

Treatment of typhus:

♦ If you think someone may have typhus, get medical advice. Special tests are often needed.

♦ Give tetracycline, adults: 2 capsules of 250 mg., 4 times a day for 4 to 10 days (see p. 353). Chloramphenicol also works, but is riskier (p. 353).

How to prevent typhus:

♦ Keep clean. De-louse the whole family regularly.

♦ Remove ticks from your dogs and do not allow dogs in your house.

♦ Kill rats and put insecticides (insect poison) in their holes or nests.

LEPROSY (HANSEN'S DISEASE)

This chronic disease develops very slowly, often over many years. It is not easily spread from one person to another, but persons who have lived for a long time in close contact with those who have leprosy sometimes get the disease.

Signs:

The signs differ greatly according to the person's natural resistance to the disease.

● Often the main sign is **loss of feeling,** usually first in the hands and feet. Persons with leprosy sometimes burn themselves without knowing it.

● Skin signs vary greatly. They include: pale spots or big ringworm-like marks that have loss of feeling in the center; swollen nerves that form thick cords or lumps under the skin; and large, chronic sores that do not hurt or itch. In one form of leprosy the skin of the face becomes thick and lumpy or the earlobes may become thick, short, and square. The eyebrows are often lost, first the outer part and then completely.

● In advanced cases, the hands and feet may become partly paralyzed and claw-like. Fingers and toes, or entire hands and feet, may gradually get shorter and become stumps.

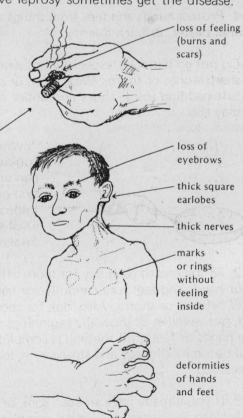

loss of feeling (burns and scars)

loss of eyebrows

thick square earlobes

thick nerves

marks or rings without feeling inside

deformities of hands and feet

POSSIBLE SIGNS OF LEPROSY

Treatment of leprosy:

Leprosy is usually curable, but medicine must be taken for years. The best medicines are the sulfones. For the dose, see page 357. If a "lepra reaction" (fever, a rash, pain and perhaps swelling of hands and feet, or eye damage) occurs or gets worse while taking the medicine, keep taking it but get medical help.

Prevention of damage to hands and feet:

The large open sores and gradual loss of hands and feet so often seen in persons with leprosy are not caused by the disease itself and can be prevented. They result because, when feeling has been lost, a person no longer protects himself against injury.

For example, if a person with normal feeling walks a long way and begins to get blisters on his feet, these hurt, so he stops walking or limps. This protects his feet from further damage. But a person with leprosy, who feels no pain, will keep on walking, and the blister turns into an open sore. This becomes infected, and because it still does not hurt, the person does not protect it or give it a chance to heal. So the infection slowly spreads into the bones and begins to destroy them. Typical deformities result. But with care they can be prevented:

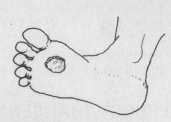

1. Protect hands and feet from things that can cut, bruise, blister, or burn them:

Do not go barefoot, especially not where there are sharp stones or thorns. Wear shoes or sandals. Put soft padding inside shoes and under straps that may rub.

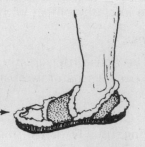

When you are working with your hands, or cooking meals, wear gloves. Never pick up a pan or other object that **might** be hot without first protecting your hand with a thick glove or folded cloth. If possible, avoid work that involves handling sharp or hot objects. Do not smoke.

2. At the end of each day (or more often if you work hard or walk far) examine your hands and feet very carefully—or have someone else examine them. Look for cuts, bruises, or thorns. Also look for spots or areas on the hands and feet that are red, hot, swollen or show the beginnings of blisters. If you find any of these, rest the hands or feet until the skin is completely normal again. In this way the skin will become calloused and stronger, instead of blistered and raw. Sores can be prevented.

3. If you already have an open sore, or one forms, keep the part with the sore very clean and at rest until it has completely healed. Then take great care not to injure the area again.

If you do these things and begin treatment early . . .

Most deformities with leprosy can be prevented.

CHAPTER

15

SKIN PROBLEMS

Some skin problems are caused by diseases or irritations that affect the skin only—such as ringworm, diaper rash, or warts. Other skin problems are signs of diseases that affect the whole body—such as the rash of measles or the sore, dry patches of pellagra (malnutrition). Certain kinds of sores or skin conditions may be signs of serious diseases—like tuberculosis, syphilis, or leprosy.

This chapter deals only with the more common skin problems in rural areas. However, there are hundreds of diseases of the skin. Some look so much alike that they are hard to tell apart—yet their causes and the specific treatments they require may be quite different.

> **If a skin problem is serious or gets worse in spite of treatment, seek medical help.**

GENERAL RULES FOR TREATING SKIN PROBLEMS

Although many skin problems need specific treatment, there are a few general measures that often help:

RULE #1

If the affected area is **hot** and painful, treat it with **heat.** Put hot, moist cloths on it *(hot compresses).*

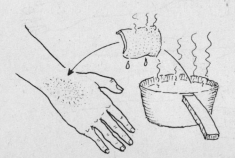

RULE #2

If the affected area itches, stings, or oozes, treat it with **cold.** Put cool, wet cloths on it *(cold compresses).*

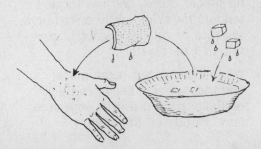

RULE #1 (in greater detail)

If the skin shows signs of serious infection such as:

- inflammation (redness of skin around the affected areas)

- swelling

- pain

- heat (it feels hot)

- pus

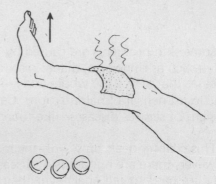

Do the following:

- Keep the affected part still and elevate it (put it higher than the rest of the body).

- Apply hot, moist cloths.

- If the infection is severe or the person has a fever, give antibiotics (penicillin or a sulfonamide).

Danger signs include: swollen lymph nodes, a red line above the infected area, or a bad smell. If these do not get better with treatment—use an antibiotic and seek medical help quickly.

RULE #2 (in greater detail)

If the affected skin forms blisters or a crust, oozes, itches, stings, or burns, do the following:

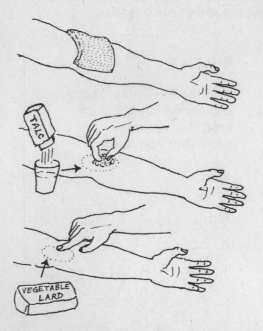

- Apply cloths soaked in cool water with white vinegar (2 tablespoons of vinegar in 1 quart of pure or boiled water).

- When the affected area feels better, no longer oozes, and has formed tender new skin, lightly spread on a mixture of talc and water (1 part talc to 1 part water).

- When healing has taken place, and the new skin begins to thicken or flake, rub on a little vegetable lard or body oil to soften it.

RULE #3

If the skin areas affected are on parts of the body often exposed to sunlight, protect them from the sun.

RULE #4

If the skin areas most affected are usually covered by clothing, expose them to direct sunlight for 20 minutes, 2 or 3 times a day.

Instructions for Using Hot Compresses (Hot Soaks):

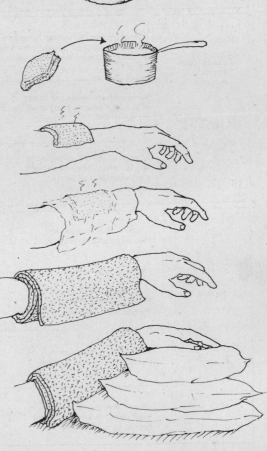

1. Boil water and allow it to cool until you can just hold your hand in it.

2. Fold a clean cloth so it is slightly larger than the area you want to treat, wet the cloth in the hot water, and squeeze out the extra water.

3. Put the cloth over the affected skin.

4. Cover the cloth with a sheet of thin plastic or cellophane.

5. Wrap it with a towel to hold in the heat.

6. Keep the affected part raised.

7. When the cloth starts to cool, put it back in the hot water and repeat.

SKIN PROBLEMS — A Guide to Identification

IF THE SKIN HAS:	AND LOOKS LIKE:	YOU MAY HAVE:	SEE PAGE:
small or pimple-like sores	Tiny bumps or sores with much itching—first between fingers, on the wrists, or the waist.	scabies	199
	Pimples or sores with pus or inflammation, often from scratching insect bites. May cause swollen lymph nodes.	infection from bacteria	201
	Irregular, spreading sores with shiny, yellow crusts.	impetigo (bacterial infection)	202
	Pimples on young people's faces, sometimes chest and back, often with small heads of pus.	acne, pimples, blackheads	211
	A sore on the genitals, without itching or pain.	syphilis / venereal lymphogranuloma	237 / 238
a large, open sore or skin ulcer	A large chronic (unhealing) sore surrounded by purplish skin—on or near the ankles of older people with varicose veins.	ulcers from bad circulation (possibly diabetes)	213 / 127
	Sores over the bones and joints of very sick persons who cannot get out of bed.	bed sores	214
	Sores with loss of feeling on the feet or hands. (They do not hurt even when pricked with a needle.)	leprosy	191
lumps under the skin	A warm, painful swelling that occasionally breaks open.	abscess or boil	202
	A warm, painful lump in the breast of a woman breast feeding.	mastitis (bacterial infection), possibly cancer	278 / 279
	A lump that keeps growing. Usually not painful at first.	cancer (also see lymph nodes)	279 / 88
	One or more round lumps on the head, neck, or upper body (or central body and thighs).	river blindness (also see lymph nodes)	227 / 88

A Guide to Identification

IF THE SKIN HAS:	AND LOOKS LIKE:		YOU MAY HAVE:	SEE PAGE:
swollen lymph nodes	Nodes on the side of the neck that continuously break open and scar.		scrofula (a type of tuberculosis)	212
	Nodes in the groin that continuously break open and scar.		venereal lymphogranuloma	238
large spots or patches	Dark patches on the forehead and cheeks of pregnant women.		mask of pregnancy	207
dark	Scaly, cracking areas that look like sunburn on the arms, legs, neck, or face.		pellagra (a type of malnutrition)	208 209
	Purple spots or peeling sores on children with swollen feet.		malnutrition	208 209
	Round or irregular patches on the face or body, especially of children.		tinea versicolor (fungus infection)	206
white	White patches, especially on hands, feet, or lips.	that begin with reddish or bluish pimples	pinta (infection)	207
		that begin without other signs.	vitiligo (loss of color, nothing more)	207
	Reddish or blistering patches on the cheeks or behind knees and elbows of young children.		eczema	216
	A reddish, hot, painful patch that spreads rapidly.		erysipelas (a very serious bacterial infection)	212
reddish	A reddish area between a baby's legs.		diaper rash from urine or heat	215
	Beef-red patches with white, milky curds in the skin folds.		moniliasis (yeast infection)	242
reddish or gray	Raised reddish or gray patches with silvery scales; especially on elbows and knees; chronic (long-term).		psoriasis (or sometimes tuberculosis)	216 212

A Guide to Identification

IF THE SKIN HAS:	AND LOOKS LIKE:	YOU MAY HAVE:	SEE PAGE:
warts	Simple warts, not very large.	common warts (virus infection)	210
	Large warts (more than 1 cm.), often on arms or feet.	a type of tuberculosis of the skin	212
rings (spots with raised or red edges, often clear in the center)	Small rings that continue to grow or spread and may itch.	ringworm (fungus infection)	205
	Large circles with a thick border that do not itch.	advanced stage of syphilis	237
	Large rings that are numb in the center. (A needle prick does not hurt them.)	leprosy	191
	Small rings, sometimes with a small pit in the middle, found on the temple, nose, or neck.	cancer of the skin	211
welts or hives	Very itchy rash, bumps, or patches. (They may appear and disappear rapidly.)	allergic reaction	203
blisters	Blisters with bumps and much itching and weeping (oozing).	contact dermatitis (like poison ivy or sumac)	204
	Small blisters over the whole body, with some fever.	chickenpox	311
	A patch of painful blisters that appears only on one part of the body, often in a stripe or cluster.	Herpes zoster (shingles)	204
	A gray or black bad-smelling area with blisters and air pockets that spread.	gas gangrene (very serious bacterial infection)	213
small reddish spots or a rash over the whole body; fever	A rash that very sick children get over the whole body.	measles	311
	After a few days of fever a few small pinkish spots appear on the body; the person is very sick.	typhoid fever	189

SCABIES (SEVEN YEAR ITCH)

Scabies is especially common in children. It causes very itchy little bumps that can appear all over the body, but are most common:

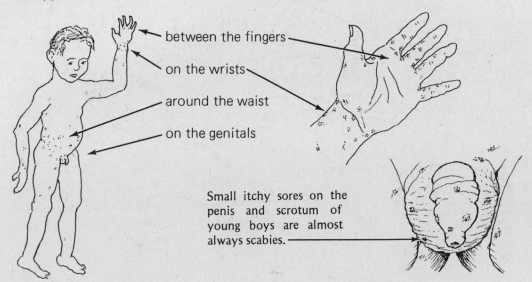

between the fingers

on the wrists

around the waist

on the genitals

Small itchy sores on the penis and scrotum of young boys are almost always scabies.

Scabies is caused by little animals—similar to tiny ticks or chiggers—which make tunnels under the skin. It is spread by touching the affected skin or by clothes and bedding. Scratching can cause infection, producing sores with pus, and sometimes swollen lymph nodes or fever.

Treatment:

- If one person has scabies, everyone in his family should be treated.
- Personal cleanliness is of first importance. Bathe and change clothes daily. Wash all clothes and bedding and hang them in the sun.
- Make the following ointment from lindane (gamma benzene hexachloride, p. 362) and *Vaseline* (petroleum jelly, p. 361). In many countries lindane is sold as a sheep or cattle 'dip'.

> lindane, 1 part
> *Vaseline* (or body oil), 15 parts

Wash the whole body vigorously with soap and hot water.

Heat the *Vaseline* and the lindane and stir well.

Smear the ointment on the whole body, except the face.
   Leave for 1 day and then bathe well.

After treating, put on clean clothes and use clean bedding.

Repeat this treatment 1 week later.

CAUTION:

Lindane is very strong and can cause poisoning if used too often. Do not apply more than once a week and be sure to bathe well the day after treatment.

- Instead of this ointment, you can put 4 drops of lindane on half a lemon. Leave it for 5 minutes and then rub the lemon over your whole body, except the face, starting with the areas most affected.

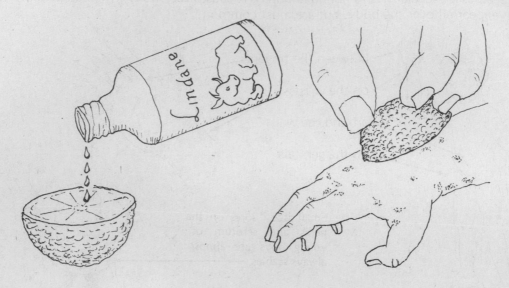

Note:

Commercial ointments or solutions of gamma benzene hexachloride or benzyl benzoate (*Kwell, Gammexane,* p. 362) also kill scabies, but are more expensive. If you cannot get these or lindane, mix sulfur with lard or body oil and apply it to the skin. Use 1 part of sulfur with 10 parts of lard.

LICE

Head lice and body lice cause itching, and sometimes skin infections and swollen lymph nodes. To avoid lice, take great care with personal cleanliness. Put cots, pillows, and bedding in the sun every day. Bathe and wash hair often. Check children's hair. If they have lice, treat them at once. Do not let a child with lice sleep with others.

Treatment:

- Make a shampoo of lindane (p. 362), water, and soap (1 part lindane to 10 parts water). Wash hair, being careful not to get lindane in the eyes. Leave the lather for 15 minutes; then rinse well with clean water. Repeat a week later.

- To get rid of nits (lice eggs), soak hair with hot vinegar water for half an hour, then comb it thoroughly with a fine-toothed comb.

TICKS AND CHIGGERS

When removing a tick that is firmly attached, take care that its head does not remain under the skin, since this can cause an infection. Never pull on the body of a tick. To make it let go:

hold a lit cigarette near it   or   put some alcohol on it.

To remove very small ticks or chiggers, use one of the remedies recommended for scabies (see p. 199).

To relieve itching or pain caused by tick or chigger bites, take aspirin and follow the instructions for treatment of itching on p. 203.

To help prevent chiggers and ticks from biting you, dust sulfur powder on your body before going into the fields or forests. Especially dust ankles, wrists, waist, and underarms.

SMALL SORES WITH PUS

Skin infections in the form of small sores with pus often result from scratching insect bites, scabies, or other irritations with dirty fingernails.

Treatment and Prevention:

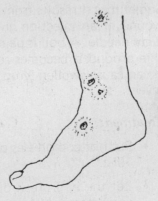

- Wash the sores well with soap and boiled water, gently soaking off the scabs. Do this daily as long as there is pus.

- Leave small sores open to the air. Bandage large sores and change the bandage frequently.

- If the skin around a sore is red and hot, or if the person has a fever, red lines coming from the sores, or swollen lymph nodes, use an antibiotic—such as penicillin tablets (p. 349) or sulfa tablets (p. 354).

- Do not scratch sores. This makes them worse and can spread infection to other parts of the body. Cut the fingernails of small children very short—or put gloves or socks over their hands so they cannot scratch.

- Never let a child with sores or any skin infection play or sleep with other children. These infections are easily spread.

IMPETIGO

This is a bacterial infection that causes rapidly spreading sores with shiny, yellow crusts. It often occurs on children's faces, especially around the mouth. Impetigo can spread easily to other people from the sores or contaminated fingers.

Treatment:

- Wash the affected part with soap and boiled water, gently soaking off the crusts.

- Paint the sores with gentian violet (p. 361) or spread on an antibiotic cream such as *Polysporin* (p. 361) or tetracycline, if that is all you have.

- If the infection is spread over a large area or causes fever, give penicillin tablets (see p. 349).

Prevention:

- Follow the Guidelines of Personal Cleanliness (p. 133). Bathe children daily and protect them from bedbugs and biting flies. If a child gets scabies, treat him as soon as possible.

- Do not let a child with impetigo sleep or play with other children. Begin treatment at the first sign.

BOILS AND ABSCESSES

A boil, or abscess, is an infection that forms a sac of pus under the skin. Sometimes it results from a puncture wound or an injection given with a dirty needle. A boil is painful and the skin around it becomes red and hot. It can cause swollen lymph nodes and fever.

Treatment:

- Put hot compresses over the boil several times a day (see instructions on p. 195).

- Let the boil break open by itself. After it breaks, continue applying hot compresses. Allow the pus to drain, but never press or squeeze the boil, since this may cause the infection to spread to other parts of the body.

- If the boil causes swollen nodes or fever, take penicillin tablets (p. 349) or erythromycin (p. 352).

ITCHING RASH, WELTS, OR HIVES (ALLERGIC REACTIONS IN THE SKIN)

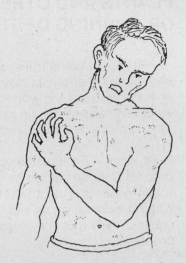

Touching, eating, injecting, or breathing certain things can cause an itching rash or *hives* in allergic persons. For more details, see Allergic Reactions, p. 166.

Hives are thick, raised spots or patches that look like bee stings and itch like mad. They may come and go rapidly or move from one spot to another.

Be on the watch for any reaction caused by certain medicines, especially injections of penicillin and the antivenins or antitoxins made from horse serum. A rash or hives may appear from a few minutes up to 10 days after the medicine has been injected.

If you get an itching rash, hives, or any other allergic reaction after taking or being injected with any medicine, stop using it and never use that medicine again in your life!

This is very important to prevent the danger of ALLERGIC SHOCK (see p. 70).

Treatment of itching:

♦ Bathe in cool water or use cool compresses—cloths soaked in cold water or ice water.

♦ Compresses of cool oatmeal water also calm itching. Boil the oatmeal in water, strain it, and use the water when cool. (Starch can be used instead of oats.)

♦ If itching is severe, take an antihistamine like chlorpheniramine (p. 371).

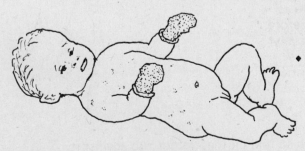

♦ To protect a baby from scratching himself, cut his fingernails very short, or put gloves or socks over his hands.

PLANTS AND OTHER THINGS THAT CAUSE ITCHING OR BURNING OF THE SKIN

Nettles, 'stinging trees', sumac, 'poison ivy', and many other plants may cause blisters, burns, or hives with itching when they touch the skin. Juices or hairs of certain caterpillars and other insects produce similar reactions.

In allergic persons rashes or 'weeping' sore patches may be caused by certain things that touch or are put on the skin. Rubber shoes, watchbands, ear drops and other medicines, face creams, perfumes, or soaps may cause such problems.

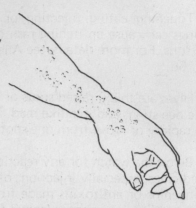

Treatment:

All these irritations go away by themselves when the things that cause them no longer touch the skin. A paste of oatmeal and water helps calm the itching. Aspirin or antihistamines (p. 371) may also help. In severe cases, you can use a cream that contains cortisone or a cortico-steroid (see p. 361).

SHINGLES (HERPES ZOSTER)

Signs:

A line or patch of painful blisters that appears all of a sudden on one side of the body is probably shingles. It is most common on the back, chest, neck, or face. The blisters usually last 2 or 3 weeks, then go away by themselves. Sometimes the pain continues or returns long after the blisters are gone.

Shingles is caused by the virus that causes chickenpox and usually affects persons who have had chickenpox before. It is not dangerous. (However, especially in older persons, it is occasionally a warning sign of some other more serious problem—perhaps cancer.)

Treatment:

• Put light bandages over the rash so that clothes do not rub against it.

• Take aspirin for the pain. (Antibiotics do not help.)

RINGWORM, TINEA (FUNGUS INFECTIONS)

Fungus infections may appear on any part of the body, but occur most frequently on:

the scalp (tinea)   the parts without hair (ringworm)   between the toes or fingers (athlete's foot)   between the legs (jock itch)

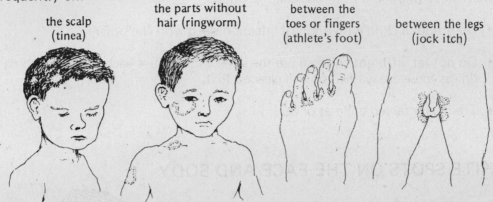

Most fungus infections grow in the form of a ring. They often itch. Ringworm of the head can produce round spots with scales and loss of hair. Fingernails infected with the fungus become rough and thick.

Treatment:

- Soap and water. Washing the infected part every day with soap and water may be all that is needed. If possible, use a soap with hexachlorophene (p. 361).

- Do your best to keep the affected areas dry and exposed to the air or sunlight. Change underwear or socks often, especially when sweaty.

- Use a cream of sulfur and lard (1 part sulfur to 10 parts lard).

- Creams with salicylic or undecylenic acid (p. 362) help cure the fungus between the fingers, toes, and groin.

- For severe tinea of the scalp, or any fungus infection that is widespread or does not get better with the above treatments, take griseofulvin, 1 gram a day for adults and half a gram a day for children (p. 362). It may be necessary to keep taking it for weeks or even months to completely control the infection.

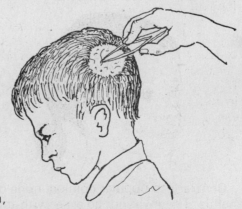

- Many tineas of the scalp clear up when a child reaches puberty (11 to 14 years old). Severe infections forming large swollen patches with pus should be treated with compresses of warm water (p. 195). It is important to pull out all of the hair from the infected part. Use griseofulvin, if possible.

How to prevent fungal infections:

Ringworm and all other fungus infections are *contagious* (easily spread). To prevent spreading them from one child to others:

• Do not let a child with a fungal infection sleep with the others.

• Do not let different children use the same comb or use each other's clothing unless these are washed or well cleaned first.

• Treat an infected child at once.

WHITE SPOTS ON THE FACE AND BODY

Small dark or light spots with a distinct and irregular border that are often seen on the neck, chest, and back may be a fungal infection called **tinea versicolor.** It usually does not itch and is of little medical importance.

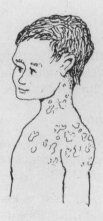

Treatment:

• Make a cream with sulfur and lard (1 part sulfur to 10 parts lard) and apply it to the spots every day until they disappear.

• Sodium thiosulfate works even better. This is the 'hypo' photographers use when developing film. Dissolve a tablespoon of sodium thiosulfate in a glass of water, apply it to the skin, and then rub the skin with a piece of cotton dipped in vinegar.

• To prevent the spots from returning, it is often necessary to repeat this treatment every 2 weeks.

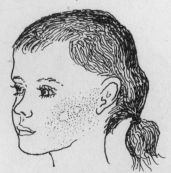

There is **another kind of small whitish spot** that is common on the cheeks of dark-skinned children who spend a lot of time in the sun. The border is less clear than in tinea versicolor. These spots are not an infection and are of no importance. Usually they go away as the child grows up. No treatment is needed.

Contrary to popular opinion, none of these types of white spots is a sign of anemia. They will not go away with tonics or vitamins. The spots that are only on the cheeks do not need any treatment.

Vitiligo (White Areas of the Skin)

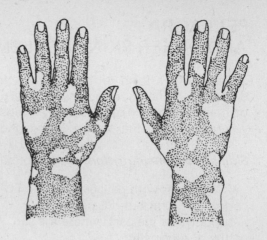

In some persons, certain areas of the skin lose their natural color (pigment). Then white patches appear. These are most common on the hands, feet, face, and upper body. This loss of normal skin color—called vitiligo—is not an illness. It can be compared to white hair in older people. No treatment helps or is needed, but the white skin should be protected from sunburn—with clothing or an ointment of zinc oxide.

Other Causes of White Skin Patches

Certain diseases may cause white spots that look like vitiligo. In Latin America an infectious disease called **pinta** starts with bluish or red pimples and later leaves pale or white patches.

Treatment of pinta is the same as for syphilis (p. 238). (But pinta does not come from sexual contact.)

Any whitish patch that **has no feeling** when pricked with a pin is probably leprosy (see p. 191).

Some fungus infections also cause whitish spots (see tinea versicolor, on the opposite page).

MASK OF PREGNANCY

During pregnancy many women develop dark, olive-colored areas on the skin of the face, breasts, and down the middle of the belly. Sometimes these disappear after the birth and sometimes not.

These marks also appear sometimes on women who are taking birth control pills.

They are completely normal and do not indicate weakness or sickness. No treatment is needed.

PELLAGRA
AND OTHER SKIN PROBLEMS DUE TO MALNUTRITION

Pellagra is a form of malnutrition that affects the skin and sometimes the digestive and nervous systems. It is very common in places where people eat a lot of maize (corn) or other starchy foods and not enough beans, meat, eggs, vegetables, and other body-building and protective foods (see p. 110 and 111).

Skin signs in malnutrition (see the pictures on the following page):

In adults with pellagra the skin is dry and cracked; it peels like sunburn on the parts where the sun hits it, especially:

In malnourished children, the skin of the legs (and sometimes arms) may have dark marks, like bruises, or even peeling sores; the feet may be swollen (see p. 112).

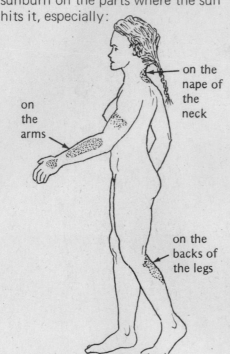

on the nape of the neck

on the arms

on the backs of the legs

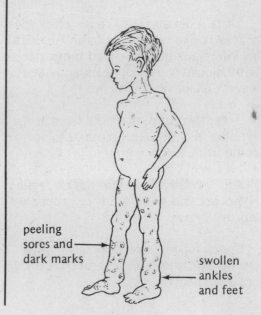

peeling sores and dark marks

swollen ankles and feet

When these conditions exist, often there are also other signs of malnutrition: swollen belly; sores in the corners of the mouth; red, sore tongue; weakness; loss of appetite; failure to gain weight; etc. (see Chapter 11, p. 112).

Treatment:

♦ Eating nutritious foods cures pellagra. Every day a person should eat beans, lentils, groundnuts, or some chicken, fish, eggs, meat, or cheese. When you have a choice, it is also better to use wheat (preferably whole wheat) instead of maize (corn).

♦ For severe pellagra and some other forms of malnutrition, it may help to take vitamins, but **good food is more important.** Be sure the vitamin formula you use is high in the B vitamins, especially niacin. Brewer's yeast is a good source of B vitamins.

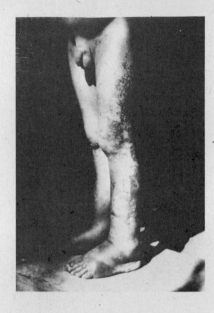

BEFORE
THIS BOY
BEGAN TO
EAT WELL

←

AND
AFTER

→

The swelling and dark spots on this boy's legs and feet are the result of poor nutrition. He was eating mostly maize (corn) without any foods rich in proteins and vitamins.

One week after he began to eat beans and eggs along with the maize, the swelling was gone and the spots had almost disappeared.

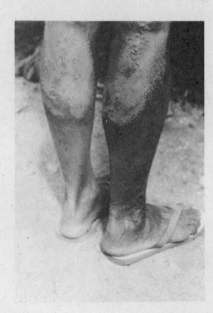

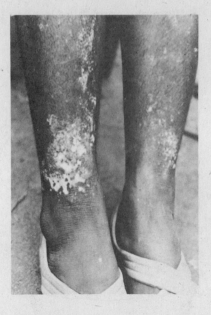

The 'burnt' skin on the legs of this woman is a sign of pellagra—which results from not eating well (see p. 208).

The white spots on the legs of this woman are due to an infectious disease called pinta (see p. 207).

WARTS (VERRUCAE)

Most warts, especially those in children, last 3 to 5 years and go away by themselves. Flat, painful wart-like spots on the sole of the foot are often 'plantar warts'. (Or they may be corns. See below.)

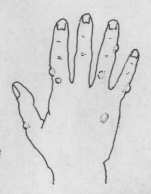

Treatment:

- ◆ Magical or household cures often get rid of warts. But do not use strong acids or poisonous plants, as these may cause burns or sores much worse than the warts.

- ◆ Painful plantar warts sometimes can be removed by a health worker.

CORNS

A corn is a hard, thick part of the skin. It forms where sandals or shoes push against the skin, or one toe presses against another. Corns can be very painful.

Treatment:

- ◆ Get sandals or shoes that do not press on the corns.

- ◆ To make corns hurt less, do this:

1. Soak the foot in warm water for 15 minutes.

2. With a file or rasp, trim down the corn until it is thin.

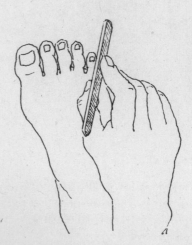

PIMPLES AND BLACKHEADS (ACNE)

Young people sometimes get pimples on their face, chest, or back—especially if their skin has too much oil in it. *Pimples* are little lumps that form tiny white 'heads' of pus or *blackheads* of dirt. Sometimes they can become quite sore and large.

Treatment:

- Wash the face twice a day with soap and hot water.

- Sunshine helps clear pimples. Let the sunlight fall on the affected parts of the body.

- Eat as well as possible, drink a lot of water, and get enough sleep.

- Before you go to bed, put a mixture of alcohol with a little sulfur on the face (10 parts alcohol to 1 part sulfur).

- For serious cases forming lumps and pockets of pus, if these do not get better with the methods already described, tetracycline may help. Take 1 capsule 4 times a day for 3 days and then 2 capsules daily. It may be necessary to take 1 or 2 capsules daily for months.

CANCER OF THE SKIN

Skin cancer is most frequent in light-skinned persons who spend a lot of time in the sun. It usually appears in places where the sun hits with most force, especially:

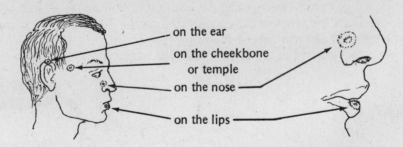

on the ear

on the cheekbone or temple

on the nose

on the lips

Skin cancer may take many forms. It usually begins as a little ring the color of pearl with a hole in the center. It grows little by little.

Most cancers of the skin are not dangerous if treated in time. Surgery is needed to remove them. If you have a chronic sore that might be skin cancer, see a health worker.

To prevent skin cancer, light-skinned persons should protect themselves from the sun and always wear a hat. Persons who have suffered from cancer of the skin and have to work in the sun can buy special creams that protect them. Zinc oxide ointment is cheap and works well.

TUBERCULOSIS OF THE SKIN OR LYMPH NODES

The same microbe that causes tuberculosis of the lungs also sometimes affects the skin, causing painless

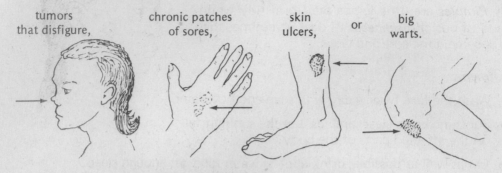

| tumors that disfigure, | chronic patches of sores, | skin ulcers, | or | big warts. |

As a rule, TB of the skin develops slowly, lasts a long time, and keeps coming back over a period of months or years.

Also, tuberculosis sometimes infects the lymph nodes—most often those of the neck or in the area behind the collar bone, between the neck and the shoulder. The nodes become large, open, drain pus, seal closed for a time, and then open and drain again. Usually **they are not painful.**

TUBERCULOSIS OF THE LYMPH NODES, OR SCROFULA

Treatment:

In the case of any chronic sore, ulcer, or swollen lymph nodes, it is best to seek medical advice. Tests may be needed to learn the cause. Tuberculosis of the skin is treated the same as tuberculosis of the lungs (see p. 180). To keep the infection from returning, the medicines must be taken for many months after the skin looks well.

ERYSIPELAS

This is a very painful, acute infection in the skin. It forms a hot, red, swollen patch with a sharp border. The patch spreads rapidly over the skin. It often begins on the face, at the edge of the nose. This usually causes swollen lymph nodes, fever, and chills.

Treatment:

Begin treatment as soon as possible. Use an antibiotic: penicillin tablets, 400,000 units, 4 times a day; in serious cases, injectable procaine penicillin, 800,000 units daily (see p. 350). Continue using the antibiotic for 2 days after all signs of infection are gone. Also use hot compresses—and aspirin for pain.

GANGRENE (GAS GANGRENE)

This is a very dangerous infection of a wound, in which a foul-smelling gray or brown liquid forms. The skin near the wound may have dark blisters and the flesh may have air bubbles in it. The infection begins between 6 hours and 3 days after the injury. It quickly gets worse and spreads fast. Without treatment it causes death in a few days.

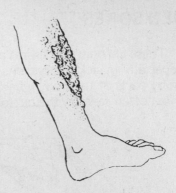

Treatment:

- Open up the wound as wide as possible. Wash it out with boiled water and soap. Clean out the dead and damaged flesh. If possible, flood the wound with hydrogen peroxide every 2 hours.

- Inject penicillin (crystalline if possible), 1,000,000 (a million) units every 3 hours.

- **Leave the wound uncovered so that air gets to it. Get medical help.**

ULCERS OF THE SKIN CAUSED BY POOR CIRCULATION

Skin ulcers, or large, open sores, have many causes (see p. 20). However, chronic ulcers on the ankles of older persons, especially in women with varicose veins, usually come from poor circulation. The blood is not moved fast enough through the legs. Such ulcers may become very large. The skin around the ulcer is dark blue, shiny, and very thin. Often the foot is swollen.

Treatment:

- These ulcers heal very slowly—and only if great care is taken. Most important: **keep the foot up** —as high and as often as possible. Sleep with it on pillows. During the day, rest with the foot up high every 15 or 20 minutes. **Walking helps the circulation, but standing in one place and sitting with the feet down are harmful.**

- Put warm compresses of weak salt water on the ulcer—1 teaspoon salt to a liter of boiled water. Cover the ulcer loosely with sterile gauze or a clean cloth. **Keep it clean.**

- Support the varicose veins with elastic stockings or bandages. Continue to use these and to keep the feet up after the ulcer heals. Take great care not to scratch or injure the delicate scar.

Prevent skin ulcers—care for varicose veins early (see p. 175).

BED SORES

These chronic open sores appear in persons so ill they cannot roll over in bed, especially in sick old persons who are very thin and weak. The sores form over bony parts of the body where the skin is pressed against the bedding. They are most often seen on the buttocks, back, elbows, or feet.

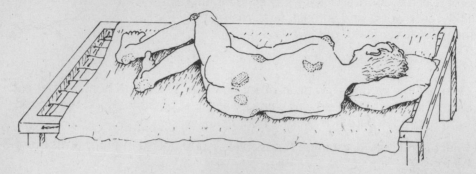

How to prevent bed sores:

- Turn the sick person over every hour: face up, face down, or from one side to the other.

- Bathe him every day and rub his skin with baby oil.

- Use soft bed sheets and padding. Change them daily and each time the bedding gets dirty with urine, stools, vomit, etc.

- Put cushions under the person in such a way that the bony parts rub less.

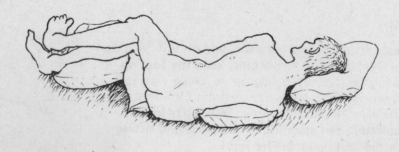

- Feed the sick person as well as possible. If he does not eat well, extra vitamins may help (see p. 119).

- A child who has a severe chronic illness should be held often on his mother's lap.

Treatment:

- Do all the things mentioned above.

- Wash the sores with boiled water mixed with a little salt or hydrogen peroxide. Protect them with sterile gauze bandages.

SKIN PROBLEMS OF BABIES

Diaper Rash

Reddish patches of irritation between a baby's legs or buttocks may be caused by urine in his diapers (nappy) or bedding.

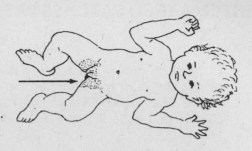

Treatment:

- Bathe the child daily with lukewarm water and mild soap.
- **To prevent or cure the rash, the child should be kept naked, without diapers, and he should be taken out into the sun.**

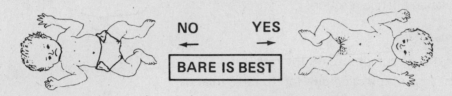

NO   YES

BARE IS BEST

- If diapers are used, change them often. After washing the diapers, rinse them in water with a little vinegar.
- Use talc (talcum powder) only after the rash is gone.

Cradle Cap (Seborrhea, Dandruff)

Cradle cap is an oily, yellow crust that forms on a baby's scalp. The skin is often red and irritated. Cradle cap usually results from not washing the baby's head often enough, or from keeping the head covered.

Treatment:

- Wash the head daily. If possible use a medicated soap (see p. 361).
- Gently clean off all the dandruff and crust. To loosen the scales and crust, first wrap the head with towels soaked in lukewarm water.
- Keep the baby's head **uncovered,** open to the air and sunlight.

DO NOT COVER A BABY'S HEAD WITH A CAP OR CLOTH. KEEP THE HEAD UNCOVERED.

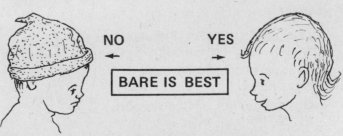

NO   YES

BARE IS BEST

- If there are signs of infection, treat as for impetigo (see p. 202).

ECZEMA (RED PATCHES WITH LITTLE BLISTERS)

Signs:

- In small children: a red patch or rash forms on the cheeks or sometimes on the arms and hands. The rash consists of small sores or blisters that ooze or weep (burst and leak fluid).

- In older children and grown-ups: eczema is usually drier and is most common behind the knees and on the inside of the elbows.

- It does not start as an infection but is more like an allergic reaction.

Treatment:

- Put cold compresses on the rash.

- If signs of infection develop (p. 88), treat as for impetigo (p. 202).

- Let the sunlight fall on the patches.

- In difficult cases, use a cortisone or cortico-steroid cream (see p. 361).

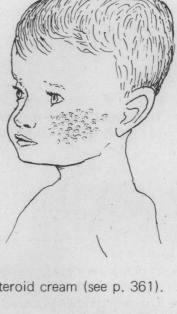

PSORIASIS

Signs:

- Thick, rough patches of reddish or blue-gray skin covered with whitish or silver-colored scales. The patches appear most commonly in the parts shown in the drawings.

- The condition usually lasts a long time or keeps coming back. It is not an infection and is not dangerous.

Treatment:

- Leaving the affected skin open to the sunlight often helps.

- Bathing in the ocean sometimes helps.

- Ointments with cortico-steroids (p. 361) or coal tar may help.

- In severe cases, seek medical advice.

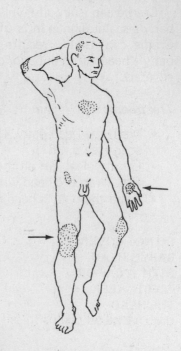

CHAPTER

16

THE EYES

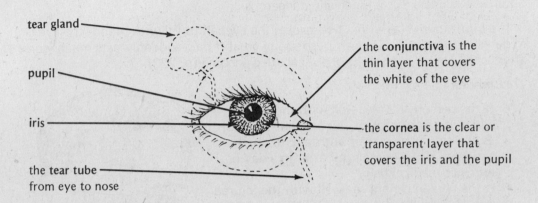

tear gland

pupil

iris

the **tear tube**
from eye to nose

the **conjunctiva** is the
thin layer that covers
the white of the eye

the **cornea** is the clear or
transparent layer that
covers the iris and the pupil

DANGER SIGNS

The eyes are delicate and need good care. Get medical help fast when any of the following danger signs occurs:

1. Any wound that cuts or ruptures (goes through) the eyeball.

2. A painful, grayish spot on the cornea, with redness around the cornea (corneal ulcer).

3. Great pain inside the eye (possibly iritis or glaucoma).

4. Difference in the size of the pupils when there is pain in the eye or the head.

A difference in the size of the pupils may come from brain damage, stroke, injury to the eye, glaucoma, or iritis. (Some difference is normal in a few people.)

5. If vision begins to fail in one or both eyes.

6. Any eye infection or inflammation that does not get better after 5 or 6 days of treatment with an antibiotic eye ointment.

INJURIES TO THE EYE

All injuries to the eyeball must be considered dangerous, for they may cause blindness.

Even small cuts on the **cornea** (the transparent layer covering the pupil and iris) may get infected and harm the vision if not cared for correctly.

If a wound to the eyeball is so deep that it reaches the black layer beneath the outer white layer, this is especially dangerous.

If a blunt injury (as with a fist) causes the eyeball to fill with blood, the eye is in danger (see p. 225). Danger is especially great if pain suddenly gets much worse after a few days, for this is probably acute glaucoma (p. 222).

Treatment:

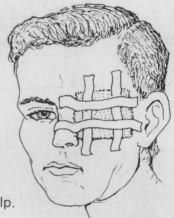

- If the person still sees well with the injured eye, put an antibiotic eye ointment (p. 365) in the eye and cover it with a soft, thick bandage. If the eye is not better in a day or two, get medical help.
- If the person cannot see well with the injured eye, if the wound is deep, or if there is blood inside the eye behind the cornea (p. 225), cover the eye with a clean bandage and go for medical help at once.
- **Do not** try to remove thorns or splinters that are tightly stuck in the eyeball. Get medical help.

HOW TO REMOVE A SPECK OF DIRT FROM THE EYE

Often you can get a bit of dirt or sand out of the eye by flooding the eye with clean water (p. 48) or by using the corner of a clean cloth or the tip of some moist cotton.

If the particle of dirt is under the upper lid, look for it by turning the lid up over a thin stick:

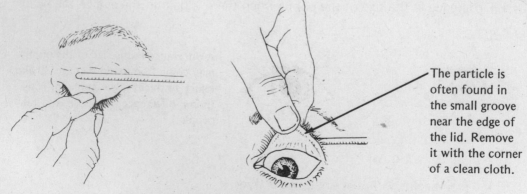

The particle is often found in the small groove near the edge of the lid. Remove it with the corner of a clean cloth.

If you cannot get the particle out easily, use an antibiotic eye ointment, cover the eye with a bandage, and go for medical help.

RED, PAINFUL EYES—DIFFERENT CAUSES

Many different problems cause red, painful eyes. This chart may help you find the cause:

foreign matter (bit of dirt, etc.) in the eye (p. 218)	usually affects **one eye only;** redness and pain variable
burns or harmful liquids (p. 48)	one or both eyes; redness and pain variable
'pink eye' (conjunctivitis, p. 219) hay fever (allergic conjunctivitis, p. 165) trachoma (p. 220) measles (p. 311)	usually **both eyes** (may start or be worse in one) usually reddest at outer edge 'burning' pain, usually mild
acute glaucoma (p. 222) iritis (p. 221) scratch or ulcer on the cornea (p. 224)	usually **one eye only;** reddest next to the cornea pain often great

The correct treatment of red, painful eyes often depends on finding out the cause. Be sure to check carefully for signs of each possibility.

'PINK EYE' (CONJUNCTIVITIS)

This infection causes redness, pus, and mild 'burning' in one or both eyes. Lids often stick together after sleep.

Treatment:

First clean pus from the eyes with a clean cloth moistened with boiled water. Then put in antibiotic eye ointment (p. 365). Pull down the lower lid and put a little bit of ointment **inside,** like this:

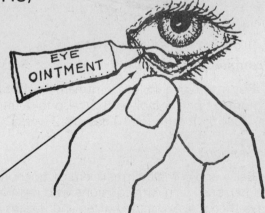

EYE OINTMENT

Putting ointment outside the eye does no good.

Prevention:

Most conjunctivitis is very contagious. The infection is easily spread from one person to another. Do not let a child with pink eye play or sleep with others, or use the same towel. Wash hands after touching eyes.

TRACHOMA

Trachoma is a chronic form of conjunctivitis that slowly gets worse. It may last for months or many years. If not treated early, it sometimes causes blindness. It is spread by touch or by flies, and is most common where people live in poor, crowded conditions.

Signs:

- Trachoma begins with red, watery eyes, like ordinary conjunctivitis.
- After a month or more, small, pinkish gray lumps, called follicles, form inside the upper lids. To see these, turn back the lid as shown on p. 218.
- The white of the eye is mildly inflamed.
- If you look very carefully, or with a magnifying glass, you may see that the top edge of the cornea looks grayish, because it has many tiny new blood vessels in it *(pannus).*
- The combination of both follicles and pannus is almost certainly trachoma.
- After several years, the follicles begin to disappear, leaving whitish scars.

These scars make the eyelids thick and may keep them from opening all the way.

Or they may pull the eyelashes down into the eye, scratching the cornea and causing blindness.

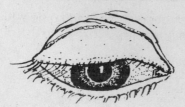

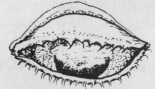

Treatment of trachoma:

Put a tetracycline eye ointment (p. 365) inside the eyes 3 times a day for a month. For a complete cure, also take tetracycline (p. 353) or a sulfonamide (p. 354) by mouth for 10 days to 2 weeks.

Prevention:

Early and complete treatment of trachoma helps prevent its spread to others. All persons living with someone who has trachoma, especially children, should have their eyes examined often and if signs appear, they should be treated early. Also, it is very important to follow the Guidelines of Cleanliness, explained in Chapter 12.

Cleanliness helps prevent trachoma.

INFECTED EYES IN NEWBORN BABIES (NEONATAL CONJUNCTIVITIS)

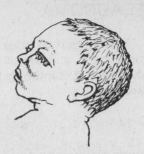

In the first 2 days of life, if a newborn baby's eyes get red, swell, and have a lot of pus in them, this is probably gonorrhea (p. 236). The baby has picked up the disease from his mother at birth. It must be treated **at once** to prevent the baby from going blind.

Treatment:

- ◆ Inject 150,000 units of crystalline penicillin twice a day for 3 days; or give 250 mg. (half a 500 mg. tablet) of triple sulfa, ground up and mixed with breast milk or boiled water, 4 times a day for a week.

- ◆ Also make penicillin eyedrops. Boil half a teaspoon of salt in half a cup of water. After cooling, add 1 million units of injectable (crystalline) penicillin. Put a drop of this mixture in the baby's eyes every 10 minutes for an hour, then every hour for 6 hours, then every 2 or 3 hours for 3 days.

- ◆ Before using drops, clean out pus as described on page 219.

Prevention:

All babies' eyes should be protected against gonorrhea, especially the eyes of babies whose mothers may have gonorrhea or whose fathers have pain when passing urine. (Mothers may have gonorrhea without knowing it.)

Put a drop of 1% silver nitrate solution **once only** in each eye at birth. If you do not have silver nitrate drops, use a tetracycline ointment 3 times a day for 3 days.

If a baby develops gonorrhea of the eyes, **both** parents should be treated for gonorrhea.

IRITIS (INFLAMMATION OF THE IRIS)

Signs:

NORMAL EYE

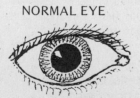

EYE WITH IRITIS

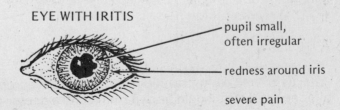

- pupil small, often irregular

- redness around iris

- severe pain

Pain may begin suddenly or gradually. The eye waters a lot. It hurts more in bright light. There is no pus as with conjunctivitis. Vision is usually blurred.

This is a medical emergency. Antibiotic ointments do not help. **Get medical help.**

GLAUCOMA

This dangerous disease is the result of too much pressure in the eye. It usually begins after the age of 40 and is a common cause of blindness. **To prevent blindness, it is important to recognize the signs of glaucoma and get medical help fast.**

There are 2 forms of glaucoma.

Acute glaucoma:

This starts suddenly with a headache or severe pain in the eye. The eye becomes red, the vision blurred. The eyeball feels hard to the touch, like a marble. There may be vomiting. The pupil of the bad eye is bigger than that of the good eye.

normal

glaucoma

If not treated very soon, acute glaucoma will cause blindness within a few days. Surgery is often needed. **Get medical help fast.**

Chronic glaucoma:

The pressure in the eye rises slowly. Usually there is no pain. Vision is lost slowly, starting from the side, and often the person does not notice the loss. Testing the side vision may help detect the disease.

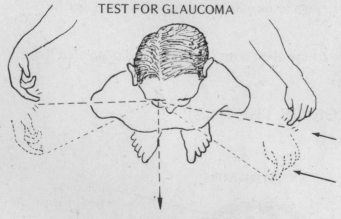

TEST FOR GLAUCOMA

Have the person cover one eye, and with the other look at an object straight ahead of him. Note when he can first see moving fingers coming from behind on each side of the head.

Normally fingers are first seen here.

In glaucoma, finger movement is first seen more toward the front.

If discovered early, treatment with special eyedrops (pilocarpine) may prevent blindness. Dosage should be determined by a doctor or health worker who can measure the eye pressure periodically. Drops must be used for the rest of one's life.

Prevention:

Persons who are over 40 years old or have relatives with glaucoma should have their eye pressure checked once a year.

INFECTION OF THE TEAR SAC (DACRYOCYSTITIS)

Signs:

Redness, pain, and swelling beneath the eye, next to the nose. The eye waters a lot. A drop of pus may appear in the corner of the eye when the swelling is gently pressed.

Treatment:

- ◆ Apply hot compresses.
- ◆ Put antibiotic eye drops or ointment in the eye.
- ◆ Take penicillin (p. 349).

TROUBLE SEEING CLEARLY

Children who have trouble seeing clearly or who get headaches or eye pain when they read may need glasses. Have their eyes examined.

In older persons, it is normal that, with passing years, it becomes more difficult to see close things clearly. Reading glasses often help. If possible, they should be carefully prescribed, so as to prevent eye strain and headache.

CROSS-EYES AND WANDERING EYES

If a baby or young child has one eye that turns in (cross-eye) or out (wall-eye) or that sometimes looks the wrong way (wanders), try covering the **good** eye with a patch.

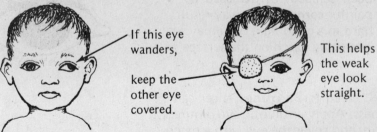

If this eye wanders,

keep the other eye covered.

This helps the weak eye look straight.

If possible, do this when the child is 6 months old. Keep the good eye covered until the other eye stays straight. For a 6-month-old baby this may only take a week or two. Older children take longer—up to a year for a 7-year-old, so for an older child discuss this with a health worker first.

Early patching of the good eye often prevents a child from staying cross-eyed or wall-eyed for life.

If one eye is always turned the wrong way, it is less likely that covering the good eye will help. Special glasses sometimes help. The eyes can perhaps be straightened by surgery, but this does not usually help the person see better.

STY (HORDEOLUM)

A red, swollen lump on the eyelid, usually near its edge. To treat, apply warm, moist compresses with a little salt in the water. Use of an antibiotic eye ointment 3 times a day will help prevent more sties from occurring.

PTERYGIUM

A fleshy thickening on the eye surface that slowly grows out from the edge of the eye and onto the cornea; caused in part by sunlight, wind, and dust. Dark glasses may help calm irritation and slow the growth of a pterygium. It should be removed by surgery before it reaches the pupil.

Folk treatments using powdered shells do more harm that good. However, eye drops of camomile tea (well boiled and without sugar) may help calm itching and burning.

A SCRAPE, ULCER, OR SCAR ON THE CORNEA

When the very thin, delicate surface of the cornea has been scraped, or damaged by infection, a painful **corneal ulcer** may result. If you look hard in a good light, you may see a grayish or less shiny patch on the surface of the cornea.

If not well cared for, a corneal ulcer can cause blindness. Apply antibiotic eye ointment, give penicillin, and cover the eye with a patch. If the eye is not better in 2 days, get medical help.

A **corneal scar** is a painless, white patch on the cornea. It may result from a corneal ulcer, burn, or other injury to the eye. Surgery (corneal transplant) is the only treatment. This is expensive and does not always give good results. Surgery should only be done if the person is blind but can still see light.

BLEEDING IN THE WHITE OF THE EYE

A painless, blood-red patch in the white part of the eye occasionally appears after lifting something heavy, coughing hard (as with whooping cough), or being hit on the eye. The condition results from the bursting of a small blood vessel. It is harmless and will slowly disappear without treatment.

Small red patches are common on the eyes of newborn babies. No treatment is needed.

BLEEDING BEHIND THE CORNEA (HYPHEMA)

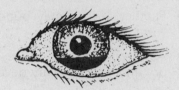

Blood behind the cornea is a dangerous sign. It usually results from an injury to the eye with a blunt object, like a fist. Treat it by patching the eyes and keeping the person at rest in bed for several days. If after a few days the pain becomes much worse, there is probably hardening of the eye (glaucoma, p. 222). Take the person to an eye doctor **at once.**

PUS BEHIND THE CORNEA (HYPOPYON)

Pus behind the cornea is a sign of severe *inflammation.* It is sometimes seen with corneal ulcers and is a sign that the eye is in danger. Give penicillin (p. 349) and get medical help at once. If the ulcer is treated correctly, the hypopyon will often clear up by itself.

CATARACT

The lens of the eye, behind the pupil, becomes cloudy, making the pupil look gray or white when you shine a light into it. Cataract is common in older persons, but also occurs, rarely, in babies. If a blind person with cataracts can still tell light from dark and notice motion, surgery may let him see again. However, he will need strong glasses afterward, which take time to get used to. Medicines do not help cataracts.

NIGHT BLINDNESS AND XEROSIS (VITAMIN A DEFICIENCY)

This eye disease is most common in children between 2 and 5 years of age. It comes from not eating enough foods with vitamin A. If not recognized and treated early, it can make the child blind.

Signs:

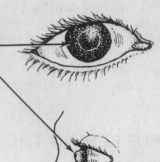

- At first, the child may have **night blindness.** He cannot see as well in the dark as other people can.

- Later, he develops **dry eyes** (xerosis). The white of the eyes loses its shine and begins to wrinkle.

- Patches of little gray bubbles (Bitot's spots) may form in the eyes.

- As the disease gets worse, the cornea also becomes dry and dull, and may develop little pits.

- Then the cornea may quickly grow soft, bulge, or even burst. Usually there is no pain. Blindness may result from infection, scarring, or other damage.

- Xerosis often begins, or gets worse, when a child is sick with another illness like diarrhea, whooping cough, or tuberculosis. **Examine the eyes of all sick and underweight children.**

Prevention and treatment:

Xerosis can easily be prevented by eating foods that contain vitamin A. Do the following:

- Breast feed the baby—up to 2 years, if possible.

- After the first 6 months, begin giving the child foods rich in vitamin A, such as dark green leafy vegetables and yellow or red fruits and vegetables. Whole milk, eggs, liver, and kidneys are also rich in vitamin A.

- If the child is not likely to get these foods, or if he is developing signs of night blindness or xerosis, give him a capsule of vitamin A, 200,000 units (60 mg. retinol) once every 6 months (p. 376). Do not give to babies under 6 months of age.

- If the condition is already fairly severe, give the child a 200,000 unit capsule of vitamin A. If the eyes are not well in a week, give another capsule.

WARNING: Too much vitamin A is poisonous. Do not give more than 200,000 units a week, or 1,000,000 U. (5 capsules) in all.

If the condition of the child's eyes is severe, with a dull, pitted, or bulging cornea, get medical help. The child's eyes should be bandaged, and he should receive vitamin A at once, preferably an injection of 100,000 units.

> **Dark green or yellow vegetables prevent blindness in children.**

SPOTS OR 'FLIES' BEFORE THE EYES (MOUCHES VOLANTES)

Sometimes older persons complain of small moving spots when they look at a bright surface (wall, sky). The spots move when the eyes move and look like tiny flies.

These spots are usually harmless and need no treatment. However, if they appear suddenly in large numbers and vision begins to fail from one side, this could be a medical emergency (detached retina). Medical help is needed at once.

DOUBLE VISION

Seeing double can have many causes.

If double vision comes suddenly, is chronic, or gradually gets worse, it is probably a sign of a serious problem. Seek medical help.

If double vision occurs only from time to time, it may be a sign of weakness or exhaustion, perhaps from malnutrition.

Read Chapter 11 on good nutrition and try to eat as well as possible. If sight does not improve, get medical help.

RIVER BLINDNESS (ONCHOCERCIASIS)

BLACK FLY

actual size →

This disease is common in many parts of Africa and certain areas of southern Mexico, Central America, and northern South America. The infection is caused by tiny worms that are carried from person to person by small, hump-backed flies or gnats known as black flies (simulids).

The worms are 'injected' into a person when an infected black fly bites him.

Signs of river blindness:

- Several months after a black fly bites and the worms enter the body, lumps begin to form under the skin. In the Americas the lumps are most common on the head and upper body; in Africa on the lower body and thighs. Often there are no more than 3 to 6 lumps. They grow slowly to a size of 2 to 3 cm. across. They are usually painless.

- There may be severe itching caused by an allergic reaction to the worms. Areas of the skin may become thick, dark, and scaly.

- Eye problems often develop. First there may be redness and tears, then signs of iritis (p. 221). The cornea becomes dull and pitted as in xerosis (p. 226). Finally sight is lost as a result of corneal scarring, cataract, glaucoma, or other problems.

Treatment of river blindness:

Early treatment can prevent blindness. In areas where river blindness is known to occur, seek treatment when the first signs appear. Once damage to the eyes has begun, treatment is much more difficult, and the medicines may actually cause the eye problems to get worse.

- Diethylcarbamazine or suramin kills the worms. Both medicines have risks in their use and sometimes do more harm than good, especially when eye damage has already begun. They should only be given by experienced health workers. For dosage and precautions, see page 365.

- Antihistamines help reduce itching (p. 371).

- Early surgical removal of the lumps lowers the number of worms.

Prevention:

- Black flies breed in fast-running water. Clearing brush and vegetation back from the banks of fast-running streams may help reduce the number of flies.

- Avoid sleeping out-of-doors—especially in the daytime, which is when the flies usually bite.

- Cooperate with programs for the control of black flies.

- **Early treatment prevents blindness and also helps limit the spread of disease.**

17

THE TEETH, GUMS, AND MOUTH

CARE OF THE TEETH AND GUMS

Taking good care of teeth and gums is important because:

- Strong, healthy teeth are needed to chew and digest food well.

- Painful cavities (holes in the teeth caused by decay) and sore gums can be prevented by good tooth care.

- Decayed or rotten teeth caused by lack of cleanliness can lead to serious infections that may affect other parts of the body.

To keep the teeth and gums healthy:

1. **Avoid sweets.** Eating many sweets (sugar cane, candy, pastry, tea or coffee with sugar, soft or fizzy drinks like colas, etc.) rots the teeth quickly.

Do not accustom children to sweets or soft drinks if you want them to have good teeth.

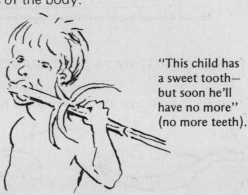

"This child has a sweet tooth— but soon he'll have no more" (no more teeth).

2. **Brush teeth well every day**—and always brush immediately after eating anything sweet. Start brushing your children's teeth as the teeth appear. Later, teach them to brush their teeth themselves, and watch to see that they do it right.

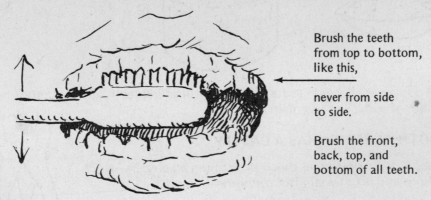

Brush the teeth from top to bottom, like this,

never from side to side.

Brush the front, back, top, and bottom of all teeth.

3. Putting **fluoride** in the drinking water or directly on teeth helps prevent cavities. Some health programs put fluoride on children's teeth once or twice a year. Be sure your children have this done if they have the chance.

CAUTION: Fluoride is poisonous if more than a small amount is swallowed. Use with care and keep it out of the reach of children.

4. **Do not bottle feed older babies.** Continual sucking on a bottle bathes the baby's teeth in sweet liquid and causes early decay. (It is best not to bottle feed at all. See p. 271.)

IF YOU DO NOT HAVE A TOOTHBRUSH:

Use the twig of a tree, like this:

Sharpen this end to clean between the teeth.

Chew on this end and use the fibers as a brush.

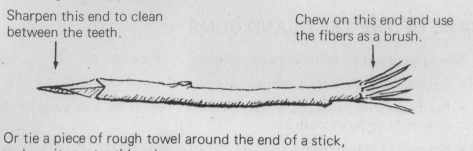

Or tie a piece of rough towel around the end of a stick, and use it as a toothbrush.

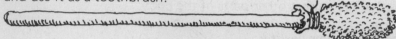

piece of rough towel

IF YOU DO NOT HAVE TOOTHPASTE:

Make a tooth powder by mixing salt and bicarbonate of soda in equal amounts. To make it stick, wet the brush before putting it in the powder.

salt

bicarbonate of soda

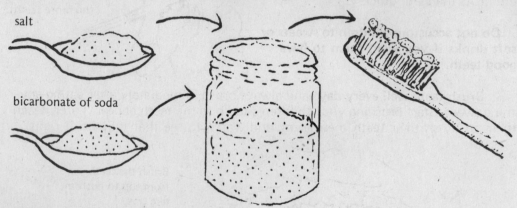

Salt with soda works as well as toothpaste for cleaning teeth. If you do not have bicarbonate of soda, just use plain salt.

IF A TOOTH ALREADY HAS A CAVITY:

To keep it from hurting as much or forming an abscess, avoid sweet things and brush well after every meal.

If possible, see a dental worker right away. If you go soon enough, he can often clean and fill the tooth so it will last for many years.

> **When you have a tooth with a cavity, do not wait until it hurts a lot. Have it filled by a dental worker right away.**

TOOTHACHES AND ABSCESSES

To calm the pain:

* Clean the hole in the tooth wall, removing all food particles. Then rinse the mouth with warm salt water.

* Take a pain reliever like aspirin.

* If the tooth infection is severe (swelling, pus, large tender lymph nodes), use an antibiotic: tablets of penicillin (p. 349) or sulfonamide (p. 354), or tetracycline capsules (p. 353).

If the pain does not go away or keeps coming back, the tooth should probably be pulled.

Treat abscesses right away— before the infection spreads to other parts of the body.

A toothache results when a cavity becomes infected.

An *abscess* results when the infection reaches the tip of a root and forms a pocket of pus.

PYORRHEA, A DISEASE OF THE GUMS

Inflamed (red and swollen), painful gums that bleed easily are caused by:

1. Not cleaning the teeth and gums well or often enough.

2. Not eating enough nutritious foods (malnutrition).

Prevention and treatment:

* Brush teeth well after each meal, removing food that sticks between the teeth. Also, if possible, scrape off the dark yellow crust (tartar) that forms where the teeth meet the gums. It helps to **clean under the gums** regularly by passing a strong thin thread (or dental floss) between the teeth. At first this will cause a lot of bleeding, but soon the gums will be healthier and bleed less.

* Eat protective foods rich in vitamins, especially eggs, meat, beans, dark green vegetables, and fruits like oranges, lemons, and tomatoes (see Chapter 11). Avoid sweet, sticky, and stringy foods that get stuck between the teeth.

Note: Sometimes medicines for fits (epilepsy) cause swelling and unhealthy growth of the gums (see p. 374). If this happens, consult a health worker and consider using a different medicine.

SORES OR CRACKS AT THE CORNERS OF THE MOUTH

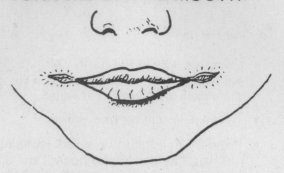

Narrow sores at the corners of children's mouths are often a sign of malnutrition.

Children with these sores should eat foods rich in vitamins and proteins: like milk, meat, fish, nuts, eggs, fruits, and green vegetables.

WHITE PATCHES OR SPOTS IN THE MOUTH

The tongue is coated with white 'fur'. Many illnesses cause a white or yellowish coating on the tongue and roof of the mouth. This is common when there is a fever. Although this coating is not serious, it helps to rinse the mouth with a solution of warm water with salt and bicarbonate of soda several times a day.

Tiny white spots, like salt grains, in the mouth of a child with fever may be an early sign of measles (p. 311).

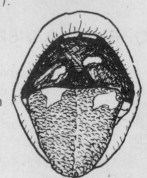

Thrush: small white patches on the inside of the mouth and tongue that look like milk curds stuck to raw meat. They are caused by a fungus or yeast infection called moniliasis (see p. 242). Thrush is common in newborn babies and in persons using certain antibiotics, especially tetracycline or ampicillin.

Unless it is very important to keep taking the antibiotic, stop taking it. Paint the inside of the mouth with gentian violet. Chewing garlic or eating yogurt may also help. In severe cases, use nystatin (p. 360).

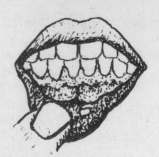

Canker sores: small, white, painful spots inside the lip or mouth. May appear after fever or stress (worry). In 1 to 3 weeks they go away. Rinse mouth with salt water, or put on a little hydrogen peroxide or cortico- steroid ointment (p. 361). Antibiotics do not help.

COLD SORES AND FEVER BLISTERS

Small painful blisters on lips (or genitals) that break and form scabs. May appear after fever or stress . Caused by a herpes virus. They heal after 1 or 2 weeks. Holding ice on the sores for 1 hour the day they begin may cure them. Putting alum, camphor, or bitter plant juices (see Cardon, p. 13) on them may help. No medications do much good.

CHAPTER

18

THE URINARY SYSTEM
AND THE GENITALS

The urinary system or *tract* serves the body by removing waste material from the blood and getting rid of it in the form of *urine:*

The *kidneys* filter the blood and form the urine.

The *ureters* are tubes that carry urine to the bladder.

The *bladder* is a bag that stores the urine. As it fills, it stretches and gets bigger.

The urine tube or *urinary canal (urethra)* carries urine out through the penis in men or to a small opening between the lips of the vagina in women.

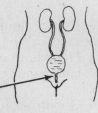

The genitals are the sex organs.

The man:

bladder

urine canal

penis or male sex organ

scrotum or sac that holds the testicles

sperm tube

The *prostate gland* makes the liquid that carries the sperm.

The *testicles* make the *sperm,* or microscopic cells with tails, that join with the egg of a woman and make her pregnant.

The woman:

outer lip of the vagina

inner lip

anus: end of the intestine

clitoris: a sensitive part somewhat like a small penis

urinary opening: hole where urine comes out

opening to the *vagina* or birth canal. (For inside view, see p. 280.)

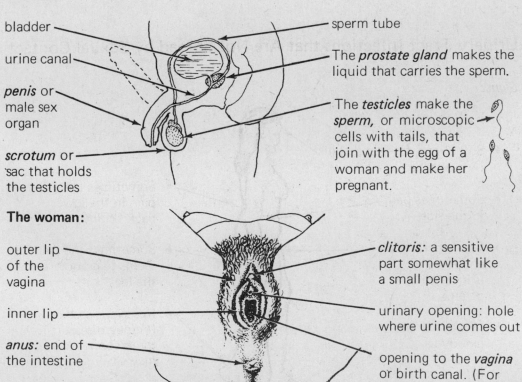

PROBLEMS OF THE URINARY TRACT

There are many different disorders of the urinary tract. They are not always easy to tell apart. Some are not serious, while others can be very dangerous. A dangerous illness may begin with only mild symptoms. It is often difficult to identify these disorders correctly by simply using a book like this one. Special knowledge and tests may be needed. When possible, seek advice from a health worker.

Common **problems with urinating** include:

1. Urinary tract infections that are not spread by sexual contact.

2. Kidney stones.

3. Prostate trouble (difficulty passing urine caused by an enlarged gland; most common in older men).

4. Gonorrhea (difficulty or pain in passing urine; an infectious disease, spread by sexual contact).

5. In some parts of the world schistosomiasis is the most common cause of blood in the urine. This is discussed with other worm infections. See page 146.

Urinary Tract Infections that Are Not Spread by Sexual Contact

Signs:

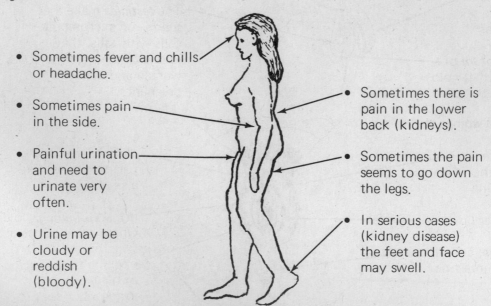

- Sometimes fever and chills or headache.

- Sometimes pain in the side.

- Painful urination and need to urinate very often.

- Urine may be cloudy or reddish (bloody).

- Sometimes there is pain in the lower back (kidneys).

- Sometimes the pain seems to go down the legs.

- In serious cases (kidney disease) the feet and face may swell.

Many women suffer from minor urinary infections. In men they are much less common. Sometimes the only symptoms are **painful urination** and the **need to urinate often.** Other common signs are **blood in the urine** and **pain in the lower belly.** Pain in the mid or lower back, often spreading around the sides below the ribs, with fever, indicates a more serious problem.

Treatment:

♦ **Drink a lot of water.** Many minor urinary infections can be cured by simply drinking a lot of water, without the need for medicine.

    (But if the person cannot urinate or has swelling of the hands and face, he should not drink much water.)

♦ If the person does not get better by drinking a lot of water, or if he has a fever, he should take pills of a sulfonamide (p. 354), ampicillin (p. 351), or tetracycline (p. 353). Pay careful attention to dosage and precautions. To completely control the infection it may be necessary to take the medicine for 10 days or more. It is very important to **continue to drink a lot of water while taking these medicines,** especially the sulfonamides.

♦ If the person does not get better quickly, seek medical advice.

Kidney or Bladder Stones:

Signs:

• The first sign is often sharp or severe pain in the lower back, the side, or the lower belly, or in the base of the penis in men.

• Sometimes the urinary tube is blocked so the person has difficulty passing urine—or cannot pass any. Or drops of blood may come out when the person begins to urinate.

• There may be a urinary infection at the same time.

Treatment:

♦ The same as for the urinary infections described above.

♦ Also give aspirin or another painkiller and an antispasmodic (see p. 367).

♦ Try to urinate while lying down. This sometimes allows a stone in the bladder to roll back and free the opening to the urinary tube.

♦ In severe cases get medical help. Sometimes surgery is needed.

Enlarged Prostate Gland:

This condition is most common in older men. It is caused by a swelling of the prostate gland, which is between the bladder and the urinary tube (urethra).

• The person has difficulty in passing urine and sometimes in having a bowel movement. The urine may only dribble or drip or become blocked completely. Sometimes the man is not able to urinate for days.

• If he has a fever, this is a sign that infection is also present.

Treatment for an enlarged prostate:

- If the person cannot urinate, he should try sitting in a tub of hot water, like this: If this does not work, a catheter may be needed (p. 239).
- If he has a fever, use an antibiotic such as ampicillin (p. 351) or tetracycline (p. 353).
- Get medical help. Serious or chronic cases may require surgery.

Note: It is important to distinguish between prostate trouble and gonorrhea, which can also make it hard to pass urine. In older men it is more likely to be an enlarged prostate. However, a younger man—especially one who has had sexual contact with an infected person (within the last few days or weeks)—probably has gonorrhea.

DISEASES SPREAD BY SEXUAL CONTACT (VENEREAL DISEASES)

Gonorrhea (clap, VD, the drip):

This is a disease usually spread by sexual contact (a venereal disease).

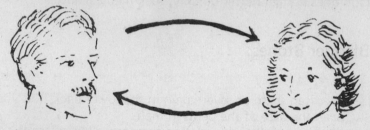

Signs:

In the man:
- Pain with urination.
- Drops of pus from the penis.
- Difficulty urinating (sometimes he cannot pass any urine at all).
- Fever (sometimes).

After months or years:
- Hard, tender swelling in one knee or other joint, or many other problems.

In the woman:
- **At first, there are often no symptoms** (she may feel a little pain when urinating or have a slight vaginal discharge).
- If a pregnant woman with gonorrhea is not treated before giving birth, the infection may get in the baby's eyes and make him blind (see p. 221).

After months or years:
- Pain in the lower belly (pelvic inflammatory disease, p. 243).
- Menstrual problems.
- She may become *sterile.*
- Other problems.

In a man, the first signs of gonorrhea begin 2 to 5 days (or up to 3 weeks or more) after sexual contact with an infected person. In a woman, years may pass before any signs show up. But even though she does not show any signs, **she can give the disease to someone else,** starting a few days after she becomes infected.

Treatment of gonorrhea:

♦ Inject procaine penicillin: 4.8 million units at one time. Put half the dose in each buttock (see p. 350). It is important to use procaine penicillin and not crystalline penicillin. If you can get probenecid, give 1 gm. half an hour before you inject the penicillin. If you do not have penicillin (or if it does not seem to work), use tetracycline. Start by taking 6 capsules of 250 mg. at once, then take two 250 mg. capsules, 4 times a day for 4 days (p. 353). If tetracycline does not work either (see Resistance to Antibiotics, p. 58), try streptomycin (p. 356).

♦ If the person cannot urinate, he should try doing so while sitting in a tub of hot water (see p. 236). If he still cannot urinate, the bladder should be drained using a *catheter* (see p. 239). Get medical help.

♦ If a man has had sex with his wife after being exposed to gonorrhea, she should be treated also. Even if the wife shows no signs of the disease, she probably has it. If she is not treated at the same time, she will give the disease right back to her husband again.

♦ The eyes of all babies should be protected from gonorrhea and possible blindness by using 1 percent silver nitrate drops at birth (see p. 365).

♦ Everyone who has had sex with a person known to have gonorrhea should also be treated, especially wives of men who are infected.

CAUTION: A person with gonorrhea may also have syphilis, without knowing it. Sometimes it is best to go ahead and give the full treatment for syphilis, because the gonorrhea treatment may prevent the first syphilis symptoms, **but may not cure the disease.**

For prevention of gonorrhea and other venereal disease, see p. 239.

Syphilis:

Syphilis is a common and dangerous disease that is spread from person to person through sexual contact.

Signs:

• The first sign is usually a sore, called a *chancre.* It appears 2 to 5 weeks after sexual contact with a person who has syphilis. The chancre may look like a pimple, a blister, or an open sore. It usually appears in the genital area of the man or woman (or less commonly on the lips, fingers, anus, or mouth). This sore is full of germs, which are easily passed on to another person. **The sore is usually painless, and if it is inside the vagina, a woman may not know she has it —but she can easily infect other persons.**

• The sore only lasts a few days and then goes away by itself without treatment. **But the disease continues spreading though the body.**

- Weeks or months later, there may be sore throat, mild fever, mouth sores, or swollen joints. Or any of these signs may appear on the skin:

a painful rash or 'pimples' all over the body	ring-shaped welts (like hives)	an itchy rash on the hands or feet

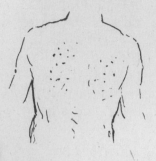  

All of these signs usually go away by themselves, and then the person often thinks he is well—but the disease continues. **Without adequate treatment, syphilis can invade any part of the body, causing heart disease, paralysis, insanity, and many other problems.**

CAUTION: If any strange rash or skin condition shows up days or weeks after a pimple or sore appears on the genitals, it may be syphilis. If unsure, get medical advice.

Treatment for syphilis:

- Inject procaine penicillin, 1 million units a day for 12 days (see p. 350). **To cure syphilis completely, it is very important to give the full 12-day treatment.** Persons who are allergic to penicillin or who do not get better with it can take tetracycline, 3 capsules of 250 mg., 4 times a day for 10 days.
- If there is any chance that someone has syphilis, he should immediately see a health worker. Special blood tests may be needed. If tests cannot be made, the person should be treated for syphilis in any case.
- Everyone who has had sexual contact with a person known to have syphilis should also be treated, especially husbands or wives of those known to be infected.

To prevent syphilis, see the next page.

Bubos: Bursting Lymph Nodes in the Groin (Lymphogranuloma Venereum)

Signs:

- **In a man:** Large, dark lumps in the groin that open to drain pus, scar up, and open again.
- **In a woman:** Lymph nodes similar to those in the man. Or painful, oozing sores in the anus.

Treatment:

- See a health worker.
- Give adults 250 mg. capsules of tetracycline, 1 or 2 capsules, 4 times a day for 2 weeks.
- Avoid all sexual contact until the sores are completely healed.

How to prevent spreading venereal disease to other people:

1. **Get treatment right away:** It is very important that all persons infected with this kind of illness get treatment at once so that they do not infect other people. Do not have sex with anyone until 3 days after treatment is finished.

2. **Tell other people if they need treatment:** When a person finds out that he or she has any form of venereal disease (VD), he should tell everyone with whom he has had sex, so that they can get treatment, too. A man is especially obligated to tell women he has slept with, because without knowing that she has it a woman can pass the disease on to other people, her babies may become blind, and in time she may become sterile or very ill herself.

3. **Be careful with whom you have sex:** Someone who has sex with many different persons is more likely to catch these diseases. Brothels or whorehouses are especially dangerous. Do not go to them! Do not be tempted when you go to the cities. Use of condoms helps (but does not always) prevent VD.

4. **Help others:** Insist that friends who may have VD get treatment at once, and that they avoid all sexual contact until they are cured.

HOW AND WHEN
TO USE A CATHETER
(A RUBBER TUBE TO DRAIN URINE FROM THE BLADDER)

When and when not to use a catheter:

- **Never use a catheter unless it is absolutely necessary** and it is impossible to get medical help in time. Even careful use of a catheter sometimes causes dangerous infection or damages the urinary canal.

- If any urine is coming out at all, do not use the catheter.

- If the person cannot urinate, first have him try to urinate while sitting in a tub of warm water (p. 236). Begin the recommended medicine (for gonorrhea or prostate trouble) at once.

- If the person has a very full, painful bladder and cannot urinate, or if he begins to show signs of poisoning from urine, then and only then use a catheter.

Signs of urine poisoning (uremia):

- The breath smells like urine.
- The feet and face swell.
- Vomiting , distress, confusion.

Note: People who have suffered from difficulty urinating, enlarged prostate, or kidney stones should buy a catheter and keep it handy in case of emergency.

HOW TO USE A CATHETER

1. Boil the catheter for 15 minutes.

2. Wash the penis and the whole area around it well with soap and warm water.

3. Wash your hands with boiled water and soap.

4. Cover the area around the penis with a very clean cloth, sterilized if possible.

5. Wash your hands with alcohol. (If you have sterile gloves, use them.)

6. Lubricate the catheter with antibiotic ointment or a sterile lubricant.

7. Insert the catheter little by little, very carefully.

BE VERY CAREFUL THAT THE CATHETER NEVER TOUCHES ANYTHING BUT THE OPENING OF THE PENIS AND YOUR HANDS.

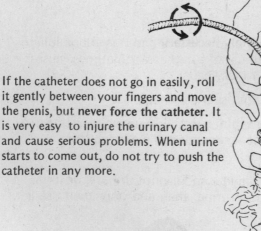

If the catheter does not go in easily, roll it gently between your fingers and move the penis, but **never force the catheter**. It is very easy to injure the urinary canal and cause serious problems. When urine starts to come out, do not try to push the catheter in any more.

Keep the penis in this position so that the urine canal is not bent.

Important:

If the person shows signs of urine poisoning, do not let the urine come out all at once: instead, let it out very slowly, little by little over an hour or 2.

Women sometimes have trouble urinating after giving birth and need a catheter put in. The method is similar, but the woman's urinary tube is much shorter.

PROBLEMS OF WOMEN

Vaginal Discharge
(a mucus or pus-like stuff that comes from the vagina):

All women normally have a small amount of vaginal discharge, which is clear, milky, or slightly yellow. If there is no itching or bad smell, there is probably no problem.

But many women, especially during pregnancy, suffer from a discharge often with itching in the vagina. This discharge may be caused by various infections. Most of them are bothersome, but not dangerous.

1. **A thin and foamy, greenish-yellow or whitish, foul-smelling discharge with itching.** This is probably an infection of **Trichomonas.** It burns to urinate. Sometimes the genitals hurt or are swollen.

Treatment:

- It is very important to keep the genitals clean.

- A vaginal wash, or *douche,* with warm water and distilled vinegar will help.

Use 3 teaspoons of vinegar
in 1 liter of boiled water.

The woman should douche 1 to 3 times a day until she gets better. If there is no vinegar, use lemon juice in water.

- In serious cases use *vaginal inserts* that contain metronidazole or other medication recommended for Trichomonas (p. 359). In very serious cases take metronidazole by mouth. Take 2 grams as a single dose. For precautions and instructions, see pages 359 and 360.

Important:

It is likely that the husband of a woman with Trichomonas has the infection, too, even though he does not feel anything. (Some men with Trichomonas have a burning feeling when urinating.) If the woman gets a severe infection again after she has been treated, both she and her husband should take 2 grams of metronidazole on the same day. Only take metronidazole by mouth if the infection is very severe.

2. **White discharge that looks like cottage cheese or buttermilk, and smells like mold, mildew, or baking bread.** This could be a yeast infection (moniliasis, 'thrush'). Itching may be severe. The lips of the vagina often look bright red and hurt. It burns to urinate. Thrush is especially common in pregnant women or in those who are sick, diabetic (p. 127), or have been taking antibiotics, or birth control pills.

Treatment:

Douche with vinegar-water (see p. 241) or dilute gentian violet, 2 parts gentian violet to 100 parts water (2 teaspoons to a half liter). Or use nystatin vaginal tablets or any other vaginal inserts for moniliasis. For dosage and instructions see page 360. Putting yogurt in the vagina is said to be a useful home remedy to help control yeast infections.

WARNING: Never use antibiotics against this kind of infection. Antibiotics make yeast infections worse.

3. **Thick, milky discharge with a rancid smell.** This could be an infection caused by a bacteria called **hemophilus.** Special tests may be needed to tell this from a trichomonas infection. Douche with vinegar-water (p. 241). Also use a vaginal tablet (insert) of sulfathiazole twice a day for 2 weeks (see p. 360).

4. **Watery, brown, or gray discharge, streaked with blood; bad smell.** These are signs of more serious infections, or possibly cancer (p. 280). If there is fever, use an antibiotic (ampicillin if possible—see p. 351). **Get medical help right away.**

Important: If any discharge lasts a long time, or does not get better with treatment, see a health worker.

How a Woman Can Avoid Many Infections:

1. Keep the genital area clean. When you bathe, wash well with mild soap.

2. Urinate after sexual contact. This helps prevent urinary infections (but will not prevent pregnancy).

3. Be sure to clean yourself carefully after each bowel movement. Always wipe from front to back:

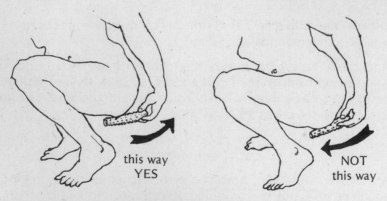

this way
YES

NOT
this way

Wiping forward can spread germs, amebas, or worms into the vagina. Also take care to wipe little girls' bottoms from front to back and to teach them, as they grow up, to do it the same way.

Pain or Discomfort
in the Lower Central Part of a Woman's Belly

This can come from many different causes, which are discussed in different parts of this book. The following list, which includes a few key questions, will help you know where to look.

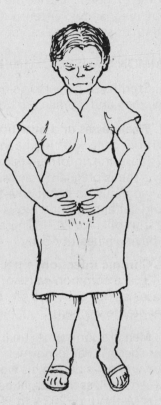

Possible causes of pain in the lower belly are:

1. **Menstrual discomfort** (p. 246). Is it worst shortly before or during the period?

2. **A bladder infection** (p. 235). One of the most common low mid-belly pains. Is urination very frequent or painful?

3. **A yeast infection** (p. 242) **or Trichomonas** (p. 241). These sometimes get into the womb or tubes to the ovaries. Is there a vaginal discharge? What is it like?

4. **Pelvic inflammatory disease.** This is often a late stage of gonorrhea (p. 236). It may be acute, with symptoms similar to those of peritonitis or appendicitis (p. 94), or chronic, with continual or intermittent pain or discomfort in the lower belly, often with periods of chills and fevers.

5. **Problems that are related to a lump or mass in the lower part of the belly.** These are discussed briefly on page 280 and include **ovarian cyst, ectopic pregnancy** (when the baby begins to develop outside the womb), and **cancer.**

6. **An infection or other problem of the gut or rectum** (p. 145). Is the pain related to eating or to bowel movements?

Some of the above problems are not serious. Others are dangerous. They are not always easy to tell apart. Special tests or examinations may be needed.

> **If you are unsure what is causing the pain,**
> **or if it does not get better soon,**
> **seek medical help.**

MEN AND WOMEN WHO ARE NOT ABLE TO HAVE CHILDREN (INFERTILITY)

Sometimes a man and woman try to have children but the woman does not become pregnant. Either the man or woman may be infertile (unable to bring about pregnancy). Often nothing can be done to make the person fertile, but sometimes something can be done, depending on the cause.

COMMON CAUSES OF INFERTILITY:

1. **Sterility.** The person's body is such that he or she can never have children. Some men and women are born sterile.

2. **Weaknesses or a nutritional lack.** In some women severe anemia, poor nutrition, or lack of iodine may lower the chance of becoming pregnant. Or it may cause the unformed baby (embryo) to die, perhaps before the mother even knows she is pregnant (see Miscarriage, p. 281).

A woman who is not able to become pregnant, or has had only miscarriages, should get enough nutritious food, use iodized salt, and if she is severely anemic, take iron pills (p. 247). These may increase her chance of becoming pregnant and having a healthy baby.

3. **Chronic infection,** especially pelvic inflammatory disease (see Gonorrhea, p. 243) is a common cause of infertility in women. Treatment may help—if the disease has not gone too far. Prevention and early treatment of gonorrhea mean fewer sterile women.

4. **Men** are sometimes unable to make their women pregnant because they have fewer sperms than is normal. It may help for the man to wait, without having sex, for several days before his woman enters her 'fertile days' each month midway between her last menstrual period and the next (see Rhythm Method and Mucus Method, p. 293 and 294). This way he will give her his full amount of sperm when they have sex together on days when she is able to become pregnant.

Warning: Hormones and other medicines commonly given to men or women who cannot have babies almost never do any good, especially in men. Home remedies and magic cures are not likely to help either. Be careful not to waste your money for things that will not help.

If you are a woman and are not able to have a baby, there are still many possibilities for leading a happy and worthwhile life:

- Perhaps you can arrange to care for or adopt children who are orphans or need a home. Many couples come to love such children just as if they were their own.
- Perhaps you can become a health worker or help your community in other ways. The love you would give to your children, you can give to others, and all will benefit.
- You may live in a village where people look with shame on a woman who cannot have children.

Perhaps you and others can form a group to help those who have special needs and to show that having babies is not the only thing that makes a woman worthwhile.

CHAPTER

19

INFORMATION FOR MOTHERS AND MIDWIVES

THE MENSTRUAL PERIOD (MONTHLY BLEEDING IN WOMEN)

Most girls have their first 'period' or monthly bleeding between the ages of 11 and 16. This means that they are now old enough to become pregnant.

The normal period comes once every 28 days or so, and lasts 3 to 6 days. However, this varies a lot in different women.

Irregular or painful periods are common in adolescent (teenage) girls. This does not usually mean there is anything wrong.

If your menstrual period is painful:

There is no need for you to stay in bed. In fact, lying quietly can make the pain worse.	It often helps to walk around and do light work or exercises . . .	or to take hot drinks, or put your feet in hot water.

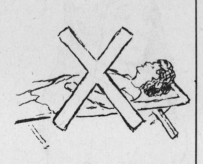  

Also, it may help to take aspirin (p. 365) or to put hot compresses on the belly.

During the period—as at all times—a woman should take care to keep clean, get enough sleep, and eat a well-balanced diet. She can eat everything she normally eats and can continue to do her usual work. It is not harmful to have sex during the menstrual period.

Signs of menstrual problems:

• Some irregularity in the length of time between periods is normal for certain women, but for others it may be a sign of chronic illness, anemia, malnutrition, or possibly an infection or tumor in the womb.

• If a period does not come when it should, this may be a sign of pregnancy. But for many girls who have recently begun to menstruate, and for women over 40, it is often normal to miss or have irregular periods. Worry or emotional upset may also cause a woman to miss her period.

• If bleeding starts during pregnancy, this almost always is the beginning of a miscarriage (death of the developing baby, see p. 281).

• **If the menstrual period lasts more than 6 days, results in unusually heavy bleeding, or comes more than once a month, seek medical advice.**

THE MENOPAUSE
(WHEN WOMEN STOP HAVING PERIODS)

The *menopause* or *climacteric* is the time in a woman's life when the menstrual periods stop coming. After menopause, she can no longer bear children. In general, this 'change of life' happens between the ages of 40 and 50. The periods often become irregular for several months before they stop completely.

During menopause, it is normal for a woman to feel many discomforts—anxiety, distress, 'hot flashes' (suddenly feeling uncomfortably hot), pains that travel all over the body, sadness, etc. After menopause is over, most women feel better again.

Women who have severe bleeding or a lot of pain in the belly during menopause, or who begin to bleed again after the bleeding has stopped for months or years, should seek medical help. An examination is needed to make sure they do not have cancer or another serious problem (see p. 280).

PREGNANCY

Signs of pregnancy:

All these signs are normal:

• The woman misses her period (often the first sign).

• 'Morning sickness' (nausea or feeling you are going to vomit, especially in the morning). This is worse during the second and third months of pregnancy.

• She may have to urinate more often.

• The belly gets bigger.

• The breasts get bigger.

• 'Mask of pregnancy' (dark areas on the face, breasts, and belly).

• Finally, during the fifth month or so, the child begins to move in the womb.

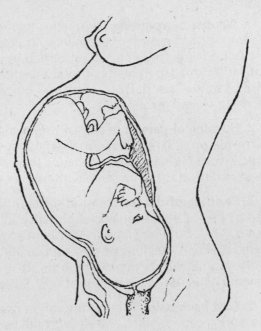

This is the normal position of the baby in the mother at 9 months.

How to Stay Healthy during Pregnancy:

• It is very important to **eat well.** The body needs food rich in proteins, vitamins, and minerals, especially iron. (Read Chapter 11 in this book.)

• **Use iodized salt** to increase the chances that the child will be born alive and will not be retarded. (But to avoid swelling of the feet and other problems, do not use very much salt.)

• **Keep clean.** Bathe or wash regularly and brush your teeth every day.

• In the last month of pregnancy, it is perhaps best to **avoid sexual contact** to keep from breaking the bag of waters and causing an infection.

• **Avoid taking medicines** if at all possible. Some medicines can harm the developing baby. As a rule, only take medicines recommended by a health worker or doctor. (If a health worker is going to prescribe a medicine, and you think that you might be pregnant, tell him so.) You can take aspirin or antacids once in a while if you need them. Vitamin and iron pills are often helpful and do no harm when taken in the right dosage.

• **Do not smoke or drink** during pregnancy. Smoking and drinking are bad for the mother and harm the developing baby.

• Stay far away from children with measles, especially **German measles** (see Rubella, p. 312).

• Continue to work and **get exercise,** but try not to get too tired.

Minor Problems during Pregnancy:

1. **Nausea or vomiting:** Normally, this is worse in the morning, during the second or third month of pregnancy. It helps to eat something dry, like crackers or dry bread, before you get out of bed in the morning. Do not eat large meals, but rather smaller amounts of food several times a day. In severe cases, take an antihistamine (see p. 371) when you go to bed and when you get up in the morning. Avoid greasy foods.

2. **Burning or pain** in the pit of the stomach or chest (acid indigestion and heartburn—see p. 128): Eat only small amounts of food at one time. If possible, drink milk. Avoid taking antacids. It helps to suck hard candy. Try to sleep with the chest and head lifted up some with pillows or blankets.

3. **Swelling of the feet:** Rest at different times during the day with your feet up (see p. 176). Eat less salt and avoid salty foods. Tea made from corn silk may help (see p. 12). If the feet are very swollen, and the hands and face also swell, seek medical advice. Swelling of the feet usually comes from the pressure of the child in the womb during the last months. It is worse in women who are anemic, malnourished, or who eat a lot of salt. So **eat nutritious food with little or no salt.**

4. **Low back pain:** This is common in pregnancy. It can be helped by exercise and taking care to stand and sit with the back straight (p. 174).

5. **Anemia and malnutrition:** Many women in rural areas are anemic even before they are pregnant, and become more anemic during pregnancy. To make a healthy baby, a woman needs foods rich in protein and iron. If she is very pale and weak or has other signs of anemia and malnutrition (see p. 107 and 125), she needs to eat more protein. She can get this by eating beans, groundnuts, chicken, milk, cheese, eggs, meat, fish, and dark green leafy vegetables. She should also take iron pills (p. 376), especially if it is hard to get enough nutritious foods. This way she will strengthen her blood to resist dangerous bleeding after childbirth. If possible, iron pills should also contain some folic acid and vitamin C.

6. **Swollen veins (varicose veins):** These are common in pregnancy, due to the weight of the baby pressing on the veins that come from the legs. Put your feet up often, as high as you can (see p. 175). If the veins get very big or hurt, wrap them like this with an elastic bandage. Take off the bandages at night.

7. **Piles (hemorrhoids):** These are varicose veins in the anus. They result from the weight of the baby in the womb.

To relieve the pain, kneel with the buttocks in the air like this:

Also see p. 175.

8. **Constipation:** Drink plenty of water. Eat fruits and food with a lot of natural fiber, like cassava or bran. Get plenty of exercise. **Do not take strong laxatives.**

Danger Signs in Pregnancy:

1. **Bleeding:** If a woman begins to bleed during pregnancy, even a little, this is a danger sign. She is probably having a miscarriage (losing the baby). The woman should lie quietly and send for a health worker. Bleeding late in pregnancy (after 6 months) may mean the *placenta* (afterbirth) is blocking the birth opening *(placenta previa).* Without expert help, the woman could bleed to death. Try to get her to a hospital at once.

2. **Severe anemia:** The woman is weak, tired, and has pale or transparent skin (see The Signs of Anemia, p. 125). If not treated, she might die from blood loss at childbirth. If anemia is severe, a good diet is not enough to correct the condition in time. See a health worker and get pills or injections of iron salts (see p. 376). If possible, she should have her baby in a hospital, in case extra blood is needed.

3. **Swelling** of the feet, hands, and face, with headache, dizziness, and sometimes blurred vision, are signs of **toxemia or poisoning of pregnancy.** Sudden weight gain, high blood pressure, and a lot of protein in the urine are other important signs. So if you can do so, go to a midwife or health worker who can measure these things.

To treat TOXEMIA OF PREGNANCY a woman should:

- Stay quiet and in bed.
- Avoid salt. (Use no salt; eat no foods that contain salt.)
- If she does not get better quickly, has trouble seeing, swells more in the face, or has fits (convulsions), get medical help fast. Her life is in danger.

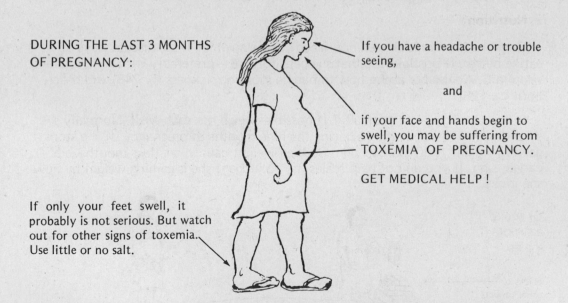

DURING THE LAST 3 MONTHS OF PREGNANCY:

If you have a headache or trouble seeing,

and

if your face and hands begin to swell, you may be suffering from TOXEMIA OF PREGNANCY.

GET MEDICAL HELP !

If only your feet swell, it probably is not serious. But watch out for other signs of toxemia. Use little or no salt.

To help prevent TOXEMIA OF PREGNANCY: eat nutritious food, making sure to get enough protein (p. 110) and use very little salt.

CHECK-UPS DURING PREGNANCY (PRENATAL CARE)

Many health centers and midwives encourage pregnant women to come for regular *prenatal* (before birth) check-ups and to talk about their health needs. If you are pregnant and have the chance to go for these check-ups, you will learn many things to help you prevent problems and have a healthier baby.

If you are a midwife, you can provide an important service to mothers-to-be (and babies-to-be) by inviting them to come for prenatal check-ups—or by going to see them. It is a good idea to see them **once a month for the first 8 months** of pregnancy, and **once a week during the last month.**

Here are some important things prenatal care should cover:

1. **Sharing information**

Ask the mother about her problems and needs. Find out how many pregnancies she has had, when she had her last baby, and any problems she may have had during pregnancy or childbirth. Talk with her about ways she can help herself and her baby be healthy, including:

* **Eating right.** Encourage her to eat foods rich in protein, vitamins, iron, and calcium (see Chapter 11).
* **Good hygiene** (Chapter 12).
* The importance of taking **few or no medicines** (p. 53).
* The importance of **not smoking** (p. 149) and **not drinking alcoholic drinks** (p. 148).
* Getting enough **exercise and rest.**
* **Tetanus vaccination** to prevent tetanus in the newborn. (Give at the 6th, 7th, and 8th month if first time. If she has been vaccinated against tetanus before, give one booster during the 7th month.)

2. **Nutrition**

Does the mother look well nourished? Is she anemic? If so, discuss ways of eating better. If possible, see that she gets iron pills—preferably with folic acid and vitamin C. Advise her about how to handle morning sickness (p. 248) and heartburn (p. 128).

Is she gaining weight normally? If possible, weigh her each visit. Normally she should gain 8 to 10 kilograms during the nine months of pregnancy. If she stops gaining weight, this is a bad sign. Sudden weight gain in the last months is a danger sign. If you do not have scales, try to judge if she is gaining weight by how she looks.

Or make a simple scales.

bricks or other objects of known weight

3. **Minor problems**

Ask the mother if she has any of the common problems of pregnancy. Explain that they are not serious, and give what advice you can (see p. 248).

4. **Signs of danger and special risk**

Check for each of the danger signs on page 249. Take the mother's **pulse** each visit. This will let you know what is normal for her in case she has problems later (for example shock from toxemia or severe bleeding). If you have a blood pressure cuff (see p. 126), take her **blood pressure.** And **weigh her.** Watch out especially for the following danger signs:

- sudden weight gain ⎫ signs of
- swelling of hands and face ⎬ toxemia of
- marked increase in blood pressure ⎭ pregnancy (p. 249)
- severe anemia (p. 125)
- any bleeding (p. 249)

Some midwives may have paper 'dip sticks' or other methods for measuring the protein and sugar in the urine. High protein may be a sign of toxemia. High sugar is a sign of diabetes (p. 127).

If any of the danger signs appear, see that the woman gets medical help as soon as possible. Also check for **signs of special risk,** page 256. If any are present, it is safer if the mother gives birth in a hospital.

5. **Growth and position of the baby in the womb**

Feel the mother's womb each time she visits; or show her how to do it herself.

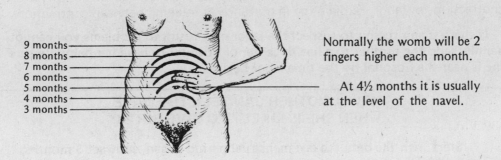

9 months
8 months
7 months
6 months
5 months
4 months
3 months

Normally the womb will be 2 fingers higher each month.

At 4½ months it is usually at the level of the navel.

Each month write down how many finger widths the womb is above or below the navel. If the womb seems too big or grows too fast, it may have more water in it than normal. If so, you may find it more difficult to feel the baby inside. Too much water in the womb means greater risk of severe bleeding during childbirth and may mean the baby is deformed.

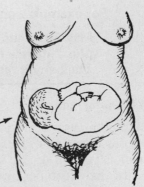

Try to feel the baby's position in the womb. If it appears to be lying sideways, the mother should go to a doctor **before** labor begins, because an operation may be needed. For checking the baby's position near the time of birth, see page 257.

252

6. Baby's heartbeat (fetal heartbeat)

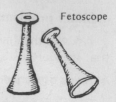

Fetoscope

After 5 months, listen for the baby's heartbeat and check for movement. You can try putting your ear against the belly, but it may be hard to hear. It will be easier if you get a *fetoscope.* (Or make one. Fired clay or hard wood works well.)

If the baby's heartbeat is heard loudest below the navel in the last month, the baby is head down and will probably be born head first.

If the heartbeat is heard loudest above the navel, his head is probably up. It may be a breech birth.

If you have a watch with a second hand, count the baby's heartbeats. From 120 to 160 per minute is normal. If less than 120, something is wrong. (Or perhaps you counted wrong or heard the mother's heartbeat. Check her pulse. The baby's heartbeat is often hard to hear. It takes practice.)

7. Preparing the mother for labor

As the birth approaches, see the mother more often. If she has other children, ask her how long labor lasted and if she had any problems. Talk with her about ways to make the birth easier and less painful (see the next pages). You may want to have her practice deep, slow breathing, so that she can do this during the contractions of labor. Explain the importance of relaxing between contractions.

If there is any reason to suspect the labor may result in problems you cannot handle, send the mother to a health center or hospital to have her baby. Be sure she is near the hospital by the time labor begins.

HOW A MOTHER CAN TELL THE DATE WHEN SHE IS LIKELY TO GIVE BIRTH:

Start with the date the last menstrual period began, subtract 3 months, and add 7 days.

For example, suppose your last period began May 10.

May 10 minus 3 months is February 10,
plus 7 days is February 17.
The baby is likely to be born around February 17.

---

8. Keeping records

To compare your findings from month to month and see how the mother is progressing, it helps to keep simple records. On the next page is a sample record sheet. Change it as you see fit. A larger sheet of paper would be better. Each mother can keep her own record sheet and bring it when she comes for her check-up.

RECORD OF PRENATAL CARE

NAME _____ AGE _____ NUMBER OF CHILDREN _____ AGES _____ DATE OF LAST CHILDBIRTH _____

DATE OF LAST MENSTRUAL PERIOD _____ PROBABLE DATE FOR BIRTH _____ PROBLEMS WITH OTHER BIRTHS _____

MONTH	DATE OF VISIT	WHAT OFTEN HAPPENS	GENERAL HEALTH AND MINOR PROBLEMS	ANEMIA (how severe)?	DANGER SIGNS (see p. 249)	SWELLING (where? how much?)	PULSE	TEMP.	WEIGHT (estimate or measure)	BLOOD PRESSURE *	PROTEIN IN URINE *	SUGAR IN URINE *	POSITION OF BABY IN WOMB	SIZE OF WOMB (how many fingers above (+) or below (−) the navel?)
1										*	*	*		−
2		tiredness, nausea, and morning sickness												−
3														−
4		womb at level of the navel												0
5		baby heartbeat & 1st movements											TETANUS VACCINE 1st	+
6														+
7		some swelling of feet											2nd or booster	+
8		constipation												+
9		heartburn											3rd	+
1st week		varicose veins												+
2nd week		shortness of breath												+
3rd week		frequent urination												+
4th week		baby moves lower in belly												+
														+
														+
BIRTH														

*These are included for midwives who have means of measuring or testing for this information.

THINGS A MOTHER SHOULD HAVE READY BEFORE GIVING BIRTH

Every pregnant woman should have the following things ready by the seventh month of pregnancy:

A lot of very clean cloths or rags.

A new razor blade. (Do not unwrap until you are ready to cut the umbilical cord.)

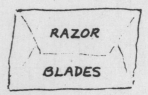

An antiseptic soap (or any soap).

(If you do not have a new razor blade, have clean, rust-free scissors ready. Boil them just before cutting the cord.)

A clean scrub brush for cleaning the hands and fingernails.

Sterile gauze or patches of thoroughly cleaned cloth for covering the navel.

Alcohol for rubbing hands after washing them.

Two ribbons or strips of clean cloth for tying the cord.

Clean cotton.

Both patches and ribbons should be wrapped and sealed in paper packets and then baked in an oven or ironed.

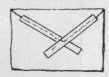

Additional Supplies
for the Well-Prepared Midwife or Birth Attendant

Flashlight (torch).

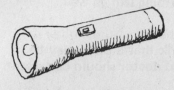

Fetoscope—or fetal stethoscope—for listening to the baby's heartbeat through the mother's belly.

Suction bulb for sucking mucus out of the baby's nose and mouth.

Blunt-tipped scissors for cutting the cord before the baby is all the way born (extreme emergency only).

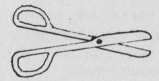

Sterile syringe and needles.

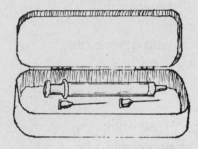

Two clamps (hemostats) for clamping the umbilical cord or clamping bleeding veins from tears of the birth opening.

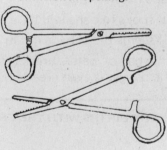

Several injections of ergonovine (or ergometrine).

Sterile needle and gut thread for sewing tears in the birth opening.

Two bowls—1 for washing hands and 1 for catching and examining the afterbirth.

Silver nitrate drops for the baby's eyes.

PREPARING FOR BIRTH

Birth is a natural event. When the mother is healthy and everything goes well, the baby can be born without help from anyone. In a normal birth, **the less the midwife or birth attendant does, the more likely everything will go well.**

Difficulties in childbirth do occur, and sometimes the life of the mother or child may be in danger. **If there is any reason to think that a birth may be difficult or dangerous, a skilled midwife or experienced doctor should be present.**

Signs of Special Risk that Make It Important that a Doctor or Skilled Midwife Attend the Birth—if Possible in a Hospital:

- If the woman begins to bleed before labor.
- If there are signs of toxemia of pregnancy (see p. 249).
- If the woman is suffering from a chronic or acute illness.
- If the woman is very anemic, or if her blood does not clot normally (when she cuts herself).
- If she is under 15, over 40, or over 35 at her first pregnancy.
- If she is especially short or has narrow hips (p. 267).
- If she has had serious trouble or severe bleeding with other births.
- If she has diabetes or heart trouble.
- If she has a hernia.
- If it looks like she will have twins (see p. 269).
- If it seems the baby is not in a normal position in the womb.
- If the bag of waters breaks and labor does not begin within a few hours. (The danger is even greater if there is fever.)

THE BIRTHS WITH THE GREATEST CHANCE OF PROBLEMS ARE:

the first birth   and   the last births after having many children

Checking if the Baby Is in a Good Position

To make sure the baby is head down, in the normal position for birth, feel for his head, like this:

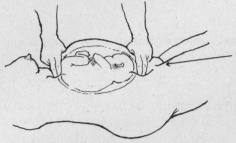

1. Have the mother breathe out all the way.

With the thumb and 2 fingers, push in here, just above the *pelvic* bone.

With the other hand, feel the top of the womb.

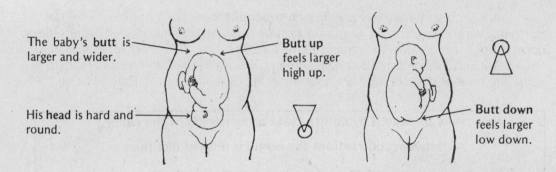

The baby's **butt** is larger and wider.

His **head** is hard and round.

Butt up feels larger high up.

Butt down feels larger low down.

2. Push gently from side to side, first with one hand, then the other.

If the baby's butt is pushed gently sideways, the baby's whole body will move too.

But if the **head** is pushed gently sideways, it will bend at the neck and the back will not move.

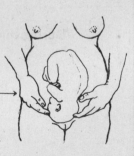

If the baby still is high in the womb, you can move the head a little. But if it has already engaged (dropped lower) getting ready for birth, you cannot move it.

A woman's first baby sometimes engages 2 weeks before labor begins. Later babies may not engage until labor starts.

> **If the baby's head is <u>down</u>, his birth is likely to go well.**
> **If the head is <u>up</u>, the birth may be more difficult (a breech birth), and it is safer for the mother to give birth in or near a hospital.**
> **If the baby is <u>sideways</u>, the mother should have her baby in a hospital. She and the baby are in danger (see p. 267).**

SIGNS THAT SHOW LABOR IS NEAR

• A few days before labor begins, **the baby moves lower** in the womb. This lets the mother breathe more easily, but she may need to urinate more often because of pressure on the bladder. (In the first birth these signs can appear up to 2 weeks before delivery.)

• A short time before the labor begins, a small **plug of mucus** (jelly) may come out. Or some mucus may come out for 2 or 3 days before labor begins. Sometimes it is tinted with blood. This is normal.

• The **contractions** (sudden tightening of the womb) or labor pains may start up to several days before childbirth; at first a long time usually passes between contractions—several minutes or even hours. When the contractions become stronger, regular, and more frequent, labor is beginning.

• Some women have a few **practice contractions** weeks before labor. This is normal. On rare occasions, a woman may have false labor. This happens when the contractions are coming strong and close together, but then stop for hours or days before childbirth actually begins. Sometimes walking or an enema will help calm the contractions if they are false or bring on childbirth if they are real.

Labor pains are caused by contractions or tightening of the womb.

Between contractions the womb is relaxed like this:

During contractions, the womb tightens and lifts up like this:

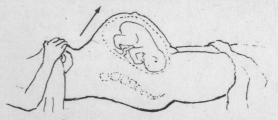

The contractions cause the *cervix* or 'door of the womb' to open—a little more each time.

• The **bag of waters** that holds the baby in the womb usually breaks with a flood of liquid sometime after labor has begun. If the waters break before the contractions start, this usually means the beginning of labor. After the waters break, the mother should keep very clean. Walking back and forth may help bring on labor more quickly.

THE STAGES OF LABOR

Labor has 3 parts or stages:

- The first stage lasts from the beginning of the strong contractions until the baby drops into the birth canal.

- The second stage lasts from the dropping of the baby into the birth canal until it is born.

- The third stage lasts from the birth of the baby until the placenta (afterbirth) comes out.

THE FIRST STAGE OF LABOR usually lasts 10 to 20 hours or more when it is the mother's first birth, and from 7 to 10 hours in later births. This varies a lot.

During the first stage of labor, the mother should not try to hurry the birth. It is natural for this stage to go slowly. The mother may not feel the progress and may begin to worry. Try to reassure her. Tell her that most women have the same concern.

The mother should not push or bear down until the child is beginning to move down into the birth canal, and she feels she has to push.

The mother should keep her bowels and bladder empty.

If the bladder and the bowels are full, they get in the way when the baby is being born.

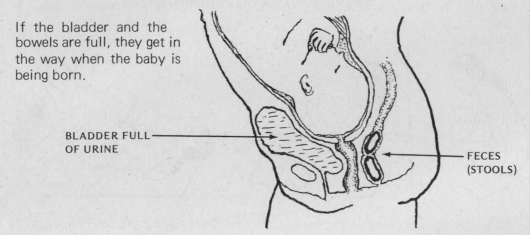

BLADDER FULL OF URINE

FECES (STOOLS)

During labor, the mother should urinate often. If she has not moved her bowels in several hours, an enema may make labor easier. During labor the mother should drink water or other liquids often. Too little liquid in the body can slow down or stop labor. If labor is long, she should eat lightly, as well. If she is vomiting, she should sip a little Rehydration Drink, herbal tea, or fruit juices between each contraction.

During labor the mother should change positions often or even get up and walk about from time to time.

During the first stage of labor, the midwife or birth attendant should:

• Wash the mother's belly, genitals, buttocks, and legs well with soap and warm water. The bed should be in a clean place with enough light to see clearly.

• Spread clean sheets, towels, or newspapers on the bed and change them whenever they get wet or dirty.

• Have a new, unopened razor blade ready for cutting the cord, or boil a pair of scissors for 15 minutes. Keep the scissors in the boiled water in a covered pan until they are needed.

The midwife should **not** massage or push on the belly. She should **not** ask the mother to push or bear down at this time.

If the mother is frightened or in great pain, have her take deep, **slow,** regular breaths during each contraction, and breathe normally between them. This will help control the pain and calm her.

THE SECOND STAGE OF LABOR, in which the child is born: Sometimes this begins when the bag of waters breaks. It is usually easier than the first stage and takes less time. During the contractions the mother bears down (pushes) with all her strength. Between contractions, she may seem exhausted and half asleep. This is normal.

To bear down, the mother should take a deep breath and push hard with her stomach muscles, as if she were having a bowel movement. If the child comes slowly after the bag of waters breaks, the mother can double her knees like this, while

| squatting, | sitting propped up, | or lying down. |

When the birth opening of the mother stretches, and the baby's head begins to show, the midwife or helper should have everything ready for the birth of the baby. At this time the mother should try **not** to push, so that the head comes out more slowly. This helps prevent tearing of the opening (see p. 269 for more details).

In a normal birth, the midwife _never_ needs to put her hand or finger inside the mother. This is the most common cause of dangerous infections of the mother after the birth.

When the head comes out, the midwife may support it, but must _never_ pull on it.

Normally the baby is born head first like this:

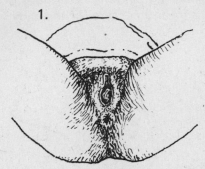

1.

Now push hard.

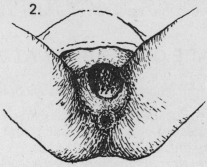

2.

Now try not to push hard. Take many short, fast breaths. This helps prevent tearing the opening (see p. 269).

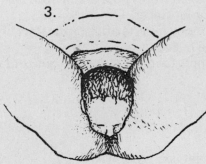

3.

The head usually comes out face down.

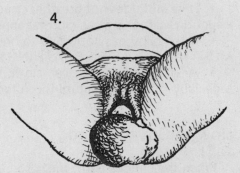

4.

Then the baby's body turns to one side so the shoulders can come out.

If the shoulders get stuck after the head comes out:

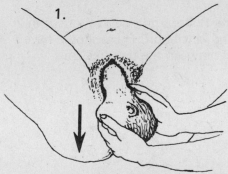

1.

The midwife can take the baby's head in her hands and lower it very carefully, so the shoulder can come out.

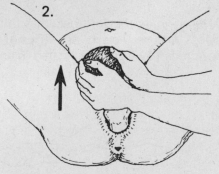

2.

Then she can raise the head a little so that the other shoulder comes out.

All the force must come from the mother. The midwife should **never pull on the head,** because pulling harms the baby.

THE THIRD STAGE OF LABOR begins when the baby has been born and lasts until the placenta (afterbirth) comes out. Usually, the placenta comes out by itself 5 mintues to an hour after the baby. In the meantime, **care for the baby.**

CARE OF THE BABY AT BIRTH

Immediately after the baby comes out:

• Put the baby's head down so that the mucus comes out of his mouth and throat. Keep it this way until he begins to breathe.

• Keep the baby *below* the level of the mother until the cord is tied. (This way, the baby gets more blood and will be stronger.)

• If the baby does not begin to breathe right away, rub his back with a towel or a cloth.

• If he still does not breathe, clean the mucus out of his nose and mouth with a suction bulb or a clean cloth wrapped around your finger.

• If the baby has not begun to breathe within one minute after birth, start MOUTH-TO-MOUTH BREATHING **at once** (see p. 80).

• Wrap the baby in a clean cloth. It is very important not to let him get cold, especially if he is premature (born too early).

How to Cut the Cord:

When the child is born, the cord pulses and is fat and blue. **WAIT.**

After a while, the cord becomes thin and white. It stops pulsing. Now tie it in 2 places with very clean, dry strips of cloth, string, or ribbon. These should have been recently ironed or heated in an oven. Cut between the ties, like this:

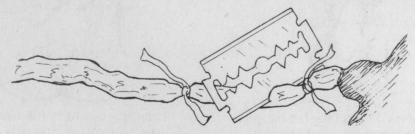

IMPORTANT: Cut the cord with a clean, unused razor blade. Before unwrapping it, wash your hands very well. If you do not have a new razor blade, use freshly boiled scissors. **Always cut the cord close to the body of the newborn baby.** Leave only about 2 centimeters attached to the baby. These precautions help prevent tetanus (see p. 182).

Care of the Cut Cord:

The most important way to protect the freshly cut cord from infection is to **keep it dry.** To help it dry out, **the air must get to it.** If the home is very clean and there are no flies, leave the cut cord uncovered and open to the air.

If there are dust and flies, cover the cord lightly. It is best to use sterile gauze. Cut it with boiled scissors. Put it on like this:

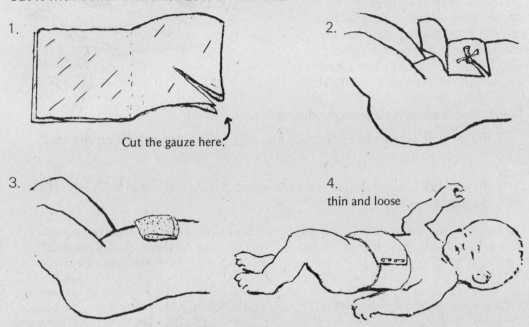

1.

Cut the gauze here.

2.

3.

4.
thin and loose

If you do not have sterile gauze, you can cover the navel with a very clean and freshly ironed cloth. It is better not to use a belly band, but if you want to use one, use a thin, light cloth, like cheesecloth, and be sure it is loose enough to let air in under it, to keep the navel dry. Do not make it tight.

Be sure the baby's nappy (diapers) does not cover the navel, so that the cord does not get wet with urine.

Cleaning the Newborn Baby:

With a warm, soft, damp cloth, gently clean away any blood or fluid.

It is better **not** to bathe the baby until after the cord drops off (usually 5 to 8 days). Then bathe him daily in warm water, using a mild soap.

Put the Newborn Baby to the Breast at Once:

Place the baby at its mother's breast as soon as the cord is cut. If the baby nurses, this will help to make the afterbirth come out sooner and to prevent or control heavy bleeding.

THE DELIVERY OF THE PLACENTA (AFTERBIRTH)

Normally, the placenta comes out 5 minutes to an hour after the baby is born, but sometimes it is delayed for many hours (see below).

Checking the afterbirth:

When the afterbirth comes out, pick it up and examine it to see if it is complete. If it is torn and there seem to be pieces missing, get medical help. A piece of placenta left inside the womb can cause continued bleeding or infection.

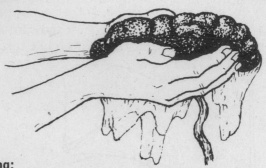

When the placenta is delayed in coming:

If the mother is not losing much blood, do nothing. **Never pull on the cord.** This could cause dangerous hemorrhage (heavy bleeding).

If the mother is losing blood, feel the womb (uterus) through the belly. If it is soft, do the following:

Massage the womb carefully, until it gets hard. This should make it contract and push out the placenta.

If the placenta does not come out soon, and bleeding continues, push downward on the top of the womb very carefully, while supporting the bottom of the womb like this.

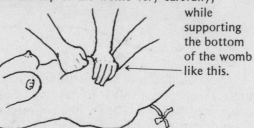

If the placenta still does not come out, and the heavy bleeding continues, try to control the bleeding as follows and seek medical help fast.

HEMORRHAGING (HEAVY BLEEDING)

When the placenta comes out, there is always a brief flow of blood. It normally lasts only a few minutes and not more than a quarter of a liter (1 cup) of blood is lost. (A little bleeding may continue for several days and is usually not serious.) Bleeding can often be slowed down by putting the baby to the breast. If he will not suck, perhaps someone can stroke or stimulate the mother's nipples.

WARNING: Sometimes a woman may be bleeding severely inside without much blood coming out. Feel her belly from time to time. If it seems to be getting bigger, it may be filling with blood. Check her pulse often and watch for signs of shock (p. 77).

If heavy bleeding continues, or if the mother is losing a great deal of blood through a steady trickle, do the following:

* Get medical help fast. If the bleeding does not stop quickly, the mother may need to be given serum blood in a vein (a transfusion).

* If you have **ergonovine** or **oxytocin,** use it, following the instructions on the next page. (Use oxytocin instead of ergonovine if the placenta is still inside.)

* The mother should drink a lot of liquid (water, fruit juices, tea, soup, or Rehydration Drink—p. 152). If she grows faint or has a fast, weak pulse or shows other signs of **shock,** put her legs up and her head down (see p. 77).

* If the mother is losing a lot of blood, and is in danger of bleeding to death, try to stop the bleeding like this:

Massage the belly until you can feel the womb get hard. Then lift the womb with one hand, and with the other hand massage the bottom of the womb.

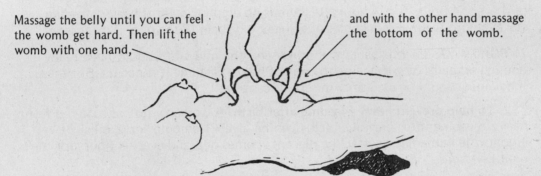

As soon as the womb gets firm and bleeding stops, stop massaging it until it gets soft again. Check it every minute or so.

* If the bleeding continues in spite of massaging the womb, do the following:

Using all of your weight, press down with both hands, one over the other, on the belly just below the navel. You should continue pressing down a long time after the bleeding stops.

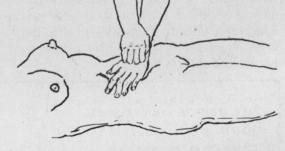

* If the bleeding is still not under control:

Grasp the womb between your hands and squeeze hard. Keep squeezing it firmly until the bleeding has stopped for several minutes or until you get medical help.

THE CORRECT USE OF OXYTOCICS:
ERGONOVINE, OXYTOCIN, *PITOCIN,* ETC.

Oxytocics are medicines that contain ergonovine, ergometrine, or oxytocin. They cause contractions of the uterus and its blood vessels. They are important but dangerous drugs. Used the wrong way, they can cause the death of the mother or the child in her womb. Used correctly, sometimes they can save lives. These are their correct uses:

1. **To control bleeding after childbirth.** This is the most important use of these medicines. In a case of heavy bleeding after the placenta has come out, inject one 0.2 mg. ampule (or give two 0.2 mg. tablets) of ergonovine or ergometrine maleate (*Ergotrate,* etc., p. 375) once every hour for 3 hours or until the bleeding is under control. After the bleeding is controlled, continue giving 1 ampule (or 1 pill) every 4 hours for 24 hours. If there is no ergonovine or if heavy bleeding starts before the placenta comes out, inject oxytocin (*Pitocin,* p. 375) instead.

IMPORTANT: Each expectant mother, and the midwife, should have ready enough ampules of ergonovine to combat heavy bleeding if it occurs. But these medicines should be used only in serious cases.

2. **To help prevent heavy bleeding after birth.** A woman who has suffered from heavy bleeding after previous births can be given 1 ampule (or 2 pills) of ergonovine immediately after the placenta comes out, and every 4 hours for the next 24 hours.

3. **To control the bleeding of a miscarriage** (p. 281). The use of oxytocics can be dangerous, and only a skilled health worker should use them. But, if the woman is rapidly losing blood and medical help is far away, use an oxytocic as suggested above. Oxytocin *(Pitocin)* is probably best.

WARNING: The use of *Ergotrate, Pitocin,* or *Pituitrin* to hasten childbirth or 'give strength' to the mother in labor is very dangerous for both her and the child. The times when oxytocics are needed before the baby is born are very rare, and it is better that only a trained birth attendant use them then. **Never use oxytocics before the child is born!**

THE USE OF OXYTOCICS
DURING CHILDBIRTH TO
'GIVE STRENGTH' TO
THE MOTHER . . .  CAN KILL THE
MOTHER, THE
BABY, OR BOTH.

There is **no** safe medicine for giving strength to the mother or for making the birth quicker or easier.

If you want the woman to have enough strength for childbirth, have her eat body-building and protective foods during the full 9 months of pregnancy. Also encourage her to have children less often. Suggest that she not get pregnant again until enough time has passed for her to regain her full strength (see Family Planning, p. 283).

DIFFICULT BIRTHS

It is important to get medical help as quickly as possible when there is any serious problem during labor. Many problems or complications may come up, some more serious than others. Here are a few of the more common ones:

1. **LABOR STOPS OR SLOWS DOWN**, or lasts a very long time after being strong or after the waters break. This has several possible causes:

■ **The woman may be frightened or upset.** This can slow down or even stop contractions. Talk to her. Try to reassure her. Explain that the birth is slow, but there are no serious problems. Encourage her to change her position often, and to drink, eat, and urinate.

■ **The baby may be in an unusual position.** Feel the belly between contractions to see if the baby is **sideways.** Sometimes the midwife can turn the baby through **gentle** handling of the woman's belly. Try to work the baby around little by little between contractions, until the head is down. But **do not use force** as this could tear the womb. If the baby cannot be turned, try to get the mother to a hospital.

■ **If the baby is facing forward** rather than backward, you may feel the lumpy arms and legs rather than the rounded back. This is usually no big problem, but labor may be longer and cause the woman more back pain. She should change positions often, as this may help turn the baby.

■ **The baby's head may be too large to fit through the woman's hip bones** (pelvis). This is more likely in a woman with very narrow hips or a woman who is very much shorter than her husband. (It is very unlikely in a woman who has given normal birth before.) You may feel that the baby does not move down. If you suspect this problem, try to get the mother to a hospital as she may need an operation (Cesarean). **Women who have very narrow hips or are especially short should have at least their first child in or near a hospital.**

■ **If the mother has been vomiting or has not been drinking,** she may be dehydrated. This can slow down or stop contractions. Have her sip Rehydration Drink or other liquids between contractions.

2. BREECH DELIVERY (the buttocks come out first). Sometimes the midwife can tell if the baby is in the breech position by feeling the mother's belly (p. 257) and listening to the baby's heartbeat (p. 252).

A breech birth may be easier in this position:

If the baby's legs come out, but not the arms, wash your hands very well, rub them with alcohol (or wear sterile gloves), and then . . .

slip your fingers inside and push the baby's shoulders toward the back, like this:

or press his arms against his body, like this:

If the head gets stuck, have the mother lie face up. Put your finger in the baby's mouth and push his head towards his chest. At the same time have someone push the baby's head down by pressing on the mother's belly like this——►

Have the mother push hard. But **never pull on the body of a baby.**

3. PRESENTATION OF AN ARM (hand first). If the baby's hand comes out first, get medical help right away. An operation may be needed to get the baby out.

4. Sometimes the **CORD IS WRAPPED AROUND THE BABY'S NECK** so tightly he cannot come out all the way. Try to slip the loop of cord from around the baby's neck. If you cannot do this, you may have to clamp or tie and cut the cord. Use boiled blunt-tipped scissors.

5. FECES IN THE BABY'S MOUTH AND NOSE. When the waters break, if you see they contain the baby's first black stools (meconium), the baby may be in danger. If he breathes any of the feces into his lungs, he may die. As soon as his head is out, tell the mother not to push, but to take short, rapid breaths. Before the baby starts breathing, take time to suck the feces out of his nose and mouth. with a suction bulb. Even if he starts breathing right away, keep sucking until you get all the feces out.

6. **TWINS.** Giving birth to twins is often more difficult and dangerous—both for the mother and babies—than giving birth to a single baby.

> **To be safe, the mother should give birth to twins in a hospital.**

Because with twins labor often begins early, **the mother should be within easy reach of a hospital after the seventh month of pregnancy.**

Signs that a woman is likely to have twins:

• The belly grows faster and the womb is larger than usual, especially in the last months (see p. 251).

• If the woman gains weight faster than normal, or the common problems of pregnancy (morning sickness, backache, varicose veins, piles, swelling, and difficult breathing) are worse than usual, be sure to check for twins.

• If you can feel 3 or more large objects (heads and buttocks) in a womb that seems extra large, twins are likely.

• Sometimes you can hear 2 different heartbeats (other than the mother's)—but this is difficult.

During the last months, if the woman rests a lot and is careful to avoid hard work, twins are less likely to be born too early.

Twins are often born small and need special care. However, there is no truth in beliefs that twins have strange or magic powers.

TEARING OF THE BIRTH OPENING

The birth opening must stretch a lot for the baby to come out. Sometimes it tears. Tearing is more likely if it is the mother's first baby.

Tearing can usually be prevented if care is taken:

The mother should try to stop pushing when the baby's head is coming out. This gives her birth opening time to stretch. In order not to push, she should pant (take many short rapid breaths).

When the birth opening is stretching, the midwife can support it with one hand and with the other hand gently keep the head from coming too fast, like this:

It may also help to put hot compresses against the skin below the birth opening. Start when it begins to stretch.

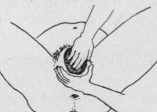 

If a tear does happen, someone who knows how should carefully sew it shut after the placenta comes out (see p. 86 and 366).

CARE OF THE NEWBORN BABY

The Cord:

To prevent the freshly cut cord from becoming infected, it should be kept **clean** and **dry.** The drier it is, the sooner it will fall off and the navel will heal. For this reason, it is better **not** to use a belly band, or if one is used, to keep it very loose (see p. 184 and 263).

The Eyes:

To protect a newborn baby's eyes from dangerous conjunctivitis, put a drop of 1% silver nitrate, or a little tetracycline eye ointment, in each eye as soon as he is born (p. 221). This is especially important if either parent has ever had signs of gonorrhea (p. 236).

Keeping the Baby Warm—But Not Too Warm:

Protect the baby from cold, but also from too much heat. Dress him as warmly as you feel like dressing yourself.

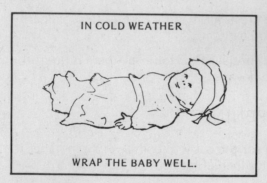

IN COLD WEATHER

WRAP THE BABY WELL.

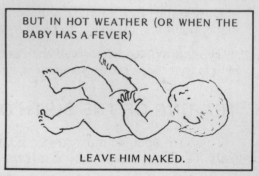

BUT IN HOT WEATHER (OR WHEN THE BABY HAS A FEVER)

LEAVE HIM NAKED.

To keep a baby just warm enough, keep him close to his mother's body.

Cleanliness:

It is important to follow the Guidelines of Cleanliness as discussed in Chapter 12. Take special care with the following:

♦ Change the baby's diapers (nappy) or bedding each time he wets or dirties them. If the skin gets red, change the diaper more often—or better, leave it off! (See p. 215.)

♦ After the cord drops off, bathe the baby daily with mild soap and warm water.

♦ If there are flies or mosquitos, cover the baby's crib with mosquito netting or a thin cloth.

♦ Persons with open sores, colds, sore throat, tuberculosis, or other infectious illnesses should not touch or go near the baby.

♦ Keep the baby in a clean place away from smoke and dust.

Feeding:

(Also see "The Best Diet for Small Children," p. 121.)

Breast milk is by far the best food for a baby. Babies who nurse on breast milk are healthier, grow stronger, and are less likely to die. This is why:

- Breast milk has a better balance of what the baby needs than does any other milk, whether fresh, canned, or powdered.

- Breast milk is clean. When other foods are given, especially by bottle feeding, it is very hard to keep things clean enough to prevent the baby from getting diarrhea and other sicknesses.

- The temperature of breast milk is always right.

- Breast milk has things in it (antibodies) that protect the baby against certain illnesses, such as measles and polio.

The mother should give her breast to the baby as soon as he is born. For the first few days the mother's breasts usually produce very little milk. This is normal. She should **not** start bottle feeding her baby, but should **nurse her baby often.** The baby's sucking will help her produce more milk.

A mother whose breasts make enough milk should give her baby **only breast milk** for the first 4 to 6 months. After that, she should continue to breast feed her baby, but should begin to give him other nourishing foods also (see p. 122).

HOW A MOTHER CAN PRODUCE MORE MILK:

She should . . .

- drink plenty of liquids,

- eat as well as possible, especially milk, milk products, and body-building foods (see p. 110),

- get plenty of sleep and avoid getting very tired or upset,

- nurse her baby more often.

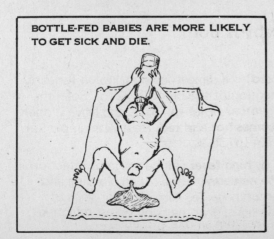

BOTTLE-FED BABIES ARE MORE LIKELY TO GET SICK AND DIE.

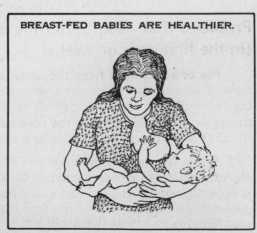

BREAST-FED BABIES ARE HEALTHIER.

Care in Giving Medicines to the Newborn:

Many medicines are dangerous for the newborn. Use only medicines you are sure are recommended for the newborn and use them only when they are absolutely necessary. Be sure you know the right dose and do not give too much. Chloramphenicol is especially dangerous to the newborn . . . and even more dangerous if the baby is premature or underweight (less than 2 kilograms).

ILLNESSES OF THE NEWBORN

It is very important to notice any problem or illness a baby may have—and to act quickly.

> **Diseases that take days or weeks to kill adults can kill a baby in a matter of hours.**

Problems the Baby is Born with: (Also see p. 316)

These may result from something that went wrong with the development of the baby in the womb or from damage to the baby while he was being born. Examine the baby carefully immediately after birth. If he shows any of the following signs, something is probably seriously wrong with him:

- If he does not breathe as soon as he is born.
- If his pulse cannot be felt or heard, or is less than 100 per minute.
- If his face and body are white, blue, or yellow after he has begun breathing.
- If his arms and legs are floppy—he does not move them by himself or when you pinch them.
- If he grunts or has difficulty breathing after the first 15 minutes.

Some of these problems may be caused by brain damage at birth. They are almost never caused by infection (unless the waters broke more than 24 hours before birth). Common medicines probably will not help. Try to get medical help.

If the baby does not urinate or have a bowel movement in the first 2 days, also seek medical help.

Problems that Result after the Baby is Born (in the first days or weeks):

1. **Pus or a bad smell from the navel (cord)** is a dangerous sign. Watch for early signs of tetanus (p. 182) or a bacterial infection of the blood (p. 275). Soak the cord in hydrogen peroxide, paint it with gentian violet (p. 361), and leave it open to the air. **If the skin around the cord becomes hot and red,** treat with ampicillin (p. 351) or with penicillin and streptomycin (p. 352).

2. Either **low temperature** (below 35°) or **high fever** can be a sign of infection. *High fever (above 39°) is dangerous for the newborn.* Take off all clothing and sponge the baby with cool water as shown on page 76. Also look for signs of dehydration (see p. 151). If you find these signs, give the baby breast milk and also Rehydration Drink (p. 152).

3. **Fits (convulsions,** see p. 178**).** If the baby also has fever, treat it as just described. Be sure to check for dehydration. Fits that begin the day of birth are probably caused by brain damage at birth. If fits begin several days later, look carefully for signs of tetanus (p. 182) or meningitis (p. 185).

4. **The baby does not gain weight.** During the first days of life, most babies lose a little weight. This is normal. After the first week, a healthy baby should gain about 200 gm. a week. By two weeks the healthy baby should weigh as much as he did at birth. If he does not gain weight, or loses weight, something is wrong. Did the baby seem healthy at birth? Does he feed well? Examine the baby carefully for signs of infection or other problems. If you cannot find out the cause of the problem and correct it, get medical help.

5. **Vomiting.** When healthy babies burp (or bring up air they have swallowed while feeding), sometimes a little milk comes up too. This is normal. Help the baby bring up air after feeding by holding him against your shoulder and patting his back gently, like this.———————————————→

If a baby vomits when you lay him down after nursing, try sitting him upright for a while after each feeding.

A baby who vomits violently, or so much and so often that he begins to lose weight or become dehydrated, is ill. If the baby also has diarrhea, he

BURP YOUR BABY AFTER FEEDING

probably has a gut infection (p. 157). Bacterial infection of the blood (see the next pages), meningitis (p. 185), and other infections may also cause vomiting.

If the vomit is yellow or green, there may be a gut obstruction (p. 94), especially if the belly is very swollen or the baby has not been having bowel movements. Take the baby to a health center **at once.**

6. **The baby stops sucking well.** If more than 4 hours pass and the baby still will not nurse, this is a danger sign—especially if the baby seems very sleepy or ill, or if he cries or moves differently from normal. Many illnesses can cause these signs, but the most common and dangerous causes in the first 2 weeks of life are a **bacterial infection of the blood** (see next 2 pages) and **tetanus** (p. 182).

A baby who stops nursing during the second to fifth day of life may have a bacterial infection of the blood.

A baby who stops nursing during the fifth to fifteenth day may have tetanus.

If a Baby Stops Sucking Well or Seems Ill:

Examine him carefully and completely as described in Chapter 3. Be sure to check the following:

- Notice if the baby has **difficulty breathing.** If the nose is stuffed up, suck it out as shown on page 164. Fast breathing (50 or more breaths a minute), blue color, grunting, and sucking in of the skin between the ribs with each breath are signs of pneumonia (p. 171). Small babies with pneumonia often do not cough; sometimes none of the common signs are present. If you suspect pneumonia, treat as for a bacterial infection of the blood (see the next page).

- Look at the baby's **skin color.**

If the lips and face are blue, consider pneumonia (or a heart defect or other problem the baby was born with).

If the face and whites of the eyes begin to get yellow (jaundiced) in the first day of life or after the fifth day, this is serious. Get medical help. Some yellow color between the second and fifth day of life is usually not serious. Give the baby plenty of liquid—Rehydration Drink is best, in addition to breast milk (p. 152). Take off all his clothes and put him in bright light near a window (but not direct sunlight).

- Feel the **soft spot on top of the head** (fontanel). See p. 9.

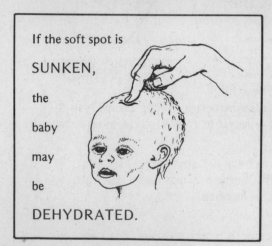

If the soft spot is

SUNKEN,

the

baby

may

be

DEHYDRATED.

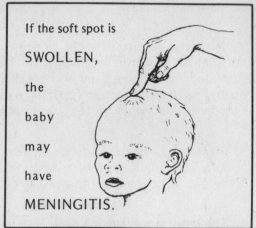

If the soft spot is

SWOLLEN,

the

baby

may

have

MENINGITIS.

IMPORTANT: If a baby has meningitis and dehydration at the same time, the soft spot may feel normal. **Be sure to check for other signs** of both dehydration (see p. 151) and meningitis (see p. 185).

- **Watch the baby's movements and expression on his face.**

Stiffness of the body and/or strange movements may be signs of tetanus, meningitis, or brain damage from birth or fever. If, when the baby is touched or moved, the muscles of his face and body suddenly tighten, this could be tetanus. See if his jaw will open and check his knee reflexes (p. 183).

If the baby's eyes roll back or flutter when he makes sudden or violent movements, he probably does **not** have tetanus. Such fits **may** be caused by meningitis, but dehydration and high fever are more common causes. Can you put the baby's head between his knees? If the baby is too stiff for this or cries out in pain, it is probably meningitis (see p. 185).

- Look for signs of a bacterial infection in the blood.

Bacterial Infection in the Blood (Septicemia):

Newborn babies cannot fight infections well. Therefore, bacteria that enter the baby's skin or cord at the time of birth often get into the blood and spread through his whole body. Since this takes a day or two, septicemia is most common after the second day of life.

Signs:

Signs of infection in newborn babies are different from those in older children. In the baby, almost any sign could be caused by a serious infection in the blood. Possible signs are:

- does not suck well
- seems very sleepy
- very pale (anemic)
- vomiting or diarrhea
- fever or low temperature (below 35°)
- swollen belly
- yellow skin (jaundice)
- fits (convulsions)
- times when the baby turns blue

Each of these signs may be caused by something other than septicemia, **but if the baby has several of these signs at once, septicemia is likely.**

Newborn babies do not always have a fever when they have a serious infection. The temperature may be high, low, or normal.

Treatment when you suspect septicemia in the newborn:

- Inject ampicillin (p. 351), 125 mg. twice a day.

- Or inject penicillin—150 mg. (250,000 units) of crystalline penicillin twice a day, together with streptomycin—20 mg. for each kilogram the baby weighs (60 mg. for a 3 kilogram baby) **once a day.** Be careful not to give too much streptomycin (see p. 352).

- Be sure the baby has enough liquids. Spoon feed breast milk and Rehydration Drink, if necessary (see p. 152).

- Try to get medical help.

Infections in newborn babies are sometimes hard to recognize. Often there is no fever. If possible, get medical help. If not, treat with ampicillin as described above. Ampicillin is one of the safest and most useful antibiotics for babies.

THE MOTHER'S HEALTH AFTER CHILDBIRTH

Diet and Cleanliness:

As was explained in Chapter 11, after she gives birth to a baby, **the mother can and should eat every kind of nutritious food she can get.** She does not need to avoid any kind of food. Foods that are especially good for her are milk, cheese, chicken, eggs, meat, fish, fruits, vegetables, grains, beans, groundnuts, etc. If all she has is corn and beans, she should eat them both together at each meal. Milk and other dairy products help the mother make plenty of milk for her baby.

The mother can and should bathe in the first few days after giving birth. In the first week it is better if she bathes with a wet towel and does not go into the water. **Bathing is not harmful following childbirth.** In fact, women who let many days go by without bathing may get infections that will make their skin unhealthy and their babies sick.

During the days and weeks following childbirth, the mother should:

eat nutritious foods   and   **bathe regularly.**

Childbirth Fever (Infection after Giving Birth):

Sometimes a mother develops fever and infection after childbirth, usually because the midwife was not careful enough to keep everything very clean or because she put her hand inside the mother.

The signs of childbirth fever are: chills or fever, headache or low back pain, sometimes pain in the belly, and a foul-smelling or bloody discharge from the vagina.

Treatment:

Penicillin, 400,000 unit pills, 1 pill 4 times a day, or injections of procaine penicillin, 250,000 units, twice a day for a week (see p. 349). Other antibiotics (ampicillin or sulfadiazine) may be used instead.

Childbirth fever can be very dangerous.
If the mother does not get well soon, get medical help.

CARE OF THE BREASTS

Taking good care of the breasts is important for the health of both the mother and her baby. Breast feeding should be started the same day the baby is born. At first the baby may not suck much, but this lets the mother's body get used to his sucking, and helps prevent sore nipples. The very first milk the breast makes (called colostrum) also protects the baby against infection and is rich in protein. Although it looks watery, this first milk is very good for the baby. So . . .

> **BEGIN BREAST FEEDING THE SAME DAY THE BABY IS BORN.**

Normally, the breasts make as much milk as the baby needs. If the baby empties them, they begin to make more. If the baby does not empty them, soon they make less. But when a baby gets sick and stops sucking, after a few days the mother's breasts stop making milk. So when the baby is able to suck again, and needs a full amount of milk, there may not be enough. For this reason,

> **When a baby is sick and unable to take much milk,
> it is important that the mother keep producing lots of milk
> by milking her breasts with her hands.**

TO MILK YOUR BREASTS:

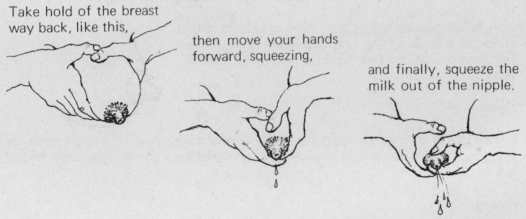

Take hold of the breast way back, like this,

then move your hands forward, squeezing,

and finally, squeeze the milk out of the nipple.

Another reason it is important to milk the breasts when the baby stops sucking is that this keeps the breasts from getting too full. When they are too full, they are painful. A breast that is painfully full is more likely to develop an abscess. Also, the baby may have trouble sucking them even if he wants to.

When your baby is too weak to suck, squeeze milk out of your breasts by hand and give it to the baby by spoon or dropper.

Always keep your breasts clean. Before breast feeding your baby, wipe your nipples with a clean, moist cloth. Do **not** use soap each time you clean your nipples, as this may lead to cracking of the skin, sore nipples, and infection.

Sore Nipples:

Sore nipples may develop when the baby bites on the nipple instead of taking the whole thing into his mouth. This is most likely to happen in women who have short nipples.

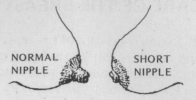

NORMAL NIPPLE   SHORT NIPPLE

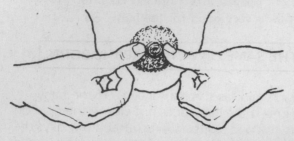

Prevention:

If a woman with short nipples squeezes her nipples like this several times a day during pregnancy, this will make it easier for her child to suck, and she will be less likely to get sore nipples.

Treatment:

It is important to keep breast feeding the baby, even though this hurts. First let him suck the side that is least sore. Only stop breast feeding if the nipple oozes a lot of blood or pus. In this case, milk the breast by hand until the nipple heals. When the baby feeds again on the breast, be sure the whole nipple enters his mouth.

Breast Abscess (Infection Inside the Breast, Mastitis):

A breast abscess may result from an infection that enters through a sore or cracked nipple. This is most common during the first weeks or months of breast feeding.

Signs:

Part of the breast becomes hot, red, swollen, and very painful. Lymph nodes in the armpit are often sore and swollen. A severe abscess sometimes bursts and drains pus.

Prevention:

- Keep the breast clean. If a sore nipple or painful cracks develop, breast feed the baby for shorter periods, but more often.

- Also put a little vegetable oil or baby oil on the nipples after each feeding.

Treatment:

- Let the baby continue to feed from the abscessed breast, or milk it by hand, whichever is less painful.

- Use cold water or ice compresses to ease the pain. Also take aspirin.

- Take an antibiotic as for childbirth fever (see p. 276).

Different kinds of breast lumps:

> A painful, hot lump in the breast of a nursing mother
> is probably a breast abscess (infection).
> A painless breast lump may be cancer.

Breast Cancer:

Cancer of the breast is fairly common in women, and is always dangerous. Successful treatment depends on spotting the first sign of possible cancer and getting medical care soon. Surgery is usually necessary.

Signs of breast cancer:

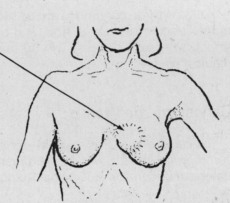

- The woman may notice a lump, often in this part of the breast.
- Or the breast may have an abnormal dent or dimple—or many tiny pits like the skin of an orange.
- Often there are large but painless lymph nodes in the armpit.
- The lump grows slowly.
- At first it usually does not hurt or get hot. Later it may hurt.

SELF-EXAMINATION OF THE BREASTS:

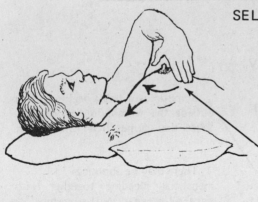

Every woman should learn how to examine her own breasts for possible signs of cancer. Once a month:

- Look at your breasts carefully for any new difference between the two in size or shape. Try to notice any of the above signs.
- While lying with a pillow or folded blanket under your back, feel your breasts with the flat of your fingers. Press your breast and roll it beneath your finger tips. Start near the nipple and go around the breast and up into the armpit.

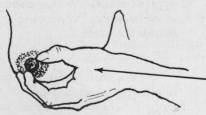

- Then squeeze your nipples and check whether blood or a *discharge* comes out.

If you find a lump or any other abnormal sign, get medical advice. Many lumps are not cancer, but it is important to find out early.

LUMPS OR GROWTHS IN THE LOWER PART OF THE BELLY

The most common lump is, of course, caused by the normal development of a baby. Abnormal lumps or masses may be caused by: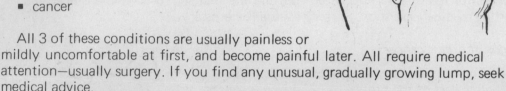

- a cyst or watery swelling in one of the ovaries
- by a baby that has accidentally begun to develop outside of the womb (ectopic pregnancy), or
- cancer

All 3 of these conditions are usually painless or mildly uncomfortable at first, and become painful later. All require medical attention—usually surgery. If you find any unusual, gradually growing lump, seek medical advice.

Cancer of the Womb:

Cancer of the uterus (womb), cervix (neck of the womb), or ovaries is most common in women over 40. The first sign may be *anemia* or unexplained bleeding. Later, an uncomfortable or painful lump in the belly may be noticed.

At the first suspicion of cancer, seek medical help.

Home remedies are not likely to help.

Out-of-Place or *Ectopic* Pregnancy:

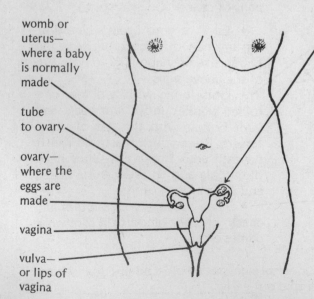

womb or uterus—where a baby is normally made

tube to ovary

ovary—where the eggs are made

vagina

vulva—or lips of vagina

Sometimes a baby begins to form outside the womb, in one of the tubes that comes from the ovaries.

There may be abnormal menstrual bleeding together with signs of pregnancy—also cramps low in the belly and a tender lump **outside** the womb.

A baby that begins to form out of place usually cannot live. Ectopic pregnancy requires surgery in a hospital. **If you suspect this problem, seek medical advice soon, as dangerous bleeding could start any time.**

MISCARRIAGE (SPONTANEOUS ABORTION)

A miscarriage is the loss of the unborn baby. Miscarriages are most frequent in the first 3 months of pregnancy. Usually the baby is imperfectly formed, and this is nature's way of taking care of the problem.

Most women have one or more miscarriages in their lifetime. Many times they do not realize that they are having a miscarriage. They may think their period was missed or delayed, and then came back in a strange way, with big blood clots. A woman should learn to know when she is having a miscarriage, because it could be dangerous.

A woman who has heavy bleeding after she has missed one or more periods probably is having a miscarriage.

A miscarriage is like a birth in that the embryo (the beginning of the baby) and the placenta (afterbirth) must both come out. Bleeding often continues until both are completely out.

The embryo of a miscarriage may be no longer than 1 or 2 centimeters.

30 days

60 days

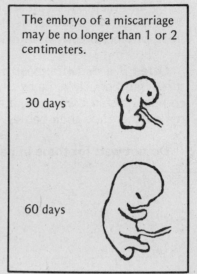

Treatment:

If there is no heavy bleeding, generally there is no problem. The woman should stay in bed, and the miscarriage should be treated with the same care and precautions as a birth.

If there is heavy bleeding, or bleeding continues for many days:

♦ Get medical help. A simple operation may be needed to clean out the womb (dilatation and curettage or D and C).

♦ Stay in bed until the heavy bleeding stops and for 2 or 3 days after the miscarriage.

♦ If the bleeding is extreme, follow the instructions on page 266.

♦ If fever or other signs of infection develop, treat as for **Childbirth Fever** (see p. 276).

If you have bleeding and suspect a miscarriage,

remain lying down until everything comes out, and the bleeding stops.

HIGH RISK MOTHERS AND BABIES

A note to midwives or health workers and anyone who cares:

Some women are more likely to have difficult births and problems following birth, and their babies are more likely to be underweight and sick. Often these are mothers who are single, homeless, poorly nourished, very young, mentally slow, or who already have malnourished or sickly children.

Often if a midwife, health worker, or someone else takes special interest in these mothers, and helps them find ways to get the food, care, and companionship they need, it can make a great difference in the well-being of both the mothers and their babies.

Do not wait for those in need to come to you. Go to them.

CHAPTER

20

FAMILY PLANNING—
HAVING THE NUMBER
OF CHILDREN YOU WANT

THIS FAMILY HAS MANY CHILDREN.

THIS FAMILY HAS FEW CHILDREN.

Some mothers and fathers want a lot of children. Where many children die young, parents feel they need a large number of children to help with work and to be sure some remain to care for them when they grow old.

Many mothers and fathers have come to realize that to have a large family may bring serious problems. For example:

- With many children it is harder to feed, clothe, and educate them all well.

- When a mother has child after child, without much space between, she often becomes weak. Her breasts produce less milk. Her babies are more likely to die (see p. 271). Also, after many pregnancies the danger is greater that she will die in childbirth, leaving many motherless children.

- If a man and woman have a lot of children, when the children grow up there may not be enough land for all of them to grow the food their families need. Children may begin to die of hunger. This is already happening in many areas.

Although most, if not all, hunger in the world today could be prevented if land and wealth were distributed fairly, the growing number of people is part of the problem. If people keep having big families, the day will come when there is not enough land or food to go around—even if people learn to share.

The situation will get better only when people—as individuals, as families, and as communities—come to understand the many factors affecting their health and take action for the good of their children and future generations.

FAMILY PLANNING AND BIRTH CONTROL

Different parents have different reasons for wanting to limit the size of their family. Some young parents may decide to delay having any children until they have worked and saved enough so that they can afford to care for them well. Some parents may decide that a small number of children is enough, and they never want more. Others may want to space their children several years apart, so that both the children and their mother will be healthier.

> **Family planning is having the number of children you want, when you want them.**

When a man and woman decide when they want to have children, and when they do not, they can choose one of several methods to prevent the woman from becoming pregnant, for as long as she wishes. These are methods of *birth control* or *contraception.*

Couples who want children but are not able to have them should see page 244.

IS BIRTH CONTROL GOOD—AND IS IT SAFE?

1. Is it good?

In some parts of the world there has been a lot of discussion about whether different forms of birth control are good or are safe. Some religions have been against any form of birth control except trying not to have sex together. But an increasing number of religious leaders are realizing how important it is to the health and well-being of families and communities that people be able to use easier and surer methods of birth control.

Also, in many places women who get pregnant when they do not want a child will go for an *abortion,* to have the developing baby destroyed or removed. Where these intentional or **provoked abortions** are legal, they can be done in health centers under sanitary conditions, and they are not usually dangerous to the woman. But where provoked abortions are not permitted, many women get abortions illegally and secretly, often in dirty conditions and performed by unskilled persons. Thousands of women die from such abortions. If women are given the chance to use birth control methods, and information to use them wisely, most provoked abortions, legal and illegal, would not be necessary. Much needless suffering and death could be prevented.

Some people feel that much of the push for family planning comes from rich countries or persons who want to keep their control over the poor by controlling their numbers. The rich and powerful find it hard to accept that the way they manage the earth's land and resources strongly contributes to world hunger. They see only the growing numbers of people. In some countries professionals sterilize poor women by force or experiment on them with new or unsafe methods. For all these reasons social reformers and spokesmen for the poor often protest against birth control.

This is unfortunate. The object of attack should not be birth control, but rather its misuse. The attack should be against social injustice and the unfair distribution of land and wealth. If used well, birth control can in fact help the poor gain strength to work for their basic human rights. But the decisions and responsibility for family planning must be in the hands of the people themselves.

> **Decide for yourself if and how you want to plan your family. Do not let anyone else decide for you.**

2. Is it safe?

Whether or not different forms of birth control are safe has been much discussed. Often those who are against birth control for religious or political reasons try to scare women by talking about the risks. Some methods do have certain risks. However, the important thing all women should realize is that **birth control is safer than pregnancy,** especially after a woman has had many children.

The risk of serious illness or death resulting from pregnancy is many times greater than the risks involved in using <u>any</u> of the common methods of birth control.

There is much talk about the risks of taking birth control pills (oral contraceptives). But the risks with pregnancy are many times greater. The pill works so well in preventing pregnancy that for most women it is safer—in terms of protecting their lives—than any of the other 'less risky' but less effective methods.

CHOOSING A METHOD OF BIRTH CONTROL

On the following pages several methods of birth control are described. Some work better for some people than others. Study these pages, and talk with your midwife, health worker, or doctor about what methods are available and are likely to work best for you. Differences in **effectiveness, safety, convenience, availability,** and **cost** should be considered. Husbands and wives should decide together, and share the responsibility.

AVERAGE EFFECTIVENESS OF DIFFERENT FORMS OF BIRTH CONTROL

Of each 20 women using this method . . .	on the average this many are likely to get pregnant in spite of the method . . .	and this many must (or should) stop the method because of problems.
PILL	🚶	🚶
CONDOM	🚶🚶	
DIAPHRAGM	🚶🚶🚶	🚶
FOAM	🚶🚶🚶🚶🚶	
I.U.D.	🚶🚶	🚶🚶🚶🚶🚶
PULLING OUT	🚶🚶🚶🚶🚶🚶🚶🚶	
STERILIZATION		*
SPONGE	🚶🚶🚶🚶🚶🚶	🚶🚶🚶
RHYTHM	🚶🚶🚶🚶🚶🚶🚶	COMBINED 🚶🚶🚶🚶🚶
MUCUS	🚶🚶🚶🚶🚶🚶	

* With sterilization, problems occasionally result from surgery but the method is permanent.

BIRTH CONTROL PILLS (ORAL CONTRACEPTIVES)

When taken correctly, the 'pill' is one of the most effective methods for avoiding pregnancy. However, certain women should not take birth control pills if they can use another method (see p. 288). If possible, birth control pills should be given by health workers, midwives, or other persons trained in their use.

The pills usually come in packets of 21 or 28 tablets. The packets of 21 are often less expensive, and of these, some brands are cheaper than others. The amount of medicine differs in different brands. To pick the kind that is right for you, see the GREEN PAGES, page 377.

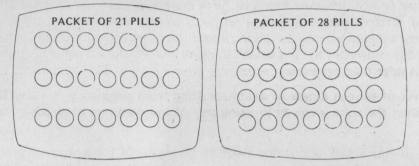

PACKET OF 21 PILLS   PACKET OF 28 PILLS

How to take the pills—packet of 21:

Take the first pill on the fifth day from the beginning of your period, counting the first day of the period as day 1. Then take 1 pill every day until the packet is finished (21 days).

After finishing the packet, wait 7 days before taking any more pills. Then begin another packet, 1 pill each day.

This way, you will take the pills for 3 weeks out of each month, then go 1 week without taking any. Normally, the menstrual period will come during the week when the pill is not taken. Even if the period does not come, start the new packet 7 days after finishing the last one.

If you do not want to get pregnant, it is important to take the pills as directed —1 every day. If you forget to take the pill one day, take 2 the next day.

Packet of 28 pills:

Take the first pill on the fifth day of the period, just as with the packets of 21. Take 1 a day. Seven of the pills will probably be a different size and color. Take these pills last (one a day) after the others have all been taken. The day after you finish the packet of 28, start another packet. Take 1 a day without ever missing a day, packet after packet, for as long as you want not to become pregnant.

No special diet must be followed when taking the pill. Even if you happen to get sick with a cold or something else while taking birth control pills, go right on taking them. If you stop taking the pills before the packet is used up, you may become pregnant.

Side effects:

Some women get a little morning sickness, swelling of the breasts, or other signs of pregnancy when they first start taking the pill. This is because the pill contains the same chemicals (hormones) that a woman's body puts into her blood when she is pregnant. These signs do not mean she is unhealthy or should stop taking the pill. They usually go away after the first 2 or 3 months. To relieve morning sickness, see page 248.

Some women may bleed a different amount than usual in their monthly period when they are taking the pill. These changes are usually not important. Sometimes they can be corrected by changing to a brand with a different amount of hormone. This is discussed in the GREEN PAGES (p. 377).

"Is it dangerous to take oral contraceptives?"

Like all medicines, birth control pills occasionally cause serious problems in certain persons (see next pages). The most serious problems related to the pill are blood clots in the heart, lungs, or brain (see stroke, p. 327). **However, the chance of getting dangerous clots is even higher when women get pregnant than when they take the pill.**

Death related to taking the pill is rare. On the average, pregnancy and childbirth are 50 times as dangerous as taking the pill.

Of 15,000 women who become pregnant, this many are likely to die from problems of pregnancy or childbirth.

Of 15,000 women who take birth control pills, only 1 is likely die from problems related to having taken the pills.

Conclusion:

IT IS MUCH SAFER TO TAKE THE PILL THAN TO BECOME PREGNANT.

For most women, birth control pills are relatively safe. Certainly they are far safer than becoming pregnant. However, **for some women both pregnancy and taking birth control pills have a higher risk. These women should use other methods of birth control.**

Who Should Not Take Birth Control Pills?

A woman who has any of the following signs should **not** take oral (or injected) contraceptives:

- **Deep or steady pain in one leg or hip.** This may be caused by an inflamed vein (phlebitis or blood clot). Do not use birth control pills. (Women with **varicose veins** that are not inflamed can usually take birth control pills without problems. But they should stop taking them if the veins become inflamed.)

- **Stroke.** A woman who has had any signs of a stroke (p. 327) should not take the pill.

- **Hepatitis (p. 172), cirrhosis (p. 328), or other liver disease.** Women with these problems, or whose eyes had a yellow color during pregnancy, should not take the pill. It is better not to take oral contraceptives for one year after having hepatitis.

- **Cancer.** If you have had or suspect cancer of the breast or womb, do not use oral contraceptives. Before beginning oral contraceptives, examine your breasts carefully (see p. 279). In some health centers you may also be able to get a simple test (Pap smear) to check for cancer of the *cervix* or opening of the womb. Birth control pills do not cause cancer, but if cancer of the breasts or womb already exists, the pill can make it worse.

Some health problems may be made worse by oral contraceptives. If you have any of the following problems, it is better to use another method if you can:

- **Migraine** (p. 162). Women who suffer from true migraine should not take oral contraceptives. But simple headache that goes away with aspirin is no reason not to take the pill.

- **Urinary infection with swelling of the feet** (p. 234).

- **Heart disease** (p. 325).

- **A great deal of blood loss during the menstrual period.**

If you suffer from asthma, tuberculosis, diabetes, or epilepsy, it is best to get medical advice before taking birth control pills. However, most women with these diseases can take oral contraceptives without harm.

Precautions Women Should Take when Using Birth Control Pills

1. Examine the breasts carefully every month for lumps or possible signs of cancer (see page 279).

2. Have your blood pressure measured every 6 months.

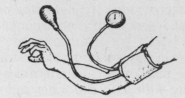

3. Watch for any of the problems mentioned on page 288, especially:

- Severe and frequent migraine headaches (p. 162).
- Dizziness, headache, or loss of consciousness that results in difficulty in seeing, speaking, or moving part of the face or body (see Stroke, p. 327).
- Pain with inflammation in a leg or hip (chance of a blood clot).
- Severe or repeated pain in the chest (see Heart Problems, p. 325).

If one of these problems develops, stop taking the pill and get medical advice. Avoid pregnancy by using another method, as these problems also make pregnancy especially dangerous.

Questions and Answers about Birth Control Pills

?	Some people claim birth control pills cause cancer. Is this true?	**No! However, if cancer of the breast or womb already exists, taking the pill may make the tumor grow faster.**
?	Can a woman have children again if she stops taking the pill?	**Yes. (Sometimes there is a delay of a month or 2 before she can become pregnant.)**
? ?	Is the chance of having twins or defective children greater if a woman has used oral contraceptives?	**No. The chances are the same as for women who have not taken the pill.**
?	Is it true that a mother's breasts will dry up if she starts taking birth control pills?	**Most women are not affected. But some mothers produce less milk, or stop making it altogether, when they start taking the pill.**

For this reason it is a good idea for women who are breast feeding to use another method of birth control during the first 6 months, and then change to the pill.

For information on the selection of birth control pills, see the Green Pages—p. 377.

OTHER METHODS OF BIRTH CONTROL

THE CONDOM (also called 'prophylactic', 'rubber', or sheath) is a narrow rubber or latex bag that the man wears on his penis while having sex. Usually it works well to prevent pregnancy. It also helps prevent spreading of venereal diseases, but is not a complete safeguard.

One can buy condoms in most pharmacies. Some are cheaper than others. To save money, wash the condom carefully with soap and water and use it several times. Before using it, fill it with water to make sure it does not leak.

THE DIAPHRAGM is a shallow cup made of soft rubber. A woman wears it in her vagina while having sexual relations. It should be left in for at least 6 hours afterward. It is a fairly sure method—especially if used together with a contraceptive cream or jelly. A health worker or midwife should help fit the diaphragm, as different women need different sizes. Check the diaphragm regularly for holes and get a new one each year. They are not expensive.

CONTRACEPTIVE FOAM comes in a tube or can. The woman puts it into her vagina with a special applicator. It must be applied no longer than 1 hour before having sex, and left in for at least 6 hours afterward. The application should be repeated before each time the couple has sex, even if this is several times in one night. It is a fairly sure method if used correctly, but a nuisance.

THE INTRAUTERINE DEVICE (IUD) is a plastic (or sometimes metal) object that a specially trained health worker or midwife places inside the womb. While in the womb, it prevents pregnancy. IUDs fall out of some women. In others they cause pain, discomfort, and sometimes serious problems, but for some women they give no trouble at all. For these women, the IUD may be the simplest and most economical method.

WITHDRAWAL OR PULLING OUT (COITUS INTERRUPTUS) is a method in which the man pulls his penis out of the woman before the sperm comes. This method is perhaps better than none, but is disturbing to the couple and does not always work, because some sperm often leaks out ahead of time and can cause pregnancy.

METHODS FOR THOSE WHO NEVER WANT TO HAVE MORE CHILDREN

INJECTIONS. There are special injections to prevent pregnancy. ***Depo-Provera*** is one. An injection is usually given every 3 months. Sometimes women cannot become pregnant ever again after they have had these injections, so generally only women who will never want more children should use this method. Side effects and precautions are similar to those for birth control pills.

Injections are useful for women who are sure they do not ever want to become pregnant again—especially those who have trouble remembering to take pills or for other reasons have difficulty taking them.

STERILIZATION. For those who never want to have more children, there are fairly safe, simple operations for both men and women. In many countries these operations are free. Ask at the health center.

- For men, the operation is called a vasectomy. It can be done in a doctor's office or a health center. Small cuts are made here so that the tubes from the man's testicles can be cut and tied.

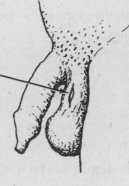

  The operation has no effect at all on the man's sexual ability or pleasure. His fluid comes just the same, but has no sperm in it.

- For women, the operation is called a tubal ligation, which means to tie the tubes. It can be done simply and quickly, and usually without putting the woman to sleep. One method is to make very small cuts in the lower belly so that the tubes coming from the ovaries, or egg-makers, can be cut and tied.

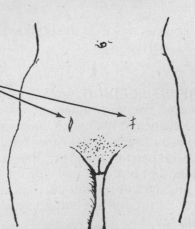

  This operation has no effect on the women's menstrual periods or sexual ability, and may make having sex more pleasant because she does not have to worry about becoming pregnant.

HOME METHODS FOR PREVENTING PREGNANCY

Every land has 'home remedies' for preventing or interrupting pregnancy. Unfortunately, most either do not work or are dangerous. For example, some women think that to wash out the vagina or to urinate after having sex will prevent pregnancy, **but this is not true.**

THE SPONGE METHOD. Here is a home method that is not harmful and sometimes works. You cannot be sure it will prevent pregnancy every time, but it can be used when no other method is available.

You will need a sponge and either **vinegar, lemons, or salt.** Either a sea sponge or an artificial sponge will work. If you do not have a sponge, try a ball of cotton, wild kapok, or soft cloth.

- ♦ Mix:

    2 tablespoons vinegar in 1 cup water

    or

    1 teaspoon lemon juice in 1 cup water

    or

    1 spoon of salt in 4 spoons water

- ♦ Wet the sponge with one of these liquids.

- ♦ Push the wet sponge deep into your vagina before having sex. You can put it in up to an hour before.

- ♦ Leave the sponge in at least 6 hours after having sex. Then take it out. If you have trouble getting it out, next time tie a ribbon or piece of string to it that you can pull.

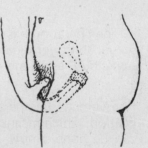

The sponge can be washed and used again, many times.

You can make up the liquid in advance and keep it in a bottle.

BREAST FEEDING. While a woman is breast feeding her baby she is less likely to become pregnant—especially when breast milk is the only food her baby receives. The chance of her becoming pregnant is much greater after 4 to 6 months, when the baby begins to get other foods in addition to breast milk. To be more sure she will not become pregnant, the mother who is breast feeding should begin some method of birth control when the baby is 3 to 4 months old. The earlier she begins the surer it will be. (Before the baby is 6 months old, a method other than birth control pills is better because the pills cause some women to produce less milk.)

METHODS THAT DO NOT WORK VERY WELL

THE RHYTHM METHOD:

This method is not very sure to prevent pregnancy, but it has the advantage of not costing anything. It is more likely to work for a woman whose periods come very regularly, more or less once every 28 days. Also, the husband and wife must be willing to pass one week out of each month without having sex the regular way.

Usually a woman has a chance of becoming pregnant only during 8 days of her monthly cycle—her 'fertile days'. These 8 days come midway between her periods, beginning 10 days after the first day of menstrual bleeding. To avoid getting pregnant, a woman should not have sex with her man during these 8 days. During the rest of the month, she is not likely to get pregnant.

To avoid confusion the woman should mark on a calendar the 8 days she is not to have sex.

For example: Suppose your period begins on the 5th day of May.

Mark it like this:

Then count 10 days. Starting with the 10th day, put a line under the 8 days that follow, like this:

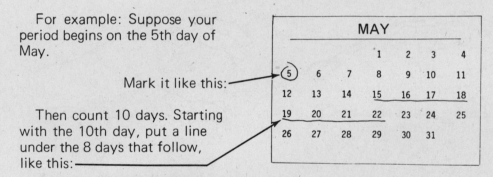

During these 8 'fertile days', do not have sexual relations.

Now suppose your next period begins on the first of June. Mark it the same way, like this:

Once again count off 10 days and underline the following 8 days in which you will not have sexual contact.

If the woman and her husband carefully avoid having sex together during these 8 days each month, it is possible that they will go years without having another child. However, few couples are successful for very long. This is not a very sure method, unless used in combination with another method such as a diaphragm or condoms.

THE MUCUS METHOD

This is a variation of the rhythm method that is being encouraged by some religious groups. It works fairly well for some people but not for others. In general it cannot be considered a very sure way of preventing pregnancy, but it costs nothing and has no other risks than those that come with pregnancy itself.

Every day, except during her period, the woman should examine the mucus from her vagina.

Take a little mucus out of your vagina with a clean finger and try to make it stretch between your thumb and forefinger, like this:

As long as the mucus is sticky like paste—not slippery or slimy—you probably cannot become pregnant, and can continue to have sexual relations.

When the mucus begins to get slippery or slimy, like raw egg, or if it stretches between your fingers, you may become pregnant if you have sexual relations—so **do not have sex when the mucus is slippery or stretches.**

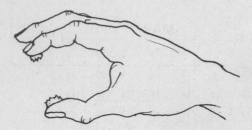 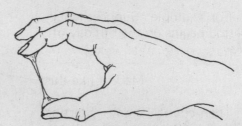

The mucus will usually become slippery during a few days midway between your periods. These are the same days you would not have sex with your man if you were using the rhythm method.

To be more sure, use the mucus and rhythm methods together. To be still more sure, see below.

Combined Methods:

If you want to be more certain not to become pregnant, it often helps to use 2 methods at the same time. The rhythm or mucus method combined with the use of a condom, diaphragm, foam, or sponge is surer than any of these methods alone. Likewise, if a man uses condoms and the woman a diaphragm or foam, the chance of pregnancy is very low.

> **Strength lies not in numbers, but in having enough to eat.**
> **Consider planning your family.**

CHAPTER

21

HEALTH AND SICKNESSES OF CHILDREN

WHAT TO DO TO PROTECT CHILDREN'S HEALTH

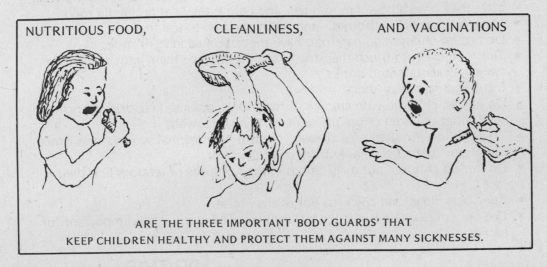

NUTRITIOUS FOOD,   CLEANLINESS,   AND VACCINATIONS

ARE THE THREE IMPORTANT 'BODY GUARDS' THAT
KEEP CHILDREN HEALTHY AND PROTECT THEM AGAINST MANY SICKNESSES.

Chapters 11 and 12 tell more about the importance of nutritious food, cleanliness, and vaccination. Parents should read these chapters carefully and use them to help care for—and teach—their children. The main points are briefly repeated here.

Nutritious Food:

It is important that children eat the most nutritious foods they can get, so that they grow well and do not get sick.

The best foods for children at different ages are:

- in the first 4 months: breast milk and nothing more.

- from 4 months to 1 year: breast milk and also other nutritious foods—such as mashed-up beans, eggs, meat, cooked fruits and vegetables, and cereals.

- from 1 year on: each meal should include body-building and protective foods—especially milk and foods made from milk, eggs, chicken, fish, meat, beans, lentils, nuts, fruits, and vegetables. These should be balanced with plenty of energy foods like rice, maize, wheat, potatoes, or cassava.

- Above all, children should get **enough** to eat.

- All parents should watch for signs of malnutrition in their children and should give them the best food they can.

Cleanliness:

Children are more likely to be healthy if their village, their homes, and they themselves are kept clean. Follow the Guidelines of Cleanliness explained in Chapter 12. Teach children to follow them—and to understand their importance. Here the most important guidelines are repeated:

- Bathe children and change their clothes often.
- Teach children always to wash their hands when they get up in the morning, after they have a bowel movement, and before they eat or handle food.
- Make latrines or 'outhouses'—and teach children to use them.
- Do not let children go barefoot; have them wear sandals or shoes.
- Teach children to brush their teeth; and do not give them a lot of candies, sweets, or carbonated drinks.
- Cut fingernails very short.
- Do not let children who are sick or have sores, scabies, lice, or ringworm sleep with other children or use the same clothing or towels.
- Treat children quickly for scabies, ringworm, intestinal worms, and other infections that spread easily from child to child.
- Do not let children put dirty things in their mouths or let dogs lick their faces.
- Keep pigs, dogs, and chickens out of the house.
- Use only pure or boiled water for drinking. This is especially important for babies.

Vaccinations:

Vaccinations protect children against many of the most dangerous diseases of childhood—whooping cough, diphtheria, tetanus, smallpox, polio, measles, and tuberculosis.

Children should be given the different vaccinations during the first months of life, as shown on page 147. Polio drops should be first given no later than 2 months of age, because the risk of developing infantile paralysis (polio) is highest in babies under 1 year old.

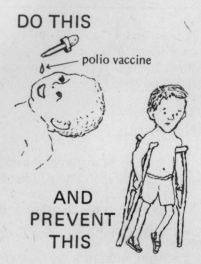

DO THIS

polio vaccine

AND PREVENT THIS

Important: For complete protection, the DPT (diphtheria, whooping cough, tetanus) and polio vaccines must be given once a month for 3 months and once again a year later.

Tetanus of the newborn can be prevented by vaccinating mothers against tetanus during pregnancy (see p. 250).

Be sure your children get all the vaccinations they need.

CHILDREN'S GROWTH—AND THE 'ROAD TO HEALTH'

A healthy child grows steadily. If he eats enough nutritious food, and if he has no serious illness, a child gains weight each month.

> **A child who grows well is healthy.**

A child who gains weight more slowly than other children, stops gaining weight, or is losing weight is not healthy. He may not be getting enough of the right kinds of foods, or he may have a serious illness, or both.

A good way to check whether a child is healthy and is getting enough nutritious food is to weigh him each month and see if he gains weight normally. If a monthly record of the child's weight is kept on a Road to Health Chart, it is easy to see at a glance whether or not the child is gaining weight normally.

On the next page is a typical Road to Health Chart. This chart can be cut out and copied. Or larger, ready-made cards can be obtained (in English, French, or Spanish) from:

Teaching Aids at Low Cost
Institute of Child Health
30 Guilford Street
London WC1N 1EH
England

Similar charts are produced in local languages by the Health Departments in many countries.

It is a good idea for every mother to keep a Road to Health Chart for each of her children under 5 years of age. If there is a health center or 'under-fives clinic' nearby, she should take her children, with their charts, to be weighed and to have a 'check-up' each month. The health worker can help explain the Chart and its use.

To protect the Road to Health Chart, keep it in a plastic envelope, like this: ⟶

Road to Health Chart

Clinic	Child's no.
Child's name	Boy/Girl
Mother's name	Registration No.
Father's name	Registration No.
Date first seen	Birthday-birthweight
Where the family live: address	

BROTHERS AND SISTERS

Year of birth	Boy/Girl	Remarks

ANTI-TUBERCULOSIS IMMUNISATION (BCG)

Date of BCG immunisation.................
....

SMALLPOX IMMUNISATION

Date of immunisation.................
Date of scar inspection.................
Date of reimmunisation.................

POLIOMYELITIS IMMUNISATION

Date of first immunisation.................
Date of second immunisation.................
Date of third immunisation.................

WHOOPING COUGH, TETANUS & DIPHTHERIA IMMUNISATION

Date of first immunisation.................
Date of second immunisation.................
Date of third immunisation.................

MEASLES IMMUNISATION

Date of immunisation.................

OTHER IMMUNISATIONS

....
....

3-4 years   **4-5 years**

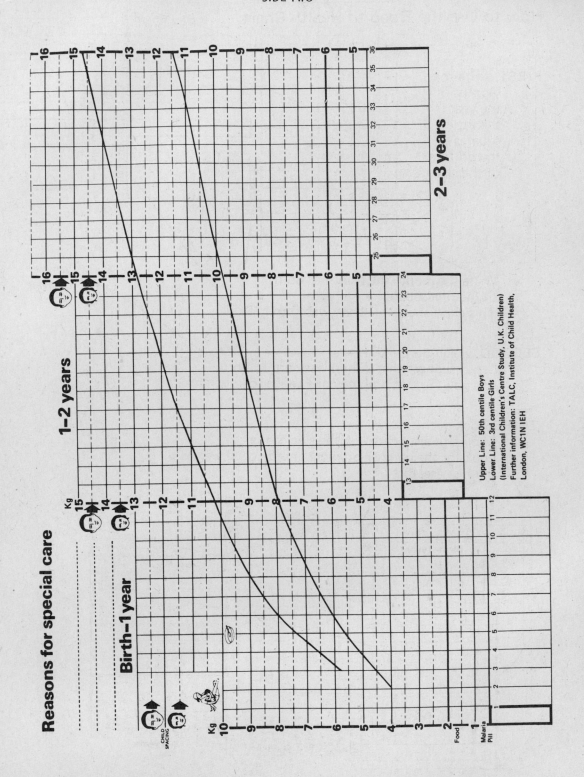

Reasons for special care

1–2 years

Birth–1 year

2–3 years

Upper Line: 50th centile Boys
Lower Line: 3rd centile Girls
(International Children's Centre Study, U.K. Children)
Further information: TALC, Institute of Child Health,
London, WC1N 1EH

CHILD SPACING

Food

Malaria Pill

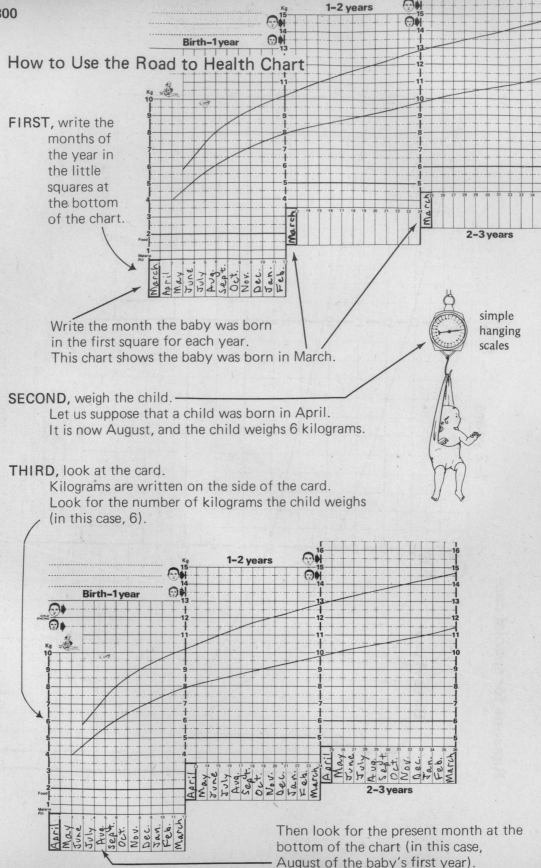

How to Use the Road to Health Chart

FIRST, write the months of the year in the little squares at the bottom of the chart.

Write the month the baby was born in the first square for each year.
This chart shows the baby was born in March.

SECOND, weigh the child.
Let us suppose that a child was born in April.
It is now August, and the child weighs 6 kilograms.

THIRD, look at the card.
Kilograms are written on the side of the card.
Look for the number of kilograms the child weighs (in this case, 6).

simple hanging scales

Then look for the present month at the bottom of the chart (in this case, August of the baby's first year).

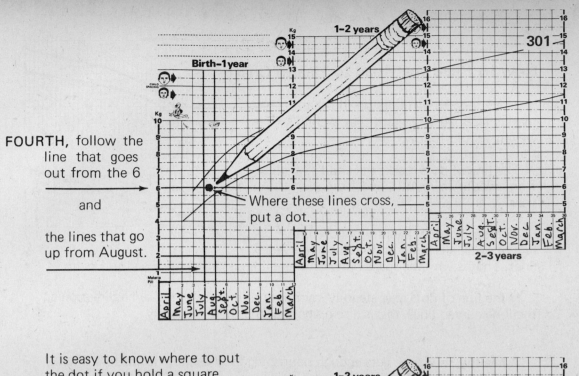

FOURTH, follow the line that goes out from the 6

and

the lines that go up from August.

Where these lines cross, put a dot.

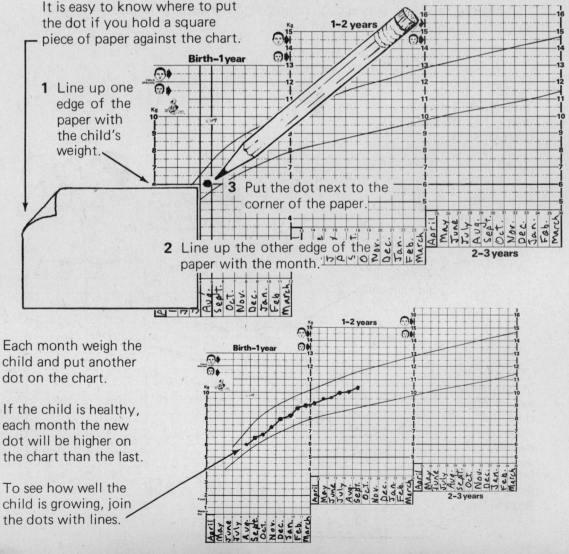

It is easy to know where to put the dot if you hold a square piece of paper against the chart.

1 Line up one edge of the paper with the child's weight.

3 Put the dot next to the corner of the paper.

2 Line up the other edge of the paper with the month.

Each month weigh the child and put another dot on the chart.

If the child is healthy, each month the new dot will be higher on the chart than the last.

To see how well the child is growing, join the dots with lines.

How to Read the Road to Health Chart

The 2 long curved lines on the chart
mark the Road to Health that a child's
weight should follow.

The line of dots marks the child's weight
from month to month, and from year to
year.

In most normal, healthy children, the
line of dots falls between the 2 long curved
lines. That is why the space between these lines is called the Road to Health.

If the line of dots rises steadily, month after month, in the same direction as
the long curved lines, this is also a sign that the child is healthy.

A healthy child who gets enough nourishing food usually begins to sit, walk,
and speak at about the times shown here.

Walks 10 steps
without help.

Typical chart of
**THE HEALTHY,
WELL-NOURISHED
CHILD**

Short
phrases.

Single
words.

Daddy
go
work.

third year

Sits
without
help.

COW,
daddy.

12 to 16
months

11 to 18
months

6 to 8 months

ROAD TO
HEALTH

In the healthy,
well-nourished
child, the
weight rises
steadily. The
dots usually lie
inside the lines
that mark the
Road to Health.

2-3 years

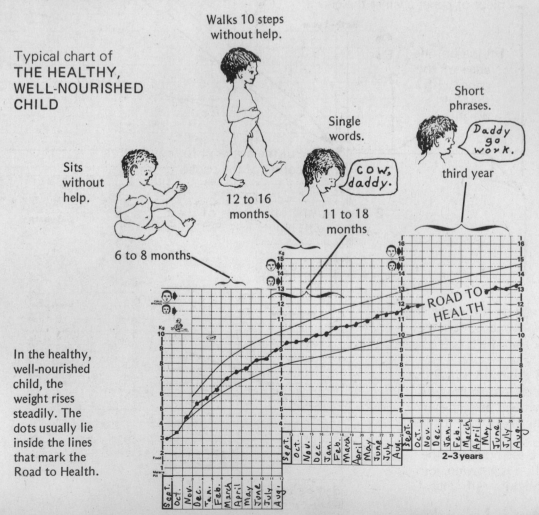

A malnourished, sickly child may have a chart like the one below. Notice that the line of dots (his weight) is below the Road to Health. The line of dots is also irregular and does not rise much. This shows the child is getting worse.

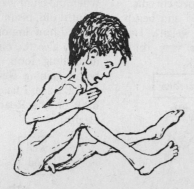

Typical chart of
**THE UNDERWEIGHT
OR MALNOURISHED
CHILD**

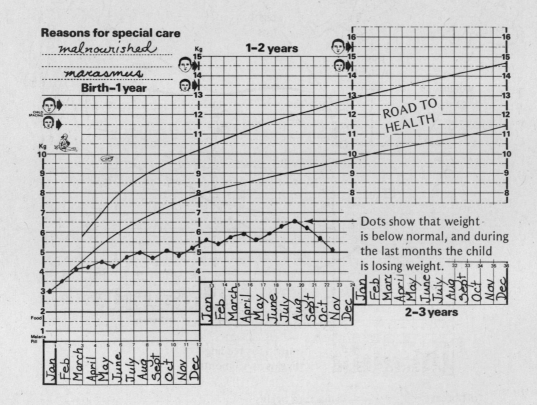

Reasons for special care
malnourished
marasmus

ROAD TO HEALTH

Dots show that weight is below normal, and during the last months the child is losing weight.

A child with a chart like the one above is seriously underweight. This may be because he is not given enough nourishing food. Or because he has some chronic disease like tuberculosis or malaria. Or both. He should be given the most nourishing food available, and if possible, he should be taken to a health worker frequently until his chart shows he is gaining weight and returning toward the Road to Health.

A typical ROAD TO HEALTH CHART SHOWING A CHILD'S PROGRESS:

This baby was healthy and gained weight well for the first 6 months of life, because his mother breast fed him.

At 6 months, the mother became pregnant again and stopped breast feeding him. The baby was fed little more than corn and rice. He stopped gaining weight.

At 10 months he developed chronic diarrhea and began losing weight. He became very thin and sick.

When the child was 13 months old, his mother learned how important it is to give the child nourishing food. He began gaining weight fast. By age 2 he was back on the Road to Health.

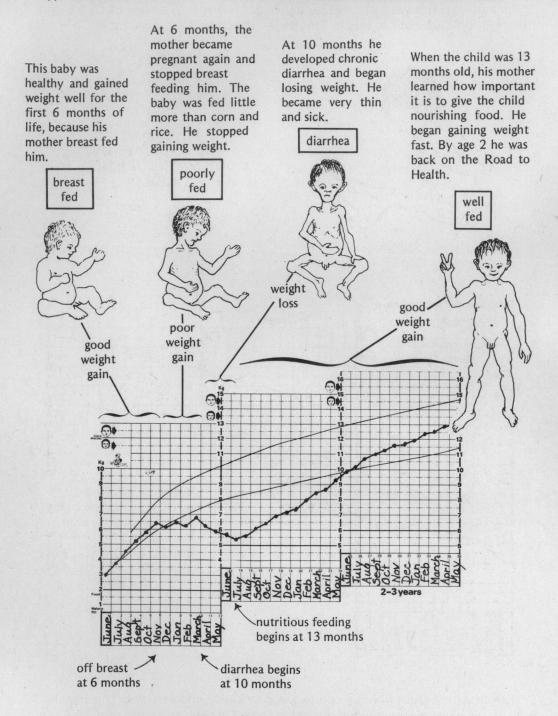

Road to Health charts are important. They help mothers know when their children need more nutritious food and special attention. They help health workers better understand the needs of the child and his family. They also let the mother know when she is doing a good job.

REVIEW OF CHILDREN'S HEALTH PROBLEMS DISCUSSED IN OTHER CHAPTERS

Many of the sicknesses discussed in other chapters of this book are found in children. Here some of the more frequent problems are reviewed in brief. For more information on each problem, see the pages indicated.

For special care and problems of newborn babies, see p. 270 to p. 275.

Remember: In children, sicknesses often become serious very quickly. An illness that takes days or weeks to severely harm or kill an adult may kill a small child in hours. So, it is important to **notice early signs of sickness and attend to them right away.**

Malnourished Children

Many children are malnourished because they do not get enough to eat. But some are malnourished because they eat a lot of starchy foods like corn, rice, cassava, or plantain, and not enough body-building and protective foods like milk, eggs, meat, beans, fruits, and vegetables. For a fuller discussion of the foods children need, read Chapter 11, especially page 123. For babies, see pages 121 and 122.

THESE TWO CHILDREN ARE MALNOURISHED

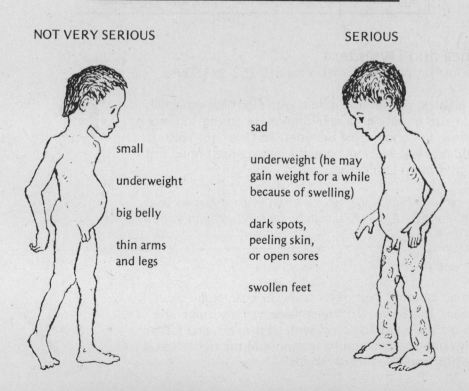

NOT VERY SERIOUS

small

underweight

big belly

thin arms
and legs

SERIOUS

sad

underweight (he may
gain weight for a while
because of swelling)

dark spots,
peeling skin,
or open sores

swollen feet

Malnutrition may cause many different problems in children, including:

In mild cases:

- slower growth
- swollen belly
- thin body
- loss of appetite
- loss of energy
- paleness (anemia)
- desire to eat dirt (anemia)
- sores in corners of mouth
- frequent colds and other infections
- night blindness

In more serious cases:

- little or no weight gain
- swelling of feet (sometimes face also)
- dark spots, 'bruises', or open peeling sores
- thinness or loss of hair
- lack of desire to laugh or play
- sores inside mouth
- failure to develop normal intelligence
- 'dry eyes' (xerosis)
- blindness (p. 226)

A comparison of 'wet' and 'dry' malnutrition, their causes, and prevention is given on page 112.

Signs of malnutrition are often first seen after an acute illness like diarrhea or measles. A child who is sick, or who is getting well after a sickness, has an even greater need for nutritious food than a child who is well.

> **Prevent and treat malnutrition by giving your children enough body-building and protective foods like milk, eggs, meat, fish, beans, lentils, fruits, and vegetables.**

Diarrhea and Dysentery
(For more complete information see p. 153 to 160.)

The greatest danger to children with diarrhea—especially if they are also vomiting—is dehydration, or losing too much liquid from the body. Give Rehydration Drink (p. 152). If the child is breast feeding, continue giving breast milk, but give Rehydration Drink also.

The second big danger to children with diarrhea is malnutrition. Give the child nutritious food as soon as he will eat.

Fever (see p. 75):

In small children, high fever (over 39°) can easily cause fits or damage the brain. To lower fever rapidly, take the clothes off the child, soak him with cool water, and fan him. Also give him acetaminophen or aspirin in the right dosage (see p. 365) and give lots of liquids.

Fits (Convulsions) (see p. 178):

Common causes of fits or convulsions in children are high fever, dehydration, epilepsy, and meningitis. If fever is high, lower it rapidly (see p. 76). Check for signs of dehydration (p. 151) and meningitis (p. 185). Fits that come suddenly without fever or other signs are probably epilepsy (p. 178), especially if the child seems well between them. Fits or spasms in which first the jaw and then the whole body becomes stiff may be tetanus (p. 182).

Meningitis (see p. 185):

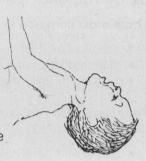

This dangerous disease may come as a complication of measles or another serious illness. Children of mothers who have tuberculosis may get tubercular meningitis. A very sick child who lies with his head tilted way back, whose neck is too stiff to bend forward, and whose body makes strange movements (fits) may have meningitis.

Anemia (see p. 125):

Common signs in children:

- pale, especially inside eyelids, gums, and fingernails

- weak, tires easily

- likes to eat dirt

Common causes:

- diet poor in iron (p. 125)

- chronic gut infections (p. 145)

- hookworm (p. 142)

- malaria (p. 186)

Prevention and Treatment:

- Eat iron-rich foods like meat and eggs. Beans, lentils, groundnuts (peanuts), and dark green vegetables also have some iron.

- Treat the cause of anemia—and do not go barefoot if hookworm is common.

- If you suspect hookworm, a health worker may be able to look at the child's stools under a microscope. If hookworm eggs are found, treat for hookworm (p. 363).

- If necessary give iron salts by mouth (ferrous sulfate, p. 376).

Worms and Other Parasites of the Gut (see p. 140):

If one child in the family has worms, all the family should be treated. To prevent worm infections, children should:

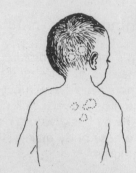

- ◆ Observe the Guidelines of Cleanliness (p. 133).
- ◆ Use latrines.
- ◆ Never go barefoot.
- ◆ Never eat raw or partly raw meat.
- ◆ Drink only boiled or pure water.

Skin Problems (see Chapter 15):

Those most common in children include:

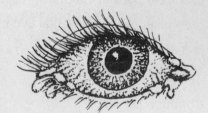

- ▪ scabies (p. 199)
- ▪ infected sores and impetigo (p. 201 and 202)
- ▪ ringworm and other fungus infections (p. 205)

To prevent skin problems, observe the Guidelines of Cleanliness (p. 133).

- ◆ Bathe and delouse children often.
- ◆ Control bedbugs, lice, and scabies.
- ◆ Do not let children with scabies, lice, ringworm, or infected sores play or sleep together with other children. Treat them early.

Pink Eye (Conjunctivitis) (see p. 219):

Put an antibiotic eye ointment (p. 365) **inside** the eyelids 4 times a day. Do not let a child with pink eye play or sleep with others. If he does not get well in a few days, see a health worker.

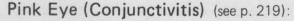

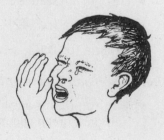

Colds and the 'Flu' (see p. 163):

The common cold, with runny nose, mild fever, cough, often sore throat, and sometimes diarrhea is a frequent but not a serious problem in children.

Treat with aspirin or acetaminophen (p. 365) and lots of liquids. Let children who want to stay in bed do so. Good food and lots of fruit help children avoid colds and get well quickly.

Penicillin, tetracycline, and other antibiotics do no good for the common cold or 'flu'. Injections are not needed for colds.

If a child with a cold becomes very ill, with high fever and shallow, rapid breathing, he may be getting **pneumonia** (see p. 171), and antibiotics should be given. Also watch for an ear infection (next page) or 'strep throat' (p. 310).

HEALTH PROBLEMS OF CHILDREN NOT DISCUSSED IN OTHER CHAPTERS

Earache and Ear Infections:

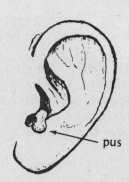

pus

Ear infections are common in small children. The infection often begins after a few days with a cold or a stuffy or plugged nose. The fever may rise, and the child often cries or rubs the side of his head. Sometimes pus can be seen in the ear. In small children an ear infection sometimes causes diarrhea. So when a child has diarrhea and fever, be sure to check his ears.

Treatment:

- It is important to treat ear infections early. Give an antibiotic like penicillin (p. 349) or sulfadiazine (p. 354). In children under 3 years of age, ampicillin (p. 351) often works better. Also give aspirin or acetaminophen for pain.
- Carefully clean pus out of the ear with cotton, but do not put a plug of cotton, leaves, or anything else in the ear.
- Children with pus coming from an ear should bathe regularly but should not swim or dive for at least 2 weeks after they are well.

Prevention:

- Teach children to wipe but **not** to blow their noses when they have a cold.
- Do not bottle feed babies—or if you do, do not let a baby feed lying on his back, as the milk can go up his nose and lead to an ear infection.
- When children's noses are plugged up, use salt drops and suck the mucus out of the nose as described on p. 164.

Infection in the ear canal:

To find out whether the canal or tube going into the ear is infected, gently pull the ear. If this causes pain, the canal is infected. Put drops of water with vinegar in the ear 3 or 4 times a day. (Mix 1 spoon of vinegar with 1 spoon of boiled water.) If there is fever or pus, also use an antibiotic.

Sore Throat and Inflamed Tonsils:

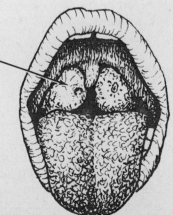

These problems often begin with the common cold. The throat may be red and hurt when the child swallows. The tonsils (two lymph nodes seen as lumps on each side at the back of the throat) may become large and painful or drain pus. Fever may reach 40°.

Treatment:

- Gargle with very warm salt water (1 teaspoon of salt in a glass of water).
- Take aspirin or acetaminophen for pain.
- If pain and fever come on suddenly or continue for more than 3 days, see the following page.

Sore throat and the danger of rheumatic fever:

For the sore throat that often comes with the common cold or flu, antibiotics should usually not be used and will do no good. Treat with gargles and aspirin.

However, one kind of sore throat—called **strep throat**—should be treated with penicillin. It is most common in children and young adults. It usually begins suddenly with severe sore throat and fever, often without signs of a cold or cough. The back of the mouth and tonsils may become very red, and the lymph nodes under the jaw may become swollen and tender.

Give penicillin (p. 349) for 10 days. If penicillin is given early and continued for 10 days, there is less danger of getting rheumatic fever. A child with strep throat should eat and sleep far apart from others, to prevent their getting it also.

Rheumatic Fever:

This is a disease of children and young adults. It usually begins 1 to 3 weeks after the person has had a strep throat (see above).

Principal signs (usually only 3 or 4 of these signs are present):

- fever
- joint pain, especially in the wrists and ankles, later the knees and elbows. Joints become swollen, and often hot and red.

- curved red lines or lumps under the skin
- in more serious cases, weakness, shortness of breath, and perhaps heart pain

Treatment:

- If you suspect rheumatic fever, see a health worker. There is a risk that the heart may become damaged.
- Take aspirin in large doses (p. 365). A 12-year-old can take up to 2 or 3 tablets of 300 mg. 6 times a day. Take them together with milk or a little bicarbonate of soda, to avoid stomach pain. If the ears begin to ring, take less.
- Give penicillin, 400,000 unit tablets, 1 tablet 4 times a day for 10 days (see p. 349).

Prevention:

- To prevent rheumatic fever, treat 'strep throat' early with penicillin—for 10 days.
- To prevent return of rheumatic fever, and added heart damage, a child who has once had rheumatic fever should take penicillin for 10 days at the first sign of a sore throat. If he already shows signs of heart damage, he should take penicillin on a regular basis or have monthly injections of benzathine penicillin (p. 350) perhaps for the rest of his life. Follow the advice of an experienced health worker or doctor.

INFECTIOUS DISEASES OF CHILDHOOD

Chickenpox:

This mild virus infection begins 2 to 3 weeks after
a child is exposed to another child who has the disease.

Signs:  spots,
blisters,
and scabs

First many small, red, itchy spots appear. These
turn into little pimples or blisters that pop and finally
form scabs. Usually they begin on the body, and later
on the face, arms, and legs. There may be spots,
blisters, and scabs, all at the same time. Fever is
usually mild.

Treatment:

The infection goes away in a week. Bathe the child daily with soap and warm
water. To calm itching, apply cool cloths soaked in water from boiled and
strained oatmeal. Cut fingernails very short. If the scabs get infected, put gentian
violet or an antibiotic ointment on them.

Measles:

This severe virus infection is especially dangerous in
children who are poorly nourished or have tuberculosis.
Ten days after being near a person with measles, it begins
with signs of a cold—fever, runny nose, red sore eyes, and
cough.

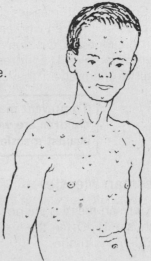

The child becomes increasingly ill. The mouth may
become very sore and he may develop diarrhea.

After 2 or 3 days a few tiny white spots like salt grains
appear in the mouth. A day or 2 later the rash appears—
first behind the ears and on the neck, then on the face and body, and last on the
arms and legs. After the rash appears, the child usually begins to get better. The
rash lasts about 5 days.

Treatment:

- The child should stay in bed, drink lots of liquids, and be given nutritious
  food. If a baby cannot breast feed, give breast milk in a spoon (see p. 121).
- For fever and discomfort, give acetaminophen (or aspirin).
- If earache develops, give an antibiotic (p. 349).
- If signs of pneumonia, meningitis, or severe pain in the ear or stomach
  develop, get medical help.

Prevention of measles:

Children with measles should keep far away from other children. Especially try to protect children who are poorly nourished or who have tuberculosis or other chronic illnesses. Children from other families should not go into a house where there is measles. If children in a family where there is measles have not yet had measles themselves, they should not go to school or into stores for 10 days.

> **To prevent measles from killing children, make sure all children are well nourished. Have your children vaccinated against measles when they are 8 to 14 months of age.**

German Measles

German measles are not as severe as regular measles. They last 3 or 4 days. The rash is mild. Often the lymph nodes on the back of the head and neck become swollen and tender.

The child should stay in bed and take aspirin if necessary.

Women who get German measles in the first 3 months of pregnancy may give birth to a child who is damaged or deformed. For this reason, pregnant women who have not yet had German measles—or are not sure—should keep far away from children who have this kind of measles.

Mumps:

The first symptoms begin 2 or 3 weeks after being exposed to someone with mumps.

Mumps begins with fever and pain on opening the mouth or eating. In 2 days, a soft swelling appears below the ears at the angle of the jaw. Often it comes first on one side, and later on the other.

Treatment:

The swelling goes away by itself in about 10 days, without need for medicine. Aspirin can be taken for pain and fever. Feed the child soft, nourishing foods and keep his mouth clean.

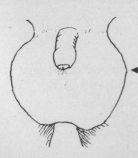

Complications:

In adults and children over 11 years of age, after the first week there may be pain in the belly or a painful swelling of the testicles (men) or the breasts (of women). Persons with such swelling should stay quiet and put ice packs or cold wet cloths on the swollen parts to help reduce the pain and swelling.

If signs of meningitis appear, get medical help (p. 185).

Whooping Cough:

Whooping cough begins a week or two after being exposed to a child who has it. It starts like a cold with fever, a runny nose, and cough.

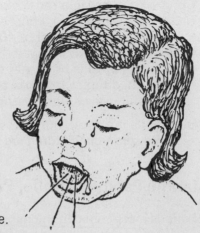

Two weeks later, the whoop begins. The child coughs rapidly many times without taking a breath, until he coughs up a plug of sticky mucus, and the air rushes back into his lungs with a loud whoop. While he is coughing, his lips and nails may turn blue for lack of air. After the whoop he may vomit. Between coughing spells the child seems fairly healthy.

Whooping cough often lasts 3 months or more.

Whooping cough is especially dangerous in babies under 1 year of age, so vaccinate children early. Small babies do not develop the typical whoop so it is hard to be sure if they have whooping cough or not. If a baby gets fits of coughing and swollen or puffy eyes when there are cases of whooping cough in your area, treat him for whooping cough **at once.**

Treatment:

- In the early stage of whooping cough, before the whoop begins, erythromycin (p. 352), tetracycline (p. 353), or ampicillin (p. 351) may help. Chloramphenicol also helps but is more risky. For the dosage for babies, see p. 354. It is especially important to treat babies under 6 months at the first sign.
- In severe cases of whooping cough, phenobarbital (p. 373) may help, especially if the cough does not let the child sleep or causes convulsions.
- To avoid weight loss and malnutrition, the child should get nutritious food and should eat soon after he vomits.

Complications:

A bright red hemorrhage in the white of the eyes may be caused by the coughing. No treatment is necessary (see p. 224). If fits or signs of pneumonia (p. 171) or meningitis (p. 185) develop, get medical help.

> **Protect your children against whooping cough. See that they are first vaccinated at 2 months of age.**

Diphtheria:

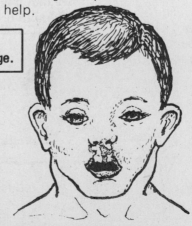

This begins like a cold with fever, headache, and sore throat. A yellow-gray coating or *membrane* may form in the back of the throat, and sometimes in the nose and on the lips. The child's neck may become swollen. His breath smells very bad.

If you suspect that a child has diphtheria:

- Put him to bed in a room separate from other persons.
- Get medical help quickly. There is a special antitoxin for diphtheria.
- Give penicillin, 1 tablet of 400,000 units, 3 times a day for older children.
- Have him gargle warm water with a little salt.
- Have him breathe hot water vapors often or continually (p. 168).
- If the child begins to choke and turn blue, try to remove the membrane from his throat using a cloth wrapped around your finger.

Diphtheria is a dangerous disease that can easily be prevented with the DPT vaccine. **Be sure your children are vaccinated.**

Infantile Paralysis (Polio, Poliomyelitis):

Polio is most common in children under 2 years of age.

This virus infection begins like a cold with fever, vomiting, and sore muscles. Sometimes that is all there is to it. But sometimes a part of the body becomes weak or paralyzed. Most often this happens to one or both legs. In time, the paralyzed limb becomes thin and does not grow as fast as the other one.

Treatment:

Once the disease has begun, no medicine can take away the paralysis. Antibiotics do not help. Calm the pain with aspirin or acetaminophen and by putting hot soaks on the painful muscles.

Prevention:

Keep the sick child in a separate room, away from other children. The mother should wash her hands after each time she touches him. The best protection against polio is the polio vaccine.

> **See that children are vaccinated against polio, with 'polio drops' at 2, 3, AND 4 months of age.**

A child who has been crippled by polio should eat nutritious food and do exercises to strengthen remaining muscles. During the first year some strength may return.

Help the child learn to walk as best he can. Fix 2 poles for support, like these, and later make him some crutches.

HOW TO MAKE SIMPLE CRUTCHES

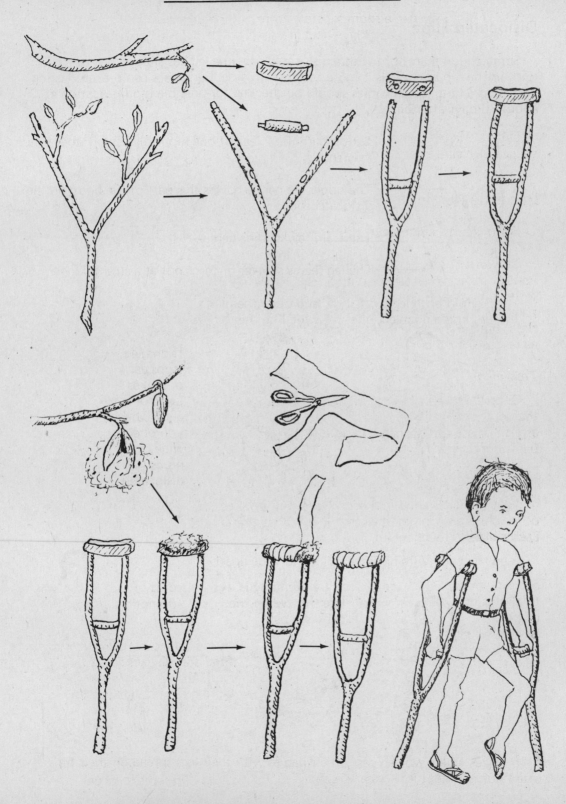

PROBLEMS CHILDREN ARE BORN WITH

Dislocated Hip:

Some children are born with a dislocated hip—the leg has slipped out of its joint in the hip bone. This is more common in girls. Early care can prevent lasting harm and a limp. So all babies should be checked for possible hip dislocation at about 10 days after birth.

1. Compare the 2 legs. If one hip is dislocated, that side may show:

The upper leg partly covers this part of the body on the dislocated side.

There are fewer folds here.

The leg seems shorter or turns out at a strange angle.

2. Hold both legs with the knees doubled, like this,

and open them wide like this.

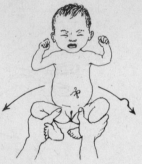

If one leg stops early or makes a jump or click when you open it wide, the hip is dislocated.

Treatment:

Keep the baby with his knees high and wide apart:

by using many thickness of diapers like this

or by pinning his legs like this (when the baby sleeps)

or by doing this.

In places where women carry their babies with their legs spread on their hips, often no treatment is necessary.

Umbilical Hernia (Belly Button that Sticks Out):

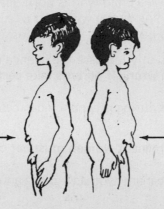

A belly button that sticks out like this is no problem. No medicine or treatment is needed. Tying a tight cloth or 'belly band' around the belly will not help.

Even a big umbilical hernia like this one is not dangerous and will often go away by itself. If it is still there after age 5, an operation may be needed. Get medical advice.

A 'Swollen Testicle' (Hydrocele or Hernia):

If a baby's *scrotum,* or bag that holds his testicles, is swollen on one side, this is usually because it is filled with liquid (a hydrocele) or because a loop of gut has slipped into it (a hernia).

To find out which is the cause, shine a light through the swelling.

If light shines through easily, it is probably a **hydrocele.**

If light does not shine through, and if the swelling gets bigger when the baby coughs or cries, it is a **hernia.**

Sometimes the **hernia** causes a swelling above and to one side of the baby's scrotum, not in it.

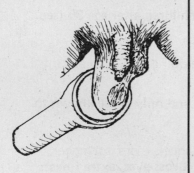

A hydrocele usually goes away in time, without treatment. If it lasts more than a year, get medical advice.

A hernia needs surgery (see p. 177).

You can tell this from a swollen lymph node (p. 88) because the hernia swells when the baby cries or is held up-right and disappears when he lies quietly.

MENTALLY SLOW, DEAF, OR DEFORMED CHILDREN

Sometimes parents will have a child who is born deaf, mentally *retarded* (slow), or with *birth defects* (something wrong with part of his body). Often no reason can be found. No one should be blamed. Often it just seems to happen by chance.

However, certain things greatly increase the chance of birth defects. **A baby is less likely to have something wrong if parents take certain precautions.**

1. **Lack of nutritious food** during pregnancy can cause mental slowness or birth defects in babies.

To have healthy babies, pregnant women must eat nutritious food (see p. 110).

2. **Lack of iodine** in a pregnant woman's diet can cause *cretinism* in her baby.

The baby's face is puffy, and he looks dull. His tongue hangs out, and his forehead may be hairy. He is weak, feeds poorly, cries little, and sleeps a lot. He is retarded and may be deaf. He will begin to walk and talk later than normal babies.

To help prevent cretinism, pregnant women should use iodized salt instead of ordinary salt (see p. 130).

If you suspect your baby may have cretinism, take him to a health worker or doctor at once. The sooner he gets special medicine (thyroid) the more normal he will be.

CRETINISM

3. **Smoking or heavy drinking** of alcoholic drinks during pregnancy causes babies to be born small or to have other problems (see p. 149). Do not drink heavily or smoke—especially during pregnancy.

4. **After age 35,** there is more chance that a mother will have a child with defects. *Mongolism* or Down's disease, which looks somewhat like cretinism, is especially common in babies of older mothers.

It is wise to plan your family so as to have no more children after age 35 (see Chapter 20).

5. **Many different medicines** can harm the baby developing inside a pregnant mother.

Use as little medicine as possible during pregnancy— and only those known to be safe.

6. **When parents are blood relatives** (cousins, for instance), there is a higher chance that their children will be defective or retarded. **Cross-eyes, extra fingers or toes, club feet, hare lip, and cleft palate** are common defects.

To lower the chance of these and other problems, do not marry a close relative. And if you have more than one child with a birth defect, consider not having more children (see Family Planning, Chapter 20).

If your child is born with a birth defect, take him to a health center. Often something can be done.

◆ For cross-eyes, see p. 225.

◆ If an extra finger or toe is very small with no bone in it, tie a string around it very tightly. It will dry up and fall off. If it is larger or has bone in it, either leave it or have it taken off by surgery.

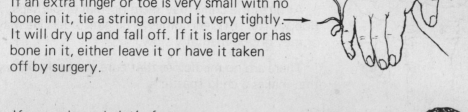

◆ If a newborn baby's feet are turned inward or have the wrong shape (clubbed), try to bend them to normal shape. If you can do this easily, repeat this several times each day. The feet (or foot) should slowly grow to be normal.

If you cannot bend the baby's feet to normal, take him **at once** to a health center where his feet can be put in casts. For the best results, it is important to **do this within 2 days after birth.**

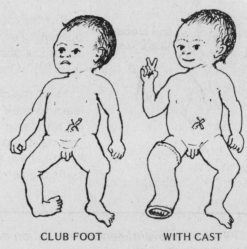

CLUB FOOT　　　WITH CAST

◆ If a baby's lip or the top of his mouth *(palate)* are divided *(cleft),* he may have trouble breast feeding and need to be fed with a spoon or dropper. With surgery, his lip and palate can be made to look almost normal. The best age for surgery is usually at 4 to 6 months for the lip, and at 18 months for the palate.

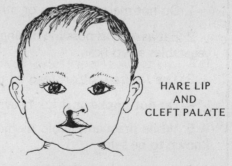

HARE LIP AND CLEFT PALATE

7. **Difficulties during birth** sometimes result in **brain damage** that causes a child to be **spastic** or have **fits.** The chance of damage is greater if at birth the baby is slow to breathe, or if the midwife injected the mother with an oxytocic (p. 266) before the baby was born.

Be careful in your choice of a midwife—and do not let your midwife use an oxytocic before the baby is born.

The Spastic Child (Cerebral Palsy):

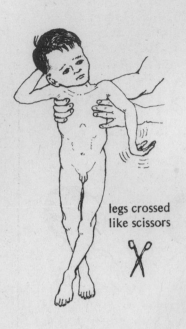

legs crossed
like scissors

A child who is spastic has tight, stiff muscles that he controls poorly. His face, neck, or body may twist, and his movements may be jerky. Often the tight muscles on the inside of his legs cause them to cross like scissors.

At birth the child may seem normal or perhaps floppy. The stiffness comes as he gets older. He may or may not be mentally slow.

There are no medicines that cure the brain damage that makes a child spastic.

But the child needs special care. To help prevent tightening of the muscles in the legs or in a foot, treat as for Dislocated Hip (p. 316) and as for Club Foot (p. 319), if necessary.

Help the child to roll over, sit and stand—then learn to walk as on p. 314. Encourage him to use both his mind and body as much as he can. Help him learn (see next page). Even if he has trouble with speaking he may have a good mind and be able to learn many skills if given a chance. **Help him to help himself.**

To help prevent mental retardation or birth defects in her child, a woman should do these things:

1. Do not marry a cousin or other close relative.

2. Eat as well as possible during pregnancy: as much meat, eggs, fruit, and vegetables as you can.

3. Use iodized salt instead of regular salt, especially during pregnancy.

4. Do not smoke or drink heavily during pregnancy (see p. 149).

5. While pregnant, avoid medicines whenever possible—use only those known to be safe.

6. While pregnant, keep away from persons with German measles.

7. Be careful in the selection of a midwife—and do not let the midwife use an oxytocic before the child is born (see p. 266).

8. Do not have more children if you have more than one child with the same birth defect, (see Family Planning, p. 283).

9. Consider not having more children after age 35.

Retardation in the First Months of Life:

Some children who are healthy when they are born do not grow well. They become mentally slow because they do not eat enough nutritious food. During the first few months of life the brain develops more rapidly than at any other time. For this reason the nutrition of the newborn is of great importance. Breast milk is the best food for a baby (see The Best Diet for Babies, p. 121).

HELPING CHILDREN LEARN:

As a child grows, he learns partly from what he is taught. Knowledge and skills he learns in school may help him to understand and do more later. School can be important.

But a child does much of his learning at home or in the forest or fields. He learns by watching, listening, and trying for himself what he sees others do. He learns not so much from what people tell him, as from how he sees them act. **Some of the most important things a child can learn—such as kindness, responsibility, and sharing—can only be taught by setting a good example.**

A child learns through adventure. He needs to learn how to do things for himself, even though he makes mistakes. When he is very young, protect a child from danger. But as he grows, help him learn to care for himself. Give him some responsibility. Respect his judgment, even if it differs from your own.

When a child is young, he thinks mostly of filling only his own needs. Later, he discovers the deeper pleasure of helping and doing things for others. Welcome the help of children and let them know how much it means.

Children who are not afraid ask many questions. If parents, teachers, and others take the time to answer their questions clearly and honestly—and to say they do not know when they do not—a child will keep asking questions, and as he grows may look for ways to make his surroundings or his village a better place to live.

22

HEALTH AND SICKNESSES OF OLDER PEOPLE

This chapter is about the prevention and treatment of problems seen mostly in older persons.

SUMMARY OF HEALTH PROBLEMS DISCUSSED IN OTHER CHAPTERS

Difficulties with Vision: (see p. 225)

After the age of 40, many people have problems seeing close objects clearly. They are becoming *farsighted.* Often glasses will help.

Everyone over age 40 should watch for signs of glaucoma, which can cause blindness if left untreated. Any person with signs of glaucoma (see p. 222) should seek medical help.

Cataracts (see p. 224) and 'flies before the eyes' (tiny moving spots—p. 227) are also common problems of old age.

Weakness, Tiredness, and Eating Habits:

Old people understandably have less energy and strength than when they were younger, but they will become even weaker if they do not eat well. Although older people often do not eat very much, they should eat some body-building and protective foods every day (see p. 110 to 111).

Swelling of the Feet: (see p. 176)

This can be caused by many diseases, but in older people it is often caused by poor circulation (see p. 213) or heart trouble (see p. 325). Whatever the cause, **keeping the feet up is the best treatment.** Walking helps too—but do not spend much time standing or sitting with the feet down. Keep the feet up whenever possible.

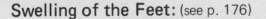

Chronic Sores of the Legs or Feet: (see p. 20)

These may result from poor circulation, often because of varicose veins (p. 175). Sometimes diabetes is part of the cause (p. 127). For other possibilities, see page 20.

Sores that result from poor circulation heal very slowly.

Keep the sore as clean as possible. Wash it with boiled water and mild soap and change the bandage often. If signs of infection develop, treat as directed on p. 88.

When sitting or sleeping, keep the foot up.

Difficulty Urinating: (see p. 235)

Older men who have difficulty urinating or whose urine drips or dribbles are probably suffering from an enlarged prostate gland. Turn to page 235.

Chronic Cough: (see p. 168)

Older people who cough a lot should not smoke and should seek medical advice. If they had symptoms of tuberculosis when they were younger, or have ever coughed up blood, they may have tuberculosis.

If an older person develops a cough with wheezing or trouble breathing (asthma) or if his feet also swell, he may have heart trouble (see the next page).

Rheumatoid Arthritis (painful joints): (see p. 173)

Many older people have arthritis.

To help arthritis:

* Rest the joints that hurt.

* Apply hot compresses (see p. 194).

* Take a medicine for pain; aspirin is best. For severe arthritis, take 2 to 3 aspirin tablets up to 6 times a day with bicarbonate of soda, milk, or a lot of water. (If the ears begin to ring, take less.)

* It is important to do exercises that help maintain as much movement as possible in the painful joints.

OTHER IMPORTANT ILLNESSES OF OLD AGE

Heart Trouble:

Heart disease is more frequent in older people, especially in those who are fat, who smoke, or who have high blood pressure.

Signs of heart problems:

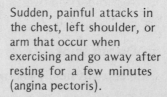
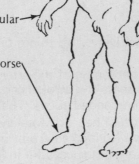

- Anxiety and difficulty in breathing after exercise; asthma-like attacks that get worse when the person lies down (cardiac asthma).

- A rapid, weak, or irregular pulse.

- Swelling of the feet—worse in the afternoons.

- Sudden, painful attacks in the chest, left shoulder, or arm that occur when exercising and go away after resting for a few minutes (angina pectoris).

- A sharp pain like a great weight crushing the chest; does not go away with rest (heart attack).

Treatment:

- Different heart diseases may require different specific medicines, which must be used with great care. If you think a person has heart trouble, seek medical help. It is important that he have the right medicine when he needs it.
- People with heart trouble should not work so hard that they get chest pain or have trouble breathing. However, regular exercise helps prevent a heart attack.
- Persons with heart problems should not eat greasy food and should lose weight if they are overweight.
- If an older person begins having attacks of difficult breathing or swelling of the feet, he should not use salt or eat food that contains salt. For the rest of his life he should eat little or no salt.
- If a person has angina pectoris or a heart attack, he should rest very quietly in a cool place until the pain goes away.

If the chest pain is very strong and does not go away with rest, or if the person shows signs of **shock** (see p. 77), the heart has probably been severely damaged. The person should stay in bed for at least a week or as long as he is in pain or shock. Then he can begin to sit up or move slowly, but should stay very quiet for a month or more. Consider getting medical help.

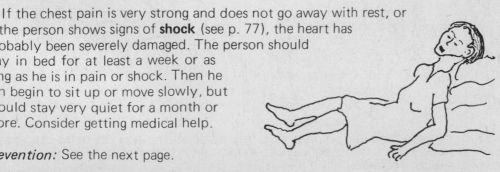

Prevention: See the next page.

Words to Younger Persons
Who Want to Stay Healthy When They Are Older

Many of the health problems of middle and old age, including high blood pressure, hardening of the arteries, heart disease, and stroke, result from the way a person has lived and what he ate, drank, and smoked when younger. Your chances for living and staying healthy longer are greater if you:

1. **Eat well**—enough nutritious foods, but not too much rich or greasy food. Avoid getting overweight or fat.

2. **Do not drink a lot of alcoholic drinks.**

3. **Do not smoke.**

4. **Keep physically and mentally active.**

5. **Try to get enough rest and sleep.**

6. **Learn how to relax** and deal positively with things that worry or upset you.

High blood pressure (p. 126) and hardening of the arteries (arteriosclerosis), which are the main causes of heart disease and stroke, can usually be prevented— or reduced—by doing the things recommended above. The lowering of high blood pressure is important in the prevention of heart disease and stroke. Persons who have high blood pressure should have it checked from time to time and take measures to lower it. For those who are not successful in lowering their blood pressure by eating less (if they are overweight), giving up smoking, getting more exercise, and learning to relax, medicines to lower blood pressure (antihypertensives) may help.

WHICH OF THESE TWO MEN IS LIKELY TO LIVE LONGER AND BE HEALTHY IN HIS OLD AGE? WHICH IS MORE LIKELY TO DIE OF A HEART ATTACK OR A STROKE? WHY? HOW MANY REASONS CAN YOU COUNT?

Stroke, (Apoplexy, Cerebro-Vascular Accident, CVA)

In older people *stroke* or *cerebro-vascular accident* (CVA) commonly results from a blood clot or from bleeding inside the brain. The word *stroke* is used because this condition often strikes without warning. The person may suddenly fall down, unconscious. His face is often reddish, his breathing hoarse, his pulse strong and slow. He may remain in a coma (unconscious) for hours or days.

If he lives, he may have trouble speaking, seeing, or thinking, or one side of his face and body may be paralyzed. In minor strokes, some of these same problems may result without loss of consciousness. The difficulties caused by stroke sometimes get better with time.

Treatment:

Put the person in bed with his head a little higher than his feet. If he is unconscious, roll his head back and to one side so his saliva (or vomit) runs out of his mouth, rather than into his lungs. While he is unconscious, give no food, drink, or medicines by mouth (see the Unconscious Person, p. 78). If possible, seek medical help.

After the stroke, if the person remains partly paralyzed, help him to walk with a cane and to use his good hand to care for himself. He should avoid heavy exercise and anger.

Prevention: See the page before this one.

Note: If a younger or middle-aged person suddenly develops paralysis on one side of his face, with no other signs of stroke, this is probably a temporary paralysis of the face nerve (Bell's Palsy). It will usually go away by itself in a few weeks or months. The cause is usually not known. No treatment is needed but hot soaks may help. If one eye does not close all the way, bandage it shut at night to prevent damage from dryness.

Deafness with Ringing of the Ears and Dizziness

Deafness that comes on gradually without pain or other symptoms is usually incurable, though a hearing aid may help. Sometimes deafness results from ear infections (see p. 309).

If an older person loses hearing in one or both ears—occasionally with severe dizziness—and hears a loud 'ringing' or buzzing, he probably has Ménière's disease. He should take an antihistamine, such as dimenhydrinate (*Dramamine,* p. 372) and go to bed until the symptoms go away. He should have no salt in his food. If he does not get better soon, or if the problem returns, he should immediately seek medical advice.

Loss of Sleep (Insomnia)

It is normal for older people to need less sleep than younger people. During long winter nights they may spend hours without being able to sleep.

Certain medicines may help bring sleep, but it is better not to use them if they are not absolutely necessary.

Here are some suggestions for sleeping:

♦ Get plenty of exercise during the day.
♦ Do not drink coffee or black tea, especially in the afternoon or evening.
♦ Drink a glass of warm milk or milk with honey before going to bed.
♦ Take a warm bath before going to bed.
♦ If you still cannot sleep, try taking an antihistamine like promethazine (*Phenergan,* p. 371) or dimenhydrinate (*Dramamine,* p. 372) half an hour before going to bed. These are less habit-forming than stronger drugs.

DISEASES FOUND MORE OFTEN IN PEOPLE OVER 40 YEARS OLD

Cirrhosis of the Liver:

Cirrhosis usually occurs in men over 40 who for years have been eating poorly and drinking a lot of liquor (alcohol).

Signs:

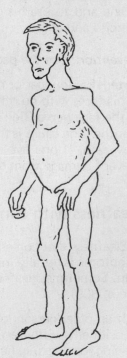

● Cirrhosis starts like hepatitis, with weakness, loss of appetite, upset stomach, and pain on the person's right side near his liver.
● As the illness gets worse, the person gets thinner and thinner. He may vomit blood. In serious cases the feet swell, and the stomach swells with liquid until it looks like a drum. The eyes and skin may turn yellowish (jaundice).

Treatment:

When cirrhosis is severe, it is hard to cure. There are no medicines that help much. Most people with severe cirrhosis die from it. If you want to stay alive, **at the first sign of cirrhosis** do the following:

♦ Never drink alcohol again! Alcohol poisons the liver.
♦ Eat as well as possible: foods high in protein and vitamins.
♦ If a person with cirrhosis has swelling, he should not use any salt in his food.

Prevention of this disease is easy: **DO NOT DRINK SO MUCH.**

Gallbladder Problems:

The gallbladder is a small sac attached to the liver. It collects a bitter, green juice called bile, which helps digest fatty foods. Gallbladder disease occurs most commonly in persons who are 'fat, female and 40'.

Signs:

- Sharp pain in the stomach at the edge of the right rib cage: This pain sometimes reaches up to the right side of the upper back.

- The pain may come an hour or more after eating rich or fatty foods. Severe pain may cause vomiting.

- Sometimes there is fever.

- Occasionally the eyes may become yellow (jaundice).

Treatment:

- Take belladonna or another antispasmodic to calm the pain (see p. 367). Strong painkillers are often needed. (Aspirin will probably not help.)

- If the person has a fever, she should take tetracycline (p. 353) or ampicillin (p. 351).

- Do not eat greasy food. Overweight (fat) people should eat small meals and lose weight.

- In severe or chronic cases, seek medical help. Sometimes surgery is needed.

Prevention:

Women who are overweight should lose weight (see p. 127). Avoid rich, sweet, and greasy food—and do not eat too much.

Biliousness:

In many countries and in different languages, bad-tempered persons are said to be 'bilious'. Some people believe that fits of anger come when a person has too much bile.

In truth, most bad-tempered persons have nothing wrong with their gallbladders or bile. However, persons who do suffer from gallbladder disease often live in fear of a return of this severe pain and perhaps for this reason are sometimes short-tempered or continually worried about their health. (In fact, the term 'hypochondria', which means to worry continually about one's own health, comes from 'hypo', meaning under, and 'chondrium', meaning rib—referring to the position of the gallbladder!)

ACCEPTING DEATH

Old people are often more ready to accept their own approaching death than are those who love them. Persons who have lived fully are not usually afraid to die. Death is, after all, the natural end of life.

We often make the mistake of trying to keep a dying person alive as long as possible, no matter what the cost. Sometimes this adds to the suffering and strain for both the person and his family. There are many occasions when the kindest thing to do is not to hunt for 'better medicine' or a 'better doctor' but to be close to and supporting of the person who is dying. Let him know that you are glad for all the time, the joy and sorrow you have shared, and that you, too, are able to accept his death. In the last hours, love and acceptance will do far more good than medicines.

Old or chronically ill persons would often prefer to be at home, in familiar surroundings with those they love, than to be in a hospital. At times this may mean that the person will die earlier. But this is not necessarily bad. We must be sensitive to the person's feelings and needs, and to our own. Sometimes a person who is dying suffers more knowing that the cost of keeping him barely alive causes his family to go into debt or children to hunger. He may ask simply to be allowed to die—and there are times when this may be the wise decision.

Yet some people fear death. Even if they are suffering, the known world may be hard to leave behind. Every culture has a system of beliefs about death and ideas about forms of life after death. These ideas, beliefs, and traditions may offer some comfort in facing death.

Death may come upon a person suddenly and unexpectedly or may be long-awaited. How to help someone we love accept and prepare for his approaching death is not an easy matter. Often the most we can do is offer support, kindness, and understanding.

The death of a younger person or child is never easy. Both kindness and honesty are important. A child—or anyone—who is dying often knows it, partly by what his own body tells him and partly by the fear or despair he sees in those who love him. Whether young or old, if a person who is dying asks for the truth, tell him, but tell him gently, and leave some room for hope. Weep if you must, but let him know that even as you love him, and because you love him, you have the strength to let him leave you. This will give him the strength and courage to accept leaving you. To let him know these things you need not say them. You need to feel and show them.

We must all die. Perhaps the most important job of the healer is to help people accept death when it can or should no longer be avoided, and to help ease the suffering of those who still live.

CHAPTER

23

THE MEDICINE KIT

Every family and every village should have certain medical supplies ready in case of emergency:

- The family should have a HOME MEDICINE KIT (see p. 334) with the necessary medicines for first aid, simple infections, and the most common health problems.

- The village should have a more complete medical kit (see VILLAGE MEDICINE KIT, p. 336) with supplies necessary to care for day-to-day problems as well as to meet a serious illness or an emergency. A responsible person should be in charge of it—a health worker, teacher, parent, store-keeper, or anyone who can be trusted by the community. If possible all members of the village should take part in setting up and paying for the medical kit. Those who can afford more should contribute more. But everyone should understand that **the medicine kit is for the benefit of all**—those who can pay and those who cannot.

On the following pages you will find suggestions for what the medicine kits might contain. You will want to change these lists to best meet the needs and resources in your area. Although the list includes mostly modern medicines, important home remedies known to be safe and to work well can also be included.

How much of each medicine should you have?

The amounts of medicines recommended for the medicine kits are the smallest amounts that should be kept on hand. In some cases there will be just enough to **begin** treatment. It may be necessary to take the sick person to a hospital or go for more medicine at once.

The amount of medicine you keep in your kit will depend on how many people it is intended to serve and how far you have to go to get more when some are used up. It will also depend on cost and how much the family or village can afford. Some of the medicines for your kit will be expensive, but it is wise to have enough of the important medicines on hand to meet emergencies.

Note: Supplies for birth kits—the things midwives and pregnant mothers need to have ready for a birth—are listed on pages 254 to 255.

HOW TO CARE FOR YOUR MEDICINE KIT

1. *CAUTION:* **Keep all medicines out of the reach of children.** Any medicine taken in large doses can be poisonous.

2. **Be sure that all medicine is well labeled and that directions for use are kept with each medicine.** Keep a copy of this book with the medicine kit.

3. **Keep all medicines and medical supplies together in a clean, dry, cool place** free from cockroaches and rats. Protect instruments, gauze, and cotton by wrapping them in sealed plastic bags.

4. **Keep an emergency supply of important medicines on hand at all times.** Each time one is used, replace it as soon as possible.

5. **Notice the DATE OF EXPIRATION on each medicine.** If the date has passed or the medicine looks spoiled, destroy it and get new medicine.

Note: Some medicines, especially tetracyclines, may be very dangerous if they have passed their expiration date. However, penicillins in dry form (tablets or powder for syrup or injection) can be used for as long as a year after the expiration date if they have been stored in a clean, dry, and fairly cool place. Old penicillin may lose some of its strength so you may want to increase the dose. (*CAUTION:* While this is safe with penicillin, with other medicines it is often dangerous to give more than the recommended dose.)

Keep medicines out of reach of children.

BUYING SUPPLIES FOR THE MEDICINE KIT

Most of the medicines recommended in this book can be bought in the pharmacies of larger towns. If several families or the village get together to buy what they need at once, often the pharmacist may sell them supplies at lower cost. Or if medicines and supplies can be bought from a wholesaler, prices will be cheaper still.

If the pharmacy does not supply a brand of medicine you want, buy another brand, but be sure that it is the same medicine and check the dosage.

When buying medicines, compare prices. Some brands are much more expensive than others even though the medicine is the same. More expensive medicines are usually no better. When possible, **buy generic medicines rather than brand-name products,** as the generic ones are often much cheaper. Sometimes you can save money by buying larger quantities. For example, a 600,000-unit vial of penicillin often costs only a little more than a 300,000-unit vial—so buy the large vial and use it for two doses.

BE PREPARED FOR EMERGENCIES: KEEP YOUR MEDICINE KIT WELL-SUPPLIED!

THE HOME MEDICINE KIT

Each family should have the following things in their medicine kit. These supplies and medicines should be enough to treat many common problems in rural areas.

Also include useful home remedies in your medicine kit.

SUPPLIES

Use	Supply	Price (write in)	Amount recommended	See page
FOR WOUNDS AND SKIN PROBLEMS:				
	sterile gauze pads in individual sealed envelopes	_____	20	97, 218 263
	1-, 2-, and 3-inch gauze bandage rolls	_____	2 each	87
	clean cotton	_____	1 small package	14, 72, 83, 254
	adhesive tape (adhesive plaster), 1-inch wide roll	_____	2 rolls	85, 218
	disinfectant soap (like *Dial*, *Betadine*, or *Phisohex*)	_____	1 bar or small bottle	361
	70% alcohol	_____	¼ liter	72, 201, 211, 254
	hydrogen peroxide, in a dark bottle	_____	1 small bottle	83, 184, 213, 214
	petroleum jelly *(Vaseline)* in a jar or tube	_____	1	91, 97, 141, 199
	white vinegar	_____	½ liter	200, 241, 292, 309
	sulfur	_____	100 gm.	200, 205, 206, 211
	scissors (clean, not rusty)	_____	1 pair	85, 254, 262
	tweezers with pointed ends	_____	1 pair	84, 175
FOR MEASURING TEMPERATURE:				
	thermometers for mouth for rectum	_____	1 each	30, 41
FOR KEEPING SUPPLIES CLEAN:				
	plastic bags	_____	several	195, 332

MEDICINES

Use	Medicine (generic name)	Local brand (write in)	Price (write in)	Amount recommended	See page
FOR BACTERIAL INFECTIONS:					
	1. Penicillin, 250 mg. tablets	_____	_____	40	349
	2. A sulfonamide, 500 mg. tablets	_____	_____	100	354
	3. Ampicillin, 250 mg. capsules	_____	_____	24	351
FOR WORMS:					
	4. Piperazine, tablets or syrup	_____	_____	40 tablets of 500 mg. or 2 bottles	363
FOR FEVER AND PAIN:					
	5. Aspirin, 300 mg. (5 grain) tablets	_____	_____	50	365
FOR DEHYDRATION:					
	6. Sodium bicarbonate (also salt and sugar)	_____	_____	½ kg.	152
	or prepackaged mix for rehydration drink	_____	_____	10 envelopes	368
FOR ANEMIA:					
	7. Iron (ferrous sulfate), 200 mg. pills (best if pills also contain vitamin C and folic acid)	_____	_____	100	376
FOR SCABIES AND LICE:					
	8. Lindane (gamma benzene hexachloride)	_____	_____	1 bottle	362
FOR ITCHING AND VOMITING:					
	9. Promethazine, 25 mg. tablets	_____	_____	12	371
FOR MILD SKIN INFECTIONS:					
	10. Gentian violet, small bottle; or an antibiotic ointment	_____	_____	1 bottle 1 tube	361
FOR EYE INFECTIONS:					
	11. Antibiotic eye ointment	_____	_____	1 tube	365

THE VILLAGE MEDICINE KIT

   This should have all the medicines and supplies mentioned in the Home
Medicine Kit, but in larger amounts, depending on the size of your village and
distance from a supply center. The Village Kit should also include the things listed
here; many of them are for treatment of more dangerous illnesses. You will have
to change or add to the list, depending on the diseases in your area.

ADDITIONAL SUPPLIES

Use	Supply	Price	Amount	Page
FOR INJECTING:	syringes, 5 ml.	_____	2	65
	needles #22, 3 cm. long	_____	3-6	
	#25, 1½ cm. long	_____	2-4	
FOR TROUBLE URINATING:	catheter (rubber or plastic #16 French)	_____	2	239
FOR SPRAINS AND SWOLLEN VEINS:	elastic bandages, 2 and 3 inches wide	_____	3-6	102, 175, 213
FOR SUCKING OUT MUCUS:	suction bulb	_____	1-2	84, 255, 262
FOR LOOKING IN EARS, ETC.:	penlight (small flashlight)	_____	1	34, 255, 309

ADDITIONAL MEDICINES

Use	Medicine	Local Brand	Price	Amount	Page
FOR SEVERE INFECTIONS:	1. Penicillin, injectable; if only one, procaine penicillin 600,000 U. per ml.	_____	_____	20-40	350
	2. Ampicillin, injectable 250 mg. ampules	_____	_____	20-40	351
	and/or streptomycin 1 gm. vials for combined use with penicillin if ampicillin is too expensive	_____	_____	20-40	352
	3. Tetracycline, capsules or tablets 250 mg.	_____	_____	40-80	353
FOR AMEBA AND GIARDIA INFECTIONS:	4. Metronidazole, 250 mg. tablets	_____	_____	40-80	359
FOR FITS, TETANUS, AND SEVERE WHOOPING COUGH:	5. Phenobarbital 15 mg. tablets	_____	_____	40-80	373
	and 200 mg. injections	_____	_____	15-30	
FOR SEVERE ALLERGIC REACTIONS AND SEVERE ASTHMA:	6. Adrenaline injections ampules with 1 mg.	_____	_____	5-10	370

Use	Medicine	Local Brand	Price	Amount	Page
FOR ASTHMA:					
	7. Ephedrine, 15 mg. tablets	_____	_____	20-100	370
FOR SEVERE BLEEDING AFTER CHILDBIRTH:					
	8. Ergonovine, injections of 0.2 mg.	_____	_____	6-12	375

OTHER MEDICINES NEEDED IN MANY BUT NOT ALL AREAS

Use	Medicine	Local Brand	Price	Amount	Page
WHERE DRY EYES (XEROSIS) IS A PROBLEM:					
	Vitamin A, 200,000 U. capsules	_____	_____	10-100	376
WHERE TETANUS IS A PROBLEM:					
	Tetanus antitoxin, 50,000 units (Lyophilized if possible)	_____	_____	2-4 bottles	373
WHERE TYPHOID IS A PROBLEM:					
	Chloramphenicol, 250 mg. capsules	_____	_____	50-200	353
WHERE SNAKEBITE OR SCORPION STING IS A PROBLEM:					
	Specific antivenin	_____	_____	2-6	372
WHERE MALARIA IS A PROBLEM:					
	Chloroquine tablets with 150 mg. of base	_____	_____	50-200	357
	(or whatever medicine works best in your area)	_____	_____		357
WHERE HOOKWORM IS A PROBLEM:					
	Thiabendazole, 500 mg. tablets (or another hookworm medicine)	_____	_____	25-100	363
TO PREVENT OR TREAT BLEEDING IN UNDERWEIGHT NEWBORNS:					
	Vitamin K, injections of 1 mg.	_____	_____	3-6	377

MEDICINES FOR CHRONIC DISEASES

It may or may not be wise to have medicines for chronic diseases such as **tuberculosis, leprosy,** and **schistosomiasis** in the Village Medicine Kit. Often, to be sure a person has one of these diseases, special tests must be made in a health center, where the necessary medicine can usually be obtained. Whether these and other medicines are included in the village medical supplies will depend on the local situation and the medical ability of those responsible.

VACCINES

Vaccines have not been included in the Village Medicine Kit because they are usually provided by the Health Department. However, a great effort should be made to see that all children are vaccinated as soon as they are old enough for the different vaccines (see p. 147). Therefore, if refrigeration is available, vaccines should be part of the village medical supplies—especially the DPT, polio, and measles vaccines.

WORDS TO THE VILLAGE STOREKEEPER (OR PHARMACIST)

Dear friend,

If you sell medicines in your store, people probably ask you about which medicines to buy and when or how to use them. You are in a position to have an important effect on people's knowledge and health.

This book can help you to give correct advice and to see that your customers buy only those medicines they really need.

As you know, people too often spend the little money they have for medicines that do not help them. But **you** can help them understand their health needs more clearly and spend their money more wisely. For example:

- If people come asking for cough syrups, for a diarrhea-thickener like *Kaopectate,* for vitamin B_{12} or liver extract to treat simple anemia, for penicillin to treat a sprain or ache, or for tetracycline when they have a cold, explain to them that these medicines are not needed and may do more harm than good. Discuss with them what to do instead.

- If someone wants to buy a vitamin tonic, encourage him to buy eggs, fruit, or vegetables instead. Help him understand that these have more vitamins and nutritional value for the money.

- If people ask for an injection when medicine by mouth would work as well and be safer—which is usually the case—tell them so.

- If someone wants to buy 'cold tablets' or some other form of 'expensive aspirin' for a cold, encourage him to save money by buying plain aspirin tablets and taking them with lots of liquids.

You may find it easier to tell people these things if you look up the information in this book, and read it together with them.

Above all, sell only useful medicines. Stock your store with the medicines and supplies listed for the Home and Village Medicine Kits, as well as other medicines and supplies that are important for common illnesses in your area. Try to stock low-cost generic products or the least expensive brands. And never sell people medicines that are expired, damaged, or useless.

Your store can become a place where people learn about caring for their own health. If you can help people use medicines intelligently, making sure that anyone who purchases a medicine is well informed as to its correct use and dosage, as well as the risks and precautions, you will provide an outstanding service to your community.

Good luck!

Sincerely,

David Werner

THE GREEN PAGES

THE USES, DOSAGE, AND PRECAUTIONS FOR
THE MEDICINES REFERRED TO IN THIS BOOK

The medicines in this section are grouped according to their uses. For example, all the medicines used to treat infections caused by worms are listed under the heading FOR WORMS.

If you want information on a medicine, look for the name of that medicine in the LIST OF MEDICINES beginning on page 341. Or look for the medicine in the INDEX OF MEDICINES beginning on page 345. When you find the name you are looking for, turn to the page number shown.

Medicines are listed according to their *generic* (scientific) names rather than their *brand names* (names given by the companies that make them). This is because generic names are similar everywhere, but brand names differ from place to place. Also, **medicines are often much cheaper when you buy generic rather than brand-name products.**

In a few cases, well-known brand names are given after the generic name. In this book brand names are written in *italics* and begin with a capital letter. For example, *Phenergan* is a brand name for an antihistamine called **promethazine** (promethazine is the generic name).

With the information on each medicine, blank spaces _____ have been left for you to **write in** the name and price of the most common or least expensive product in your area. For example, if the cheapest or only available form of tetracycline in your area is *Terramycin,* you would write in the blank spaces as follows:

Tetracycline (tetracycline HCl, oxytetracycline, etc.)

Name: _____*Terramycin*_____ price: *$1.25* for *6 capsules*

If, however, you find you can buy generic **tetracycline** more cheaply than *Terramycin*, write instead:

Name: _____*oxytetracycline*_____ price: *$1.00* for *60 capsules*

Note: Not all the medicines listed in the Green Pages are needed in your Home or Village Medicine kit. Because different medicines are available in different countries, information has sometimes been given for a number of medicines that do the same job. However, it is wise to

KEEP AND USE ONLY A SMALL NUMBER OF MEDICINES.

Dosage Information:

HOW FRACTIONS ARE SOMETIMES WRITTEN

1/2 tablet   = half a tablet =

1 1/2 tablets = one and a half tablets =

1/4 tablet   = one quarter or one fourth of a tablet =

1/8 tablet   = one eighth of a tablet (dividing it
into 8 equal pieces and taking 1 piece) =

DECIDING DOSAGE BY HOW MUCH A PERSON WEIGHS

In these pages most instructions for dosage are given according to the age of a person—so that children get smaller doses than adults. However, it is more exact to determine dosage according to a person's weight. Information for doing this is sometimes included briefly in parentheses ( ), for use of health workers who have scales. If you read . . .

$$(100 \text{ mg./kg./day}),$$

this means 100 mg. per kilogram of body weight per day. In other words, during a 24 hour period you give 100 mg. of the medicine for each kilogram the person weighs.

For example, suppose you want to give aspirin to a boy with rheumatic fever who weighs 36 kilograms. The recommended dose of aspirin for rheumatic fever is 100 mg./kg./day. So multiply:

$$100 \text{ mg.} \times 36 = 3600 \text{ mg.}$$

The boy should get 3600 mg. of aspirin a day. One aspirin tablet contains 300 mg. of aspirin. 3600 mg. comes to 12 tablets. So give the boy 2 tablets 6 times a day (or 2 tablets every 4 hours).

This is one way to figure the dosages for different medicines. For more information on measuring and deciding on dosages, see Chapter 8.

Note to educators and planners of health care programs and to local distributors of this book:

If this book is to be used in training programs for village health workers or is distributed by a local health care program, **information about local names and prices of medicines should accompany the book.**

Local distributors are encouraged to duplicate a sheet with this information, so that it can be copied into the book by the user. Wherever possible, include local sources for **generic or low-cost medicines and supplies.** (See "Buying Supplies for the Medicine Kit," page 333.)

LIST OF MEDICINES IN THE GREEN PAGES

Listed in the order in which they appear

INDEX OF MEDICINES IN THE GREEN PAGES

Listed in this order: A B C D E F G H I J K L M N O P Q R S T U V W X Y Z

Note: Medicines not listed in the GREEN PAGES, but mentioned in the book are listed in the main Index (yellow pages).

ONLY USE A MEDICINE WHEN YOU ARE SURE IT IS NEEDED
AND WHEN YOU ARE SURE HOW TO USE IT.

ANTIBIOTICS

THE PENICILLINS: VERY IMPORTANT ANTIBIOTICS

Penicillin is one of the most useful antibiotics. It fights certain kinds of infections, including many that produce pus. It does no good for most diarrheas, most urinary infections, backache, bruises, the common cold, chickenpox, or other virus infections (see p. 18 and 19).

Penicillin is measured in milligrams (mg.) or units (U.). For penicillin G, 250 mg. = 400,000 U.

Risks and precautions for all kinds of penicillin (including ampicillin):

For most people penicillin is one of the safest medicines. Too much does no harm and only wastes money. Too little does not completely stop the infection and may make the bacteria *resistant* (more difficult to kill).

In certain persons penicillin causes **allergic reactions.** Mild allergic reactions include itchy raised spots or rashes. Often these come several hours or days after taking penicillin and may last for days. Antihistamines (p. 371) help calm the itching.

Rarely, penicillin causes a dangerous reaction called **allergic shock.** Soon after penicillin is injected, the person suddenly gets pale, has trouble breathing, and goes into the state of shock (see p. 70). *Adrenalin* **must be injected at once.**

Always have *Adrenalin* **ready when you inject penicillin (see p. 370).**

A person who has once had **any** allergic reaction to penicillin should **never** be given any kind of penicillin or ampicillin again. This is because the next time the reaction would likely be far worse and might kill him.

Most infections that can be treated with penicillin can be treated quite well with penicillin taken by mouth. Injected forms of penicillin are more dangerous than those taken by mouth.

Use injectable penicillin only for severe or dangerous infections.

Before injecting penicillin or any medicine that contains it, take the precautions given on page 70.

Resistance to penicillin:

Sometimes penicillin does not work against an infection it would normally control. This may be because the bacteria have become resistant, so that penicillin no longer harms them. Infections that are at times resistant to penicillin include impetigo, sores on the skin with pus, and infections of the bone (osteomyelitis).

If one of these infections does not respond to ordinary penicillin, another antibiotic may be tried. Or special forms of penicillin (methacillin, nafcillin, oxacillin, cloxacillin, dicloxacillin) may work.

If a case of gonorrhea is resistant to penicillin, use tetracycline or streptomycin as indicated on pages 236 and 356.

PENICILLIN BY MOUTH

Penicillin G or V

Name:_____ price:_____ for:____

Often comes in: 250 mg. (400,000 U.) tablets
also: suspensions or powders for suspension, 125 or 250 mg. per teaspoon

(Penicillin V is used by the body more easily than penicillin G, but is more expensive.)

Penicillin by mouth (rather than injections) should be used for mild and moderately severe infections, including:

abscessed or infected teeth
infected wounds or many infected sores
widespread impetigo
erysipelas
ear infections
sinusitis
sore throat with sudden, high fever
   (strep throat)
some cases of bronchitis
prevention of tetanus in persons who have
   not been vaccinated and who have deep
   or dirty wounds

If infection is severe, it may be best to start with injections of penicillin, but often penicillin by mouth can be given instead once improvement begins.

If improvement does not begin within 2 or 3 days, consider using another antibiotic and try to get medical advice.

Dosage of penicillin by mouth—using tablets of 250 mg. (20 mg./kg./day):

For mild infections:
  adults: 250 mg. (1 tablet) 4 times a day
  children 6 to 12 years old: 125 mg.
    (½ tablet) 3 or 4 times a day
  children under 6 years: 50 to 75 mg.
    (¼ tablet) 3 or 4 times a day
For more serious infections: double the above dosage.

Important: Keep taking the penicillin for at least 2 or 3 days after fever and other signs of infection are gone.

To help the body make better use of the medicine, **always take penicillin on an empty stomach,** an hour before meals. (This is more important for penicillin G than for penicillin V.)

INJECTABLE PENICILLIN

Injectable penicillin should be used for certain severe infections, including:

  meningitis
  septicemia
  tetanus
  severe pneumonia
  badly infected wounds
  gangrene
  infected bones and to prevent infection
    when a bone pokes through the skin
  gonorrhea
  syphilis

Injectable penicillin comes in many different preparations. Before you inject any penicillin, be sure to check the **amount** and the **kind.**

Choosing the right kind of penicillin for injection:

Some kinds of penicillin do their job quickly but do not last long. Others work more slowly but last longer. There are times when it is better to use one kind than another.

Short-acting penicillin: These are known by many names, including crystalline penicillin, benzylpenicillin, aqueous penicillin, soluble penicillin, sodium penicillin, potassium penicillin, and penicillin G injections. These penicillins act quickly but only stay in the body a short time, so that they must be injected every 6 hours (4 times a day). A short-acting penicillin is the best choice for very severe infections when high doses of penicillin are needed. For example, for gas gangrene or when a broken bone pokes through the skin.

Intermediate-acting penicillin: Procaine penicillin or procaine penicillin aluminum monostearate (PAM). These work more slowly and last about a day in the body, so injections should be given once daily. Procaine penicillin, or a combination of procaine and a short-acting penicillin, is the best choice for most infections when injectable penicillin is needed.

Long-acting penicillin: Benzathine or benethamine penicillin. This penicillin goes into the blood slowly and lasts up to a month. Its main use is in the treatment of strep throat and prevention of rheumatic fever. It is useful when a person lives far away from someone who injects or cannot be counted upon to take penicillin by mouth. For mild infections a single shot may be enough. Benzathine penicillin often comes combined with faster-acting penicillins.

Crystalline penicillin (a short-acting penicillin)

Name:_____ price:_____ for___

Often comes in: vials of 1 million U. (625 mg.)

Dosage of crystalline penicillin or any short-acting penicillin—for severe infections:

  Give an injection every 4 to 6 hours.

  In each injection give:

    adults: 1 million U.
    children age 8 to 12: 500,000 U.
    children age 3 to 7: 250,000 U.
    children under 3: 125,000 U.
    newborn babies: 150,000 U. **twice** a day
    only

Procaine penicillin (intermediate-acting)

Name:_____ price:_____ for___

Often comes in: vials of 300,000 U., 400,000 U., and more

Dosage of procaine penicillin—for moderately severe infections:

Give **1** injection a day.

With each injection give:

> adults: 600,000 to 1,200,000 U.
> children age 8 to 12: 600,000 U.
> children age 3 to 7: 300,000 U.
> children under 3: 150,000 U.
> newborn babies: DO NOT USE unless no other penicillin or ampicillin is available. In emergencies, 75,000 U.

For very severe infections, give twice the above dose. However, it is better to use a short-acting penicillin.

The dosage for procaine penicillin combined with a short-acting penicillin is the same as for procaine penicillin alone.

For treatment of gonorrhea and syphilis, procaine penicillin is best. Very high doses are needed. For dosage, see pages 237 and 238.

Benzathine penicillin (long-acting)

Name:_____ price:_____ for:___

Often comes in: vials of 1,200,000 or 2,400,000 U.

Dosage of benzathine penicillin—for mild to moderately severe infections:

Give 1 injection every 4 days. For mild infections, 1 injection may be enough.

> adults: 1,200,000 U.
> children age 8 to 12: 600,000 U.
> children age 3 to 8: 300,000 U.
> children under 3 years: 150,000 U.

To prevent return infection in persons who have had rheumatic fever, give twice the above dose once every 3 or 4 weeks (see p. 310).

AMPICILLIN: A WIDE-RANGE (BROAD-SPECTRUM PENICILLIN)

Ampicillin

Name:_____
Often comes in:
solutions,
    125 or 250 mg./tsp.   price:_____ for___
capsules, 250 mg.   price:_____ for___
injections, 250 mg.   price:_____ for___

Ampicillin is a *broad-spectrum* (wide-range) penicillin that kills many more kinds of bacteria than are killed by other penicillins. It is safer than other broad-spectrum antibiotics and is especially useful for babies and small children.

Because it is expensive, and sometimes causes diarrhea or 'thrush', ampicillin should not be used when regular penicillin is likely to do the job as well.

Ampicillin works well when taken by mouth. Injections should only be used for severe illnesses such as meningitis, peritonitis, and appendicitis, or when the sick person vomits or cannot swallow the medicine.

Ampicillin is especially useful in treating the following:

> septicemia and unexplained illness in the newborn
> pneumonia or ear infections of children under 6 years
> severe diarrhea or dysentery **with fever**
> meningitis
> peritonitis and appendicitis
> severe urinary tract infections
> typhoid fever (after illness has been controlled with chloramphenicol or if it is resistant to chloramphenicol)

Persons allergic to penicillin should not take ampicillin. See *Risks and Precautions* for penicillin, page 349.

Dosage for ampicillin:
By mouth—(25 to 50 mg./kg./day):
    capsules of 250 mg.; syrup with 125 mg. per teaspoon (5 ml.)

Give 4 doses a day.

In each dose give:

> adults: 2 capsules or 4 teaspoons (500 mg.)
> children age 8 to 12: 1 capsule or 2 teaspoons (250 mg.)
> children 3 to 7: ½ capsule or 1 teaspoon (125 mg.)
> children under 3: ¼ capsule or ½ teaspoon (62 mg.)
> newborn babies: same as for children under 3 years

By injection, for severe infections—(50 to 100 mg./kg./day—up to 300 mg./kg./day for meningitis):
vials of 250 mg.

Give 4 doses a day, once every 6 hours.

In each dose give:

> adults: 500 mg. (two 250 mg. vials)
> children age 8 to 12: 250 mg. (one 250 mg. vial)
> children 3 to 7: 125 mg. (½ of a 250 mg. vial)
> children under 3: 62 mg. (¼ of a 250 mg. vial)
> newborn babies: 125 mg. (½ of a 250 mg. vial) **twice** a day only

Keep giving the ampicillin for at least 2 days after signs of infection have gone.

PENICILLIN WITH STREPTOMYCIN

Products that combine penicillin with streptomycin are found in most countries and are often used more than they should be. If one of these products is widely used in your area, write down its name, contents, and price:

Name:_____ mg. of penicillin:_____

mg. of streptomycin:_____ price:_____ for___

Penicillin and streptomycin should be used together only in special cases, as an alternative to ampicillin, when ampicillin cannot be obtained or is too expensive. They should not be used for minor infections or for the common cold or 'flu'.

Frequent use of streptomycin for illnesses other than tuberculosis makes the tuberculosis bacteria in a community resistant to streptomycin, and therefore harder to treat. Also, streptomycin may cause deafness.

Streptomycin with penicillin can be used for most of the illnesses for which ampicillin is recommended (see p. 351), but ampicillin is safer, especially for babies.

Usually, it is cheaper, as well as easier to figure the correct dosage, if streptomycin and penicillin are injected separately, rather than in a combination.

Dosage of penicillin with streptomycin—**for severe infections:**

Give short-acting penicillin, at least 25,000 U./kg. 4 times a day, and streptomycin, no more than 30 to 50 mg. /kg./day.

In newborns, give short-acting penicillin, 50,000 U./kg. twice a day together with streptomycin, 20 mg./kg. once a day.

	Give this much short-acting penicillin	with this much streptomycin
adults.	.1,000,000 U. 4 to 6 times a day	1 gm. (usually 2 ml.) once a day
children . . . . 8 to 12 years	.500,000 U. 4 to 6 times a day	750 mg. (1½ ml.)once a day
children . . . . 3 to 7 years	.250,000 U. 4 to 6 times a day	500 mg. (1 ml.) once a day
children . . . . under 3	.125,000 U. 4 to 6 times a day	250 mg. (½ ml.) once a day
newborn babies	.150,000 U. twice a day	60 mg. (1/8 ml.) once a day

For very severe infections, such as peritonitis, appendicitis, meningitis, or an acute infection of the bone (osteomyelitis), even higher doses of penicillin may be given, but **the dosage of streptomycin must never be higher than what is suggested here.**

For less severe infections calling for penicillin with streptomycin, procaine penicillin can be used with streptomycin. For the dosage of procaine penicillin, see page 351. The dosage for streptomycin is the same as that given above.

Be sure to read the *Risks and Precautions* for both penicillin and streptomycin, pages 349 and 355.

ERYTHROMYCIN: AN ALTERNATIVE TO PENICILLIN

Erythromycin

Name:_____

Often comes in:
tablets or capsules of 250 mg.   Price:_____ for___
syrups with 125 or 200 mg.
in 5 ml.   Price:_____ for___

Erythromycin is not as strong as penicillin and is more expensive. It may be used instead of penicillin by persons allergic to penicillin. It should be included in the family or village medical kit when someone is known to be allergic to penicillin.

Erythromycin is fairly safe, but care should be taken not to give more than the recommended dose. Do not use for more than 2 weeks, as it may cause jaundice.

Dosage of erythromycin—for persons allergic to penicillin:
Take erythromycin with meals to avoid stomach upset.

Give 1 dose 4 times a day.

In each dose give:

    adults: 500 mg. (2 tablets or 4 teaspoons)
    children 8 to 12 years: 250 mg. (1 tablet or
      2 teaspoons)
    children 3 to 7 years: 150 mg. (½ tablet or 1
      teaspoon)
    children under 3 years: 75 to 150 mg. (¼
      to ½ tablet or ½ to 1 teaspoon)

TETRACYCLINES: WIDE-RANGE ANTIBIOTICS

Tetracycline (tetracycline HCl, oxytetracycline, etc.)
(Familiar but expensive brand: *Terramycin*)

Name:_____

Often comes in:
    capsules of 250 mg.   Price:____ for____
    mixture, 125 mg./5 ml.   Price:____ for____

Tetracyclines are *broad-spectrum* antibiotics; that is, they fight a wide range of different kinds of bacteria.

Tetracycline should be taken by mouth, as this works as well and causes less problems than when it is injected.

Tetracycline can be used for:

    diarrhea or dysentery caused by bacteria or
      amebas
    sinusitis
    respiratory infections (bronchitis, etc.)
    infections of the urinary tract
    typhus
    brucellosis (tetracycline with streptomycin)
    cholera
    trachoma
    gallbladder infections

Tetracycline does no good for the common cold. For many common infections it does not work as well as penicillin or sulfas. It is also more expensive. Its use should be limited.

Risks and Precautions:

1. Pregnant women should not take tetracycline after the fourth month, as it can damage or stain the baby's teeth. For the same reason, children under 6 years old should take tetracycline only when absolutely necessary, and for short periods only.

2. Tetracycline may cause diarrhea or upset stomach, especially if taken for a long time.
3. It is dangerous to use tetracycline that is 'old' or has passed the expiration date.

Dosage for tetracycline—(20 to 40 mg./kg./day):
—capsules of 250 mg. and mixture of 125 mg. in 5 ml.—

Give tetracycline by mouth 4 times a day.

In each dose give:

    adults: 250 mg. (1 capsule)
    children 8 to 12 years: 125 mg. (½ capsule
      or 1 teaspoon)
    children 4 to 7 years: 80 mg. (1/3 capsule or
      2/3 teaspoon)
    children 1 to 3 years: 60 mg. (¼ capsule or
      1/2 teaspoon)
    babies under 1 year: 25 mg. (1/10 capsule
      or 1/5 teaspoon)
    newborn babies (when other antibiotics
      are not available): 8 mg. (1/30 capsule
      or 6 drops of the mixture)

In severe cases, and for infections like typhus and brucellosis, twice the above dose should be given (except to small children).

For the body to make the best use of tetracycline, milk should not be taken within 1 hour before or after taking the medicine.

For most infections, tetracycline should be continued for 1 or 2 days after the signs of infection are gone. Some forms of diarrhea will clear up after only a few doses. (For choice of medicines for diarrhea, see pages 156 to 158.) For some illnesses, prolonged treatment is needed: typhus 6 to 10 days; brucellosis 2 to 3 weeks.

CHLORAMPHENICOL: AN ANTIBIOTIC FOR TYPHOID

Chloramphenicol *(Chloromycetin)*

Name:_____

Often comes in:
    capsules of 250 mg.   Price:____ for____
    mixture, 125 mg. in 5 ml.   Price:____ for____
    (injections, 250 mg. per vial) Price: ____ for____

This broad-spectrum antibiotic fights a wide range of different bacteria. It is cheap, but there is some danger in using it. For this reason. its use must be very limited.

Chloramphenicol should be used only for **typhoid** and for very serious diarrhea or other infections that are not cured by sulfas, penicillin, tetracycline, or ampicillin.

Except for typhoid, ampicillin usually works as well as or better than chloramphenicol, and is much safer. Unfortunately, ampicillin is very expensive, so there are times when chloramphenicol must be used instead.

WARNING: Chloramphenicol harms the blood of some persons. It is even more dangerous for newborn babies, especially premature babies. **To newborn babies with serious infections, give ampicillin rather than chloramphenicol** if this is at all possible. As a rule, **do not give chloramphenicol to babies under 1 month of age.**

Take care not to give more than the recommended dose of chloramphenicol. **For babies, the dose is very small** (see below).

Avoid long or repeated use.

In treating typhoid, change from chloramphenicol to ampicillin as soon as the illness is under control. (In regions where typhoid is known to be resistant to chloramphenicol, the entire treatment should be with ampicillin.)

Chloramphenicol taken by mouth often does more good than when it is injected, and is less dangerous. Except in rare cases when the person cannot swallow, **do not inject chloramphenicol.**

Dosage for chloramphenicol—(50 to 100 mg./kg./ day):—capsules of 250 mg., or a mixture of 125 mg. in 5 ml.—

Give by mouth 4 times a day.

In each dose give:

adults: 500 to 1000 mg. (2 to 4 capsules). For typhoid, peritonitis, and other dangerous infections the higher dose should be given. (3 capsules 4 times a day is 12 capsules a day.)

children 8 to 12 years: 250 mg. (1 capsule or 2 teaspoons of mixture)

children 3 to 7 years: 125 mg. (½ capsule or 1 teaspoon)

babies 1 month to 2 years: give 12 mg. (½ ml. of the mixture or 1/20 part of a capsule) for *each* kg. of body weight. (This way, a 5 kg. baby would get 60 mg., which is ½ teaspoon of mixture, or ¼ capsule, at each dose. With 4 doses, this means the 5 kg. baby will get 1 capsule, or 2 teaspoons of mixture, a day.)

newborn babies: *As a general rule, do not use chloramphenicol.* If there is no other choice, give 5 mg. (¼ ml. or 5 drops of the mixture) for each kg. of body weight. Give a 3 kg. baby 15 mg. (15 drops of the mixture) 4 times a day, or about ¼ capsule a day. Do not give more.

THE SULFAS (OR SULFONAMIDES): INEXPENSIVE MEDICINE FOR COMMON INFECTIONS

Sulfadiazine, sulfisoxazole, sulfadimidine, or 'triple sulfa'

Name:_____

Often comes in:
tablets of 500 mg.   Price:_____ for___
mixture, 500 mg. in 5 ml.   Price:_____ for___

The sulfas or sulfonamides fight many kinds of bacteria, but they are weaker than many antibiotics and more likely to cause allergic reactions (itching) and other problems. Because they are cheap and can be taken by mouth, they are still useful.

The most important use of sulfas is for urinary infections. They may also be used for some ear infections and for impetigo and other skin infections with pus.

Not all the sulfas are used the same way or have the same dosage. If you have a sulfonamide other than one of those listed above, be sure of the correct use and dosage before you use it. Sulfathiazole is similar to the sulfas named above, and is very cheap, but is not recommended because it is more likely to cause side effects.

The sulfas do not work as well for diarrhea as they used to, because many of the microbes that cause diarrhea have become resistant to them.

WARNING:

It is important to **drink lots of water** when taking sulfa, to prevent harm to the kidneys.

If the sulfa causes a rash, itching, joint pain, fever, lower back pain or blood in the urine, **stop taking it and drink lots of water.**

Never give sulfa to a person who is dehydrated.

Note: To do any good, these sulfas must be taken in the right dose, which is large. Be sure to take enough—but not too much!

Dosage for sulfadiazine, sulfisoxazole, sulfa-dimidine, or triple sulfa (200 mg./kg./day):
    —tablets of 500 mg., or a mixture with 500 mg. in 5 ml.—

Give 4 doses a day—**with lots of water!**

In each dose give:

> adults: 3 to 4 gm. (6 to 8 tablets) for the first dose; then 1 gm. (2 tablets) for the other doses
> children 8 to 12 years: 2 gm. (4 tablets or teaspoons of the mixture) for the first dose, then 1 gm. (2 tablets or teaspoons) for the other doses
> children 4 to 8 years: 750 mg. (1½ tablets or teaspoons) in each dose
> children 2 to 4 years: 500 mg. (1 tablet or 1 teaspoon) in each dose
> babies 1 year and under: **Do not give sulfa.** If you have no choice, give 250 mg. (½ tablet or teaspoon) 4 times a day

MEDICINES FOR TUBERCULOSIS

In treating tuberculosis, it is very important always to use 2 or 3 anti-tuberculosis medicines at the same time. If only 1 medicine is used, the TB bacteria often become resistant to it and make the disease harder to treat.

To keep it from coming back, **tuberculosis must be treated for a long time,** usually at least a year after there are no more symptoms.

The medicines for tuberculosis are often expensive if you buy them in a pharmacy, but most governments have programs that test for tuberculosis and give medicine free or at low cost. Ask at the nearest health center.

To treat tuberculosis, it is best to start with 3 medicines—**streptomycin, isoniazid,** and 1 other anti-TB medicine. Three examples are given below. Of these, **ethambutol** is the best and usually causes few side effects, but is very expensive. The least expensive is **thiacetazone,** but it causes side effects so often that many persons cannot use it. **Aminosalicylic acid** (PAS) is halfway between the other 2, both in cost and frequency of side effects, and is often the best choice.

Streptomycin should be continued as a part of the treatment for at least 2 months after the person shows no more symptoms of TB. Isoniazid and 1 other anti-tuberculosis medicine should be continued for 1 or 2 years after the person shows no symptom of TB. To keep tuberculosis from coming back again the **full, long-term treatment is extremely important.**

Streptomycin

Name:_____ price:_____ for_____

Often comes in: vials for injection 500 mg. in each ml.

Streptomycin is an important medicine for treating tuberculosis. **It should always be used in combination with other medicines.** Streptomycin and penicillin together can be used to treat certain severe infections (see STREPTOMYCIN WITH PENICILLIN, p. 352). However, the use of strepto-mycin for other than tuberculosis should be very limited, because frequent use of streptomycin for other illnesses helps make tuberculosis resistant to it, and therefore harder to treat.

Risks and Precautions:

Great care must be taken not to give more than the correct dose. Too much streptomycin for too long may cause deafness. If ringing of the ears or deafness begins, stop taking the medicine and see a health worker.

Dosage for streptomycin (30 to 50 mg./kg./day):
    —vials of liquid; or powder for mixing with water to give 1 gm. of streptomycin in 2 ml.—

> *For treatment of tuberculosis:*
> **very severe cases,** give 1 injection daily for 3 weeks or until person shows improvement
> **for mild cases,** give 1 injection 2 or 3 times a week for 2 months

With each injection give:

> adults: 1 gm. (or 2 ml.)
> children 8 to 12 years: 750 mg. (1½ ml.)
> children 3 to 7 years: 500 mg. (1 ml.)
> children under 3 years: 250 mg. (½ ml.)
> newborn babies: give 20 mg. for each kg. of
> body weight; thus a 3 kg. baby gets 60
> mg. (1/8 ml.)

Always give streptomycin together with other anti-tuberculosis medicines.

Streptomycin in the treatment of gonorrhea:

Adults with gonorrhea who are allergic to penicillin or who do not get well using penicillin (see **Resistance,** p. 349) can be given a single dose of 4 gm. (8 ml.) of streptomycin. Inject half the medicine into each buttock. Do not use except when the infection is resistant to other antibiotics.

Isoniazid (INH)

Name:_____ price:_____ for_____

Often comes in: tablets of 100 mg.

This is the most active anti-TB medicine. Whenever possible, it should be given with at least 1 other anti-TB medicine.

Risks and Precautions:

Rarely, isoniazid causes anemia, nerve pains in the hands and feet, muscle twitching, or even fits. These side effects can usually be prevented by giving 100 mg. of pyridoxine (vitamin B_6) daily, by mouth. Or, since these side effects are rare, to save money, pyridoxine can be given only to persons who begin to develop side effects.

Dosage for isoniazid—(10 to 20 mg./kg./day):
—tablets of 100 mg.—

Give isoniazid once a day for at least a year.

In each dose give:

> adults: 400 mg. (4 tablets)
> children: 50 mg. (½ tablet) for each 5 kg.
> the child weighs.

For children with severe TB, or tubercular meningitis, the above dose should be doubled until improvement takes place.

Aminosalicylic acid (PAS)

Name:_____ price:_____ for_____

Often comes in: 500 mg. tablets

Risks and Precautions:

PAS may cause vomiting, diarrhea, and stomach upset. Acid indigestion can often be avoided by taking it with meals or with milk. Persons with stomach ulcers should not take PAS.

Dosage for PAS—(250 mg./kg./day):
—500 mg. tablets—

Give PAS 3 times a day, with meals, for at least a year.

In each dose give:

> adults: 4 gm. (8 tablets)
> children 8 to 12 years: 3 gm. (6 tablets)
> children 3 to 7 years: 2 gm. (4 tablets)
> children under 3 years: 1 gm. (2 tablets)

Thiacetazone

Name:_____ price:_____ for_____

Often comes in: tablets with 50 mg. of thiacetazone (often in combination with 100 or 133 mg. of isoniazid)

Side effects: May cause rashes, vomiting, dizziness, or loss of appetite. Side effects occur often.

Dosage for thiacetazone—(3 to 5 mg./kg./day):
—tablets with 50 mg. thiacetazone, with or without isoniazid—

Give once a day for at least a year.

In each dose give:

> adults: 3 tablets (150 mg.)
> children 8 to 12 years: 2 tablets (100 mg.)
> children 3 to 7 years: 1 tablet (50 mg.)
> children under 3 years: ½ tablet (25 mg.)

Ethambutol (familiar brand name: *Myambutol*)

Name:_____ price:_____ for_____

Often comes in: tablets of 100 or 400 mg.

Side effects: May cause eye pain or damage if taken in large doses for a long time.

357

Dosage of ethambutol—(15 to 25 mg./kg./day):
—100 mg. tablets or 400 mg. tablets—

Give once a day for at least 6 months.

In each dose give:

adults: 400 mg. (one 400 mg. tablet or
four 100 mg. tablets)
children: Give 15 mg. for each kg. the child
weighs. For tubercular meningitis give 25
mg. for each kg. the child weighs.

FOR LEPROSY: SULFONES

Dapsone (diaminodiphenylsulfone, DDS) —for
leprosy

Name:_____ price:_____ for_____

Often comes in: tablets of 5 and 50 and 100 mg.

Treatment of leprosy must continue for at least
2 years and sometimes for life. To prevent the
bacteria that cause leprosy from becoming
resistant to DDS, it is important to keep taking the
medicine regularly. Be sure you get more before
your supply runs out.

Side effects: Occasionally, DDS causes a serious
problem called 'lepra reaction'. There may be
fever, swollen and tender nerves, and lumpy
inflamed spots. It may also cause joint pains,
swelling of the hands and feet, or severe eye
damage leading to blindness.

In case of a 'lepra reaction', it is usually best to
keep taking the DDS but to also take an anti-
inflammatory medicine (cortico-steroid). This
should be done with the advice of an experienced
health worker or doctor because the cortico-
steroid can also cause serious problems and
the dose may need to be raised or lowered.

WARNING: DDS is a dangerous drug. Keep it
where children cannot reach it.

Dosage for DDS:
—using tablets of 5 and 50 mg.—

Not long ago, persons were started with very
small doses, which were increased slowly over a
period of months. It was thought that this
helped prevent lepra reaction. Now, it is usually
considered best to start with the full dose. This
helps prevent the bacteria from becoming
resistant to the medicine. Take DDS once a day:

adults: 50 mg. (one 50 mg. tablet)
children from 5 to 10 years: 25 mg. (half
a 50 mg. tablet or five 5 mg. tablets)
children under 5 years: 10 mg. (two 5 mg.
tablets)

OTHER MEDICINES

MEDICINES FOR MALARIA

Medicines for malaria can be used in three different
ways:

1. **Treatment** of the person who is ill with
malaria. Medicine is given daily for just a
few days.
2. **Suppression:** to keep any malaria parasites
that may be in the blood from doing harm.
Suppression is used in areas where marlaria
is very common, especially to protect
children who are weak or sick for other
reasons. Medicines are given weekly.
3. **Semi-suppression (half- suppression):** this
partly protects a person against malaria,
but lets his body build up defenses against
it. It is used where malaria is very common.
Medicine is given every 2 to 4 weeks.

There are several medicines that fight malaria.
Unfortunately, in many parts of the world, malaria
parasites have become resistant to some of the
better and less dangerous medicines, so other
medicine must be used. It is important to learn
from the Health Department or at a health center
what medicines work best in your area.

In many areas, **chloroquine** is still the most
useful medicine for malaria. To completely get
rid of some kinds of malaria, it may be necessary
to take **primaquine** together with chloroquine.

Pyrimethamine is mostly used for suppression
of malaria.

Chloroquine (familiar brand name: *Aralen*)

Name:_____

Often comes in:
250 mg. tablets) both have
of chloroquine   150 mg. of   Price:____ for___
phosphate; or   **chloroquine**
150 mg. tablets   **base**
of chloroquine
sulfate

injections, 200 mg. in 5 ml.   Price:____ for___

Dosage for chloroquine by mouth:
—tablets with 150 mg. of chloroquine base—

For treatment of someone who has acute attacks of malaria:

Give chloroquine tablets once daily for 3 days:

Each day give:

>   adults: 4 tablets (600 mg. of base)
>   children 10 to 15 years: 3 tablets (450 mg. base)
>   children 6 to 9 years: 2 tablets (300 mg. base)
>   children 3 to 5 years: 1 tablet (150 mg. base)
>   children 1 to 2 years: ½ tablet (75 mg. base)
>   babies under 1 year: ¼ tablet (37 mg. base)

For suppression of malaria with chloroquine:

Give each week:

>   adults: 2 tablets (300 mg. of base)
>   children 8 to 12 years: 1 tablet (150 mg. base)
>   children 3 to 7 years: ½ a tablet (75 mg. base)
>   children under 3: ¼ a tablet (37 mg. base)

For semi-suppression of malaria give the same dose as for suppression, but only once every 2 or 4 weeks.

For treatment of liver abscess caused by amebas:

>   adults: 3 or 4 tablets (500 mg. of base) twice daily for 2 days and then 1½ or 2 tablets (250 mg. of base) daily for 3 weeks.
>   Give children less, according to age or weight.

Injections of chloroquine: when to give them:

Injections of chloroquine should be given only rarely, in cases of great emergency. If a person who shows signs of malaria, or lives in an area where there is a lot of malaria, is vomiting, having fits, (convulsions), or showing other signs of meningitis (see p. 185), he may have cerebral malaria (malaria in the brain). **Inject chloroquine at once.** Great care must be taken to **be sure the dose is right.**

Dosage for injecting chloroquine—(4 mg./kg.): —an ampule of 200 mg. in 5 ml.—

Give the dose once only (inject ½ into each buttock):

>   adults: 200 mg. (the entire ampule of 5 ml.)
>   children: inject 0.1 ml. (1/10 ml.) for each kg. the child weighs. (A one-year-old baby who weighs 10 kg. would get 1 ml.)

The dose may be repeated 1 day later if improvement has not taken place. Try to get medical help.

Primaquine

Name:_____ price:_____ for_____

Often comes in: tablets with 26.3 mg. of primaquine phosphate, which contains 15 mg. of primaquine base

Primaquine is added to chloroquine treatment to keep some kinds of malaria from coming back. It does not work well by itself for acute attacks.

Dosage for primaquine:

Give once a day for 14 days.

In each dose give:

>   adults: 1 tablet (15 mg. base)
>   children 8 to 12 years: ½ tablet (7 mg. base)
>   children 3 to 7 years: ¼ tablet (4 mg. base)

Pyrimethamine

Name:_____ price:_____ for_____

Often comes in: 25 mg. tablets

Used mostly for suppression of malaria.

Dosage of pyrimethamine **for suppression** of malaria:

Each week give:

>   adults: 1 tablet (25 mg.)
>   children 8 to 12 years: 1 tablet (25 mg.)
>   children 3 to 7 years: ½ a tablet (12 mg.)
>   children under 2 years: ¼ a tablet (6 mg.)

For semi-suppression of malaria give the same dose, but only once every 2 or 4 weeks.

WARNING: Too much pyrimethamine is dangerous. Keep it where children cannot reach it.

FOR AMEBAS AND GIARDIA

In diarrhea or dysentery caused by amebas there are usually frequent stools with much mucus and sometimes blood. Often there are gut cramps, but little or no fever. Amebic dysentery can be treated with **metronidazole, tetracycline** (see p. 353), or better, both together. Unfortunately, metronidazole is very expensive. A less expensive (but not as good) medicine, which can be used together with tetracycline, is **diiodohydroxyquin.**

In order to kill all the amebas in the gut, very long (2 to 3 weeks) and expensive treatment is necessary. It often makes more sense to stop giving medicines when the person has no more symptoms and then let the body defend itself against the few amebas that are left. This is especially true in areas where the chance of getting a new infection is high.

In diarrhea caused by giardia the stools are often yellow and frothy, but without blood or mucus. Metronidazole is the best medicine, but **quinacrine** is cheaper.

Tetracycline (see p. 353)

Metronidazole (familiar brand name: *Flagyl*)

Name:_____

Often comes in:
    tablets of 250 mg.   Price:____ for____
    vaginal inserts, 500 mg.   Price:____ for____

Metronidazole is useful for gut infections caused by amebas and giardia, and also for vaginal infections caused by trichomonas.

CAUTION: Metronidazole should be used only for severe infections, as there is suspicion that it may, in rare cases, cause cancer. **Do not drink alcoholic drinks when taking metronidazole,** as this causes severe nausea.

Dosage for **amebic dysentery**—(25 to 50 mg./kg./ day):—250 mg. tablets—

Give metronidazole 3 times a day for 5 days.

In each dose give:
    adults: 500 to 750 mg. (2 to 3 tablets)
    children 8 to 12 years: 500 mg. (2 tablets)
    children 4 to 7 years: 375 mg. (1½ tablets)
    children 2 to 3 years: 250 mg. (1 tablet)
    children under 2 years: 80 to 125 mg. (1/3 to ½ tablet)

Dosage for **giardia** infection:

Give metronidazole 3 times a day for 5 days.

In each dose give:
    adults: 250 mg. (1 tablet)
    children 8 to 12 years: 250 mg. (1 tablet)
    children 3 to 7 years: 125 mg. (½ a tablet)
    children under 3 years: 62 mg. (¼ a tablet)

Dosage for **trichomonas** infections of the vagina:

The woman should take 8 tablets (2 gm.) in one single dose, and should put an insert inside her vagina twice daily for 10 to 20 days. If the infection returns, both the woman and man should take 8 tablets at the same time. (He should do this even if he has no symptoms.)

WARNING: Only take metronidazole by mouth for trichomonas infections of the vagina if the infection is very severe.

Quinacrine (mepacrine)
(familiar brand name: *Atabrine*)

Name:_____ price:_____ for____

Often comes in: 100 mg. tablets

Quinacrine can be used in treating giardia, malaria, and tapeworm, but is not the best medicine for any of these. It is used because it is cheap.

Dosage of quinacrine for treating **giardia:**

Give quinacrine 3 times a day for a week.

In each dose give:
    adults: one 100 mg. tablet
    children under 10 years: 50 mg. (½ a tablet)

Dosage of quinacrine for treating **tapeworm:**

(Half an hour before giving quinacrine, give an antihistamine like **promethazine** to help prevent vomiting.)

Give 1 large dose only:

    adults: 1 gm. (10 tablets)
    children 8 to 12 years: 600 mg. (6 tablets)
    children 3 to 7 years: 400 mg. (4 tablets)

Diiodohydroxyquin
(familiar brand name: *Diodoquin*)

Name:_____

Often comes in:
    tablets of 650 mg.   Price:_____ for___
    vaginal inserts   Price:_____ for___

Diiodohydroxyquin can be used to treat mild infections of the gut caused by amebas, or following treatment with tetracycline or metronidazole. Diiodohydroxyquin does no good for prevention and should not be used for long periods of time, because it may cause eye damage. **Iodochlorhydroxyquin** (*Entero-Vioform*, 250 mg. tablets) can be used instead, but the risk of eye damage is greater.

Dosage of diiodohydroxyquin for treating amebas
    (40 mg./kg./day):
    —tablets of 650 mg.—

Give the medicine 3 times (mild disease) or 4 times (more severe disease) a day. For complete treatment take for 10 to 14 days.

In each dose give:

    adults: 1 tablet (650 mg.)
    children 8 to 12 years: ½ tablet (325 mg.)
    children 3 to 7 years: ¼ tablet (160 mg.)
    children under 3 years: do not give

Dosage of diiodohydroxyquin vaginal inserts for treating trichomonas infections of the vagina:

Put an insert deep inside the vagina once or
    twice a day for 4 to 8 weeks.

FOR VAGINAL INFECTIONS

Vaginal discharge, itching, and discomfort can be caused by different infections, the most common of which are **trichomonas** and **thrush** (yeast infection or moniliasis). Cleanliness and vinegar-and-water douches (vaginal washes) help any vaginal infection. Specific medicines are also listed below.

White vinegar for vaginal douches (washes):

Price:_____ for_____

Mix 2 or 3 tablespoons of white vinegar in a liter of boiled water. As shown on page 241, give 1 douche a day for a week, then 1 every other day. It helps to give a douche before using a vaginal cream or insert.

Metronidazole, tablets to be taken by mouth and vaginal inserts (see p. 359):

    For trichomonas infections of the vagina.

Diiodohydroxyquin vaginal inserts (see this page):

    For trichomonas infections of the vagina.

Nystatin, tablets, cream, and vaginal inserts
(see p. 362):

    For moniliasis (yeast infection) of the vagina.

Gentian violet (crystal violet) 1 percent solution
(see p. 361):

Price:_____ for_____

For treatment of moniliasis (yeast infection) and other infections of the vulva and vagina.

    Paint on gentian violet once daily for 3 weeks.

Sulfathiazole vaginal inserts

Price:_____ for_____

For treatment of bacterial infections *(Hemophilus)* of the vagina.

    Put 1 insert deep inside the vagina twice a day.

FOR SKIN PROBLEMS

Washing the hands and bathing frequently with soap and water helps prevent many infections, both of the skin and of the gut. Wounds should be carefully washed with soap and boiled water before they are closed or bandaged.

Frequent scrubbing with soap and water is often the only treatment necessary for dandruff, cradle cap (seborrhea), pimples, mild impetigo, as well as for minor ringworm, tinia, and other fungus infections of the skin or scalp. For these purposes it is better if the soap has in it an antiseptic like **hexachlorophene,** such as *Phisohex* or *Gamophen;* or like iodine, such as *Betadine.*

Soap with hexachlorophene

Name:_____

Often comes in: bars   Price:____ for____
          liquid   Price:____ for____

Use as described above. Health workers who wash their hands daily with hexachlorophene soap have cleaner hands (fewer bacteria). It is good to wash babies with hexachlorophene soap **occasionally,** but daily use for a long time may cause nerve damage to babies.

Sulfur

Often comes as a yellow powder.
                    Price:____ for____
Also comes in many skin lotions and ointments.

Sulfur is useful for many skin problems:

1. To avoid or discourage ticks, mites, chiggers, jiggers, and fleas. Before going into fields or forests where these are common, dust the skin—especially legs or ankles, wrists, waist, and neck—with sulfur.
2. To help treat scabies, burrowing fleas, mites, and tiny ticks in or on the skin. Make an ointment: Mix 1 part of sulfur with 10 parts of petrolatum *(Vaseline)* or lard, and smear this on the skin (see p. 199).
3. For ringworm, tinia, and other fungus infections, use the same ointment, 3 or 4 times a day, or a lotion of sulfur and vinegar (see p. 205).
4. For cradle cap (seborrhea) and severe dandruff, the same ointment can be used, or the scalp can be dusted with sulfur.

Gentian violet (crystal violet)

Often comes as dark blue crystals.
                    Price:____ for____

Gentian violet helps fight certain skin infections, including impetigo and sores with pus. It can also be used to treat thrush (moniliasis) or yeast infection in the mouth, the vulva, and in skin folds.

Dissolve a teaspoon of gentian violet in half a liter of water. This makes a 2 percent solution. Paint it on the skin or in the mouth or the vulva.

Potassium permanganate

Comes in dark red crystals. Price:____ for____

This makes a good antiseptic (germ-killing) solution for soaking infected sores. Put a pinch of the crystals in a liter of water (1 part potassium permanganate to 1000 parts of water).

Antibiotic ointments

Name:_____ price:_____ for_____

These are expensive and often do no more good than gentian violet. However, they do not color the skin or clothes and are of use in treating minor skin infections like impetigo. A good ointment is one that contains a neomycin/polymyxin combination (for example *Neosporin* or *Polysporin*). An ointment of tetracycline can also be used.

Cortico-steroid ointments or lotions

Name:_____ price:_____ for_____

These can be used for 'weeping' or itching skin irritations caused by insect bites, by touching certain 'poisonous' plants, and other things. They are also useful in treating severe eczema (see p. 216) and psoriasis (p. 216). Use 3 or 4 times a day.

Petroleum jelly (petrolatum, *Vaseline*)

Price:_____ for____

Useful for preparing ointments or dressings in the treatment of: scabies (see p. 199 and 363)
                            ringworm (p. 362)
                            itching from pinworm (p. 141)
                            burns (p. 96 and 97)
                            chest wound (p. 91)

FOR RINGWORM
AND OTHER FUNGUS INFECTIONS

Many fungus infections are very difficult to get rid of. For complete control, treatment must be continued for days or weeks after the signs disappear. Bathing and cleanliness are also important.

Ointments with undecylenic, benzoic, or salicylic acid

Name:_____ price:_____ for_____

Ointments with these acids can be used to treat ringworm, tinia of the scalp, and other fungus infections of the skin. Often they are (or can be) combined with sulfur. Ointments with salicylic acid and sulfur can also be used for cradle cap (seborrhea).

Ointments and lotions are cheaper if you make them yourself. Mix 3 parts of salicylic acid and/or 6 parts of benzoic acid with 100 parts of *Vaseline,* petrolatum, mineral oil, lard, or 40 percent alcohol (or rum). Rub onto skin 3 or 4 times a day.

Sulfur and vinegar

A lotion of 5 parts of sulfur to 100 parts vinegar helps fight fungus infections of the skin. Let dry on the skin. Also, an ointment can be made using 1 part sulfur to 10 parts of lard.

Sodium thiosulfate ('hypo')

Comes as white crystals, sold in photographic supply stores as 'hypo'.   Price:_____ for_____

Used for **tinea versicolor** infections of the skin (see p. 206).

Dissolve a tablespoon of 'hypo' in ½ cup of water and spread it on the skin with a piece of cotton or cloth. Then rub the skin with a piece of cotton soaked in vinegar. Do this twice daily until the 'spots' go away and then once every 2 weeks to keep them from coming back.

Griseofulvin

Name:_____ price:_____ for_____

Often comes in: tablets or capsules of 250 or 500 mg.

Preparations in 'microsized' particles are best.

This is very expensive and should be used only for severe fungus infections of the skin and deep tinia infections of the scalp.

Dosage of griseofulvin—(15 mg./kg./day):
—for microsized particle form, 250 mg. capsules—

Give once a day.

adults: 500 to 1000 mg. (2 to 4 capsules)
children 8 to 12 years: 250 to 500 mg. (1 to 2 capsules)
children 3 to 7 years: 125 to 250 mg. (½ to 1 capsule)
children under 3 years: 125 mg. (½ capsule)

Gentian violet—for thrush (yeast infection) (see p. 361)

Nystatin—for thrush

Name:_____ price:_____ for_____

Comes in: solutions, dusting powders, vaginal tablets, and ointments

Used for treating thrush (moniliasis) in the mouth, the vagina, or in the folds of the skin. It does no good for any other infections.

Dosage for nystatin—the same for children and adults:

Thrush in the mouth: put 1 ml. of solution in the mouth and hold it there for at least 1 minute before swallowing. Do this 3 or 4 times a day.

Yeast infection on the skin: keep as dry as possible and use nystatin dusting powder or ointment 3 or 4 times a day.

Yeast infection in the vulva or vagina: put dusting powder inside the vagina twice daily or a vaginal tablet inside the vagina nightly for 2 weeks.

FOR SCABIES AND LICE:
INSECTICIDES

Gamma benzene hexachloride (lindane)
(familar brand names: *Kwell, Gammezane*)

Name:_____ price:_____ for_____

This comes in expensive preparations for people and cheap preparations for animals which work just as well for people. Lindane for a sheep or cattle dip is quite cheap, but it often comes concentrated in a 15 percent solution and must be diluted to 1 percent. Mix 1 part of 15 percent lindane concentrate with 15 parts of water or *Vaseline,* and use on the skin following the instructions on page 199. For head lice, see page 200. Make only one application; if necessary repeat once more a week later.

Benzyl benzoate, cream or lotion

Name:_____ price:_____ for_____

Use the same as gamma benzene hexachloride cream or lotion.

Sulfur in petroleum jelly *(Vaseline)* or lard

Use this for scabies if you cannot get the above.

Mix 1 part of sulfur in 20 parts of *Vaseline,* mineral oil, or lard to form a 5 percent sulfur ointment.

FOR WORMS

Medicines by themselves are not enough to get rid of worm infections for very long. Guidelines of personal and public cleanliness must also be followed. When 1 person in the family has worms, it is wise to treat the whole family.

Piperazine—for Ascaris (roundworm) and Enterobius (threadworm or pinworm)

Name:_____

Comes as piperazine citrate, tartrate, hydrate, adipate, or phosphate
Often comes in:
    500 mg. tablets   Price:____ for____
    Mixture, 500 mg. in 5 ml.   Price:____ for____

One large dose is given for Ascaris. Smaller doses every day for a week are given for Enterobius. There are few side effects.

Dosage of piperazine for **roundworm** (Ascaris)—(120 mg./kg.)
    —500 mg. tablets or mixture with 500 mg. in 5 ml.—

Give 1 dose only.
    adults: 4 gm. (8 tablets or 8 teaspoons)
    children 8 to 12 years: 3 gm. (6 tablets or 6 teaspoons)
    children 3 to 7 years: 2 gm. (4 tablets or 4 teaspoons)
    children 1 to 3 years: 1½ gm. (3 tablets or 3 teaspoons)
    babies under 1 year: 1 gm. (2 tablets or 2 teaspoons)

Dosage of piperazine for **pinworm** (Enterobius)—(40 mg./kg./day):

Give 2 doses daily for a week.

adults: 1 gm. (2 tablets or 2 teaspoons)
children 8 to 12 years: 750 mg. (1½ tablets or 1½ teaspoons)
children 3 to 7 years: 500 mg. (1 tablet or 1 teaspoon)
children under 3 years: 250 mg. (½ tablet or ½ teaspoon)

Thiabendazole—for many different worm infections

Name:_____ price:_____ for_____

Often comes as: 500 mg. tablets or mixture with 1 gm. in 5 ml.

This can be used to treat hookworm, whipworm (Trichuris), and another worm called Strongyloides. It works for roundworm and pinworm, but piperazine has fewer side effects. It may do some good in cases of trichinosis.

CAUTION: Thiabendazole may cause Ascaris (roundworm) to crawl up the throat. This can block breathing. Therefore, if you suspect a person has Ascaris in addition to other worms, it is wise to treat first with piperazine before giving thiabendazole.

Side effects: Thiabendazole often causes tiredness, a sick feeling, and sometimes vomiting.

Dosage for thiabendazole—(50 mg./kg./day):
    —500 mg. tablets or mixture with 1 gm. in 5 ml.—

Give twice a day for 3 days. Tablets should be chewed.

In each dose give:
    adults: 1500 mg. (3 tablets or 1½ teaspoons)
    children 8 to 12 years: 1000 mg. (2 tablets or 1 teaspoon)
    children 3 to 7 years: 500 mg. (1 tablet or ½ teaspoon)
    children under 3 years: 250 mg. (½ tablet or ¼ teaspoon)

Tetrachlorethylene (TCE)—for hookworm

Name:_____ price:_____ for____

Comes as a clear liquid or in gelatin capsules

This is the cheapest medicine for hookworm, but it causes the most *side effects* (pain in the belly and headache). It should not be given to pregnant women or to children who are greatly malnourished or anemic, until their condition is improved. Always give on an empty stomach.

(TCE can also be used to treat liver flukes. Dose is the same as for hookworm.)

WARNING: Keep TCE in a dark bottle with the lid on tight. Sunlight can make it poisonous. Take great care to be sure the dose is right.

Always treat for Ascaris **before** using TCE for hookworm.

Dosage of TCE—(0.12 ml./kg. but never more than 5 ml.):

Give 1 dose by mouth. Two days later give another dose.

In each dose give:

adults: 1 teaspoonful (5 ml.)
children: ½ ml. for each 5 kg. the child weighs, but never more than 4 ml. (a little less than a teaspoon)

Mebendazole *(Vermox)*

Name:_____ price:_____ for____

Often comes in: tablets of 100 mg.

A new medicine similar to Thiabendazole, but better. Works against hookworm, whipworm, Strongyloides, roundworm, and pinworm (threadworm). Works well for mixed infections. When treating heavy worm infections there may be some gut pain or diarrhea, but mebendazole does not cause vomiting or the severe side effects common when taking Thiabendazole. With mebendazole, roundworm need not be treated first with other medicine.

WARNING: Do not give mebendazole to pregnant women or children under 2 years old.

Dosage of mebendazole—using 100 mg. tablets—

Give the same amount to children and adults.

For pinworm: one tablet one time only.

For roundworm (Ascaris), whipworm (Trichuris), hookworm, and Strongyloides: one tablet twice a day (morning and evening) for 3 days (6 tablets in all).

Bephenium—for hookworm

Name:_____ price:_____ for____

Often comes in: packets of 5 gm.

Bephenium should not be given to pregnant women, or to children who are very anemic or malnourished, until they are better. It works fairly well for Ascaris as well as hookworm, and the person need not be treated for Ascaris first.

Dosage of Bephenium for hookworm—using packet of 5 gm.:

Give 1 dose only, by mouth.

adults and children over 5 years: 5 gm. (1 packet)
children under 5 years old: 2½ gm. (½ packet)

FOR TAPEWORM

Niclosamide *(Yomesan)*—for tapeworm infection

Name:_____ price:_____ for____

Often comes in: chewable tablets of 500 mg.

Niclosamide is probably the best medicine for tapeworm and has the least side effects, but is expensive. It works against most kinds of tapeworm in the gut, but not against cysts outside the gut.

Dosage of niclosamide for tapeworm—500 mg. tablets:

Chew well and swallow 1 dose only. Do not eat before or until 2 hours after taking the medicine.

adults and children over 8 years: 2 gm. (4 tablets)
children 2 to 8 years: 1 gm. (2 tablets)
children under 2 years: 500 mg. (1 tablet)

Dichlorophen *(Antiphen)*—for tapeworm

Name:_____ price:_____ for____

Often comes in: tablets of 500 mg.

A fairly safe medicine. May cause diarrhea, sometimes vomiting and gut cramps, and rarely jaundice.

Dosage of dichlorophen for tapeworm— (70 mg./kg.):

Take once only, 2 hours before breakfast.

adults: 3 to 4 gm. (6 to 8 tablets)
children 8 to 12 years: 2 gm. (4 tablets)
children 4 to 7 years: 1½ gm. (3 tablets)
children 2 to 4 years: 500 mg. to 1 gm.
(1 or 2 tablets)

Quinacrine (mepacrine, _Atabrine_)—for tapeworm, (see p. 359).

FOR SCHISTOSOMIASIS
(BILHARZIA, SCHISTOSOMA HAEMATOBIUM)

Niridazole _(Ambilhar)_—for schistosomiasis

Name:_____ price:_____ for___

Often comes in: 500 mg. tablets

Niridazole causes side effects such as headache, dizziness, nervousness, vomiting, gut cramps, or diarrhea in most persons, but treatment need not be stopped because of them. It also colors the urine brown.

Dosage of Niridazole for schistosomiasis—
(25 mg./kg./day):

Give twice a day by mouth for a week.

In each dose give:

adults: 750 mg. (1½ tablets)
children 8 to 12 years: 500 mg. (1 tablet)
children 3 to 7 years: 250 mg. (½ tablet)
children under 3 years: 125 mg. (¼ tablet)

FOR RIVER BLINDNESS

Diethylcarbamazine _(Hetrazan, Banocide)_

Name:_____ price:_____ for___

To avoid severe damage to the eyes it is important to start with a low daily dose of 1½ mg. for adults and gradually increase the amount to 150 mg. 3 times a day. Give the full dose for 2 to 3 weeks. Use of the medicine may result in severe allergic reactions. These can be partly controlled with antihistamines. Diethylcarbamazine kills the young worms but not the adults.

The medicine should be used only under the direction of an experienced health worker.

Suramin _(Naphuride, Bayer 205, Antrypol, Germanin)_

Name:_____ price:_____ for___

This is more effective than diethylcarbamazine in killing adult worms but sometimes poisons the kidneys. If swelling of the feet or other signs of urinary poisoning occur, stop using this medicine. Persons with kidney problems should not use it.

Suramin must be given intravenously and should only be used with the assistance of an experienced health worker. For adults inject 1 gm. of Suramin in 10 ml. of distilled water **once a week** for 5 to 7 weeks. Start with a small test dose of 200 mg. Treat allergic reactions with antihistamines.

FOR THE EYES

Antibiotic eye ointment—
for 'pink eye' (conjunctivitis)

Useful examples: oxytetracycline or chlortetracycline eye ointments

Name:_____ price:_____ for___

These eye ointments can be used for 'pink eye' caused by bacteria and for trachoma. For complete cure of trachoma, tetracycline should be taken by mouth also (see p. 353).

For an eye ointment to do any good, it must be put **inside** the eyelid, not outside. Use it 3 or 4 times a day.

Silver nitrate eye drops, 1 percent—to protect eyes of newborn babies

Name:_____ price:_____ for___

At birth, put a drop of 1 percent silver nitrate in each eye. This protects the baby's eyes against gonorrhea. All babies should receive this protection.

FOR PAIN: ANALGESICS

Note: There are many different kinds of pain medicine, many of which are dangerous (especially those containing **dipyrone**). Use only those you are sure are relatively safe like **aspirin** and **acetaminophen.** For a stronger painkiller see **codeine** (p. 369).

Aspirin (acetylsalicylic acid)

Often comes in:
300 mg. (5 grain) tablets Price:_____ for___
75 mg. (1¼ grain) tablets for children
(or 'child's aspirin') Price:_____ for___

Aspirin is a very useful, low-cost 'painkiller' or analgesic. It helps to calm pain, lower fever, and reduce inflammation. It also helps a little to calm cough and reduce itching.

Many different medicines sold for pain, arthritis, or colds contain aspirin, but they are more expensive and often do not do any more good than aspirin alone.

Risks and Precautions:

1. Do not use aspirin for stomach pain or indigestion. Aspirin is acid and may make the problem worse. For the same reason, **persons with stomach ulcers should never use aspirin.**
2. Aspirin causes stomach pain or 'heartburn' in some persons. To avoid this, take aspirin with milk, a little bicarbonate of soda, or a lot of water—or together with meals.
3. Do not give more than 1 dose of aspirin to a dehydrated person until he begins to urinate well.
4. It is better not to give aspirin to babies under 1 year old or to persons with asthma (this may bring on an attack).
5. Keep aspirin where children cannot reach it. Large amounts can poison them.

Dosage of aspirin—for pain or fever:
—tablets of 300 mg. (5 grains)—

Take once every 4 to 6 hours (or 4 to 6 times a day)

    adults: 1 or 2 tablets (300 to 600 mg.)
    children 8 to 12 years: 1 tablet (300 mg.)
    children 3 to 7 years: ½ tablet (150 mg.)
    children 1 to 2 years old: ¼ tablet (75 mg.)

(Dose may be doubled for severe arthritis or rheumatic fever. Or give 100 mg./kg./day. If ringing of the ears develops, lower the dose.)

—75 mg. 'child's aspirin' tablets—

Give children aspirin 4 times a day:

    children 8 to 12 years: 4 tablets (300 mg.)
    children 3 to 7 years: 2 to 3 tablets (150 to 225 mg.)
    children 1 to 2 years: 1 tablet (75 mg.)
    do not give aspirin to children under 1 year old

Acetaminophen (paracetamol)—for pain and fever

Name:_____ price:_____ for___

Often comes in: 500 mg. tablets
    Also comes in syrups

Acetaminophen is safer for children than aspirin. It does not cause stomach irritation and so can be used instead of aspirin by persons with stomach ulcers.

Dosage of acetaminophen—for pain and fever:
—500 mg. tablets—

Give acetaminophen by mouth 4 times a day.

In each dose give:

    adults: 500 mg. to 1 gm. (1 or 2 tablets)
    children 8 to 12 years: 500 mg. (1 tablet)
    children 3 to 7 years: 250 mg. (½ tablet)
    children 6 months to 2 years: 125 mg.
        (¼ tablet)
    babies under 6 months: 62 mg. (1/8 tablet)

Ergotamine with caffeine *(Cafergot)*—for migraine headache

Name:_____ price:_____ for___

Often comes in: tablets with 1 mg. of ergotamine

Dosage of ergotamine with caffeine for migraine:

    adults: Take 2 tablets at the first sign of a migraine, then 1 tablet every half hour until the pain goes. But do not take more than 6 tablets in all.

WARNING: Do not take this medicine often. Do not take when pregnant.

FOR STOPPING PAIN WHEN CLOSING WOUNDS: ANESTHETICS

Lidocaine *(Xylocaine)*
2 percent (with or without epinephrine)

Name:_____ price:_____ for___

Often comes in: ampules or bottles for injection

Lidocaine can be injected around the edges of a wound before sewing it, to make the area *anesthetic* or numb so it will not hurt.

Inject both into and under the skin at points about 1 cm. apart. Be sure to pull back on the plunger before injecting. Use about 1 ml. of anesthetic for each 2 cm. of skin. If the wound is clean, you can inject into the sides of the wound itself. If the wound is dirty, inject through the skin (after cleaning it) around the wound and then **clean the wound with great care** before closing it.

Use lidocaine with epinephrine for sewing most wounds. The epinephrine makes the numbness last longer and helps control bleeding.

Use lidocaine without epinephrine for wounds on fingers, toes, penis, ears, and nose. This is important because the epinephrine can stop the flow of blood to these areas and cause great damage.

Another use of lidocaine with epinephrine: **For severe nosebleed,** soak a little into some cotton and pack it into the nose. The epinephrine will cause the veins to squeeze shut and help control bleeding.

FOR GUT CRAMPS: ANTISPASMODICS

Belladonna (with or without phenobarbital)

Name:_____ price:_____ for___

Often comes in: tablets with 8 mg. belladonna

There are many different antispasmodic preparations. Most contain belladonna or something like it (atropine, hyoscyamine) and often phenobarbital (phenobarbitone). These medicines should not be used on a regular basis, but can be used occasionally for treatment of pain or cramps (colic) in the stomach or gut. They may help calm the pain of a bladder infection or inflamed gallbladder. They are sometimes useful in the treatment of ulcers.

Dosage for belladonna—for gut cramps:
 —tablets with 8 mg. belladonna—

   adults: 1 tablet, 3 to 6 times a day
   children 8 to 12 years: 1 tablet, 2 or 3 times a day
   children 5 to 7 years: ½ tablet, 2 or 3 times a day
   do not give to children under 5 years

WARNING: These medicines are poisonous if too much is taken. Keep out of reach of children.

Persons with glaucoma should not take medicines that contain belladonna or atropine.

FOR ACID INDIGESTION, HEARTBURN, AND STOMACH ULCERS: ANTACIDS

Aluminum hydroxide with magnesium hydroxide (or trisilicate)

Name:_____ price:_____ for___

Often comes in tablets of 500 to 750 mg., or in mixtures with 300 to 500 mg. in 5 ml.

These can be used occasionally for acid indigestion or heartburn or as a regular part of treatment of a stomach (peptic) ulcer. The most important time to take antacids is 1 hour after meals and at bedtime. Chew 2 or 3 tablets. For severe stomach ulcers, it may be necessary to take 3 to 6 tablets (or teaspoons) every hour.

Sodium bicarbonate (bicarbonate of soda, baking soda)

Comes as a white powder   Price:_____ for___

As an antacid, this should be used in a very limited way, when someone has an occasional stomach upset, with 'heartburn' or acid indigestion. **It should not be used in treating chronic indigestion or stomach (peptic) ulcers.** Although it seems to help at first, it causes the stomach to produce more acid, which soon makes things worse. 'Soda' is also useful for the 'hangover' of a person who has drunk too much alcohol the night before. For this purpose (but not for acid indigestion) it can be taken with aspirin. *Alka-Seltzer* is a combination of sodium bicarbonate and aspirin. As an **occasional** antacid, mix ½ teaspoon of sodium bicarbonate with water and drink it. Do not use often.

For cleaning teeth, baking soda or a mixture of 'soda' and salt, can be used instead of toothpaste (see p. 230).

To prepare **Rehydration Drink** using sodium bicarbonate, see p. 152 and also the next page.

WARNING: Persons with certain heart problems (failure) or with swelling of the feet or face should not take sodium bicarbonate or other products high in sodium (like salt).

FOR DEHYDRATION

Rehydration Mix

Name:_____ price:_____ for____

Often comes in: packets for making 1 liter

Instructions for making Rehydration Drink with ordinary sugar are on page 152.

Health Departments of some countries supply rehydration mix in individual envelopes, for making 1 liter of Rehydration Drink. These mixes contain *glucose,* instead of ordinary sugar, or *sucrose.* Glucose is a simpler form of sugar that is more easily used by the child's body than regular sugar. Glucose also helps the liquid get into the baby's body more quickly. It is especially important to use glucose rather than sucrose if a child has very severe diarrhea or is very malnourished. Standard rehydration mixes also contain potassium salt, which helps balance the ordinary salt.

If you can get both glucose and potassium chloride, make the following Rehydration Drink instead of the one on page 152. Mix:

> boiled water, 1 liter (4 cups)
> glucose powder, 20 gm. or 8 level teaspoons
> ordinary salt (sodium chloride), 2 gm. or ½ level teaspoon
> baking soda (sodium bicarbonate) 2 gm. or ½ level teaspoon
> potassium chloride, 1.5 gm. or 1/3 level teaspoon

If you have glucose, but not potassium chloride, use only half the above amounts of salt and baking soda.

For the treatment of dehydration, see page 152.

FOR HARD STOOLS (CONSTIPATION): LAXATIVES

A discussion of the use and misuse of different laxatives and purges is found on page 15. Laxatives are used far too much. They should be used only **occasionally** to help soften hard, painful stools (constipation). **Never give laxatives to anyone who has diarrhea or gut pain or who is dehydrated.** Do not give laxatives to small children under 2 years old.

Generally the best stool softeners are foods high in roughage or fiber, like bran or cassava. Drinking a lot of liquid and eating lots of fruit also help.

Milk of magnesia (magnesium hydroxide)—laxative and antacid

Name:_____ price:_____ for____

Often comes as a milky solution

Dosage for milk of magnesia:

As an antacid:
adults and older children: ½ to 1 teaspoon 3 or 4 times a day
As a mild laxative give 1 dose at bedtime:
adults and children over 8 years: 1 to 2 tablespoons
children 2 to 7 years: ½ to 1 tablespoon
do not give to children under 2 years old

Epsom salts (magnesium sulfate)—as a laxative and for itching

Name:_____ price:_____ for____

Often comes in white powder or crystals

Dosage for Epsom salts:

As a mild laxative—mix the following amount of Epsom salts with water and drink:
adults: 1 to 2 teaspoons
children 6 to 12 years: ½ to 1 teaspoon
children 2 to 6 years: ¼ to ½ teaspoon
do not give to children under 2 years old

To help stop itching—mix 8 teaspoons of Epsom salts in a liter of water and put on itching skin as cool soaks or compresses.

Mineral oil—as a laxative

Name:_____ price:_____ for____

This is sometimes taken by persons with piles (hemorrhoids) who have hard, painful stools. However, it does not really soften the stools, but merely greases them. Foods high in fiber, like bran or cassava are far better.

Dosage of mineral oil as a laxative:

adults only: 1 or 2 tablespoons by mouth at least 1 hour after the evening meal. Do not take with meals because the oil will rob some of the vitamins from the food.

FOR MILD DIARRHEA: ANTI-DIARRHEA MEDICINE

Kaolin with pectin (Kaopectate)

Name:_____ price:_____ for____

Often comes as a milky mixture

This can be used to make mild diarrhea thicker (less watery) and less troublesome. **It does not cure the cause of the diarrhea and does not help prevent or cure dehydration.** It is never necessary in the treatment of diarrhea, and its common use is a great waste of money. **It should not be given to persons who are very ill or to small children.**

Dosage of kaolin with pectin, for **mild diarrhea only:**
—using a standard mixture such as *Kaopectate*—

Give 1 dose after each stool, or 4 or 5 times a day.

In each dose give:

adults: 2 to 8 tablespoons
children 6 to 12 years: 1 to 2 tablespoons
children 2 to 6 years: 1 to 2 tablespoons
children under 2 years: DO NOT GIVE

FOR STUFFY NOSE

To help open a stuffy nose, often all that is needed is to sniff water with a little salt in it, as described on page 164. Occasionally, decongestant drops may be used, as follows:

Nose drops with ephedrine or phenylephrine (Neo-Synephrine)

Name:_____ price:_____ for____

These may be used for stuffy or 'runny' nose, especially if a person has (or often gets) infection of the inner ear.

Dosage for decongestant nose drops:

Put 1 or 2 drops in each nostril as shown on page 164. Do this 4 times a day. Do not use for many days or make a habit of using these drops.

For nose drops made from ephedrine tablets, see page 370.

FOR COUGH

Cough is the body's method for cleaning the air tubes that go to the lungs and preventing germs and mucus in these tubes from getting into the lungs. Because cough is part of the body's defense, medicines that stop or calm cough sometimes do more harm than good. These **cough-calmers** (or cough *suppressants*) should be used only for irritating, dry coughs that do not let a person sleep. There are other medicines, called **cough-helpers** (or *expectorants*) that help make mucus more liquid and easier to cough up. For most coughs, it is better to use a cough-helper than a cough-calmer.

In truth, both kinds of cough syrups (cough-calmers and cough-helpers) are used far more than they need to be. Most popular cough syrups do little or no good and are a waste of money. **The best and most important cough medicine is water.** Drinking a lot of water and breathing hot water vapors loosens mucus and helps calm cough far better than most cough syrups. For instructions, see page 168. Also, instructions for a homemade cough syrup are given on page 169.

Cough-calmers (cough suppressants): codeine and chloral hydrate

Name:_____ price:_____ for____

Often comes in: cough syrups or liquid (Codeine also comes in tablets, with or without aspirin.)

Codeine is a strong painkiller and also one of the most powerful cough-calmers, but because it is habit-forming (narcotic), it may be hard to get. It often comes in cough syrup combinations or in tablet form. For dosage, follow the instructions that come with the preparation. Less is needed to calm cough than to control pain. To calm cough in adults, 7 to 15 mg. of codeine is usually enough. Children should be given less, according to age or weight (see p. 62).

Chloral hydrate is a sedative that can be given to a child who coughs so much at night he cannot sleep. It is especially useful for whooping cough. Phenobarbital can also be used for whooping cough (see p. 373).

Dosage of chloral hydrate to calm cough:
—using standard chloral cough mixture (Chloral elixir BPC)—

(turn page)

Give up to 4 doses a day, not more.

> children over 2 years old: 10 ml.
> (2 teaspoons)
> babies under 2 years: from 1¼ teaspoon to
> 1½ teaspoon. Smaller babies should be
> given smaller doses.

Cough-helpers (expectorants): potassium iodide

Name:_____ price:_____ for___

Often comes in tablets of 300 mg. or in a standard (saturated) solution

Potassium iodide helps loosen thick mucus in the tubes to the lungs.

Dosage of potassium iodide as a cough-helper:

Give 3 or 4 times a day.

In each dose give:

> adults: one 300 mg. tablet, or 10 drops of
> the solution.
> children should be given less according to
> age or weight (see p. 62)

FOR ASTHMA

To help prevent and manage asthma correctly, see page 167.

Ephedrine

Name:_____ price:_____ for___

Often comes in: tablets of 15 mg. (also 25 mg.)

Ephedrine is useful to control mild attacks of asthma and between severe attacks to prevent them. It works by helping open the tubes that lead into the lungs, so that air can pass more easily. It can also be used when there is difficulty breathing due to pneumonia or bronchitis.

Ephedrine often comes in combination with **theophylline** or **aminophylline,** and sometimes **phenobarbital.** *Tedral* is a well-known brand-name medicine for asthma with this combination, but it is expensive.

Dosage of ephedrine for asthma—
(1 mg./kg./ 3 times a day):
—using 15 mg. tablets—

Give by mouth 3 times a day.

In each dose give:

> adults: 15 to 60 mg. (1 to 4 tablets)
> children 5 to 10 years: 15 to 30 mg.
> (1 or 2 tablets)
> children 1 to 4 years: 15 mg. (1 tablet)
> children under 1 year: DO NOT GIVE

For stuffy nose, nose drops with ephedrine can be used. They can be made by dissolving 1 tablet in a teaspoon of water.

Theophylline or Aminophylline

Name:_____ price:_____ for___

Often comes in: tablets and syrups of different strengths

For controlling asthma and preventing attacks

Dosage—(3 to 5 mg./kg. every 6 hours):

Using 100 mg. tablets

> adults: 2 tablets every 6 hours
> children 7 to 12 years: 1 tablet every 6
> hours
> children under 7 years: ½ tablet every 6
> hours
> babies: DO NOT GIVE

In severe cases or if asthma is not controlled with the above dosage, double this dosage may be given, but no more.

Adrenaline (epinephrine, *Adrenalin*)

Name:_____ price:_____ for___

Often comes in: ampules of 1 mg. in 1 ml.

Adrenaline should be used for:

1. **severe attacks of asthma** when there is trouble breathing
2. **severe allergic reactions** or allergic shock due to penicillin injections, tetanus antitoxin, or other antitoxins made from horse serum (see p. 70).

Dosage of adrenaline for asthma or allergic shock:
—using ampules of 1 mg. in 1 ml. of liquid—

First count the pulse (in the case of asthma). Then inject:

> adults: ½ ml.
> children 7 to 12 years: 1/3 ml.
> children 1 to 6 years: ¼ ml.
> children under 1 year: DO NOT GIVE

If needed, a second dose can be given after half an hour, and a third dose 2 hours later. Do not give more than 3 doses. If the pulse goes up by more than 30 beats per minute after the first injection, do not give another dose.

In using adrenaline, be careful never to give more than the recommended amount.

FOR ALLERGIC REACTIONS
AND VOMITING:
THE ANTIHISTAMINES

Antihistamines are medicines that affect the body in several ways:

1. They help calm or prevent allergic reactions, such as itchy rashes or lumps on the skin, hives, 'hay fever', and allergic shock.
2. They help prevent or control motion sickness or vomiting.
3. They often cause sleepiness (sedation). Avoid doing dangerous work or operating machines when taking antihistamines.

Promethazine *(Phenergan)* and **diphenhydramine** *(Benadryl)* are strong antihistamines that cause a lot of sleepiness. **Dimenhydrinate** *(Dramamine)* is similar to diphenhydramine and is most used for motion sickness. However, for vomiting due to other causes, promethazine often works better. **Chlorpheniramine** is a less expensive antihistamine and causes less sleepiness. For this reason, it is sometimes best to use chlorpheniramine to calm itching in the daytime. Promethazine is useful at night because it encourages sleep at the same time that it calms the itching.

There is no proof that the antihistamines do any good for the common cold. They are often used more than they need to be. They should not be used much.

Generally antihistamines should **not** be used for asthma, because they make the mucus thicker and can make breathing more difficult.

One antihistamine is all that is usually needed in a medical kit. Promethazine is a good choice. Because it is not always available, doses for other antihistamines are also given.

As a general rule, antihistamines are best given by mouth. Injections should be used only to help control severe vomiting or before giving antitoxins (for tetanus, snakebite, etc.) when there is special danger of allergic shock.

Promethazine *(Phenergan)*

Name:_____

Often comes in:
    tablets of 12.5 mg.   Price:_____ for___
    injections—ampules of 25 mg. in 1 ml.
                     Price:_____ for___

Dosage of promethazine—(1mg./kg./day):
    —using tablets of 12.5 mg.—

Give by mouth 2 times a day.

In each dose give:

    adults: 25 to 50 mg. (2 to 4 tablets)
    children 7 to 12 years: 12.5 to 25 mg.
       (1 or 2 tablets)
    children 2 to 6 years: 6 to 12 mg.
       (½ to 1 tablet)
    babies 1 year old: 4 mg. (1/3 tablet)
    babies under 1 year: 3 mg. (¼ tablet)

    —using intramuscular (IM) injections, 25 mg. in a ml.—

Inject once, and again in 2 to 4 hours, if necessary.

In 1 dose inject:

    adults: 25 to 50 mg. (1 to 2 ml.)
    children 7 to 12 years: 12.5 to 25 mg.
       (½ to 1 ml.)
    children under 7 years: 6 to 12 mg.
       (¼ to ½ ml.)
    babies under 1 year: 2.5 mg. (0.1 ml.)

Diphenhydramine *(Benadryl)*

Name:_____ price:_____ for___

Often comes in: ampules with 10 mg. in each ml.

Dosage of diphenhydramine—(5 mg./kg./day):

Inject once, and again in 2 to 4 hours if necessary

    adults: 30 to 50 mg. (3 to 5 ml.)
    children: 10 to 30 mg., depending on size
       (1 to 3 ml.)
    babies: 5 mg. (½ ml.)

Chlorpheniramine

Name:_____ price:_____ for___

Often comes in: 4 mg. tablets (also tablets of other sizes, syrups, etc.)

Dosage for chlorpheniramine:

Take 1 dose 3 or 4 times a day.

In each dose give:

adults: 4 mg. (1 tablet)
children under 12: 2 mg. (½ tablet)
babies: 1 mg. (¼ tablet)

Dimenhydrinate *(Dramamine)*

Name:_____ price:_____ for___

Often comes in: 50 mg. tablets; also syrups with
12.5 mg. in a teaspoon; also suppositories to
put up the anus

This is sold mostly for motion sickness, but can
be used like other antihistamines to calm allergic
reactions and to encourage sleep.

Dosage of dimenhydrinate:

Take up to 4 times a day.

In each dose give:

adults: 50 to 100 mg. (1 or 2 tablets)
children 7 to 12 years of age: 25 to 50 mg.
(½ to 1 tablet)
children 2 to 6 years: 12 to 25 mg. (¼ to
½ tablet)
children under 2 years: 6 to 12 mg. (1/8 to
¼ tablet)

ANTITOXINS

WARNING:
All antitoxins made from horse serum, such as
tetanus antitoxin and the antivenins for snakebite
and scorpion sting, run a risk of causing a
dangerous allergic reaction (allergic shock, see
p. 70). Before you inject an antitoxin, **always have
Adrenalin ready in case of an emergency.** In persons
who are allergic, or who have been given any kind
of antitoxin made of horse serum before, it is a
good idea to inject an antihistamine like
promethazine *(Phenergan)* or diphenhydramine
(Benadryl) 15 minutes before giving the antitoxin.

Scorpion antitoxin or antivenin

Name:_____ price:_____ for___

Often comes *lyophilized* (in powdered form) for
injection

Different antivenins are produced for scorpion
sting in different parts of the world. In Mexico,
Antialacrán Myn is produced by Laboratorios Myn
in México, D.F.

Antivenins for scorpion sting should be used
only in those areas where there are dangerous or
deadly kinds of scorpions. Antivenins are usually
needed only when a small child is stung, especially
if stung on the main upper part of the body or
head. To do most good, the antivenin should be
injected as soon as possible after the child has been
stung.

Antivenins usually come with full instructions.
Follow them carefully. Small children often need
more antivenin than larger children. Two or 3 vials
may be necessary.

Most scorpions are not dangerous to adults.
Because the antivenin itself has some danger in its
use, it is usually better not to give it to adults.

Snakebite antivenin or antitoxin

Name:_____ price:_____ for___

Often comes in: bottles or kits for injection

Antivenins, or medicines that protect the body
against poisons, have been developed for the bites
of poisonous snakes in many parts of the world. If
you live where people are sometimes bitten or
killed by poisonous snakes, find out what
antivenins are available, **get them ahead of time,**
and keep them on hand.

The following are a few of the products sold
in different parts of the world:

North America: *Polyvalent Crotalid Antivenin.*
Through Wyeth Laboratories. For rattlesnakes
and other pit vipers.

Mexico and Central America: *Suero Anticrotálico*
(rattlesnakes) and *Suero Antiviperino* (rattlesnakes,
pit vipers, fer de lance, and many other poisonous
snakes). Through Laboratorios Myn, México, D.F.

Thailand: Specific antivenins for different snakes.
Through the Red Cross Pasteur Institute, Bangkok.

India: A polyvalent antivenin (for different snakes).
Through Hoffkins Institute, Bombay.

Ethiopia: Polyvalent antivenin.
From Behringwerke Laboratories.

Egypt: Polyvalent antivenin.
Available only through government.

Instructions for the use of snakebite antivenins usually come with the kit. Study them **before** you need to use them. The bigger the snake, or the smaller the person, the larger the amount of antivenin needed. Often 2 or more vials are necessary. To be most helpful, antivenin should be injected as soon as possible after the bite.

Be sure to take the necessary precautions to avoid allergic shock (see p. 70).

(see p. 70)

Tetanus antitoxin

Name:_____ price:_____ for____

Often comes in: vials of 20-; 40-; and 50-
thousand units

In remote villages where there are people who have not been vaccinated against tetanus, the medical kit should have tetanus antitoxin in at least 50,000 units. In some countries there is a lyophilized (powdered) form that can be mixed with sterile water for injection and does not need refrigeration (Laboratorios Myn, México, D.F.).

If a person develops the signs of tetanus, inject 50,000 units of tetanus antitoxin. The full amount should be given within a period of a few minutes. Give it in many intramuscular injections in the large muscles of the body (buttocks and thighs). Or it can be given intravenously if someone knows how. If the person suffers from asthma or other allergies, or has ever received any kind of antitoxin made with horse serum, give an injection of antihistamine such as promethazine 15 minutes before injecting the antitoxin.

The signs of tetanus usually continue to get worse in spite of treatment with antitoxin. The other measures of treatment described on page 184 are equally or more important. Begin treatment at once and get medical help fast.

FOR SWALLOWED POISONS

Syrup of Ipecac—to cause vomiting

Name:_____ price:_____ for____

Often comes in: syrup (**Do not use the elixir.**)

To cause vomiting when a person has swallowed a poison. **Do not use if the person has swallowed strong acid, lye, gasoline, or kerosene.**

Dosage of Ipecac:

1 tablespoon for any age. Repeat in half an hour if the person has not vomited.

Powdered charcoal (or activated charcoal)—
for swallowed poison

Price:_____ for____

Charcoal soaks up swallowed poisons and makes them less harmful.

Dosage of powdered charcoal:

1 tablespoon mixed in water.

FOR FITS (CONVULSIONS)

Phenobarbital (phenobarbitone)

Often comes in:
tablets of 15 mg.   Price:_____ for____
ampules of 200 mg. in 1 ml.
                               Price:_____ for____

Phenobarbital can be taken by mouth to help prevent fits (convulsions) and the spasms of tetanus. For the fits or convulsions of epilepsy, sometimes it is necessary to take it in combination with **diphenylhydantoin.** For epilepsy, it is often necessary to continue the medicine for life. The lowest dose that prevents fits should be used. Low doses of phenobarbital can also be used to help lessen the cough of whooping cough or to help control severe vomiting.

WARNING: Too much phenobarbital can slow down or stop breathing. Its action begins slowly and lasts a long time (up to 24 hours, or longer if the person is not urinating). **Be careful not to give too much!**

Dosage of phenobarbital—(3 to 6 mg./kg./day):
—using tablets of 15 mg.—

Give 1 dose by mouth 3 times a day.

In each dose give:

> adults: 30 to 120 mg. (2 to 8 tablets)
> children from 7 to 12 years: 15 to 30 mg.
> (1 or 2 tablets)
> children under 7 years: 15 mg. (1 tablet)

To control the spasms of tetanus, it may be necessary to give twice the dose of phenobarbital shown above—but do not give more than that.

Phenobarbital injections can be given to stop an epileptic fit or the spasms of advanced tetanus.

Dosage for phenobarbital injections:
—using ampules with 200 mg. in 1 ml.—

Give 1 injection, intramuscular

> adults: 200 mg. (1 ml.)
> children 7 to 12 years: 150 mg. (3/4 ml.)
> children 2 to 6 years: 100 mg. (½ ml.)
> children under 2 years: 50 mg. (¼ ml.)

If the fit does not stop, 1 more dose can be given after 15 minutes, but then give no more. For tetanus repeat the dose 3 times a day, and if the spasms are controlled, begin to lower the dose a little at a time.

Diphenylhydantoin (phenytoin, *Dilantin*)

Name:_____ price:_____ for___

Often comes in capsules of 100 mg.

This helps prevent the fits of epilepsy. The medicine must often be taken for life. Sometimes it works better, or in smaller doses, when taken together with phenobarbital. The lowest dosage that prevents fits should be used.

Side effects: Diphenylhydantoin causes swelling and abnormal growth of the gums in some people. If this is severe, another medicine should be used instead.

Dosage of diphenylhydantoin for fits—
(5 mg./kg./day):
—using capsules of 100 mg.—

Start with the following dose once a day:

In each dose take:

> adults: 100 to 300 mg. (1 to 3 capsules)
> children 6 to 12 years: 100 mg. (1 capsule)
> children under 6 years: 50 mg. (½ capsule)

If fits are not completely prevented with this dose, up to twice this dose can be given but not more.

If fits are prevented, try lowering the dose a little at a time, until you find the lowest dose that prevents the fits.

Diazepam *(Valium)*

Name:_____ price:_____ for___

Often comes in: injections of 5 mg. in 1 ml. of liquid

The uses of diazepam are similar to those of phenobarbital, but it is far more expensive. It is included here because sometimes it can be obtained when phenobarbital cannot.

For stopping epileptic fits the adult dose is 5 to 10 mg. Repeat in 2 hours if necessary.

For tetanus give enough to control most of the spasms. Start with 5 mg. (less in children) and give more as needed, but not more than 10 mg. at a time or 50 mg. a day. If necessary, diazepam can be given together with phenobarbital, but care must be taken not to give too much.

Valium may also be useful in cases of extreme fright (hysteria) or anxiety, but its use for these should be very limited.

WARNING: It is safer to inject diazepam in the muscle (IM) than the vein (IV). If you inject in the vein, pick a large vein and inject very slowly.

Too much diazepam can slow down or stop breathing. Be careful not to give too much!

FOR SEVERE BLEEDING AFTER BIRTH (POSTPARTUM HEMORRHAGE)

For information on the right and wrong use of medicines to control bleeding after a woman gives birth, see page 266. As a general rule, **oxytocics (ergonovine, oxytocin, etc.) should only be used to control bleeding after the baby is born.** Their use to speed up labor or to give strength to the mother in labor can be dangerous both to the mother and child. These medicines should never be given until the baby is born, and better, not until the placenta or afterbirth has come out, too. If there is much bleeding before the afterbirth comes out (but after the child has been born), ½ ml. (5 units) of oxytocin can be given by intramuscular injection. **Do not use ergonovine before the afterbirth comes out,** as this may prevent it from coming out.

Pituitrin is similar to oxytocin, but more dangerous, and should never be used except in a case of emergency bleeding when oxytocin and ergonovine are not available.

For bleeding in the newborn child, use vitamin K (see p. 377).

Ergonovine or ergometrine maleate *(Ergotrate, Methergine)*

Name:_____

Often comes in:
 injections of 0.2 mg. in a 1 ml. ampule
  Price:_____ for____
 tablets of 0.2 mg.   Price:_____ for____

To prevent or control severe bleeding **after** the placenta has come out.

Dosage of injectable ergonovine:

For severe bleeding (more than 2 cups) after the afterbirth has come out, give 1 or 2 ampules (0.2 to 0.4 ml.) of ergonovine by intramuscular injection (or 1 ampule by intravenous injection in extreme emergencies). Dose may be repeated if necessary in half an hour to an hour. Change to ergonovine tablets as soon as bleeding is under control.

Dosage for ergonovine by mouth—using tablets of 0.2 mg.:

To prevent severe bleeding after giving birth or to lessen the amount of blood loss (especially in mothers who are anemic) give 1 tablet 3 or 4 times daily, beginning when the afterbirth comes out. If bleeding is heavy, 2 tablets can be given in each dose.

Oxytocin *(Pitocin)*

Name:_____ price:_____ for____

Often comes in: ampules of 10 units in 1 ml.

To help stop severe bleeding of the mother **after** the baby is born and **before** the afterbirth comes out. (Also helps bring the afterbirth out, but should not be used for this unless there is severe bleeding or great delay.)

Dosage of oxytocin for the mother after the baby is born:

Inject ½ ml. (5 units). If severe bleeding continues, inject another ½ ml. in 15 minutes.

FOR PILES (HEMORRHOIDS)

Suppositories for hemorrhoids

Name:_____ price:_____ for____

These are special bullet-shaped tablets to be put up the anus. They help make hemorrhoids smaller and less painful. There are many different preparations. Those that are often most helpful, but are more expensive, contain **cortisone** or a **cortico-steroid.** Special ointments are also available.

Dosage:

Put a suppository up the anus after the daily bowel movement, and another on going to bed.

FOR MALNUTRITION AND ANEMIA

Powdered milk (dried skim milk)

Name:_____ price:_____ for____

Milk is one of the best foods for preventing and treating malnutrition. For babies, mother's milk is best. Milk is rich in body-building proteins and in body-protecting vitamins and minerals. Every village health station or medical kit should contain a supply of powdered milk for treating malnourished children. Dried skim milk is cheapest and keeps best. To allow a baby to make full use of the protein it contains, mix the powdered milk with some sugar and cooking oil.

In 1 cup of boiled water, put:
 12 level teaspoons of powdered milk,
  2 level teaspoons of sugar,
 and 3 teaspoons of oil.

Mixed (or multi) vitamins

Name:_____ price:_____ for____

These come in many forms, but tablets are usually cheapest and work well. Injections of vitamins are rarely necessary, are a waste of money, cause unnecessary pain and sometimes abscesses. Tonics and elixirs often do not have the most important vitamins and are usually too expensive for the good they do. Nutritious food is the best source of vitamins. If additional vitamins are needed, use vitamin tablets.

In some cases of poor nutrition added vitamins may help. Be sure the tablets used contain the important vitamins the person needs (see p. 119).

Using standard tablets, 1 tablet daily is usually enough.

<u>Vitamin A</u>—for night blindness and xerosis

Name:_____ price:_____ for___

Often comes as: capsules of 200,000 units,
60 mg. of retinol
(also in smaller doses)

injections of 100,000 units

WARNING: Too much vitamin A can cause fits.
Do not give too much, and keep out of the reach
of children.

For prevention: In areas where night blindness
and xerosis are common problems in children, they
should eat more yellow fruits and vegetables and
dark green leafy foods as well as animal foods, such
as eggs and liver. Fish liver oil is high in vitamin A.
Or vitamin A capsules can be given. Give 1 capsule
once every 6 months—no more for prevention.

For treatment: Give 1 vitamin A capsule
(200,000 units) by mouth. If eyes are not normal
in a week, give another capsule. In severe cases
give an injection of 100,000 units vitamin A at
once.

<u>Iron sulfate (ferrous sulfate)</u>—for anemia

Name:_____ price:_____ for___

Often comes in: tablets of 200, 300, or 500 mg.
(also in drops, mixtures, and elixirs for
children)

Ferrous sulfate is useful in the treatment of
most anemias. Treatment with ferrous sulfate by
mouth usually takes at least 3 months. If
improvement does not take place, the anemia is
probably caused by something other than lack of
iron. Get medical help. If this is difficult, try
treating with folic acid.

Ferrous sulfate sometimes upsets the stomach
and is best taken with meals. For children under 3
years, a piece of a tablet can be ground up very
fine and mixed with the food.

WARNING: Be sure the dose is right. Too much
ferrous sulfate is poisonous. Keep tablets out of
the reach of children.

Dosage of ferrous sulfate for anemia:
—using tablets of 200 mg.—

Give 3 times a day, with meals.

In each dose give:

adults: 200 to 400 mg. (1 or 2 tablets)
children over 6 years old: 200 mg. (1 tablet)
children 3 to 6 years: 100 mg. (½ tablet)
children under 3 years: 25 to 50 mg. (1/8 to
¼ tablet) ground up fine and mixed with
food.

<u>Folic acid</u>—for some kinds of anemia

Name:_____ price:_____ for___

Often comes in: tablets of 5 mg.

Folic acid can be important in the treatment of
kinds of anemia in which blood cells have been
destroyed in the veins, as is the case with malaria.
An anemic person who has a large spleen or looks
yellow may need folic acid, especially if his anemia
does not get much better with ferrous sulfate.
Babies who are fed goat's milk and pregnant
women who are anemic or malnourished often
need folic acid as well as iron.

Folic acid can be obtained by eating dark green
leafy foods, meat, and liver, or by taking folic acid
tablets. Usually 2 weeks treatment is enough for
children, although in some areas children with a
kind of anemia called *thalassemia* may need it for
years. Pregnant women who are anemic and
malnourished would be helped by taking folic acid
tablets daily throughout pregnancy.

Dosage of folic acid for anemia:
—using 5 mg. tablets—

Give by mouth once a day.

adults and children over 3 years: 1 tablet
(5 mg.)
children under 3 years: ½ tablet (2½ mg.)

<u>Vitamin B$_{12}$ (cyanocobalamin)</u>—for pernicious
anemia **only**

This is mentioned only to discourage its use.
Vitamin B$_{12}$ is useful only for a rare type of
anemia that is almost never found in persons under
35 years old or in Orientals. Many doctors
prescribe it when it is not needed, just to be giving
their patients something. **Do not waste your money
on vitamin B$_{12}$** or let a doctor or health worker
give it to you unless a blood analysis has been
done, and it has been shown that you have
pernicious anemia.

Vitamin K (phytomenadione, phytonadione)

Name:_____ price:_____ for___

Often comes in: ampules of 1 mg. in 2.5 ml. of milky solution.

If a newborn child begins to bleed from any part of his body (mouth, cord, anus), this may be caused by a lack of vitamin K. Inject 1 mg. (1 ampule) of vitamin K into the outer part of the thigh. Do not inject more, even if the bleeding continues. In babies who are born very small (under 2 kg.) an injection of vitamin K may be given to reduce the risk of bleeding.

Vitamin K is of no use to control bleeding of the mother after childbirth.

Vitamin B$_6$ (pyridoxine)

Often comes in: 100 mg. tablets
Price:_____ for___

Persons with tuberculosis being treated with **isoniazid** sometimes develop a lack of vitamin B$_6$. To prevent this 100 mg. of vitamin B$_6$ (pyridoxine) may be taken daily while taking isoniazid. Or the vitamin can be given only to persons who develop problems because of its lack. Signs include pain or tingling in the hands or feet, muscle twitching, nervousness, and being unable to sleep.

Dosage of vitamin B$_6$—while taking isoniazid:

Take one 100 mg. tablet daily.

FAMILY PLANNING METHODS: BIRTH CONTROL

Oral Contraceptives (Birth Control Pills)

Information about the use, risks, and precautions for birth control pills can be found on pages 286 to 289. The following information is about choosing the right pill for individual women.

Birth control pills contain 2 chemicals, or *hormones,* similar to those produced in a woman's body to control her period. These hormones are called *estrogen* and *progesterone.* The pills come under many different brand names, with different strengths and combinations of the 2 hormones.

Generally speaking, brands that contain a relatively small amount of both hormones are safest and work best for most women. For example:

Group 1. fairly low amounts of estrogen and progesterone (.05 mg. estrogen)

Norinyl 1/50 "Blue Lady" brands
Ortho-Novum 1/50 without a diagonal
Eugynon blue line across
Nordiol the package are
Neogynon also in this group.

Name:_____ price:_____

Name:_____ price:_____

Most women should start with pills from Group 1.

For women who are very fat, suffer from acne (pimples), or who have very brief or irregular periods, it may help to start with a pill that has a little more estrogen. For example:

Group 2. a somewhat higher amount of estrogen (.08 mg.)

Norinyl 1/80 "Blue Lady" brands
Ortho-Novum 1/80 with a diagonal blue
Demulen line across the package.

Name:_____ price:_____

Name:_____ price:_____

Women who begin with a brand from Group 1 and are bothered by 'spotting' of blood during the second week after the period can often lessen the problem by taking 2 pills daily instead of 1 during the days when spotting takes place. (To avoid confusion, take the extra pills from a separate package.)

If spotting continues after 3 or 4 months, you can change to one of the brands in Group 2. (The brand *Ovulen* will often control spotting that continues even when taking pills from Group 2, but it is so strong in estrogen that it is likely to cause other problems, and for this reason is rarely recommended.)

As a rule, women who take birth control pills have less bleeding with their periods. This may be a benefit, especially for women who are anemic. But if a woman misses her period for months or is disturbed by the small amount of blood with her period, she can change to a brand with more estrogen, in Group 2.

For women who have very heavy menstrual bleeding, or whose breasts become painful before their period begins, a brand low in estrogen but high in progesterone may be better. For example:

Group 3.
high in progesterone
low in estrogen

Lindiol
Ovral
Norlestrin 2.5
(*Norinyl 1/50* and
Ortho-Novum 1/50
are also relatively high
in progesterone)

Name:_____ price:_____

Brands from Group 3 are not recommended for women who have pimples, a lot of hair on their arms or lip, or reduced menstrual bleeding, for the high progesterone may make these conditions worse—or even cause them.

Women who are disturbed by morning sickness or other side effects after 2 or 3 months of taking the pill, and women who have a higher risk for blood clots (see p. 288) can use a brand of birth control pill that is very low in both estrogen and progesterone. For example:

Group 4.
very low in
both estrogen
and progesterone

Lo-ovral
Brevicon
Modican
Loestrin
Zorane
Microgynon

Name:_____ price:_____

The disadvantages of brands in Group 4 are that they often cause mid-period spotting, and that there is an increased chance of pregnancy if only 1 pill is forgotten.

Condoms (Rubbers, Prophylactics, Sheaths)

Name:_____ price:_____ for___

Often come in packages of 3.

There are many different brands of condoms; some far more costly than others. Some are lubricated (oiled). Some come in different colors.

Use and care of condoms is described on page 290.

Diaphragm

Name:_____ price:_____

To be most effective, the diaphragm should be used with a special cream or jelly, which should be spread on the rim before it is put into the vagina (see p. 290).

Name of jelly or cream:_____ price:_____

Contraceptive Foam (Well-known brands: *Emko, Lempko, Delfen*)

Name:_____ price:_____

For discussion of the use of foam, see page 290.

Intrauterine Device (IUD)

Name:_____ price:_____
fee for putting it in:_____

For information on IUDs, see page 290. There are several different kinds. One of the first and best kinds is the **Lippes loop.** A newer kind that works well is called the **Copper 7.** One kind of IUD, the **Dalkon Shield,** causes more problems than other kinds and should not be used.

IUDs can be used by women who have never had a child, but are more likely to come out or cause other problems.

The best time to have an IUD put in is while the woman is having her period or just after.

Injectable Contraceptives
Common brand: *Depo-Provera*

Name:_____ price:_____

This is being used in many countries, but there are still arguments over its safety. It should probably not be used by women who may want to have more children at a later date (see p. 291).

VOCABULARY

This vocabulary is listed in the order of the alphabet:
A B C D E F G H I J K L M N O P Q R S T U V W X Y Z

Words marked with a star (*) are usually not used in this book but are often used by doctors or found on package information of medicines.

Most names of sicknesses are not included in this vocabulary. See the Index (yellow pages) and read about the sickness in the book.

A

Abdomen   The part of the body that contains the stomach, liver, and guts. The belly.

Abnormal   Different from what is usual, natural, or average. Not normal.

Abscess   A sac of pus caused by bacterial or other infection. For example, a boil.

Acne (pimples)   A skin problem causing bumps on the face, chest, or back that form small white 'heads' of pus or sometimes 'blackheads' of dirt. Most common in young people (adolescents).

Acute   Sudden and short-lived. An acute illness is one that starts suddenly and lasts a short time. The opposite of 'chronic'.

Acute abdomen   An emergency condition of the abdomen that often requires a surgical operation. Severe pain in the belly with vomiting and no diarrhea may mean an acute abdomen.

Adolescent   The years in which a child becomes an adult. The teens: 13 to 19 years old.

Afterbirth   See **Placenta.**

Alcoholism   A continual need a person cannot control to overuse alcoholic drinks such as beer, rum, wine, etc.

Allergy, allergic reaction   A problem such as an itching rash, hives, sneezing, and sometimes difficult breathing or shock that affects certain people when specific things are breathed in, eaten, injected, or touched.

Amebas (also amoebas)   Tiny animals that live in water or in the gut and can only be seen with a microscope. They can cause diarrhea, dysentery, and liver abscess.

Analgesic   Medicine to calm pain.

Anemia   A disease in which the blood gets thin for lack of red blood cells. Signs include tiredness, pale skin, and lack of energy. See also **Pernicious anemia.**

Antacid   Medicine used to control too much stomach acid and to calm stomach upset.

Antibiotic   Medicine that fights infections caused by bacteria.

*Antiemetic   Vomit-control medicine. A medicine that helps keep people from vomiting or feeling nauseous.

Antihistamine   Medicine used to treat allergies such as hay fever and itching. Also helps control vomiting and causes sleepiness.

Antiseptic   A soap or cleaning liquid that prevents growth of bacteria.

Antispasmodic   Medicine used to relieve cramps or spasms of the gut.

Antitoxin   Medicine that acts against or neutralizes a poison or toxin. Often made from the blood serum of horses.

Antivenin (anti-venom)   An antitoxin used to treat poisoning from a venom, such as snake poison.

Anus   The opening at the end of the gut between the legs; asshole.

Aorta   The main artery or vessel that carries blood out of the heart to the body.

Apoplexy   An old word for stroke. See **Stroke.**

Appendix   A finger-like sac attached to the large intestine (gut).

Appropriate   Something that is easiest, safest, and most likely to work in a particular situation or condition.

Artery   A vessel carrying blood from the heart through the body. Arteries have a pulse. Veins, which return blood to the heart, have no pulse.

Ascaris (roundworm)   Large worms that live in people's intestines and cause discomfort, indigestion, weakness, and sometimes gut obstruction (blocking of the gut).

B

Bacteria   Tiny germs that can only be seen with a microscope and that cause many different infectious diseases.

Bag of waters   The sac inside the womb that holds the baby; amniotic sac. When it breaks, releasing its fluid, this usually means that labor has begun.

Bedsores   Chronic open sores that appear in people who are so ill they do not roll over or change position in bed.

Bewitchment   The act of casting a spell or influencing by witchcraft; hexing. Some people believe that they get sick because a witch has bewitched them or given them the 'evil eye'.

Bile   A bitter, green liquid made by the liver and stored in the gallbladder. It helps digest fat.

Birth defects   See **Defects.**

Blackhead   A small plug or 'head' of dirt blocking a pore in the skin of the face, chest, or back. A kind of pimple.

Bladder stones   See **Kidney stones.**

Blood pressure   The force or pressure of the blood upon the walls of the blood vessels (arteries and veins); it varies with the age and health of the person.

Boil   A swollen, inflamed lump with a pocket of pus under the skin. A kind of abscess.

Booster   A repeat vaccination to renew the effect of an earlier series of vaccinations.

Bowel movement   To have a bowel movement is to defecate; to shit; the way of passing solid waste out of the body.

Brand name   Trade name. The name a company gives to its product. A brand-name medicine is sold under a special name and is often more expensive than the same generic medicine.

Breast abscess   See **Mastitis.**

Breech delivery   A birth in which the baby comes out buttocks or legs first.

Broad-spectrum antibiotic   A medicine that works against many kinds of micro-organisms. Compare with a narrow-spectrum antibiotic, which works against only a few.

Bronchi   The tubes leading to the lungs, through which air passes when a person breathes.

Bronchitis   An infection of the bronchi.

Bubo   A very swollen lymph node. **Bubos** is a common name for lymphogranuloma venereum.

Buttocks   The part of the body a person sits on; ass, arse, rump, behind, backside, butt.

C

Cancer   A tumor or lump that grows and may keep growing until it finally causes death.

Carbohydrates   Starches and sugars. Foods that provide energy.

Cassava (manioc, yuca)   A starchy root grown in the tropics.

Cast   A stiff bandage of gauze and plaster that holds a broken bone in place until it heals.

Cataract   An eye problem in which the lens of the eye becomes cloudy, making it more and more difficult for the person to see. The pupil looks gray or white when you shine a light into it.

Catheter   A rubber tube used to drain urine from the bladder.

Cavity   A hole or spot of decay in a tooth where bacteria have got in and destroyed part of the tooth.

Centigrade (C.)   A measure or scale of heat and cold. A healthy person's temperature (normal temperature) is 37°C. Water freezes at 0°C. and boils at 100°C.

Cerebro-vascular accident, CVA   See **Stroke.**

Cervix   The opening or neck of the womb at the back of the vagina.

Chancre   A painless sore or ulcer on the genitals, finger, or lip that is one of the first signs of syphilis.

Chigger   A tiny, crawling spider or tick-like animal that buries its head under the skin and sucks blood.

Childbirth fever   (This is also called childbed fever, postpartum infection, or puerperal infection.) The fever and infection that mothers sometimes develop after childbirth.

Chronic   Long-term or frequently recurring (compare with acute). A chronic disease is one that lasts a long time.

Circulation   The flow of blood through the arteries and veins by the pumping of the heart.

Cleft   Divided, separated. A child born with a cleft palate has a separation or abnormal opening in the roof of his mouth.

Climacteric   Menopause.

Colic   Sharp abdominal pains caused by spasms or cramps in the gut.

Colostrum   The first milk a mother's breasts produce. It looks watery but is rich in protein and helps protect the baby against infection.

Coma   A state of unconsciousness from which a person cannot be wakened. It is caused by disease, injury, or poison, and often ends in death.

Community   A group of people living in the same village or area who have similar living conditions, interests, and problems.

*Complications   Secondary health problems that sometimes develop in the course of a disease. For example, meningitis may result as a dangerous complication of measles.

Compost   A mixture of plant and animal waste that is allowed to rot for use as a fertilizer. Hay, dead leaves, vegetable waste, animal droppings, and manure all make good compost.

Compress   A folded cloth or pad put on a part of the body. It may be soaked in hot or cold water.

Conjunctiva   A thin, protective layer that covers the white of the eye and inner side of the eyelids.

Consciousness   See **Loss of consciousness.**

Constipation   Dry, hard, difficult stools (bowel movements) that do not come often.

Consumption   An old name for tuberculosis.

Contact   Touch. Contagious diseases can be spread by a sick person coming in contact with (touching or being close to) another person.

Contagious disease   A sickness that can be spread easily from one person to another.

Contaminate   To dirty, stain, or infect by contact. A syringe that has not been boiled is often contaminated and can cause infections, even though it looks clean.

Contraceptive   Any method of preventing pregnancy.

Contractions   Tightening or shortening of muscles. The strong contractions of the womb when a woman is in labor help to push the baby out of the womb.

*Contraindication   A situation or condition when a particular medicine should not be taken. (Many medicines are contraindicated in pregnancy.)

Convulsions   An uncontrolled fit. A sudden jerking of part or all of the person's body, as in meningitis or epilepsy.

Cornea   The clear outer layer or 'window' of the eye, covering the iris and pupil.

Corns   Hard, thick, painful parts of the skin formed where sandals or shoes push against the skin or one toe presses against another.

Cramp   A painful tightening or contraction of a muscle.

Cretinism   A condition in which a child is born mentally slow and often deaf. It is usually due to lack of iodine in the mother's diet.

Cupping   A home remedy that consists of drawing blood to the surface of the body by use of a glass or cup with a flame under it.

Cyst   An abnormal, sac-like, liquid-filled growth developing in the body.

D

Dandruff   Oily white or grayish flakes or scales that appear in the hair. Seborrhea of the scalp.

Decongestant   A medicine that helps relieve swelling or stuffiness of the nose or sinuses.

Defects   Birth defects are physical or mental problems a child is born with, such as a hare lip, club foot, or an extra finger or toe.

Deficiency   Not having enough of something; a lack.

Deformed   Abnormally formed, not having the right shape.

Dehydration   A condition in which the body loses more liquid than it takes in. This lack of water is especially dangerous in babies.

Delirium   A state of mental confusion with strange movements and speech; it may come with high fever or severe illness.

*Dermal   Of the skin.

Dermatitis   An infection or irritation of the skin.

Diaper rash   Reddish, irritated patches between a baby's legs caused by urine in his diapers (nappy) or bedding.

Diarrhea   Frequent runny or liquid stools.

Diet   The kinds and amounts of foods that a person should eat or avoid eating.

Discharge   A release or flowing out of fluid, mucus, or pus.

Dislocations   Bones that have slipped out of place at a joint.

Douche   A way to wash out the vagina by squirting a stream of water up into it.

Drowning   When a person stops breathing (suffocates) from being under water.

Dysentery   Diarrhea with mucus and blood. It is usually caused by an infection.

E

*Eclampsia   Sudden fits, especially during pregnancy or childbirth. The result of toxemia of pregnancy.

Embryo   The beginnings of an unborn baby when it is still very small.

Emergency   A sudden sickness or injury that calls for immediate attention.

*Emetic   A medicine or drink that makes people vomit. Used when poisons have been swallowed.

Enema   A solution of water put up the anus to cause a bowel movement.

Epidemic   An outbreak of disease affecting many persons in a community or region at the same time.

Evaluation   A study to find out the worth or value of something, or how much has been accomplished. Often done by comparing different factors or conditions before and after a project or activity is underway.

Evil eye   A glance or look from someone believed to have the power to bewitch or do harm to people.

Exhaustion   Extreme fatigue and tiredness.

*Expectorant   A medicine that helps a person cough up mucus from the respiratory tract (lungs, bronchi, etc.); a cough-helper.

Expiration date   The month and year marked on a medicine that tells when it will no longer be good. Throw away most medicines after this date.

F

Fahrenheit (F.)   A measure or scale of heat and cold. A healthy person's temperature (normal temperature) is 98.6°F. Water freezes at 32°F. and boils at 212°F.

Family planning   Using birth control methods to plan when to have and not have children.

Farsighted   Being able to see things at a distance better than things close at hand.

Feces   Stools; shit; the waste from the body that is moved out through the bowels in a 'bowel movement'.

Feces-to-mouth   Spread or transmitted from the stools of one person to his or another person's mouth, usually by food or drink, or on fingers.

Fetoscope   An instrument or tool for listening to sounds made by the unborn baby (fetus) inside the womb.

Fetus (foetus)   The developing baby inside the womb.

Fever   A body temperature higher than normal.

First aid   Emergency care or treatment for someone who is sick or injured.

Fit   A sudden, violent attack of a disease, causing convulsions or spasms (jerking of the body that the person cannot control), and sometimes unconsciousness.

Flu   A bad cold, often with fever, pain in the joints, and sometimes diarrhea.

Flukes   Worms that infect the liver or other parts of the body and cause different diseases. Blood flukes get into the blood and cause schistosomiasis.

Foetus   See **Fetus**.

Folic acid   A nutritious substance found in leafy green vegetables.

Follicles   Small lumps.

Fontanel   The 'soft spot' on the top of a young baby's head.

Fracture   A broken bone.

Fright   A great or sudden fear.

G

Gallbladder   A small, muscular sac attached to the liver. The gallbladder collects bile, a liquid that helps digest fatty foods.

Gauze   A soft, loosely woven kind of cloth used for bandages.

Generic name   The scientific name of a medicine, as distinct from the brand names given it by different companies that make it.

Genitals   The organs of the reproductive system, especially the sex organs.

Germs   Very small organisms that can grow in the body and cause some infectious diseases; micro-organisms.

Giardia   A tiny, microscopic parasite that can infect the intestines, causing frothy yellow diarrhea.

Glucose   A simple form of sugar that the body can use quickly and easily. It is found in fruits and honey, and can be bought as a white powder for use in Rehydration Drinks.

Goiter   A swelling on the lower front of the neck (enlargement of the thyroid gland) caused by lack of iodine in the diet.

Grain (gr.)   A unit of weight based on the weight of a grain of wheat. 1 grain weighs 65 mg.

Gram (gm.)   A metric unit of weight. There are about 28 grams in an ounce. There are 1000 gm. in 1 kilogram.

Groin   The front part of the body where the legs join. The genital area.

Gut   Intestines.

Gut thread or gut suture material   A special thread for sewing or stitching tears from childbirth. The gut thread is slowly absorbed (disappears) so that the stitches do not need to be taken out.

History (medical history)   What you can learn through asking questions about a person's sickness—how it began, when it gets better or worse, what seems to help, whether others in the family or village have it, etc.

Hives   Hard, thick, raised spots on the skin that itch severely. They may come and go all at once or move from one place to another. A form of allergic reaction.

Hormones   Chemicals made in parts of the body to do a special job. For example, estrogen and progesterone are hormones that regulate a woman's period and chance of pregnancy.

Hygiene   Actions or practices of personal cleanliness that lead to good health.

*Hypertension   High blood pressure.

Hyperventilation   Very rapid, deep breathing in a person who is frightened.

*Hypochondria   Extreme worry or concern over an imagined sickness.

Hysteria   (1) In common language, a condition of great nervousness, fear, and emotional distress.   (2) In medical terms, signs of sickness caused by fear or the power of belief.

H

Hare lip   A split in the upper lip, going from the mouth up to the nose (like a hare, or rabbit). Some babies are born with a hare lip.

Health worker   A person who takes part in making his community a healthier place to live.

Heartburn   A burning feeling in the lower chest or upper part of the stomach.

Hemorrhage   Severe or dangerous bleeding.

Hemorrhoids (piles)   Small, painful bumps or lumps at the edge of the anus or inside it. These are actually swollen or varicose veins.

Herb   A plant, especially one valued for its medicinal or healing qualities.

Hereditary   Passed on from parent to child.

Hernia (rupture)   An opening or tear in the muscles covering the belly that allows a loop of the gut to push through and form a ball or lump under the skin.

Hex   A magic spell or jinx said to be caused by a witch.

I

Immunizations (vaccinations)   Medicines that give protection against specific diseases, for example: diphtheria, whooping cough, tetanus, polio, tuberculosis, measles, and smallpox.

Infection   A sickness caused by bacteria or other germs. Infections may affect part of the body only (such as an infected finger) or all of it (such as measles).

Infectious disease   A disease that is easily spread or communicated (passed from one person to another); contagious.

Inflammation   An area that is red, hot, and painful, often because of infection.

Insecticide   A poison that kills insects. DDT and lindane are insecticides.

*Insomnia   A condition in which a person is not able to sleep, even though he wants and needs to.

Insulin   A substance (enzyme) produced by the pancreas, which controls the amount of sugar in the blood. Injections of insulin are sometimes needed by persons with diabetes.

Intestinal parasites   Worms and tiny animals that get in people's intestines and cause diseases.

Intestines   The guts or tube-like part of the food canal that carries food and finally waste from the stomach to the anus.

Intramuscular (IM) injection   An injection put into a muscle, usually of the arm or the buttock—different from an intravenous (IV) injection, put directly into a vein.

Intussusception   The slipping of one portion of the gut into one nearby, usually causing a dangerous obstruction or blocking of the gut.

Iris   The colored or dark part of the eye around the pupil.

J

Jaundice   A yellow color of the eyes and skin. It is a sign of disease in the liver, gallbladder, pancreas, or blood.

K

*****Keratomalacia**   A dullness and softening of the eye, ending in blindness. It is caused by a lack of vitamin A.

Kidneys   Large, bean-shaped organs in the lower back that filter waste from the blood, forming urine.

Kidney stones   Small stones that form in the kidneys and pass down to the urinary tube. They can cause a sharp pain in the lower back, side, urinary tube, or lower belly. In the bladder they may block the urinary tube and make urination painful or impossible.

Kilogram (kg.)   One thousand grams. A 'kilo' is equal to a little over 2 pounds.

Kwashiorkor (wet malnutrition)   Severe malnutrition caused by not eating enough protein. A child with kwashiorkor has swollen feet, hands, and face, and peeling sores.

L

Labor   The sudden tightening or contractions of the womb that mean the baby will soon be born.

Larva (larvae)   The young worm-like form that comes from the egg of many insects or parasites. It changes form when it becomes an adult.

Latrine   An outhouse; privy; a hole or pit in the ground to use as a toilet.

Laxative   A medicine used for constipation that makes stools softer and more frequent.

Ligaments   Tough cords in a persons's joints that help hold them in place.

*****Lingual**   Of or relating to the tongue.

Liter (l.)   A metric measure equal to about one quart. A liter of water weighs one kilogram.

Liver   A large organ under the lower right ribs that helps clean the blood and get rid of poisons.

Loss of consciousness   The condition of a sick or injured person who seems to be asleep and cannot be wakened. Unconsciousness.

*****Lubricant**   An oil or cream used to make surfaces slippery.

Lymph nodes   Small lumps under the skin in different parts of the body that are traps for germs. They become painful and swollen when they get infected. In tuberculosis and cancer they are often swollen but not painful.

Lyophilized   Powdered; a way of preparing injectable medicine so that it does not have to be kept cold.

M

Malnutrition   Health problems caused by not eating enough of the foods that the body needs.

Marasmus (dry malnutrition)   A condition caused by not eating enough. Starvation. The person is very thin and underweight, often with a pot belly.

Mask of pregnancy   Dark, olive-colored areas on face, breasts, or middle of the belly that are normal in a pregnant woman.

Mastitis (breast abscess)   An infection of the breast, usually in the first weeks or months of nursing a baby. It causes part of the breast to become hot, red, and swollen.

Membrane   A thin, soft sheet or layer that lines or protects some part of an animal or plant.

Menopause (climacteric)   The time when a woman naturally stops having monthly bleeding, usually between the ages of 40 and 50.

Menstrual period, menstruation   Monthly bleeding in women.

Mental   Of or relating to the mind (thinking, brain).

Micro-organism   A tiny plant or animal so small it can only be seen with the aid of a microscope.

Microscope   An instrument with lenses that make very tiny objects look larger.

Microscopic   Something so small that it can only be seen with a microscope.

Migraine   A severe, throbbing headache, sometimes on one side of the head only. It often causes vomiting.

Milligram (mg.)   One thousandth of a gram.

Milliliter (ml.)   One thousandth of a liter.

Minerals   Simple metals or other things the body needs, such as iron, calcium, and iodine.

Miscarriage (spontaneous abortion)   The death of the developing baby or fetus in the womb, sometimes followed by heavy bleeding with blood clots.

Mongolism (Down's syndrome)   A disease in which a child is born mentally slow with slanted eyes, a round dull face, and wide hands with short fingers.

Morning sickness   Nausea and vomiting that occur especially in the morning in the early months of pregnancy.

Mouth-to-mouth breathing   Artificial respiration. A method of helping a person who has stopped breathing to start breathing again.

Mucus   A thick, slippery liquid that moistens and protects the linings of the nose, throat, stomach, guts, and vagina.

N

Narrow-spectrum antibiotic   A medicine that works against a limited number of different kinds of bacteria.

*Nasal   Of or relating to the nose.

Nausea   Stomach distress or upset; feeling like you need to vomit.

Navel   Belly button; umbilicus; the place in the middle of the belly where the umbilical cord was attached.

Nerves   Thin threads or strings that run from the brain to every part of the body and carry messages for feeling and movement.

Non-infectious disease   A disease that does not spread from person to person.

Normal   Usual, natural, or average. Something that is normal has nothing wrong with it.

Nutritious   Nourishing. Nutritious foods are those that have the things the body needs to grow, be healthy, and fight off disease.

O

Obstruction   A condition of being blocked or clogged. An obstructed gut is a medical emergency.

Ointment   A salve or lotion to use on the skin.

*Ophthalmic   Of the eyes.

*Oral   By mouth. An oral medicine is one taken by mouth.

Organ   A part of the body that is more or less complete in itself and does a specific job. For example, the lungs are organs for breathing.

Organisms   Living things (animals or plants).

*Otic   Having to do with the ears.

Ounce   A measure of weight equal to about 28 grams. There are 16 ounces in one pound.

Ovaries   Small sacs in a woman's belly next to her womb. They produce the eggs that join with a man's sperm to make a baby.

Oxytocics   Dangerous medicines that cause the womb and blood vessels in it to contract. They should only be used to control a mother's heavy bleeding after her child is born.

P

Palate   The roof or top part of the mouth.

Pancreas   An organ below the stomach, on the left side, that produces insulin.

Pannus   Tiny blood vessels that appear in the top edge of the cornea in certain eye diseases, like trachoma.

Paralysis   Loss of the ability to move part or all of the body.

Parasites   Worms and tiny animals that live in or on another animal or person and cause harm. Fleas, intestinal worms, and amebas are parasites.

*Parenteral   Not by mouth but by injection.

Pasteurization   The process of heating milk or other liquids to a certain temperature ($60°C$) for about 30 minutes in order to kill harmful bacteria.

Pelvis   Hip bones.

Peritoneum   The thin lining between the guts and body wall. The bag that holds the guts.

Peritonitis   A very dangerous inflammation of the peritoneum. The belly gets hard like a board, and the person is in great pain, especially when he tries to lie with his legs straight.

Pernicious anemia   A rare kind of anemia caused by a lack of vitamin B_{12}. Pernicious means harmful.

Petroleum jelly (petrolatum, *Vaseline*)   A grease-like jelly used in preparing skin ointments.

Pharmacy   A store that sells medicines and health care supplies.

Phlegm   Mucus with pus that forms in abnormal amounts in the lungs and must be coughed out.

Piles   See **Hemorrhoids.**

Pimples   See **Acne.**

Placenta (afterbirth)   The dark and spongy lining inside the womb where the fetus joins the mother's body. The placenta normally comes out 15 minutes to half an hour after the baby is born.

Placenta previa   A condition in which the placenta is too low in the womb and blocks the mouth of the womb. The risk of dangerous bleeding is high. Women who have bleeding late in pregnancy—a possible sign of placenta previa—should go to a hospital at once.

Plantain   A kind of banana with a lot of starch and fiber. It is often cooked and eaten when green.

Pollen   The fine dust made in the flower of a seed plant. People who are **allergic** to pollen often have hay fever at times of the year when plants put a lot of this dust into the air.

Postpartum   After childbirth.

Postpartum hemorrhaging   Heavy bleeding of the mother following childbirth.

Power of suggestion or power of belief   The influence of belief or strong ideas. For example, sick people can feel better because they have faith in a remedy, even if the remedy does not have any medical effect.

Precaution   Care taken in advance to prevent harm or prepare for emergencies before they happen.

Pregnancy   The period (normally 9 months) when a woman carries a child inside her.

Premature baby   A baby born before the full 9 months of pregnancy and weighing less than 2 kilos.

Presentation of an arm   An abnormal position of delivery in which the baby's hand comes out first during the birth. This is an emergency needing a doctor.

Prevention   Action taken to stop sickness before it starts.

Prolapse   The slipping or falling down of a part of the body from its normal position, for example, a prolapsed rectum or womb.

Prophylactic   The word prophylactic means preventive, but condoms are sometimes called prophylactics.

Prostate gland   A firm, muscular gland at the base of the man's urinary tube, or urethra. Often in older men the prostate becomes enlarged, causing difficulty in urinating.

Protective foods   Foods that are rich in vitamins and minerals. They help build healthy bodies and make people more able to resist or fight diseases.

Proteins   Body-building foods necessary for proper growth and strength.

Pterygium   A fleshy growth that slowly extends from the edge of the eye onto the cornea.

Pulse   The number of times a person's heart beats in one minute.

Pupil   The round opening or black center in the iris of the eye. It gets smaller in bright light and larger in the dark.

Purge   A very strong laxative that causes diarrhea.

R

Rate   The number of times something happens in a given amount of time.

Rebound pain   A very sharp pain in the abdomen that occurs after the belly is pressed firmly and slowly, when the hand is removed suddenly. This pain is a sign of an acute abdomen.

Rectum   The end of the large intestine close to the anus.

Reflex   An automatic reaction or movement that happens without a person's trying to do it.

Rehydration Drink   A drink to correct dehydration, which you can make with boiled water, sugar, salt, and bicarbonate of soda.

Resistance   The ability of something to defend itself against something that would normally harm or kill it. Many bacteria become resistant to the effects of certain antibiotics.

Resource   What is needed or available for doing or making something. People, land, animals, money, skills, and plants are resources that can be used for improving health.

Respiration   Breathing. The **respiratory system** includes the bronchi, lungs, and other organs used in breathing.

Respiration rate   The number of times a person breathes in one minute.

Retardation   Abnormal slowness of thought, action, or mental and emotional growth.

Rhinitis   An inflammation of the lining of the nose, often caused by allergies. Hay fever.

Risk   The possibility of injury, loss, or harm. Danger.

Road to Health Chart   A monthly record of a child's weight that shows whether the child is gaining weight normally.

Rotation of crops   To grow different crops one after the other in the same field, so that the soil becomes richer rather than weaker from year to year.

Rupture   See **Hernia**.

S

Sanitation   Public cleanliness involving community efforts in disease prevention, promoting hygiene, and keeping public places free of waste.

Scrotum   The bag between a man's legs that holds his testicles or balls.

Septicemia   An infection of the blood—sometimes called 'blood poisoning'.

Shock   A dangerous condition with severe weakness or unconsciousness, cold sweat, and fast, weak pulse. It is caused by dehydration, hemorrhage, injury, burns, or a severe illness.

Side effects   Problems caused by using a medicine.

Signs   The things or conditions one looks for when examining a sick person, to find out what sickness he has. In this book symptoms, or the problems a person feels, are included with signs.

Sinus trouble (sinusitis)   Sinuses are hollows in the bone that open into the nose. Sinusitis is inflammation causing pain above and below the eyes.

Soft drinks   Fizzy, carbonated drinks like Coca-Cola.

Soft spot   See **Fontanel**.

Spasm   A sudden muscle contraction that a person cannot control. Spasms of the gut produce cramps, or colic. Spasms of the bronchi occur in asthma. Spasms of the jaw and other muscles occur in tetanus.

Spastic   Having chronic abnormal muscle contraction due to brain damage. The legs of spastic children often cross like scissors.

Spleen   An organ normally the size of a fist under the lower edge of the ribs on the left side. Its job is to help make and filter the blood.

Spontaneous abortion   See **Miscarriage**.

Sprain (strain)   Bruising, stretching, or tearing of ligaments or tendons in a twisted joint. A sprain is worse than a strain.

Sputum   Mucus and pus (phlegm) coughed up from the lungs and bronchi of a sick person.

Starches   Energy foods like maize, rice, wheat, cassava, potatoes, and squash.

Sterile   (1) Completely clean and free from living micro-organisms. Things are usually sterilized by boiling or heating.
(2) Sterile also means permanently unable to have children.

Sterilization   (1) To sterilize instruments, bottles, and other things by boiling or heating in an oven.   (2) Also, a permanent way of making a man or a woman unable to reproduce (have children).

Stethoscope   An instrument used to listen to sounds in the body, such as the heartbeat.

Stomach   The sac-like organ in the belly where food is digested. In common language 'stomach' is often used to mean the whole belly or abdomen.

Stools   See **Feces**.

Stroke (apoplexy, cerebro-vascular accident)   A sudden loss of consciousness, feeling, or ability to move, caused by bleeding or a clot inside the brain. Also see heat stroke (p. 81).

Sty   A red, swollen lump on the eyelid, usually near the edge, caused by infection.

Sucrose   The common sugar that comes from sugarcane or sugar beets. It is more complex and more difficult for the body to use than glucose.

Sugars   Sweet foods like honey, sugar, or fruit that give energy.

Suppository   A bullet-shaped tablet of medicine to put up the anus or vagina.

*Suppressant   A medicine that helps to check, hold back, or stop something, such as a medicine to stop coughing (cough suppressant).

Suspension   A powder mixed in a liquid.

Suture   A stitch made with needle and thread to sew up an opening or wound.

Symptoms   The feelings or conditions a person reports about his sickness. In this book symptoms are included with signs.

T

Tablespoon   A measuring spoon that holds 3 teaspoons or 15 ml.

Taboo   Something that is avoided, banned, or not allowed because of a cultural belief.

Teaspoon   A measuring spoon that holds 5 ml. Three teaspoons equal 1 tablespoon.

Temperature   The degree of heat of a person's body.

Tendons   Tough cords that join muscles to bones (distinct from ligaments, which join bones with bones at joints).

*Thalassemia   A form of hereditary anemia seen only in certain countries. A child may become very anemic by age 2, with a large liver and spleen.

Thermometer   An instrument used to measure how hot a person's body temperature is.

Tick   A crawling insect-like animal that buries its head under the skin and sucks blood.

*Topical   For the skin. A topical medicine is to be put on the skin.

Toxemia   A sickness resulting from certain poisons in the body; for example, toxemia of pregnancy and urine toxemia (or uremia).

Toxic   Poisonous.

Tract   A system of body organs and parts that work together to do a special job; for example, the urinary tract cleans the blood and gets rid of urine.

Traditions   Practices, beliefs, or customs handed down from one generation to another by example or word of mouth.

Transmit   To pass on, transfer, or allow to spread from one person to another.

Tropical   Having to do with the tropics or hot regions of the world.

Tumor   An abnormal mass of tissue without inflammation. Some tumors are due to cancer.

U

Ulcer   A break in the skin or mucus membrane; a chronic open sore of the skin, the surface of the eye, the stomach, or gut.

Umbilical cord   The cord that connects a baby from its navel to the placenta on the inside of its mother's womb.

Umbilical hernia   A large, outward bulge of the navel—caused by a loop of intestine that has pushed through the sac holding the guts.

Umbilicus   See **Navel**.

Unconsciousness   See **Loss of consciousness**.

Under-Fives Program   A plan that helps mothers learn about their children's health needs, make regular visits to a clinic for check-ups, and keep a record (Road to Health Chart) of the growth of their children under five years old.

Urethra   Urinary tube or canal. The tube that runs from the bladder to the hole a person urinates from.

Urinary tract   The system of organs concerned with the formation and getting rid of urine—such as kidneys, bladder, and urinary tube (urethra).

Urine   Liquid waste from the body; piss; pee.

Uterus   Womb.

V

Vaccinations   See **Immunizations**.

Vagina   The tube or canal that goes from the opening of a woman's sex organs to the entrance of her womb.

Vaginal   Of or relating to the vagina.

Varicose veins   Abnormally swollen veins, often lumpy and winding, usually on the legs of older people, pregnant women, and women who have had a lot of children.

Vaseline   See **Petroleum jelly.**

Venereal disease   A disease spread by sexual contact.

Vessels   Tubes. Blood vessels are the veins and arteries that carry the blood through the body.

Virus   Germs smaller than bacteria, which cause some infectious (easily spread) diseases.

Vitamins   Protective foods that our bodies need to work properly.

Vomiting   Throwing up the contents out of the stomach through the mouth.

W

Welts   Lumps or ridges raised on the body, usually caused by a blow or an allergy (hives).

Womb   The sac inside a woman's belly where a baby is made. The uterus.

X

Xerosis or xerophthalmia   Abnormal dryness of the eye due to lack of vitamin A.

ADDRESSES FOR TEACHING MATERIALS

Teaching Aids at Low Cost (TALC)
Institute of Child Health
30 Guilford Street
London WC1N 1EH
England

Slide sets, weight charts, aids to weight charts (flannelgraphs, etc.). Free booklist. English, French, and Spanish.

Courtejoie, Dr. J.
Centre pour le Promotion de la Santé
Kangu Majumbe, République du Zaire

Excellent simple material for villages in French, some English, and local languages.

Voluntary Health Association of India (CAHP)
C-45, South Extension, Part II
New Delhi 110049, India

Flannelgraphs, books, flip charts, etc. List available. Material in English and local languages.

Christian Medical College and Hospital
Vellore 4
Madras, India

Posters, flash cards, flannelgraphs in English and local languages.

F. A. O.
Nutrition and Home Economic Division
Rome, Italy

Wide variety of material, some useful at village level. English, French, and Spanish.

W. H. O.
Geneva, Switzerland

Material in English, French, and Spanish.

Health Education Department
Addis Ababa, Ethiopia

Teaching kits. Material in English and some local languages.

International Development Research Centre (IRDC)
P. O. Box 8500
Ottawa, Canada, K19 3HG

Booklets on China. Also on the place of doctors and auxiliaries in health care. Free to those in poorer countries.

National Food and Nutrition Commission
P. O. Box 2669
Lusaka, Zambia

Posters and teaching material on nutrition. English and local languages.

Chief Education Officer
Public Health Department, Ministry of Health
Ibadan, Nigeria

Posters and material in English and main Nigerian languages.

Matériel Réalisé à l'Atelier de Matériel Didactique
Busiga, B. P. 18
Ngozi, Burundi

Good flip charts; a teaching plan using flip charts in French local languages.

World Neighbours
5116 North Portland Avenue
Oklahoma City, Oklahoma 73112, U.S.A.

Filmstrips, manuals, flip charts in English, French, and Spanish.

Shanta Bhawan Community Health Program
Box 252, Kathmandu, Nepal

Slides, flip charts.

Carlos Campesino Apartado 2444 Guatemala City, Guatemala	Battery-powered projectors and film strip sets.
O. C. E. A. C. B. P. 288 Yaounde, Cameroun	Material in French.
Health Education Supply Centre P. O. Box 922 Loma Linda, California 92354, U.S.A.	Books and visual aids (hard and soft).
The Philippine Lutheran Church P. O. Box 507 Manila, Philippines, D404	Flip charts.
Saidpur Concern, Teaching Aids Workshop c/o CONCERN, P. O. Box 650 Dacca, Bangladesh	Flip charts.
I. L. O. Geneva, Switzerland	Booklets on use of the flannelgraph, etc.
I. T. D. G. Parnell House, Wilton Road London SW1, England	Booklets on simple technology. Will send advice on technical problems.
V. I. T. A. 3706 Rhode Island Avenue Mt. Rainier, Maryland 20822, U.S.A.	Village equipment handbook.
ENI Communication Centre P. O. Box 2361 Addis Ababa, Ethiopia	Education packages and visual aids in child health and nutrition.
African Medical and Research Foundation Wilson Airport, P. O. Box 30125 Nairobi, Kenya	Booklets for auxiliaries.
American Foundation for Overseas Blind, Inc. 22 West 17th Street New York, New York 10011, U.S.A.	Material on blindness from lack of vitamin A.
Alfalit Boliviano Junin 6305, Casilla 1466 Cochabamba, Bolivia	Simple booklets on health in Spanish and English.
Centro Andino de Comunicaciones Casilla 2774 Cochabamba, Bolivia	Flip charts in Spanish.
Nutrition Center of the Philippines Communications Department Nichols Interchange, South Superhighway Makati, Rizal, Philippines	Leaflets and fact sheets in English.
The Nutrition Section Public Health Department, Box 2084 Konedobu, Papua New Guinea	Posters and booklets.

INDEX

Things in this book are listed in the order of the alphabet:

A B C D E F G H I J K L M N O P Q R S T U V W X Y Z

Page numbers in **bold** tell you where to find the main reference in this book. Medicines included in the Green Pages are in the Index of Medicines, p. 341.

(see p. 64)

cut out and use as needed

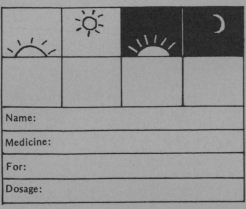

Name:

Medicine:

For:

Dosage:

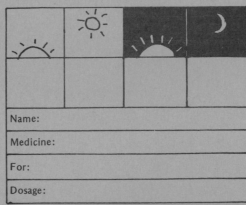

Name:

Medicine:

For:

Dosage:

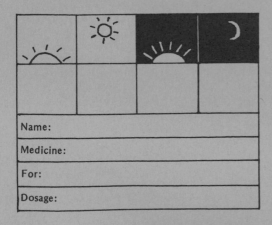

Name:

Medicine:

For:

Dosage:

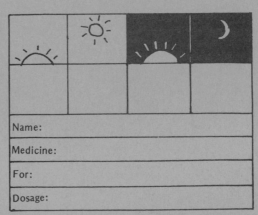

Name:

Medicine:

For:

Dosage:

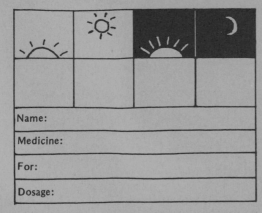

Name:

Medicine:

For:

Dosage:

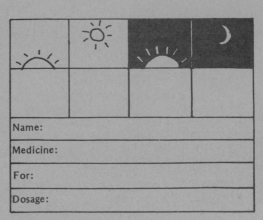

Name:

Medicine:

For:

Dosage:

PATIENT REPORT

TO USE WHEN SENDING FOR MEDICAL HELP.

Name of the sick person:_____ Age:_____

Male_____ Female_____ Where is he (she)?_____

What is the main sickness or problem right now?_____

_____

_____

_____

When did it begin?_____

How did it begin?_____

Has the person had the same problem before?_____ When?_____

Is there fever?_____ How high?_____° When and for how long?_____

Pain?_____ Where?_____ What kind?_____

What is wrong or different from normal in any of the following?

Skin:_____ **Ears:**_____

Eyes:_____ **Mouth and throat:**_____

Genitals:_____

Urine: Much or little?_____ Color?_____ Trouble urinating?_____

Describe:_____ Times in 24 hours:_____ Times at night:_____

Stools: Color?_____ Blood or mucus?_____ Diarrhea?_____

Number of times a day:_____ Cramps?_____ Dehydration?_____ Mild or

severe?_____ Worms?_____ What kind?_____

Breathing: Breaths per minute:_____ Deep, shallow, or normal?_____

Difficulty breathing (describe):_____ Cough (describe):_____

_____ Wheezing?_____ Mucus?_____ With blood?_____

Does the person have any of the SIGNS OF DANGEROUS ILLNESS listed on

page 42?_____ Which? (give details)_____

_____

Other signs:_____

Is the person taking medicine?_____ What?_____

Has the person ever used medicine that has caused hives (or bumps) with itching,

or other allergic reactions?_____ What?_____

The state of the sick person is: Not very serious:_____ Serious:_____

Very serious:_____

On the back of this form write any other information you think may be important.

Tear along this line.

PATIENT REPORT

TO USE WHEN SENDING FOR MEDICAL HELP.

Name of the sick person:_____ Age:_____

Male_____ Female_____ Where is he (she)?_____

What is the main sickness or problem right now?_____

_____

_____

_____

When did it begin?_____

How did it begin?_____

Has the person had the same problem before?_____ When?_____

Is there fever?_____ How high?_____° When and for how long?_____

Pain?_____ Where?_____ What kind?_____

What is wrong or different from normal in any of the following?

Skin:_____ **Ears:**_____

Eyes:_____ **Mouth and throat:**_____

Genitals:_____

Urine: Much or little?_____ Color?_____ Trouble urinating?_____

Describe:_____ Times in 24 hours:_____ Times at night:_____

Stools: Color?_____ Blood or mucus?_____ Diarrhea?_____

Number of times a day:_____ Cramps?_____ Dehydration?_____ Mild or

severe?_____ Worms?_____ What kind?_____

Breathing: Breaths per minute:_____ Deep, shallow, or normal?_____

Difficulty breathing (describe):_____ Cough (describe):_____

_____ Wheezing?_____ Mucus?_____ With blood?_____

Does the person have any of the SIGNS OF DANGEROUS ILLNESS listed on

page 42?_____ Which? (give details)_____

_____

Other signs:_____

Is the person taking medicine?_____ What?_____

Has the person ever used medicine that has caused hives (or bumps) with itching,

or other allergic reactions?_____ What?_____

The state of the sick person is: Not very serious:_____ Serious:_____

Very serious:_____

On the back of this form write any other information you think may be important.

PATIENT REPORT

TO USE WHEN SENDING FOR MEDICAL HELP.

Name of the sick person:_____ Age:_____

Male_____ Female_____ Where is he (she)?_____

What is the main sickness or problem right now?_____

_____

_____

_____

When did it begin?_____

How did it begin?_____

Has the person had the same problem before?_____ When?_____

Is there fever?_____ How high?_____° When and for how long?_____

Pain?_____ Where?_____ What kind?_____

What is wrong or different from normal in any of the following?

Skin:_____ **Ears:**_____

Eyes:_____ **Mouth and throat:**_____

Genitals:_____

Urine: Much or little?_____ Color?_____ Trouble urinating?_____

Describe:_____ Times in 24 hours:_____ Times at night:_____

Stools: Color?_____ Blood or mucus?_____ Diarrhea?_____

Number of times a day:_____ Cramps?_____ Dehydration?_____ Mild or

severe?_____ Worms?_____ What kind?_____

Breathing: Breaths per minute:_____ Deep, shallow, or normal?_____

Difficulty breathing (describe):_____ Cough (describe):_____

_____ Wheezing?_____ Mucus?_____ With blood?_____

Does the person have any of the SIGNS OF DANGEROUS ILLNESS listed on

page 42?_____ Which? (give details)_____

_____

Other signs:_____

Is the person taking medicine?_____ What?_____

Has the person ever used medicine that has caused hives (or bumps) with itching,

or other allergic reactions?_____ What?_____

The state of the sick person is: Not very serious:_____ Serious:_____

Very serious:_____

On the back of this form write any other information you think may be important.

Tear along this line.

INFORMATION ON VITAL SIGNS

TEMPERATURE

There are two kinds of thermometer scales. Centigrade (C.) and Fahrenheit (F.). Either can be used to measure a persons's temperature.

Here is how they compare:

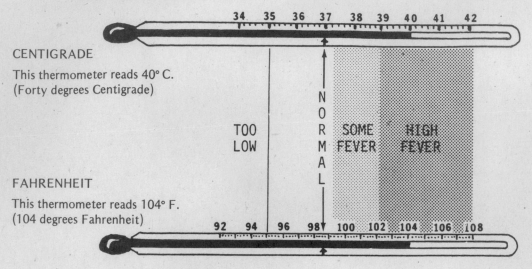

CENTIGRADE

This thermometer reads 40° C.
(Forty degrees Centigrade)

FAHRENHEIT

This thermometer reads 104° F.
(104 degrees Fahrenheit)

PULSE OR HEARTBEAT

For a person at rest
{
ADULTS......:. 60–80 beats per minute is normal.
CHILDREN..... 80-100
BABIES.......: 100–140
}

For each degree Centigrade (°C.) of fever, the heartbeat usually increases about 20 beats per minute.

RESPIRATION

For a person at rest
{
ADULTS AND
LARGE CHILDREN......... 12-20 breaths per minute is normal.
CHILDREN...............up to 30 breaths per minute is normal.
BABIES.................up to 40 breaths per minute is normal.
}

More than 40 shallow breaths a minute usually means pneumonia (see p. 171).

BLOOD PRESSURE (This is included for health workers who have the equipment to measure blood pressure.)

For a person at rest
}
120/80 is normal, but this varies a lot.

If the second reading, when the sound disappears, is over 100, this is a danger sign of high blood pressure (see p. 126).